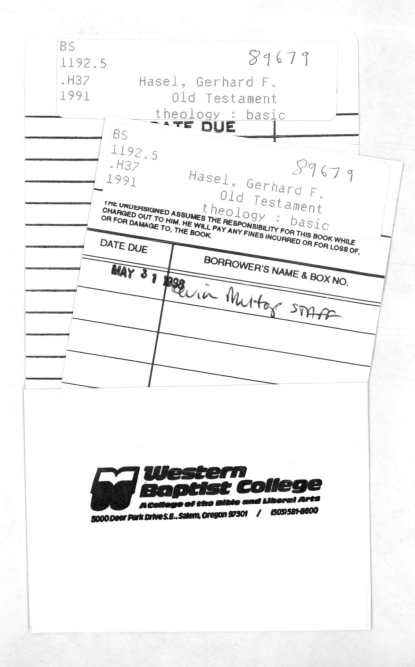

OLD TESTAMENT THEOLOGY

Basic Issues in the Current Debate

GERHARD F. HASEL

FOURTH EDITION

WILLIAM B. EERDMANS PUBLISHING COMPANY
GRAND RAPIDS, MICHIGAN

Printed in the United States of America

First printing, October 1972
Revised edition, 1975
Revised & updated, 1982
Revised, updated & enlarged, 1991

Library of Congress Cataloging-in-Publication Data

Hasel, Gerhard F.
    Old Testament theology: basic issues in the current debate /
Gerhard F. Hasel. — 4th ed., rev., updated, and enl.
        p.   cm.
    Includes bibliographical references and indexes.
    ISBN 0-8028-0537-X
    1. Bible. O.T.—Theology.   I. Title.
BS1192.5.H37   1991
230—dc20   91-6676
                                                           CIP

89679

Contents

ABBREVIATIONS   vii

PREFACE   ix

INTRODUCTION   1

 I. BEGINNINGS AND DEVELOPMENT
    OF OT THEOLOGY   10

 II. THE QUESTION OF METHODOLOGY   28

III. THE QUESTION OF HISTORY, HISTORY
     OF TRADITION, SALVATION HISTORY, AND STORY   115

 IV. THE CENTER OF THE OT AND OT THEOLOGY   139

  V. THE RELATIONSHIP BETWEEN THE TESTAMENTS   172

 VI. BASIC PROPOSALS FOR DOING OT THEOLOGY   194

    SELECTED BIBLIOGRAPHY   209

    INDEX OF SUBJECTS   252

    INDEX OF AUTHORS   258

Abbreviations

AnBib	Analecta Biblica
ASTI	*Annual of the Swedish Theological Institute*
AUSS	*Andrews University Seminary Studies*
Bib	*Biblica*
BibSac	*Bibliotheca Sacra*
BTB	*Biblical Theology Bulletin*
BZAW	Beihefte zur *Zeitschrift für die alttestamentliche Wissenschaft*
CBQ	*Catholic Biblical Quarterly*
CJT	*Canadian Journal of Theology*
CTM	*Concordia Theological Monthly*
EOTH	*Essays on Old Testament Hermeneutics*, ed. C. Westermann (repr. Atlanta, 1979)
EvQ	*Evangelical Quarterly*
EvT	*Evangelische Theologie*
ExpTim	*Expository Times*
FRLANT	Forschungen zur Religion und Literatur des Alten und Neuen Testaments
HBT	*Horizons in Biblical Theology*
IDB	*Interpreter's Dictionary of the Bible* (4 vols.; Nashville, 1962)
Interp	*Interpretation*
IRT	Issues in Religion and Theology
JAAR	*Journal of the American Academy of Religion*
JBL	*Journal of Biblical Literature*
JBR	*Journal of Bible and Religion*

JETS	*Journal of the Evangelical Theological Society*
JR	*Journal of Religion*
JSOT	*Journal for the Study of the Old Testament*
KuD	*Kerygma und Dogma*
OaG	*Offenbarung als Geschichte*, ed. W. Pannenberg (2nd ed.; Göttingen, 1963)
OBT	Overtures to Biblical Theology
OTCF	*The Old Testament and Christian Faith*, ed. B. W. Anderson (New York, 1963)
OTT	G. von Rad, *Old Testament Theology* (2 vols.; New York, 1962, 1965)
RHPR	*Revue d'histoire et de philosophie religieuses*
RSPT	*Revue des sciences philosophiques et théologiques*
RSR	*Recherches de science religieuse*
SBLDS	Society of Biblical Literature Dissertation Series
SBT	Studies in Biblical Theology
SJT	*Scottish Journal of Theology*
TAT	G. von Rad, *Theologie des Alten Testaments* (5th ed.; Munich, 1966)
TBl	*Theologische Blätter*
TBü	Theologische Bücherei
TDNT	*Theological Dictionary of the New Testament* (10 vols.; Grand Rapids, 1964-1976)
TDOT	*Theological Dictionary of the Old Testament* (Grand Rapids, 1974-)
TLZ	*Theologische Literaturzeitung*
TOT	W. Eichrodt, *Theology of the Old Testament* (2 vols.; Philadelphia, 1961, 1967)
TRu	*Theologische Rundschau*
TToday	*Theology Today*
TynBul	*Tyndale Bulletin*
TZ	*Theologische Zeitschrift*
VT	*Vetus Testamentum*
WMANT	Wissenschaftliche Monographien zum Alten und Neuen Testament
WuD	*Wort und Dienst*
ZAW	*Zeitschrift für die alttestamentliche Wissenschaft*
ZTK	*Zeitschrift für Theologie und Kirche*

Preface

The subject of OT theology remains at the center of the most debated issues in the study of the OT. Here the questions of objectivity/subjectivity, "what it meant/what it means," Christian and/or Jewish OT theology, the descriptive and/or normative nature of OT theology, "above the fray" and/or "in the fray," transcendence and/or immanence, confessional or nonconfessional OT theology, and the like remain of core importance. Such matters as whether OT theology is a historical or a theological discipline remain hotly debated, although it appears that there is a growing trend in the direction of affirming it as a theological enterprise. How do the shifts from a historical paradigm to a literary and/or structuralist paradigm in the study of the OT reflect on OT theology? The new emphasis on "canon criticism" and the "canonical approach" have had an impact on the doing of OT theology. These and many other items are part of this new edition.

It is certain that the volume of material in English, German, French, Spanish, and Italian, to mention but these languages, on the topic of OT theology and its subject areas has increased in the last few years as never before. Thus it has been necessary to produce this fourth revised, updated, and enlarged edition. Nearly a decade has passed since the third edition had been produced and several reprintings had been necessary. All of this testifies to the wide use of this volume by

ix

research and teaching staffs and students in seminaries and universities around the world.

We have attempted to update the various chapters with additions and revisions to keep this volume current. There have been a dozen or so new OT theologies and nearly inexhaustible numbers of articles on a variety of aspects of OT theology. It was, therefore, felt imperative to provide for the first time a comprehensive bibliography on OT theology with nearly 950 entries, unequaled anywhere in current literature. While such a bibliography can never be complete, it is designed to provide a working tool for those who wish to pursue any subject in greater detail.

My appreciation and gratitude go first of all to those seminary and university teachers of mine who introduced me to the subject of OT theology and Biblical theology. My professional and academic graduate students make their own contributions in stimulating discussions. Special thanks goes to Mr. Gary Lee, Editor, William B. Eerdmans Publishing Company, for his expert assistance in getting this edition off the press. I must express my thanks to all those who contributed to bringing this edition into existence, particularly Mrs. Betty Jean Mader, whose computer skills made a world of difference, and my doctoral student Mr. Reinaldo Siqueira, who assisted in the preparation of the bibliography.

Theological Seminary   GERHARD F. HASEL
Andrews University

Introduction

Old Testament theology today is undeniably in crisis. Recent monographs and articles by European and American scholars[1] show that the fundamental issues and crucial questions are presently undecided and matters of intense debate. Though it is centuries old, OT theology is now uncertain of its true identity.

George Ernest Wright tells us in *The OT and Theology* (New York, 1969) that he has now changed and "must side with Eichrodt . . ." (p. 62). Earlier, in his well-known study *God Who Acts: Biblical Theology as Recital* (SBT, 8; London, 1952), he found himself close to the theological views of Gerhard von Rad with regard to the question of what constitutes OT theology.[2] The French theologian Edmond Jacob, on the other hand, has re-entered the ongoing discussion about the nature, function, and method of OT theology in his most recent contribution *Grundfragen alttestamentlicher Theologie* (Stuttgart, 1970), in which he further undergirds and defends his own position.[3] The same is true of the Dutch

---

1. See Bibliography, pp. 209-251.
2. *The OT and Theology*, pp. 61f. Note also Wright's essays "Reflections Concerning OT Theology," in *Studia Biblica et Semitica. Festschrift Th. C. Vriezen* (Wageningen, 1966), pp. 376-388; and "Historical Knowledge and Revelation," in *Translating and Understanding the OT: Essays in Honor of Herbert G. May*, ed. H. T. Frank and W. L. Reed (New York, 1970), pp. 279-303.
3. The new French edition of *Théologie de l'AT* (2nd ed.; Neuchâtel, 1968)

scholar Th. C. Vriezen. His thoroughly revised and expanded second English edition of *An Outline of OT Theology* (Newton, Mass., 1970)[4] exhibits a new emphasis in regard to the communion concept. B. S. Childs has presented his penetrating and daring monograph *Biblical Theology in Crisis* (1970) in which he reports on the substance, achievements, and failures of the so-called Biblical Theology Movement in the United States, which is said to have reached its "end" and "demise."[5] He also proposes a new methodology for engaging in a "new Biblical Theology."[6] The European counterpart to the monograph by Childs comes from the pen of the German theologian Hans-Joachim Kraus, whose *Die Biblische Theologie. Ihre Geschichte und Problematik* (1970) is mainly concerned with the European history of the discipline since 1770.[7] This indispensable tome focuses at length on problems crucial to the discipline of OT theology (pp. 307-395).

The volume by Wilfred J. Harrington, OP, *The Path of Biblical Theology* (Dublin, 1973), depicts "the method, the scope and the range of Biblical theology." It surveys OT and NT theology primarily on the basis of representative theologies

---

deals in the preface also with the problems here under discussion. Two recent articles by Jacob are also very pertinent, "Possibilitiés et limites d'une théologie biblique," *RHPR*, 46 (1966), 116-130; and "La théologie de l'AT," *Ephemerides theologicae lovanienses*, 44 (1969), 420-432.

4. The 2nd English ed. is based upon the 3rd Dutch ed. of 1966, inclusive, however, of additions from the literature published after 1966.

5. The exact date for the "end" of the Biblical Theology Movement as a dominant force in American theology is supposedly May 1963, the date of the publication of J. A. T. Robinson's *Honest to God;* so B. S. Childs, *Biblical Theology in Crisis* (Philadelphia, 1970), pp. 85, 91. See the reviews and critiques by M. Barth, "Whither Biblical Theology," *Interp*, 25/3 (July, 1971), 350-354, and Gerhard F. Hasel, *AUSS*, 10 (1972), 179-183.

6. See here especially chs. 5 and 6 entitled "The Need for a New Biblical Theology" and "The Shape of a New Biblical Theology" in Childs, pp. 91-96, 97-122.

7. It is surprising that Kraus mentions in only a few instances names of Anglo-Saxon scholars (pp. 2, 4, 5, 334, 336, 344, 373f.). Though he covers in greater detail much of what R. C. Dentan has covered (see Bibliography), he apparently does not even once refer to the latter's study.

but is generally less successful in depicting the complex and contradictory relations of Biblical theology. In this respect Kraus is much more comprehensive and sensitive to the issues and problems, while Harrington brings in valuable aspects of Roman Catholic contributions.

Five new OT theologies have appeared within a four-year period, a record never before achieved and not easily duplicated in the future. The Catholic scholar A. Deissler presents his OT theology under the title *The Basic Message of the OT*,[8] which reveals immediately a theological stance opposed to that of G. von Rad, namely that the OT contains a unifying center. It is God in his relationship to the world and man.[9] The basic message of the OT consists of its witness to the only, nonworldly, supratemporal, holy, personal God who is presented along the lines of the testimonies of Genesis, Exodus, Deuteronomy, the writing prophets, the priestly and wisdom traditions. W. Zimmerli[10] shares with Deissler the conviction that a single center can serve as an organizing principle. OT theology "is combined throughout of OT expressions about God"[11] and it is therefore "the task [of OT theology] to present OT speaking about God in its inner connection."[12] In Zimmerli's *OT Theology in Outline* the OT is considered a "book of address *(Buche der Anrede)*," which reveals his distance from von Rad for whom the OT is a "history book *(Geschichtsbuch)*."[13] The volume entitled *Theological Founding Structures of the OT* by G. Fohrer[14] is built primarily on the dual concept of the *rulership* of God and

8. *Die Grundbotschaft des AT* (Freiburg i. Br., 1972).

9. At this point there is agreement with the thesis advanced by W. Zimmerli in his review of von Rad's *OTT* in *VT*, 13 (1969), 109.

10. *Grundriss der alttestamentlichen Theologie* (Stuttgart, 1972). Note the extensive discussion of this work by C. Westermann, "Zu zwei Theologien des AT," *EvT*, 34 (1974), 102-110.

11. Zimmerli, *Grundriss*, p. 7.

12. P. 9.

13. G. von Rad, *OTT*, II, 415.

14. *Theologische Grundstrukturen des AT* (Berlin, 1972). Note also the discussion by Westermann, *EvT*, 34 (1974), 96-102.

the *communion* between God and man. He seems to be influenced by both Th. C. Vriezen[15] and M. Buber.[16] Fohrer's work lacks a coherent structure.[17] The same may be said of J. L. McKenzie's *A Theology of the OT* (Garden City, 1974), which begins with a chapter on "Cult" (not covered at all by Zimmerli), then discusses "Revelation," "History," "Nature," "Wisdom," "Political and Social Institutions," and concludes with "The Future of Israel." Instead of following an organizing principle (a center, concept, or motif) or a particular structure McKenzie's approach is to choose "particular topics" which are "usually selected according to the personal studies and interests. . . ."[18] Accordingly his tome is far from being a comprehensive guide to OT theology and for that matter does not claim to be one. Over against these four theologies which consider their task to be purely descriptive is the presentation by C. R. Lehman, *Biblical Theology I: Old Testament* (Scottdale, Pa., 1971). OT theology is understood as part of Biblical theology and is built on "the fundamental idea of progressive revelation" and the "grand unity of the entire Bible."[19] "Biblical theology studies God's revelation in the setting of biblical history," which means "the unfolding of divine revelation concerning the covenants recorded in the Bible."[20] Lehman, therefore, provides a combination of the history of Israel's religion and OT theology under the rubric of Biblical theology.

Never in the history of OT theology has such a short span of time produced as many OT theologies as the years 1978-1981. In that period no less than seven tomes were published in English or German on OT theology by scholars from Europe

---

15. Especially in the concept of "communion" which is Vriezen's center of the OT (*infra,* Chapter IV) and the selection "The Personal Structure" (pp. 133ff.).

16. This is evident in the "correlation" principle and the strong emphasis on "the faith of the prophets."

17. There is essentially no relationship between Chapters 1-3 and 4-7.

18. McKenzie, *Theology of the OT,* p. 23.

19. Lehman, *Biblical Theology I: OT,* p. 8.

20. P. 37.

and North America. Claus Westermann published his *Elements of OT Theology* (Atlanta, 1982),[21] and Walther Zimmerli's *Grundriss der alttestmentlichen Theologie* was translated into English as *OT Theology in Outline* (Atlanta, 1978).[22] Professor Ronald E. Clements published his *OT Theology: A Fresh Approach* (Suffolk, 1978; Atlanta, 1979). His "fresh approach" consists of emphasizing the two major categories of "law" and "promise" as the fundamental unifying themes of the OT for Jews and Christians respectively.

In North America three evangelical scholars entered the fray of OT theology writing. Walter C. Kaiser produced his *Toward an OT Theology* (Grand Rapids, 1978), which centers on the promise theme along a chronological axis. Elmer A. Martens published his OT theology under the title *God's Design: A Focus on OT Theology* (Grand Rapids, 1981).[23] The title *Themes in OT Theology* (Downers Grove, IL, 1979) was given to a volume by W. A. Dyrness, who uses the conventional God-Man-Salvation scheme for his presentation.

Samuel Terrien enriched the scholarly and larger theological reading community with his impressive tome *The Elusive Presence: Toward a New Biblical Theology* (San Francisco, 1978), in which he produced a major new paradigm for the discipline by challenging the prevailing covenant-oriented Biblical theology.

In 1985 Brevard S. Childs constructed the "canonical approach" for the discipline of OT theology with the publication of his long-awaited *OT Theology in a Canonical Context* (London, 1985; Philadelphia, 1986), breaking new ground in the discipline and departing from well-established approaches. Paul D. Hanson had published several books,[24] preparing the

---

21. Westermann's German original appeared in 1978 under the title *Theologie des AT in Grundzügen* (Göttingen, 1978).

22. The 5th German ed., which was revised and enlarged, was published posthumously in 1985. Zimmerli died in 1983.

23. This volume was copublished in Great Britain under the title *Plot and Purpose in the OT* (Leicester, 1981).

24. Paul D. Hanson, *Dynamic Transcendence: The Correlation of Con-*

way for his substantive volume, *The People Called: The Growth of the Community in the Bible* (San Francisco, 1986), in which he stresses the interaction of ancient and modern communities of faith who witness confessionally to the divine activity in history. His emphasis is built on the view that the OT as well as the Bible as a whole does not wish to be understood as absolute truth that was revealed in the past and is to remain the standard for faith of the community of faith in the present. It is rather a process of the unfolding divine encounter. Hanson significantly departs in this approach from Brevard Childs, one of his esteemed teachers. These scholars present actually two divergent approaches that seem to pose an either/or choice for doing OT theology.

Now, there is a debate that has just begun regarding the question whether OT theology is a distinctly Christian enterprise or whether Jews can and should have a part in it. Is OT theology or the theology of the Hebrew Bible an enterprise in which Jews and Christians can cooperate or join forces? Is it built on such neutral—or better, "objective" or scientific—methods and procedures that it does not matter what the personal faith stance of the scholar is who engages in this enterprise? Can a pure "what it meant" stance be maintained? Since the Scripture designated the OT is so designated from the Christian point of view, where it is the first part of one Bible, consisting of two testaments with the NT concluding the entire Bible,[25] some have suggested that OT theology should rather be called "theology of the Hebrew Bible." The latter is the designation chosen in recent years for the section on OT theology at the annual meetings of the Society of

---

fessional Heritage and Contemporary Experience in a Biblical Model of Divine Activity (Philadelphia, 1978); idem, *The Diversity of Scripture: A Theological Interpretation* (OBT, 11; Philadelphia, 1982).

25. See D. L. Baker, *Two Testaments, One Bible* (Downers Grove/Leicester, 1977); S. M. Mayo, *The Relevance of the OT for the Christian Faith: Biblical Theology and Interpretative Methodology* (Washington, D.C., 1982); H. D. Preuss, *Das AT in christlicher Predigt* (Stuttgart/Berlin/Köln/Mainz, 1984); Henning Graf Reventlow, *Problems of Biblical Theology in the Twentieth Century* (Philadelphia, 1986), among others.

Biblical Literature.[26] Such renaming of the discipline is indicative of a host of important issues that we will reflect upon later.

For now it will suffice that some Jewish scholars are willing to be participants in the debate and in some sense the enterprise of a theology of the Hebrew Bible, but with significant distinctions.[27] For example, Professor Jon D. Levenson writes on the subject[28] and has published a book entitled *Creation and the Persistence of Evil: The Jewish Drama of Divine Omnipotence* (San Francisco, 1988), which is a (kind of) theology of the Hebrew Bible. He believes that the OT, or Hebrew Bible, is "contextualized" within either the Jewish or the Christian traditions and, therefore, an "ecumenical [interfaith] biblical theology" is possible at best only within a very limited area "of smaller literary and historical contexts."[29]

Before we break up our highlighting of current trends, we need to make reference to two new studies on the history and development of the discipline of OT theology. Henning Graf Reventlow published his *Problems of OT Theology in the Twentieth Century* (Philadelphia, 1985).[30] This concise volume is filled with bibliographical information and has been appropriately described as "an extended bibliographical essay con-

26. It is to be noted in this connection that articles in the journal *BTB* in recent years have refrained from using the designation "Old Testament," which has been replaced by "First Testament." The "New Testament" is called "Second Testament."

27. See Chapter II below, under "The Descriptive and/or Normative Tasks."

28. See, e.g., Jon D. Levenson, "Why Jews Are Not Interested in Biblical Theology," in *Judaic Perspectives on Ancient Israel*, ed. J. Neusner, B. A. Levine, and E. S. Frerichs (Philadelphia, 1987), pp. 281-307; idem, "The Eighth Principle of Judaism and the Literary Simultaneity of Scripture," *JR*, 68 (1988), 205-225. See also M. Goshen-Gottstein, "Tanakh Theology: The Religion of the OT and the Place of Jewish Biblical Theology," in *Ancient Israelite Religion: Essays in Honor of Frank Moore Cross*, ed. P. D. Miller, P. D. Hanson, and S. D. McBride (Philadelphia, 1987), pp. 617-644; M. Tsevat, "Theology of the OT—A Jewish View," *HBT*, 8/2 (1986), 33-50.

29. Levenson, *Creation and the Persistence of Evil*, p. 225.

30. The translation of *Hauptprobleme der alttestamentlichen Theologie im 20. Jahrhundert* (Darmstadt, 1982).

cerning the major questions arising from attempts to present
an Old Testament theology in the twentieth century" (R. E.
Clements on the dust jacket). It is an excellent work for the
advanced student or specialist with a particular interest in the
problem of "history" and how it has affected the study of OT
theology and is still exercising issues at present. But it hardly
deals with the matter of the current appropriation or "actualization" attempts on the part of OT theologians, and it was
published too long ago to deal much with the significant
influence of the literary paradigms on Scripture study. Any
discussion of the relationship between the OT and NT is
excluded from this volume.[31]

The best history of the developments of OT theology, in
the English language, was published by John H. Hayes and
Frederick Prussner under the title *OT Theology: Its History and
Development* (Atlanta, 1985). John Hayes expanded, revised,
and updated the first part of Prussner's doctoral dissertation,
which he completed in 1952. It is a very respectable study
and is particularly significant for the early period and into
1950. The succeeding thirty years are touched on in much
briefer fashion, although this is the period of greatest activity
and greatest divergence in the 20th century. But this may not
have been the interest of the authors. It is, however, the focus
of the present volume.

The issues connected with the discipline of OT theology
are legion and, as we shall see, are evidently becoming even
more complex. Is OT theology a confessional enterprise? Or
is OT theology a "neutral" and "objective" scientific enterprise
from which any religious commitment is shut out? Is it an
enterprise built on the canonical form of the biblical witness
or is it to penetrate below or behind the text as it is available?
Is it to describe the reconstructed layers and the socio-cultural
forces that were at work in their production as a theology of

---

31. Reventlow published a second volume dealing with this subject and
other matters under the title *Problems of Biblical Theology in the Twentieth
Century* (Philadelphia, 1986).

the tradition-building processes? Is it to describe the intentions of the authors of the biblical texts or is it to describe the forces that were at work in the production of the text? Is it to bridge the gap between the past and the present by means of one or more philosophical systems? Is it a part of historical study, or the history-of-religions study, or literary study, or theological study, or a combination of these and other approaches? These and many other penetrating issues and matters will receive attention in the following pages.

These recent major contributions in monograph form indicate that the debate concerning the nature, function, method, and shape of OT theology continues unabated. The recent OT theologies demonstrate that the whole enterprise of OT theology and more broadly Biblical theology remains in a state of flux. Recent developments have made the situation even more complex than before.

Each responsible exegete and theologian will continue to probe into the basic issues that determine the character of OT (and NT) theology and thus Biblical theology. Our presentation does not aim to be exhaustive or complete but seeks to touch on those factors and issues that in the present writer's view are major unresolved problems. We attempt to focus on the origin and development of Biblical and then OT theology in order to highlight major roots of basic issues in the current debate on OT theology. Our focus on crucial issues which are at the center of the fundamental problems in the current debate have thus a broad foundation. On the basis of this discussion our own suggestions for doing OT theology will be put forth in the last chapter.

I. Beginnings and Development of OT Theology

This chapter is designed to survey major trends in the history of Biblical and OT theology from their beginnings to the revival of OT theology after World War I.[1] This historical survey is to provide the background for the current debate about the scope, purpose, nature, and function of OT theology. Since OT theology is part of Biblical theology, the former cannot be studied in isolation from the latter.

A. *From the Reformation to the Enlightenment.* The Protestant principle of "sola scriptura,"[2] which became the battle cry of the Reformation against scholastic theology and ecclesiastical tradition, provides with its call for the self-interpretation of Scripture *(sui ipsius interpres)* the source for the subsequent development of Biblical theology.[3] The Reformers did not create the phrase "Biblical theology" nor did they engage in Biblical theology as a discipline as subsequently understood.

1. Among histories of Biblical theology are the following: R. C. Dentan, *Preface to OT Theology* (2nd ed.; New York, 1963); H.-J. Kraus, *Die biblische Theologie, Ihre Geschischte und Problematik* (Neukirchen-Vluyn, 1970); O. Merk, *Biblische Theologie des NT in ihrer Anfangszeit* (Marburg, 1972); C. T. Fritsch, "New Trends in OT Theology," *BibSac,* 103 (1946), 293-305; E. Würthwein, "Zur Theologie des AT," *ThR,* 36 (1971), 185-208.

2. For the use of this principle in the pre-Reformation period, see H. Oberman, *The Harvest of Medieval Theology* (2nd ed.; Grand Rapids, 1967), pp. 201, 361-363, 377, 380-390.

3. G. Ebeling, "The Meaning of 'Biblical Theology,'" in *Word and Faith* (London, 1963), pp. 81-86.

The phrase "Biblical theology" is used in a twofold sense: (1) It can designate a theology which is rooted in its teachings in Scripture and bases its foundation on Scripture, or (2) it can designate the theology which the Bible itself contains.[4] In the latter sense it is a specific theological discipline, the origin and development of which we briefly describe.

Luther's hermeneutic of "sola scriptura" *and* his principle "was Christum treibet" together with the "letter-spirit" dualism[5] prevented him from developing a Biblical theology. Among some representatives of the Radical Reformation an approach resembling that of later Biblical theology was developed in the early 1530s by O. Glait and Andreas Fischer.[6]

It was not until a hundred years after the Reformation that the phrase "Biblical theology" actually appears for the first time in Wolfgang Jacob Christmann's *Teutsche Biblische Theologie* (Kempten, 1629). His work is presently not extant.[7] But the work of Henricus A. Diest entitled *Theologia biblica* (Daventri, 1643) is available and permits the earliest insight into the nature of an emerging discipline. "Biblical theology" is understood to consist of "proof-texts" from Scripture, taken indiscriminately from both Testaments in order to support the traditional "systems of doctrine" of early Protestant Orthodoxy. The subsidiary role of "Biblical theology" over against dogmatics was firmly established by Abraham Calovius, one of the most significant representatives of Protestant Orthodoxy, when he applied "Biblical theology" as a

---

4. W. Wrede, *Über Aufgabe und Methode der sogenannten Neutestamentlichen Theologie* (Göttingen, 1897), p. 79; Ebeling, *Word and Faith*, pp. 79-81; K. Stendahl, "Method in the Study of Biblical Theology," in *The Bible in Modern Scholarship*, ed. J. P. Hyatt (Nashville, 1965), pp. 202-205; Merk, *Biblische Theologie*, p. 7.

5. G. Ebeling, "Die Anfänge von Luthers Hermeneutik," *ZTK*, 48 (1951), 172-230, esp. 187-208.

6. G. F. Hasel, "Capito, Schwenckfeld and Crautwald on Sabbatarian Anabaptist Theology," *Mennonite Quarterly Review*, 46 (1972), 41-57.

7. Quoted in M. Lipenius, *Bibliotheca realis theologica omnium marteriarum* (Frankfurt, 1685), tom. I, col. 1709, and first referred to by Ebeling, *Word and Faith*, p. 84 n. 3.

designation of what was before called *theologia exegetica*.[8] In his work Biblical "proof-texts," which were called *dicta probantia* and later designated *collegia biblica*, had the role of supporting dogmatics. Calovius' lasting contribution was to assign to Biblical theology the role of a subsidiary discipline that supported Protestant orthodox doctrines. Biblical theology as a subsidiary discipline of orthodox dogmatics is evident in the Biblical theologies of Sebastian Schmidt (1671), Johann Hülsemann (1679), Johann Heinrich Maius (1689), Johann Wilhelm Baier (1716-19), and Christian Eberhard Weismann (1739).[9]

The back-to-the-Bible emphasis of German Pietism brought about a changing direction for Biblical theology.[10] In Pietism Biblical theology became a tool in the reaction against arid Protestant Orthodoxy.[11] Philipp Jacob Spener (1635-1705), a founding father of Pietism, opposed Protestant scholasticism with "Biblical theology."[12] The influence of Pietism is reflected in the works of Carl Haymann (1708), J. Deutschmann (1710), and J. C. Weidner (1722), which oppose orthodox systems of doctrine with "Biblical theology."[13]

As early as 1745 "Biblical theology" is clearly separated from dogmatic (systematic) theology and the former is conceived of as being the foundation of the latter.[14] This means

---

8. Calovius, *Systema locorum theologicorum I* (Withenbergae, 1655).

9. Schmidt, *Collegium Biblicum in quo dicta et Novi Testamenti iuxta seriem locorum communium theologicorum explinatur* (Strassburg, 1671); Hülsemann, *Vindiciae Sanctae Scripturae per loca classica systematis theologici* (Lipsiae, 1679); Maius, *Synopsis theologiae judicae veteris et nova* (Giessen, 1698); Baier, *Analysis et vindicatio illustrium scripturae* (Altdorf, 1716-19); Weismann, *Institutiones theologiae exegetico-dogmaticae* (Tübingen, 1739).

10. O. Betz, "History of Biblical Theology," *IDB*, I, 432.

11. Dentan, *Preface to OT Theology*, p. 17; Merk, *Biblische Theologie*, pp. 18-20; Kraus, *Biblische Theologie*, pp. 24-30.

12. P. J. Spener, *Pia Desideria* (Frankfurt, 1675), trans. and ed. T. G. Tappert (Philadelphia, 1964), pp. 54f.

13. Haymann, *Biblische Theologie* (Leipzig, 1708); Deutschmann, *Theologia Biblica* (1710); Weidner, *Deutsche Theologia Biblica* (Leipzig, 1722).

14. So in an unsigned article in J. H. Zedler, ed., *Grosses vollständiges Universallexikon* (Leipzig and Halle, 1745; repr. Graz, 1962), Vol. 43, col. 849, 866f., 920f. Cf. Merk, *Biblische Theologie*, p. 20.

that Biblical theology is emancipated from a role merely subsidiary to dogmatics. Inherent in this new development is the possibility that Biblical theology can become the rival of dogmatics and turn into a completely separate and independent discipline. These possibilities realized themselves under the influence of rationalism in the age of Enlightenment.

B. *The Age of Enlightenment.* In the age of Enlightenment *(Aufklärung)* a totally new approach for the study of the Bible was developed under several influences. First and foremost was rationalism's reaction against any form of supernaturalism.[15] Human reason was set up as the final criterion and chief source of knowledge, which meant that the authority of the Bible as the infallible record of divine revelation was rejected. The second major contribution of the period of the Enlightenment was the development of a new hermeneutic, the historical-critical method[16] which holds sway to the present day in liberalism and beyond. Third, there is the application of radical literary criticism to the Bible by J. B. Witter, J. Astruc, and others. Finally, rationalism by its very nature was led to abandon the orthodox view of the inspiration of the Bible so that ultimately the Bible became simply one of the ancient documents, to be studied as any other ancient document.[17]

15. English deism as represented by John Locke (1632-1704), John Toland (1670-1722). Matthew Tindal (1657-1733), and Thomas Chubb (1679-1747) with its emphasis on reason's supremacy over revelation was paralleled on the Continent with the "rational orthodoxy" of Jean A. Turretini (1671-1737), and such figures as S. J. Baumgarten, J. S. Semler (1725-1791). J. D. Michaelis (1717-1791). See W. G. Kümmel, *The NT: The History of the Investigation of its Problems* (Nashville, 1972), pp. 51-72 (hereafter cited as *History*); H.-J. Kraus, *Geschichte der historisch-kritischen Erforschung des AT* (2nd ed.; Neukirchen-Vluyn, 1969), pp. 70ff.

16. G. Ebeling, "The Significance of the Critical Historical Method for Church and Theology in Protestantism," in *Word and Faith*, pp. 17-61; U. Wilckens, "Über die Bedeutung historischer Kritik in der Bibelexegese," *Was heisst Auslegung der Heiligen Schrift?* ed. W. Joest et al. (Regensburg, 1966), pp. 85ff.; J. E. Benson, "The History of the Historical-Critical Method in the Church," *Dialog*, 12 (1973), 94-103; K. Scholder, *Ursprünge und Probleme der Bibelkritik im 17. Jahrhundert. Ein Beitrag zur Entstehung der historisch-kritischen Theologie* (Munich, 1966).

17. The key figure is J. S. Semler, whose four-volume *Abhandlung von*

Under the partial impetus of Pietism and with a strong dose of rationalism Anton Friedrich Büsching's publications (1756-58) reveal for the first time that "Biblical theology" becomes the rival of dogmatics.[18] Protestant dogmatics, also called "scholastic theology," is criticized for its empty speculations and lifeless theories. G. Ebeling has aptly summarized that "from being merely a subsidiary discipline of dogmatics 'biblical theology' now became a rival of the prevailing dogmatics."[19]

A chief catalyst in the "revolution of hermeneutics"[20] was the rationalist Johann Solomo Semler (1725-1791), whose four-volume *Treatise on the Free Investigation of the Canon* (1771-75) claimed that the Word of God and Holy Scripture are not at all identical.[21] This implied that not all parts of the Bible were inspired[22] and that the Bible is a purely historical document which as any other such document is to be investigated with a purely historical and thus critical methodology.[23] As a result Biblical theology can be nothing else but a historical discipline which stands in antithesis to traditional dogmatics.[24]

A highly significant step toward a separation of Biblical theology from dogmatics came in the four-volume work of Biblical theology (1771-75) by Gotthilf Traugott Zachariä (1729-1777).[25] Under the influence of the new orientation in

der freien Untersuchung des Kanons (1771-75) fought the orthodox doctrine of inspiration. Kraus, *Geschichte*, pp. 103ff.

18. A. F. Büsching, *Dissertatio inauguralis exhibens epitomen theologiae e solis literis sacris concinnatae* (Göttingen, 1756); idem, *Epitome Theologiae* (Lemgoviae, 1757); idem, *Gedanken von der Beschaffenheit und dem Vorzug der biblisch-dogmatischen Theologie vor der scholastischen* (Lemgo, 1758).

19. Ebeling, *Word and Faith*, p. 87.

20. Dentan, *Preface*, p. 19.

21. Kümmel, *History*, p. 63.

22. G. Hornig, *Die Anfänge der historisch-kritischen Theologie* (Göttingen, 1961), pp. 56ff.

23. Merk, *Biblische Theologie*, p. 22.

24. Hornig, *Die Anfänge*, pp. 57f.; Merk, *Biblische Theologie*, pp. 23f.

25. G. T. Zachariä, *Biblische Theologie oder Untersuchung des biblischen Grundes der vornehmsten theologischen Lehren* (Göttingen and Kiel, 1771-75); Dentan, *Preface*, p. 21; Kraus, *Biblische Theologie*, pp. 31-39; Merk, *Biblische Theologie*, pp. 23-26.

dogmatics and hermeneutics he attempted to build a system of theological teachings based upon careful exegetical work. Each book of Scripture has its own time, place, and intention. But Zachariä held to the inspiration of the Bible,[26] as did J. A. Ernesti (1707-1781)[27] whose Biblical-exegetical method he followed.[28] Historical exegesis and canonical understanding of Scripture do not collide in Zachariä's thought because "the historical aspect is a matter of secondary importance in theology."[29] On this basis there is no need to distinguish between the Testaments; they stand in reciprocal relationship to each other. Most basically Zachariä's interest was still in the dogmatic system, which he wished to cleanse from impurities.

The works of W. F. Hufnagel (1785-89)[30] and the rationalist C. F. von Ammon (1792)[31] hardly distinguish themselves in structure and design from that of Zachariä. Hufnagel's Biblical theology consists of a "historical-critical collection of Biblical proof-texts supporting dogmatics."[32] Von Ammon took up ideas of Semler and the philosophers Lessing and Kant and presented actually more a "philosophical theology." Significant in his treatment is the higher evaluation of the NT than the OT,[33] which is a first step toward an independent treatment of OT theology[34] which was realized four years later by G. L. Bauer.

The late Neologist and rationalist Johann Philipp Gabler (1753-1826), who never wrote or even intended to write a Biblical theology, made a most decisive and far-reaching con-

---

26. Zachariä, *Biblische Theologie*, I, p. VI.
27. J. A. Ernesti, *Institutio interpres Novi Testamenti* (Leipzig, 1761); Kümmel, *History*, pp. 60f.
28. Kraus, *Biblische Theologie*, p. 35.
29. Zachariä, *Biblische Theologie*, I, p. LXVI.
30. W. F. Hufnagel, *Handbuch der biblischen Theologie* (Erlangen, Vol. I, 1785; Vol. II, 1789).
31. C. F. von Ammon, *Entwurf einer reinen biblischen Theologie*, 3 vols. (Erlangen, 1792). Cf. Kraus, *Biblische Theologie*, pp. 40-51.
32. D. G. C. von Cölln, *Biblische Theologie* (Leipzig, 1836), I, 22.
33. Kraus, *Biblische Theologie*, p. 51.
34. Dentan, *Preface*, p. 26.

tribution to the development of the new discipline in his inaugural lecture at the University of Altdorf on March 30, 1787.[35] This year marks the beginning of Biblical theology's role as a purely historical discipline, completely independent from dogmatics. Gabler's famous definition reads: "Biblical theology possesses a historical character, transmitting what the sacred writers thought about divine matters; dogmatic theology, on the contrary, possesses a didactic character, teaching what a particular theologian philosophizes about divine matters in accordance to his ability, time, age, place, sect or school, and other similar things."[36] Gabler's inductive, historical, and descriptive approach to Biblical theology is based on three essential methodological considerations: (1) Inspiration is to be left out of consideration, because "the Spirit of God most emphatically did not destroy in every holy man his own ability to understand and the measure of natural insight into things."[37] What counts is not "divine authority" but "only what they [Biblical writers] thought."[38] (2) Biblical theology has the task of gathering carefully the concepts and ideas of the individual Bible writers, because the Bible does not contain the ideas of just a single man. Therefore the opinions of Bible writers need to be "carefully assembled" from Holy Writ, suitably arranged, properly related to general concepts, and carefully compared with one another. . . ."[39] This task can be accomplished by means of a consistent application of the historical-critical method with the aid of lit-

35. J. P. Gabler, "Oratio de iusto discrimine theologicae biblicae et dogmaticae regundisque recte utriusque finibus" ["About the Correct Distinction of Biblical and Dogmatic Theology and the Right Definition of their Goals"], in *Kleine theologische Schriften*, ed. Th. A. Gabler and J. G. Gabler (Ulm, 1831), II, 179-198. A complete German translation is provided by Merk, *Biblische Theologie*, pp. 273-284; a partial English translation is found in Kümmel, *History*, pp. 98-100.

36. "Oratio," in *Kleine theologische Schriften*, II, 183-184. Cf. R. Smend, "J. P. Gablers Begründung der biblischen Theologie," *EvT*, 22 (1962), 345-367; Kraus, *Biblische Theologie*, pp. 52-59; Merk, *Biblische Theologie*, pp. 29-140.

37. *Kleine theologische Schriften*, II, 186.

38. P. 186; Kümmel, *History*, p. 99.

39. P. 187; Kümmel, *History*, p. 100.

erary criticism, historical criticism, and philosophical criticism.[40] (3) Biblical theology as a historical discipline is by definition obliged to "distinguish between the several periods of the old and new religion."[41] The main task is to investigate which ideas are of importance for Christian doctrine, namely which ones "apply today" and which ones have no "validity for our time."[42] These programmatic declarations gave direction to the future of Biblical (OT and NT) theology despite the fact that Gabler's program for Biblical theology was conditioned by his time and contains significant limitations.[43]

The goal of a strictly historical Biblical theology is for the first time realized by Georg Lorenz Bauer (1755-1806),[44] a student of J. G. Eichhorn. Bauer is to be credited as the first to publish an OT theology, under the title *Theologie des AT* (Leipzig, 1796).[45] Bauer has the credit, for better or for worse, for having separated Biblical theology into OT and NT theology.[46] Bauer's *Theologie des AT* has the threefold structure of (1) Theology, (2) Anthropology, and (3) Christology. This reveals his dependence on the system of dogmatic theology. As a "historical-critical rationalist"[47] Bauer's determining position in the development of Biblical (OT and NT) theology was his consistent application of the historical-critical method supported with rationalism's emphasis on historical reason.[48] His historical-critical reconstruction of the manifoldness of the Biblical witnesses raised among other problems the matter of the relationship between the Testaments, a problem under

40. Merk, *Biblische Theologie*, pp. 68-81.

41. Gabler, "Oratio," in *Kleine theologische Schriften*, II, 186; Kümmel, *History*, p. 99.

42. P. 191; Kümmel, *History*, p. 100.

43. Merk, *Biblische Theologie*, pp. 87-90, 111-113.

44. See especially Kraus, *Biblische Theologie*, pp. 87-91 and Merk, *Biblische Theologie*, pp. 141-203.

45. Shortly later he published in four volumes a *Biblische Theologie des NT* (Leipzig, 1800-1802).

46. This separate treatment Gabler had called for in his inaugural lecture of March 30, 1787.

47. Merk, *Biblische Theologie*, p. 202.

48. P. 199.

vigorous debate today. Furthermore, the whole issue of Biblical theology's nature as a purely historical discipline as vigorously maintained by Gabler and consequently by Bauer and others is again questioned in the recent debate, as is the question of the nature of the descriptive task. Nevertheless, Gabler and Bauer are the founders of the independent discipline of Biblical and OT theology.

C. *From the Enlightenment to Dialectical Theology.* It has been shown how during the age of the Enlightenment the discipline of Biblical theology freed itself from a role subsidiary to dogmatics to become its rival. The subsequent development reveals that the new historical discipline succumbed to and was dominated by various philosophical systems, then experienced the challenge of conservative Biblical scholarship, and finally was eclipsed by the "history-of-religions" *(Religionsgeschichte)* approach. In the decades after World War I it received new life in the period of dialectical theology.

The early decades of the nineteenth century witness the appearance of several significant works. Gottlob Ph. Chr. Kaiser published three volumes on Biblical theology between 1813 and 1821.[49] Along with his rationalistic approach he rejected any kind of supernaturalism and attempted to delineate the historio-genetic development of OT religion. He was the first to apply a "history-of-religions" approach, and subordinated all Biblical and nonbiblical aspects under the principle of "universal religion."

The work of W. M. L. de Wette, *Biblische Dogmatik* (1813), a student of Gabler, marked the first move away from rationalism. He adopted Kantian philosophy as mediated by J. F. Fries and became the first Biblical theologian who combined Biblical theology with a system of philosophy.[50] His higher synthesis of faith and feeling moved in a "genetic develop-

49. G. P. C. Kaiser, *Die biblische Theologie*, 3 vols. (Erlangen, 1813, 1814, 1821). Cf. Dentan, *Preface*, pp. 28f.; Kraus, *Biblische Theologie*, pp. 57f.; Merk, *Biblische Theologie*, pp. 214-216.

50. Kraus, *Biblische Theologie*, p. 72.

ment" of religion from Hebraism via Judaism to Christianism.[51]

The two-volume work of the moderate rationalist D. C. von Cölln, which was published in 1836, deals in its first part with the *Biblical Theology of the OT*.[52] It reacts strongly to de Wette's introduction of philosophy into Biblical theology. Von Cölln presented a historical Biblical theology with a strong theocratic emphasis. As others before him, he moved within the tension of particularism and universalism and delineated a historical developmentalism of Hebraism-Judaism-Christianism.

Wilhelm Vatke (1806-1882)[53] regarded the "rationalistic period of Biblical theology as a necessary but now superseded development. He was the first to adopt the Hegelian philosophy of thesis (nature religion), antithesis (spiritual religion = Hebrew religion), and synthesis (absolute or universal religion = Christianity), in his *Die biblische Theologie. Die Religion des AT* (Berlin, 1835). He claimed that the system for the arrangement of the OT material must *not* be set forth on the basis of categories derived from the Bible but must be imposed from the outside,[54] and formulated the dogma of the "history-of-religion" approach concerning the "independent totality" of the OT.[55] Three years after the publication of Vatke's tome, which later had great influence on J. Wellhausen,[56] a second "history-of-religions" OT theology based on Hegelianism was published by Bruno Bauer (1809-1882),[57] who arrived at opposite conclusions from his teacher Vatke.[58]

---

51. Merk, *Biblische Theologie*, pp. 210-214.

52. *Biblische Theologie*, 2 vols. (Leipzig, 1836). Cf. Kraus, *Biblische Theologie*, pp. 60-69.

53. L. Perlitt, *Vatke und Wellhausen* (Berlin, 1965).

54. W. Vatke, *Biblische Theologie. Die Religion des AT* (Berlin, 1835), pp. 4f.

55. Kraus, *Biblische Theologie*, pp. 93-96.

56. Dentan, *Preface*, p. 36.

57. B. Bauer, *Die Religion des AT in der geschichtlichen Entwicklung ihrer Principien*, 2 vols. (Berlin, 1838).

58. Moderate Hegelianism is also present in L. Noack, *Die Biblische*

During the middle of the nineteenth century a very power-
ful conservative reaction against the rationalistic and philosophical approaches to OT (and Biblical) theology arose on
the part of those who denied the validity of the historical-
critical approach and from those who attempted to combine
a moderate historical approach with the acceptance of divine
revelation. E. W. Hengstenberg's *Christology of the OT* (1829-
1835)[59] argued against the validity of the historical-critical
methodology as applied to the Bible and made little distinction between the Testaments.

A moderate historical approach with due allowance for the
authority and inspiration of the OT is manifested in the posthumously published OT theologies of J. C. F. Steudel (1840),[60]
H. A. C. Haevernick (1848),[61] and G. F. Oehler (1873-74).[62]
Steudel insisted on the grammatical-historical method and
rejected the destructive historical-critical method. He maintained the divine origin of the OT but rejected the narrow
view of "verbal inspiration."[63] He was strongly critical of the
subjectivity of the Hegelians[64] but has been classified himself
as a "rational supernaturalist." In his structure of OT theology
he followed the God-Man-Salvation system of dogmatics.
Haevernick adopted the idea of developmentalism of OT religion in the form of "primitive religion-law-prophets," and
held on to the God-Man-Salvation scheme. At the same time

---

*Theologie, Einleitung ins Alte und Neue Testament und Darstellung des Lehrge-
haltes der biblischen Bücher* (Halle, 1853), who combined a strange conglom-
eration of ideas of historical-critical research of de Wette and Vatke for the
OT and F. C. Baur for the NT.

59. The German original is entitled *Christologie des AT* (Berlin, 1829-
1835) and was first translated into English in 1854. It was a collector's item
until recently when it was reprinted by MacDonald Publ. Comp., P.O. Box
6006, MacDill AFB, Florida 33608.

60. J. C. F. Steudel, *Vorlesungen über die Theologie des AT,* ed. G. F. Oehler
(Berlin, 1840).

61. H. A. C. Haevernick, *Vorlesungen über die Theologie des AT,* ed.
E. Hahn (Erlangen, 1848).

62. G. F. Oehler, *Theologie des AT,* 2 vols. (Tübingen, 1873, 1874).

63. Steudel, *Vorlesungen,* pp. 44-51, 64.

64. Dentan, *Preface,* p. 42.

he sought to distinguish between the Testaments and neutral-
ized dogmatic-orthodox axioms.

Oehler's contribution was the most significant and lasting.
He was the first since Gabler to publish a volume dealing
extensively with the theory and method of a Biblical-theological
understanding of OT theology.[65] His massive *Theology of the OT*
appeared in French and English.[66] Oehler reacted both against
the Marcionite strain introduced by F. Schleiermacher with the
depreciation of the OT and the total uniformity of OT and NT
as maintained by Hengstenberg.[67] But he himself does not give
up the unity of the Testaments. There is unity in diversity.[68]
Oehler accepts the division of OT and NT theology,[69] but OT
theology can function properly only within the larger canonical
context. OT theology is a "historical science which is based
upon grammatical-historical exegesis whose task it is to repro-
duce the content of the Biblical writings according to the rules
of language under consideration of the historical circumstances
during which the writings originated and the individual condi-
tions of the sacred writers."[70] The proper method for Biblical
theology is "the historico-genetic" approach according to which
grammatical-historical exegesis, not historical-critical exegesis,
is to be combined with an "organic process of development" of
OT religion.[71] Oehler's OT theology is considered to be "the
outstanding salvation-historical presentation of Biblical theology of the 19th century."[72] However, it is "today almost
completely outmoded, largely because Oehler attempted to deal
with the material genetically"[73] under the influence of Hegel.[74]

---

65. G. F. Oehler, *Prolegomena zur Theologie des AT* (Stuttgart, 1845).
66. English translations by E. D. Smith and S. Taylor (Edinburgh, 1874-
75) and G. E. Day (New York, 1883).
67. Oehler, *Theologie*, I, 3-4.
68. Pp. 29-31, 70.
69. P. 33.
70. P. 66.
71. Pp. 67-68.
72. Kraus, *Biblische Theologie*, p. 106.
73. Dentan, *Preface*, pp. 45f.
74. Oehler, *Prolegomena*, p. x.

A significant part of the conservative reaction came to expression in the "salvation-history school" with such theologians as Gottfried Menken (1768-1831),[75] Johann T. Beck (1804-1878),[76] and especially J. Ch. Konrad von Hofmann (1810-1877).[77] The "salvation-history school" of the nineteenth century is based upon (1) the history of the people of God as "expressed in the Word"; (2) the idea of the inspiration of the Bible; and (3) the (preliminary) result of the history between God and man in Jesus Christ. Von Hofmann found in the Bible a record of linear saving history in which the active Lord of history is the triune God whose purpose and goal it is to redeem mankind. Since Jesus Christ is the primordial goal of the world to which salvation history aims and from which it receives its meaning,[78] the OT contains salvation-historical proclamation. This an OT theology has to expound. Each book of the Bible is assigned its logical place in the scheme of salvation history. The Bible is not to be regarded primarily as a collection of proof-texts or a repository of doctrine but a witness to God's activity in history which will not be fully completed until the eschatological consummation. The influence of the "salvation-history school" on the development of both OT and NT theology has been considerable and is felt to the present day, though with great variation and in new forms.[79]

Just before OT theology was eclipsed by the "history-of-religions" approach, which dealt it a virtual deathblow, Henrich Ewald's four-volume monumental *magnum opus* was

75. The importance of his place in this school has been demonstrated by Kraus, *Biblische Theologie*, pp. 240-244.

76. Pp. 244-247.

77. J. Ch. K. von Hofmann, *Weissagung und Erfüllung im Alten und Neuen Testamente* (Nördlingen, 1841-44); idem, *Der Schriftbeweis* (Nördlingen, 1852-56); idem, *Biblische Hermeneutik*, ed. J. Hofmeister and Volck (Nördlingen, 1880), trans. *Interpreting the Bible* (Minneapolis, 1959).

78. *Weissagung und Erfüllung*, I, 40.

79. In the field of OT theology an influence is explicit in O. Procksch, *Theologie des AT* (Gütersloh, 1950), pp. 17-19, 44-47; G. von Rad, *OTT*, II, 357ff.; and others (see below, Ch. III). In the field of NT theology, see G. E. Ladd, *A Theology of the NT* (Grand Rapids, 1974), pp. 16-21, for those who may be counted among present-day scholars using this approach.

published.[80] For a whole generation Ewald's conservative influence held back German scholarship from accepting the modernistic reconstruction of Israelite religion as popularized by Wellhausen.[81] Ewald's students Ferdinand Hitzig (1807-1875)[82] and August Dillmann (1823-1894)[83] wrote OT theologies which were posthumously published. Ewald defended a systematic treatment of his subject; Hitzig wrote a "history of ideas"; and Dillmann a "history of revelation" with salvation-historical emphases.

The year 1878 marks the beginning of the triumph of the "history-of-religions" *(Religionsgeschichte)* approach over OT theology with the publication of the *Prolegomena to the History of Israel* by Julius Wellhausen (1844-1918). OT (and Biblical) theology was from now on deeply influenced by (1) the late date assigned to the P document in Pentateuchal criticism as advanced by K. H. Graf and A. Kuenen and popularized by Wellhausen,[84] and (2) the new total picture of the development of the history of Israelite religion as reconstructed on the basis of the new dates assigned to OT materials by the Graf-Kuenen-Wellhausen school. Another distinguishing feature of the "history-of-religions" school is the historical-genetic method of evolutionary development. The new school is in accord with the intellectual temper of that age "which had been taught by Hegel and Darwin to regard the principles of evolution as the magic key to unlock all the secrets of history."[85] The title of OT theology is used (misused) for the

80. H. Ewald, *Die Lehre der Bibel von Gott oder Theologie des Alten und Neuen Bundes* (Leipzig, 1871-76). Vols. I-III were translated under the title *Old and New Testament Theology* (Edinburgh, 1888).

81. So according to J. Wellhausen as referred to by A. Bertholet, "H. Ewald," *Die Religion in Geschichte und Gegenwart* (Tübingen, 1901), II, 767.

82. F. Hitzig, *Vorlesungen über Biblische Theologie und messianische Weissagungen des AT,* ed. J. J. Kneucher (Karlsruhe, 1880); cf. Dentan, *Preface,* p. 49; Kraus, *Biblische Theologie,* pp. 107-110.

83. A. Dillmann, *Handbuch der alttestamentlichen Theologie,* ed. R. Kittel (Leipzig, 1895); cf. Kraus, *Biblische Theologie,* pp. 110-113.

84. R. J. Thompson, *Moses and the Law in a Century of Criticism Since Graf* (Leiden, 1970), pp. 53-101.

85. Dentan, *Preface,* p. 51.

publications in this the new era by August Kayser (1886),[86] Hermann Schultz (five editions from 1869-1896),[87] C. Piepenbring (1886),[88] A. B. Davidson (1904),[89] and Bernhard Stade (1905),[90] whereas Rudolf Smend (1893) was more exact.[91]

For over four decades OT theology was eclipsed by *Religionsgeschichte.*[92] The full-fledged historicism of the "history-of-religions" approach had led to the final destruction of the unity of the OT, which was reduced to a collection of materials from detached periods and consisted simply of Israelite reflections of as many different pagan religions. This approach had a particularly destructive influence both on OT theology and on the understanding of the OT in every other aspect. In addition "the essential inner coherence of the Old and New Testaments was reduced, so to speak, to a thin thread of historical connection and causal sequence between the two, with the result that an external causality—not even susceptible in every case of secure demonstration—was substituted for a homogeneity that was real because it rested on the similar content of their experience of life."[93] It took a "real act of courage" to break "the tyranny of historicism in OT studies"[94] and to rediscover and revive OT theology.

D. *The Revival of OT Theology.* In the decades following

86. A. Kayser, *Die Theologie des AT in ihrer Geschichtlichen Entwicklung dargestellt,* ed. E. Reuss (Strassburg, 1886). The latest edition was retitled *Geschichte der israelitischen Religion* (Strassburg, 1903).

87. H. Schultz, *Alttestamentliche Theologie* (Braunschweig, 1869). In the 2nd ed. of 1878 Schultz adopted Wellhausen's theory. A translation was made of the 4th ed. of 1889 under the title *OT Theology* (Edinburgh, 1892). The 5th German ed. appeared in Göttingen, 1896.

88. C. Piepenbring, *Théologie de l'Ancien Testament* (Paris, 1886). The English translation appeared in New York, 1893.

89. A. B. Davidson, *The Theology of the OT,* ed. S. D. F. Salmond (Edinburgh, 1904).

90. B. Stade, *Biblische Theologie des AT* (Tübingen, 1905).

91. R. Smend, *Lehrbuch der alttestamentlichen Religionsgeschichte* (Freiburg-Leipzig, 1893).

92. Not until 1922 with the publication of E. König, *Theologie des AT kritisch und vergleichend dargestellt* (Stuttgart, 1922), did an OT theology appear "which attempted to take its title seriously" (Eichrodt, *OTT,* I, 31).

93. Eichrodt, *OTT,* I, 30.

94. Eichrodt, *OTT,* I, 31.

World War I several factors, aside from the changing *Zeitgeist*, brought about a revival of OT (and NT) theology. R. C. Dentan suggests three major factors that contributed to the "renaissance of OT theology": (1) a general loss of faith in evolutionary naturalism; (2) a reaction against the conviction that historical truth can be attained by pure scientific "objectivity" or that such objectivity is indeed attainable; and (3) the trend of a return to the idea of revelation in dialectical (neo-orthodox) theology.[95] The historicism of liberalism[96] was found to be totally inadequate and a new approach needed to be developed.

In 1922 came the first clear sign of reviving interest in OT theology with the publication of E. König's *Theologie des AT.* He had a high opinion of the reliability of the OT, rejected the Wellhausenistic evolution of OT religion, and called for an exact use of the grammatical-historical method of interpretation. His OT theology is, however, a "hybrid" in that he combines a history of the development of Israelite religion with a history of particular theological factors of OT faith.[97]

The 1920s are characterized by a rousing debate over the nature of OT theology.[98] In 1923 W. Staerk[99] raised the question of the relationship between *Religionsgeschichte* and philosophy of religion and Biblical theology. Two years later appeared the significant essay by C. Steuernagel,[100] who pleaded for the autonomy of OT theology as a purely historical subject, sup-

95. Dentan, *Preface*, p. 61.
96. See especially C. T. Craig, "Biblical Theology and the Rise of Historicism," *JBL*, 62 (1943), 281-294; M. Kähler, "Biblical Theology," *The New Schaff-Herzog Encyclopedia of Religious Knowledge* (repr. Grand Rapids, 1952), II, 183ff.; C. R. North, "OT Theology and the History of Hebrew Religion," *SJT*, 2 (1949), 113-126.
97. König, *Theologie des AT*, p. 1.
98. For surveys, see N. W. Porteous, "OT Theology," in *The OT and Modern Study*, ed. H. H. Rowley (London, 1951), pp. 316-324; Emil G. Kraeling, *The OT Since the Reformation* (New York, 1955), pp. 268-284; Dentan, *Preface*, pp. 62-71; and for details below, Chapter II.
99. W. Staerk, "Religionsgeschichte und Religionsphilosophie in ihrer Bedeutung für die biblische Theologie," *ZTK*, 4 (1923), 289-300.
100. C. Steuernagel, "Alttestamentliche Theologie und alttestamentliche Religionsgeschichte," in *Vom AT. Festschrift für K. Marti*, ed. K. Budde (BZAW, 41; Giessen, 1925), pp. 266-273.

plementary to the history of Israel's religion. In 1926 O. Eissfeldt[101] entered the discussion by asserting that OT theology is a nonhistorical discipline, determined by the faith stance of the theologian, and is thus subjective, whereas the study of the religion of Israel is historical and objective. This dichotomy between knowledge and faith, objectivity and subjectivity, that which is relative and that which is normative, was directly challenged in an essay by W. Eichrodt,[102] who keeps both feet planted in history and finds Eissfeldt's suggestions unsatisfactory. Eichrodt points out that Gabler's heritage of OT theology as a historical discipline is essentially sound and that there is no such thing as a history of the religion of Israel which is entirely free from presuppositions. A subjective element is present in every science because the process of selection and organization cannot be purely objective.

The "golden age" of OT theology began in the 1930s and continues to the present. Significant volumes on OT theology were published by E. Sellin (1933) and L. Köhler (1936), both of which follow the God-Man-Salvation arrangement.[103] W. Eichrodt (1933-39) pioneered the cross-section method based on a unifying principle,[104] and W. Vischer (1934) published the first volume of his *The Witness of the OT to Christ*.[105] An important contribution to the subject was made by H. Wheeler Robinson.[106] Among major contributions to OT theology are those by W. and H. Moeller (1938), P. Heinisch (1940), O. Procksch (1949), O. J. Baab (1949), G. E. Wright

101. O. Eissfeldt, "Israelitisch-jüdische Religionsgeschichte und alttestamentliche Theologie," *ZAW*, 44 (1926), 1-12.

102. W. Eichrodt, "Hat die alttestamentliche Theologie noch selbständige Bedeutung innerhalb der alttestamentlichen Wissenschaft?" *ZAW*, 47 (1929), 83-91.

103. E. Sellin, *Theologie des AT* (Leipzig, 1933); L. Köhler, *Theologie des AT* (Tübingen, 1936), trans. as *OT Theology* (London, 1957).

104. W. Eichrodt, *Theologie des AT*, 3 vols. (Leipzig, 1933, 1935, 1939), trans. as *Theology of the OT*, 2 vols. (Philadelphia, 1961, 1967).

105. W. Vischer, *Das Christuszeugnis des AT* (Zurich, 1934), trans. London, 1949.

106. H. W. Robinson, *Inspiration and Revelation in the OT* (Oxford, 1946); idem, *Record and Revelation* (London, 1938), pp. 303-348.

(1952, 1970), Th. C. Vriezen (1949), P. van Imschoot (1954), G. von Rad (1957, 1960), J. B. Payne (1962), A. Deissler (1972), G. Fohrer (1972), W. Zimmerli (1972), and T. L. McKenzie (1974).[107] Works with the title "Biblical theology" were published by M. Burrows (1946), G. Vos (1948), J. Blenkinsopp (1968), and C. R. Lehman (1971).[108] E. J. Young (1959) and J. N. Schofield (1964) came out with short studies on OT methodology from conservative and moderate perspectives respectively.[109] B. S. Childs provides a valuable survey of the "Biblical Theology Movement" in America which, although derivative of European Biblical theology, is primarily an outgrowth of the polarity of the battle over the Bible in the Fundamentalist-Modernist controversy fought from 1910 to the 1930s in the USA.[110]

There is no consensus on any of the major problems of OT (and Biblical) theology. Fundamental issues are widely debated among scholars of various backgrounds and schools of thought. The historical survey of this chapter highlights major roots of the basic issues in the current debate on OT theology with which the following chapters (II-V) deal.

---

107. P. Heinisch, *Theologie des AT* (Bonn, 1940), trans. *Theology of the OT* (Collegeville, MN, 1950); O. Procksch, *Theologie des AT* (Gütersloh, 1949); O. J. Baab, *The Theology of the OT* (Nashville, 1949); G. E. Wright, *God Who Acts: Biblical Theology as Recital* (SBT, 1/8; London, 1952); idem, *The OT and Theology* (New York, 1970); Th. C. Vriezen, *Hoofdlijnen der Theologie van het Oude Testament* (Wageningen, 1954), 2nd rev. ed. *An Outline of OT Theology* (Newton, MA, 1970); P. van Imschoot, *Théologie de l'AT* (Tournai, 1943), trans. *Theology of the OT* (New York, 1965); J. B. Payne, *The Theology of the Older Testament* (Grand Rapids, 1962); A. Deissler, *Die Grundbotschaft des AT* (Freiburg i. Br., 1972); G. Fohrer, *Theologische Grundstrukturen des AT* (Berlin, 1972); W. Zimmerli, *Grundriss der alttestamentlichen Theologie* (Stuttgart, 1972); J. L. McKenzie, *A Theology of the OT* (New York, 1974).

108. M. Burrows, *An Outline of Biblical Theology* (Philadelphia, 1946); G. Vos, *Biblical Theology* (Grand Rapids, 1948); J. Blenkinsopp, *A Sketchbook of Biblical Theology* (London, 1968); C. R. Lehman, *Biblical Theology I: OT* (Scottdale, PA, 1971).

109. E. J. Young, *The Study of OT Theology Today* (London, 1959); J. N. Schofield, *Introducing OT Theology* (Philadelphia, 1964).

110. B. S. Childs, *Biblical Theology in Crisis* (Philadelphia, 1970), pp. 13-87.

II. The Question of Methodology

The issues related to the question of methodology in OT theology are complex. In the years following World War I a debate regarding an aspect of the question of methodology was renewed and has remained with us to the present. It relates to the question of whether OT theology is purely descriptive and historical or whether it is a normative and theological enterprise. In this chapter we will address this question first. Then we will attempt to classify various ways in which scholars have conceived OT theology in order to analyze major current methodological approaches and the questions they raise.

The Descriptive and/or Normative Tasks

The descriptive task in the scholarly tradition of Gabler-Wrede-Stendahl[1] has its proponents to the present day in

---

1. Johann Philipp Gabler's inaugural lecture "Oratio de iusto discrimine theologiae biblicae et dogmaticae, regundisque recte utriusque finibus," delivered at the University of Altdorf, March 30, 1787, marked the beginning of a new phase in the study of Biblical theology through its claim that "Biblical theology is historical in character [*e genere historico*] in that it sets forth what sacred writers thought about divine matters . . ." (in *Gableri Opuscula Academica II* [1831], pp. 183f.). Cf. R. Smend, "J. Ph. Gablers Begründung der biblischen Theologie," *EvT,* 22 (1962), 345ff. Wilhelm Wrede's programmatic essay *Über Aufgabe und Methode der sogenannten Neutestamentlischen Theo-*

E. Jacob,[2] G. E. Wright,[3] P. Wernberg-Möller,[4] and P. S. Watson,[5] among others. The Biblical theologian is said to have to place his attention on describing "what the text meant" and not "what it means," to use Stendahl's distinctions.[6] The progress of Biblical theology is dependent upon a rigorous application of this distinction,[7] which is to be understood as a "wedge"[8] that separates once and for all the descriptive ap-

---

logie (Göttingen, 1897), p. 8, emphasizes again the "strictly historical character" of NT (Biblical) Theology. The penetrating and influential article of Krister Stendahl, "Biblical Theology, Contemporary, " in *IDB*, I, 418-432, followed by his paper "Method in the Study of Biblical Theology," in *The Bible in Modern Scholarship*, ed. J. Philip Hyatt (Nashville, 1965), pp. 196-209, presents arguments for the rigorous distinction between "what it meant" and "what it means."

2. E. Jacob, *Theology of the OT* (London, 1958), p. 31, states that OT theology is a "strictly historical subject." In a somewhat more cautious tone he maintained recently that no method may claim absolute priority over another, because a theology is always *"unterwegs"* (*Grundfragen alttestamentlicher Theologie*, p. 17) and for doing OT theology there are various ways open (p. 16). At the same time he maintains that a theology of the OT has the task of presenting or expressing what is present in the OT itself (p. 14).

3. G. E. Wright, *God Who Acts*, pp. 37f., expresses at length that he believes Biblical theology to be a "historical discipline" which is best described as a "theology of recital, in which man confesses his faith by reciting the formative events of his history as the redemptive handiwork of God. The later Wright, who now feels closer to Eichrodt than von Rad, holds on to the notion that Biblical theology is a "descriptive discipline." See G. E. Wright, "Biblical Archaeology Today," in *New Directions in Biblical Archaeology*, ed. D. N. Freedman and J. C. Greenfield (New York, 1969), p. 159.

4. P. Wernberg-Möller, "Is There an OT Theology?" *Hibbert Journal*, 59 (1960), 29, argues for a "descriptive, disinterested theology."

5. P. S. Watson, "The Nature and Function of Biblical Theology," *ExpTim*, 73 (1962), 200: "As a scientific discipline, Biblical theology has a purely descriptive task. . . ." See the critique by H. Cunliffe-Jones, "The 'Truth' of the Bible," *ExpTim*, 73 (1962), 287.

6. Stendahl, *IDB*, I, 419.

7. Here Stendahl follows the position of the contributors from Uppsala University of the volume *The Root of the Vine: Essays in Biblical Theology*, ed. A. Fridrichsen (London, 1953), who agree that Biblical theology is primarily a historical and descriptive task to be distinguished from later normative reflections.

8. Childs, *Biblical Theology in Crisis*, p. 79, objects to the dichotomy reaffirmed by Stendahl on the basis that it drives a "wedge between the Biblical and theological disciplines" which the Biblical Theology Movement sought to remove.

proach to the Bible from the normative approach often assigned to the systematic theologian, whose task it is to translate its meaning for the present. The latter task, "what it
means" for today, is not to be considered a proper part of the
strictly historical descriptive method.

The distinction between what a text meant and what a text
means is at the core of the most fundamental problem of OT
theology, because "what it meant" is not simply discovering the
meaning of the Biblical text within its own canonical Biblical
context; it is historical reconstruction. By historical reconstruction the modern scholar means a presentation of the thought-
world of the OT (or NT) as reconstructed on the basis of its
socio-cultural surroundings. Historical reconstruction, or
"what the text meant," understands the Bible as conditioned by
its time and by its surroundings. The Bible's time and place, the
Bible's socio-cultural environment, its social setting, and its
cultural environment among other nations and religions become the virtually exclusive key to its meaning. In this sense
the Bible is interpreted in the same way as any other ancient
document. Just as "what it meant" is historical reconstruction
done with the principles of the historical-critical method, so
"what it means" is theological interpretation. Theological interpretation is the translation of the historically reconstructed text
into the situation of the modern world. Normally this means
that the key to theological interpretation is the modern worldview of the individual interpreter. Regardless of what the interpreter's worldview is and what kind of philosophical system
may be adopted for theological interpretation or "what it
means," the theological and interpretative approach of "what it
means" is doing theology and is conceived of as normative for
faith and life.

It is evident that the distinction of modern times between
"what it meant" and "what it means," i.e., theological interpretation which is normative, is problematical in both its distinction and its task. D. H. Kelsey, e.g., has stated succinctly
that there are several ways in which both "what it meant" and
"what it means" can be related to each other with varying

results.[9] First, it may be decided that the descriptive approach that seeks to determine "what it meant" by whatever methods of inquiry is considered to be identical with "what it means." Second, it may be decided that "what it meant" contains propositions, ideas, etc. that are to be decoded and translated systematically and explicated and that this is "what it means," even though those explications may never have occurred to the original authors and might have been rejected by them. Third, it may be decided that "what it meant" is an archaic way of speaking dependent upon its own culture and time that needs to be redescribed in contemporary ways of speaking of the same phenomena, and that this redescription is "what it means." "This assumes that the theologian has access to the phenomena independent of scripture and 'what it meant,' so that he can check the archaic description and have a basis for his own."[10] Fourth, it may be decided that "what it meant" refers to the way in which early Christians used Biblical texts and that "what it means" is simply the way these are used by modern Christians. In this case there is a genetic relationship. Kelsey notes, "None of these decisions can itself be either validated or invalidated by exegetical study of the text, for what is at issue is precisely how exegetical study is related to doing theology."[11] If this is the case, then one must ask on what grounds one makes a theological judgment in favor of one over the other of these or other ways of relating "what it meant" to "what it means."

Criticisms of the distinction between "what it meant" and "what it means," i.e., between historical reconstruction or what is historical, descriptive, and objective, and theological interpretation or what is theological and normative, have been advanced from several quarters. B. S. Childs[12] objects to the historical and descriptive approach on account of its limiting

9. D. H. Kelsey, *The Uses of Scripture in Recent Theology* (Philadelphia, 1975), pp. 202f. n. 18.
10. Ibid., p. 203.
11. Ibid.
12. Childs, "Interpretation in Faith: The Theological Responsibility of an OT Commentary," *Interp*, 18 (1964), 432-449.

nature. The historical and descriptive task cannot be seen as a neutral stage leading to later genuine theological interpretation.[13] The text, says Childs, is "a witness beyond itself to the divine purpose of God."[14] There must be "the movement from the level of the witness to the reality itself."[15] Stendahl concedes that the descriptive task is "able to describe scriptural texts as aiming beyond themselves . . . in their intention and their function through the ages. . . ."[16] But Stendahl denies that the explication of this reality is a part of the task of the Biblical theologian. Childs, however, insists that "what the text 'meant' is determined in large measure by its relation to the one to whom it is directed." He argues that "when seen from the context of the canon both the question of what the text meant and what it means are inseparably linked and both belong to the task of the interpretation of the Bible as Scripture."[17] A. Dulles makes a similar point when he speaks of the "uneasiness at the radical separation . . . between what the Bible meant and what it means."[18] Whereas Stendahl gives normative value to the task of what the Bible means, i.e., theological interpretation, Dulles maintains that normative value must be given also to what the Bible meant, and we may add what it meant in its own canonical context in speaking with Childs. If this is the case, then Stendahl's dichotomy is seriously impaired because "the possibility of an 'objective' or non-committed descriptive approach, and thus . . . one of the most attractive features of Stendahl's position" is done away with.[19] Similar points are made by R. A. F. MacKenzie, C. Spicq, and R. de Vaux.[20]

13. Ibid., p. 437.

14. Ibid., p. 440.

15. Ibid., p. 444.

16. Stendahl, *The Bible in Modern Scholarship*, p. 203 n. 13.

17. Childs, *Biblical Theology in Crisis*, p. 141.

18. A. Dulles, "Response to Krister Stendahl's 'Method in the Study of Biblical Theology,'" in *The Bible in Modern Scholarship*, p. 210.

19. Ibid., pp. 210f. Stendahl, of course, maintains that there is no "Absolute objectivity" (*IDB*, I, 422; *The Bible in Modern Scholarship*, p. 202) to be had. He is completely right in emphasizing that the relativity of human objectivity does not give us an excuse to "excel in bias," but neither, we insist, does it give us the possibility of doing purely descriptive work.

20. R. A. F. MacKenzie, "The Concept of Biblical Theology," *TToday*, 4

Perhaps we need to be reminded by O. Eissfeldt that "we cannot penetrate on the basis of historical grounds to the nature of OT religion."[21] How can the nonnormative descriptive approach with its limiting historical emphasis lead us to the totality of the theological reality contained in the text? By definition and presupposition the descriptive and historical approach is limited to such an extent that the total theological reality of the text does not come fully to expression. Does OT theology need to be restricted to be nothing more than a "first chapter" of historical theology? If Biblical theology also has normative value on the basis of the recognition that what the Bible meant is normative in itself, then would it not be expected that Biblical theology must engage in more than just to describe what the Biblical texts meant? Biblical theology is not aiming to take the place of or be in competition with systematic theology as the latter expresses itself in the form of system building based on its own categories either with or without the aid of philosophy. Is it not possible for Biblical theology to have normative value on the basis of its recognition that it is done within the Biblical context first of all and that the Bible is normative in itself? Can Biblical theology draw its very principles of content and organization from the Biblical documents rather than ecclesiastical documents or scholastic and modern philosophy? Would it not be one of the tasks of Biblical theology to come to grips with the nature of the Biblical texts as aiming beyond themselves, as ontologi-

---

(1956), 131-135, esp. 134: "Coldly scientific—in the sense of rationalistic—objectivity is quite incapable of even perceiving, let alone exploiting, the religious values of Scripture. There must be first the commitment, the recognition of faith of the divine origin and authority of the book, then the believer can properly and profitably apply all the most conscientious techniques of the subordinate sciences, without in the least infringing on their due autonomy or being disloyal to the scientific ideal." C. Spicq as quoted in J. Harvey, "The New Diachronic Biblical Theology of the OT (1960-1970)," BTB, 1 (1971), 18f. Cf. R. de Vaux, "Method in the Study of Early Hebrew History," in The Bible in Modern Scholarship, pp. 15-17; idem, "Is It Possible to Write a 'Theology of the OT'?," in The Bible and the Ancient Near East (Garden City, NY, 1971), pp. 49-62.

21. O. Eissfeldt, "Israelitisch-jüdische Religionsgeschichte und alttestamentliche Theologie," ZAW, 44 (1926), 1-12.

cal and theological in their intention and function through the ages, without defining in advance the nature of Biblical reality?

In the latter part of the 1980s another development has raised serious questions regarding the meant/means, descriptive/prescriptive, nonnormative/normative dichotomy of the Gabler-Wrede-Stendahl approach in which OT (and Biblical) theology is perceived as a purely historical enterprise. Indeed, this new development is so disturbing to key figures who wish to maintain OT (and Biblical) theology on that foundation that some of them speak of a bleak future for these undertakings of OT theology on a purely descriptive basis.[22]

Some have raised the question whether Jewish scholars should not also engage in OT theology or the theology of the Hebrew Bible. Why have Jewish scholars not been involved in writing a "theology of the Hebrew Bible"? In 1986 the issue came to the fore with an essay on the matter of a Jewish OT theology by M. Tsevat in the journal *Horizons in Biblical Theology*. Tsevat argues against the notion of a "Jewish biblical [OT] theology."[23] He insists that the "theology of the Old Testament" is to be practiced from an "objective" point of view as "that branch of study of the literature which has the Old Testament as its subject; it is philology of the Old Testament."[24] In his view the OT, or the Hebrew Bible, is literature and not theology. He suggests that literature is a category of philological study, but theology is a category of study which is embedded for the Jew in Jewish tradition and for the Christian in Christian tradition. These two traditions or contextualizations are so pervasive that the theological enterprise done by Jews will Judaize OT theology and that done by Christians will Christianize it.

Pure "objectivity" is not to be had! This seems to be Bern-

22. See the discussion on James Barr below, section H. "Recent 'Critical' OT Theology Methods."

23. M. Tsevat, "Theology of the OT — A Jewish View," *HBT,* 8/2 (1986), 50.

24. Ibid., p. 48.

hard W. Anderson's response to Tsevat when he suggests that "our epistemological starting point should not become our epistemological norm; otherwise the hermeneutical circle would become a confining solipsism in which we are shut up in our own world and talk only to our own circle."[25] Anderson comes from the point of view of H.-G. Gadamer and Paul Ricoeur. Gadamer is particularly known for the concept of the hermeneutical melting of the horizons of the past and the present to complete the hermeneutical circle.[26] Following the Gadamer-Ricoeur hermeneutic, Anderson insists, "Obviously, the meaning of a text cannot be sharply separated from our appropriation, and it may be falsified by our appropriation."[27] Evidently there are two differing epistemologies at work and two differing hermeneutics. But the issue coming to the forefront here is whether OT theology is indeed an enterprise where scholars of differing religious persuasions can participate in such a way that their religious traditions, i.e., their present horizons, do not enter into the interpretational process.

In contrast to Tsevat, other voices in Jewish scholarship today see things from a different though not entirely unrelated perspective. M. H. Goshen-Gottstein argues that the time is here for Jewish scholarship to engage in what he calls a

25. Bernhard W. Anderson, "Response to Matitahu Tsevat 'Theology of the OT — A Jewish View,'" HBT, 8/2 (1986), 55.

26. Hans-Georg Gadamer, Truth and Method (New York, 1975; 2nd ed. 1989). See the penetrating analysis of Gadamer's hermeneutic by Joel C. Weinsheimer, Gadamer's Hermeneutics: A Reading of Truth and Method (New Haven/London, 1985), with rich bibliography. Of importance for the hermeneutical enterprise as a whole is the application of Gadamer's hermeneutic by Anthony Thiselton, The Two Horizons: NT Hermeneutics and Philosophical Description (Grand Rapids, 1980). Another approach to hermeneutics is based on the massive work of Emilio Betti. Most of his publications are not available in English, but see his "Hermeneutics as the General Science of the Geisteswissenschaften," in Contemporary Hermeneutics: Hermeneutics as Method, Philosophy, and Critique, ed. Josef Bleicher (London, 1980), pp. 51-94. E. D. Hirsch, Validity in Interpretation (New Haven, 1967); idem, The Aims of Interpretation (Chicago, 1976), is in line with Betti as an opponent of Gadamer and his followers.

27. Anderson, "Response," p. 55.

"Jewish Biblical Theology" or "Tanakh Theology."[28] In his view this enterprise is a separate discipline but complementary to that of the one called "history of ancient Israel." "Tanakh Theology must be created as a parallel field of study"[29] to that of OT theology in which Christians are engaged. He maintains that it cannot be a purely historical enterprise— OT theology is not a purely historical enterprise either— because such a theology would be a "nontheology." He clearly separates himself from the Gabler-Wrede-Stendahl approach of a "descriptive" undertaking. Goshen-Gottstein shares the conviction also held by others, both Jews and Christians, that scholars cannot isolate themselves from the communities of faith in which they function and cannot be outside their religious traditions that shape in some form or another their theologizing.[30] As will be seen later in this chapter, more and more scholars are departing from the notion of a "what it meant" or purely descriptive enterprise for OT theology.[31]

A third Jewish scholar entering this newest debate is Jon D. Levenson.[32] He argues with vigor that Jewish scholars are not interested in "Biblical theology," because it assumes an "ex-

28. M. H. Goshen-Gottstein, "Tanakh Theology: The Religion of the OT and the Place of Jewish Biblical Theology," in *Ancient Israelite Religion: Essays in Honor of Frank Moore Cross*, ed. P. D. Miller, P. D. Hanson, and S. D. McBride (Philadelphia, 1987), pp. 617-644.

29. Ibid., p. 626.

30. This is the point of view held by, among others, R. E. Clements, John Goldingay, and particularly Brevard Childs.

31. See also the essay and sensitive analysis of Ben C. Ollenburger, "What Krister Stendahl 'Meant'—A Normative Critique of 'Descriptive Biblical Theology,'" *HBT*, 8/1 (1986), 61-98.

32. See Jon D. Levenson, "Why Jews Are Not Interested in Biblical Theology," in *Jewish Perspectives on Ancient Israel*, ed. J. Neusner, B. A. Levine, and E. S. Frerichs (Philadelphia, 1987), pp. 281-307. Levenson is a very perceptive and analytical scholar; see also particularly idem, "The Hebrew Bible, the OT, and Historical Criticism," in *The Future of Biblical Studies: The Hebrew Scriptures*, ed. R. E. Friedman and H. G. M. Williamson (Atlanta, 1987), pp. 19-60; idem, "The Eighth Principle of Judaism and the Literary Simultaneity of Scripture," *JR*, 68 (1988), 205-225; idem, *Sinai and Zion: An Entry Into the Jewish Bible* (Minneapolis, 1985); idem, *Creation and the Persistence of Evil: The Jewish Drama of Omnipotence* (San Francisco, 1988).

istential commitment" that "will necessarily include other sources of truth (the Talmud, the New Testament, and so on)."[33] Due to the fact that "Biblical" is not a neutral term since it means different things to Jews (namely, the Tanakh) and to Christians (namely, the one Bible of both Testaments), one can pursue either a "Jewish biblical theology" or a "Christian biblical theology." He has shown in his article how OT theology in the last hundred years has been colored by shades of anti-Semitism, and until recently was non-Catholic and non-Jewish (and one may add non-evangelical).[34] He maintains that "the effort to construct a systematic, harmonious theological statement out of the unsystematic and polydox materials in the Hebrew Bible fits Christianity better than Judaism because systematic theology in general is more prominent and more at home in the church than in the yeshivah and the synagogue."[35] He feels that a "contexualized" Jewish or Christian "biblical theology" will be able to serve the respective Jewish or Christian religious communities.[36]

These voices of Jewish scholarship make it clear that in their minds no "Biblical theology" of a purely descriptive type is to be had. No wonder that those who insist on such an enterprise feel that we are moving away from OT theology so perceived. As a result some see a diminished role and an altered future for such an undertaking.[37]

It can be stated without hesitation that there is today a renewed attempt on the part of Biblical theologians to view the enterprise of Biblical theology as more than merely descriptive and nonnormative. This will emerge more clearly as

33. Levenson, "Why Jews Are Not Interested in Biblical Theology," p. 286.
34. Ibid., pp. 287-293.
35. Ibid., p. 296.
36. Levenson, *Creation and the Persistence of Evil*, pp. 224-225.
37. So, e.g., James Barr, "Are We Moving Toward an OT Theology, or Away From It?," paper read at the annual meeting of the Society of Biblical Literature in Anaheim CA, November 1989, with an abstract published in *Abstracts: American Academy of Religion, Society of Biblical Literature*, ed. J. B. Wiggins and D. J. Lull (Atlanta, 1989), p. 20.

we survey significant approaches to OT theology in the last
five decades with an emphasis on the period since the 1970s.

Methodology in OT Theology

In a comprehensive review of five decades of literature on OT
theology E. Würthwein concluded his penetrating analysis in
a sobering sentence: "We are today further apart regarding an
agreement on the context and method of OT theology than
we were fifty years ago."[38] Despite this lack of agreement, in

38. E. Würthwein, "Zur Theologie des AT," *TRu*, 36 (1971), 188. Among
the useful earlier surveys are the ones by C. T. Fritsch, "New Trends in OT
Theology," *BibSac*, 103 (1946), 293-305; N. Porteous, "OT Theology," in *The
OT and Modern Study*, ed. H. H. Rowley (London, 1951), pp. 311-345; R. C.
Dentan, *Preface to OT Theology* (2nd ed.; New York, 1963); F. M. Braun, "La
Théologie Biblique," *Revue thomiste*, 61 (1953), 221-253; E. G. Kraeling, *The
OT since the Reformation* (New York, 1955), pp. 265-284; E. J. Young, *The
Study of OT Theology Today* (New York, 1959); R. Martin-Achard, "Les voies
de la théologie de l'AT," *RSPT*, 3 (1959), 217-226; A. M. Barnett, "Trends in
OT Theology," *CJT*, 6 (1960), 91-101; O. Betz, "Biblical Theology, History of,"
IDB, I, 432-437; F. Festorazzi, "Rassegna di teologia dell'AT," *Revista biblica*,
10 (1962), 297-316; 12 (1964), 27-48; L. Ramlot, "Une décade de théologie
biblique," *Revue thomiste*, 64 (1964), 65-96; 65 (1965), 95-135; R. E. Clements,
"The Problem of OT Theology," *London Quarterly and Holborn Review* (Jan.,
1965), 11-17; P. Benoit, "Exégèse et théologie biblique," *Exégèse et Théologie*
(Paris, 1968), III, 1-13; J. Harvey, "The New Diachronic Biblical Theology of
the OT (1960-1970)," *BTB*, 1 (1971), 5-29; W. H. Schmidt, " 'Theologie des
AT' vor und nach Gerhard von Rad," *Verkündigung und Forschung*, 17 (1972),
1-25; W. Zimmerli, "Erwägungen zur Gestalt einer alttestamentlichen Theo-
logie," *TLZ*, 98 (1973), 81-98; E. Osswald, "Theologie des AT — eine bleibende
Aufgabe alttestamentlicher Wissenschaft," *TLZ*, 99 (1974), 641-658; C. Wes-
termann, "Zu zwei Theologien des AT," *EvT*, 34 (1974), 96-112; J. Goldingay,
"The Study of OT Theology: Its Aims and Purpose," *TynBul*, 26 (1975), 34-52;
R. E. Clements, "Recent Developments in OT Theology," *Epworth Review*, 3
(1976), 99-107; R. L. Hicks, "G. Ernest Wright and OT Theology," *Anglican
Theological Review*, 58 (1976), 158-178; J. J. Scullion, "Recent OT Theologies:
Three Contributions," *Australian Biblical Review*, 24 (1976), 6-17; J. J. Burden,
"Methods of OT Theology: Past, Present and Future," *Theologia Evangelica*,
10 (1977), 14-33; E. Jacob, "De la théologie de l'AT à la théologie biblique,"
RHPR, 57 (1977), 513-518; E. A. Martens, "Tackling OT Theology," *JETS*, 20
(1977), 123-132; H. Graf Reventlow, "Basic Problems in OT Theology," *JSOT*,
11 (1979), 2-22; A. H. J. Gunneweg, " 'Theologie' des AT oder 'Biblische Theologie'?," in *Textgemäss. Aufsätze und Beiträge zur Hermeneutik des AT. Fest-*

the years following this assessment more than a dozen different volumes were published on OT theology alone.[39] This output is unmatched in any decade in the roughly 180 years of the existence of the discipline of OT theology. It will now be our task to survey and to classify the various OT theologies, even though it is at times difficult to do this adequately.

A. *The Dogmatic-Didactic Method.* The traditional method of organizing OT theology is the approach borrowed from dogmatic (or systematic) theology and its division (for its loci) of God-Man-Salvation or Theology-Anthropology-Soteriology. Georg Lorenz Bauer employed this scheme in 1796 for the first *Theology of the OT* ever published under this name.[40]

The strongest case for the dogmatic-didactic method in recent years comes from R. C. Dentan, whose monographs are an eloquent defense for what most have discarded as an out-

---

schrift für Ernst Würthwein zum 70. Geburtstag, ed. A. H. J. Gunneweg and O. Kaiser (Göttingen, 1979), pp. 38-46; J. J. Collins, "The 'Historical Character' of the OT in Recent Biblical Theology," *CBQ,* 41 (1979), 185-204; W. Brueggemann, "A Convergence in Recent OT Theologies," *JSOT,* 18 (1980), 2-18; G. F. Hasel, "A Decade of OT Theology: Retrospect and Prospect," *ZAW,* 93 (1981), 165-184.

39. G. E. Wright, *The OT and Theology* (New York, 1970); Th. C. Vriezen, *An Outline of OT Theology* (2nd ed.; Newton, MA, 1970); M. García Cordero, *Teologia de la Biblia, I: Antiguo Testamento* (Madrid, 1970); C. K. Lehman, *Biblical Theology I: OT* (Scottdale, PA, 1971); A. Deissler, *Die Grundbotschaft des AT* (Freiburg i. Br., 1972); G. Fohrer, *Theologische Grundstrukturen des AT* (Berlin/New York, 1972); W. Zimmerli, *Grundriss der alttestamentlichen Theologie* (Stuttgart, 1972), trans. *OT Theology in Outline* (Atlanta, 1978); J. L. McKenzie, *A Theology of the OT* (Garden City, NY, 1974); D. F. Hinson, *Theology of the OT* (London, 1976); S. Terrien, *The Elusive Presence: Toward a New Biblical Theology* (San Francisco, 1978); W. C. Kaiser, *Toward an OT Theology* (Grand Rapids, 1978); R. E. Clements, *OT Theology: A Fresh Approach* (Atlanta, 1978); E. A. Martens, *God's Design: A Focus on OT Theology* (Grand Rapids, 1981); C. Westermann, *Theologie des AT in Grundzügen* (Göttingen, 1978), trans. *Elements of OT Theology* (Atlanta, 1982).

40. Georg L. Bauer (1755-1806) was the first to publish a separate *Theologie des AT oder Abriss der religiösen Begriffe der alten Hebräer* (Leipzig, 1796), which was followed by a four-volume *Biblische Theologie des NT* (Leipzig, 1800-1802). See also Kraus, *Biblische Theologie,* pp. 87-91; O. Merk, *Biblische Theologie des NT in ihrer Anfangszeit* (Marburg, 1972), pp. 143-202; W. Dyrness, *Themes in OT Theology* (Downers Grove, IL, 1979).

moded model.[41] Dentan's *The Knowledge of God in Ancient Israel* (1968) attempts to treat only the first of the three major loci, namely, "the Old Testament doctrine of God," because "all other aspects of the normative religion of ancient Israel 'have their center in a distinctive doctrine of God (theology)."[42] Dentan affirms that "the most basic affirmation of Old Testament religion is that Yahweh is the God of Israel, and Israel is the people of Yahweh."[43] It is surprising that this "covenant formula," which is conceived by J. Wellhausen, B. Duhm, B. Stade, M. Noth, and most recently by R. Smend[44] as the center of the OT[45] and by Smend as the "material framework for organizing the [OT] materials"[46] into an OT theology, remains unrecognized as providing the framework for the structure of an OT theology. It is possible that Dentan was unwilling to move in this direction because of his earlier commitment to the Theology-Anthropology-Soteriology scheme.

A glance at Dentan's structure for his OT "doctrine" of God reveals that the first two chapters on "The Mystery of Israel" and "The Nature of Israel's Knowledge" are preliminary to the book. Chapters 3, 4, and 9 treat God in the past, present, and future respectively, whereas the chapters on "The Being of God" and "The Character of God" (Chapters 6 and 7) are the

41. See his *Preface to OT Theology* and *The Knowledge of God in Ancient Israel* (New York, 1968). See also R. de Vaux, "Is It Possible to Write a 'Theology of the OT'?," in *The Bible and the Ancient Near East* (New York, 1971), pp. 61f.

42. Dentan, *The Knowledge of God in Ancient Israel*, p. vii.

43. Ibid.

44. R. Smend, *Die Bundesformel* (Zurich, 1963).

45. On the issue of the center or centers of the OT, see G. F. Hasel, "The Problem of the Center in the OT Theology Debate," *ZAW*, 86 (1974), 65-82; below, Chapter IV; W. Zimmerli, "Zum Problem der 'Mitte des AT,'" *EvT*, 35 (1975), 97-118; S. Wagner, "'Biblische Theologien' und 'Biblische Theologie,'" *TLZ*, 103 (1978), 791-793; on the issue of the center or centers for the NT, see Hasel, *NT Theology: Basic Issues in the Current Debate* (Grand Rapids, 1978), pp. 140-170 with literature; S. Schulz, *Die Mitte der Schrift* (Stuttgart, 1976), pp. 403-433; O. Betz, "The Problem of Variety and Unity in the NT," *HBT*, 2 (1980), 3-14.

46. R. Smend, *Die Mitte des AT* (Zurich, 1970), p. 55.

heart of Dentan's exposition. Chapters 5 and 8 are digressions under the titles "God and the Natural World" and "The Names of God," which Dentan suggests are "not central to the main argument of the book."[47] This structure reveals the difficulty of organizing the OT materials under traditional rubrics. It would be interesting to see how Dentan would handle OT anthropology, with which he has not yet dealt, and then to compare it with H. W. Wolff's timely and rich contribution in this field.[48]

In contrast to Dentan, whose monograph is limited to the "doctrine of God," two other OT theologies reflect in full-fledged form the Theology-Anthropology-Soteriology scheme. The detailed study of the Spanish scholar M. García Cordero[49] begins with the OT concept of God, followed by anthropology. Soteriology is discussed in Parts II and III, where he elucidates the hopes of the OT with emphasis on Messianic expectations, the kingdom of God, eschatology, and man's religious and moral obligations with personal salvation.

The OT theology by D. F. Hinson is much more modest in length.[50] The Theology-Anthropology-Soteriology scheme is evident from the titles and the sequence of his work. Upon a preliminary section follow eight chapters with the headings: God, Other Spiritual Beings, Man, Fall, Salvation, New Life, The Ultimate Goal, and The OT in the NT. Hinson has a didactic aim. He conceives the nature of OT theology as God's revelation "about Himself, about mankind, and about the world which is contained in the books of the Old Testament."[51] He does not explain how the material structure can grasp the totality of that revelation. Hinson is concerned to show that the OT is the preparation for the NT; Dentan, on

---

47. Dentan, *The Knowledge of God in Ancient Israel*, p. x.
48. H. W. Wolff, *Anthropologie des AT* (Munich, 1973), trans. *Anthropology of the OT* (London, 1974).
49. García Cordero, *Teología de la Biblia, I: Antiguo Testamento*, pp. 17-732.
50. D. F. Hinson, *Theology of the OT.*
51. Ibid., p. xi.

the other hand, "deliberately tried to keep any specifically Christian point of view out of the chapters."[52]

The dogmatic-didactic method has certain advantages. However, among the problems is the deductive nature of the enterprise. The OT cannot speak for itself, because outside interests seem to dominate. The OT patterns of thought are not structured along the lines of the Theology-Anthropology-Soteriology scheme. Did any particular individual or group in ancient Israel think about God, man, and salvation in just the way a dogmatic method depicts the "doctrines" of the OT? Does the dogmatic approach not ultimately present a theology rooted in the OT rather than the OT's own theology? Is it really able to present the theology that the OT (or the Bible) contains? The center of the OT does not even become an issue or bear much weight in the dogmatic approach because the center is predetermined by the scheme; it is Theology-Anthropology-Soteriology. These and other issues will concern OT theologians in our period and probably for some time to come.

B. *The Genetic-Progressive Method.* In regard to the scope, function, and structure of OT theology this is another time-honored method which has been employed in a variety of ways.[53] Chester K. Lehman defines the "method of biblical theology" as one "determined in the main by the principle of historic progression."[54] This is understood as "the unfolding of God's revelation as the Bible presents it."[55] The historic progression of the unfolding revelation is evidenced in "periods or eras of divine revelation [which] are determined in strict agreement with the lines of cleavage drawn by revelation itself." More specifically this means that divine revelation centers in the several covenants made by God with Noah, Abraham, Moses,

52. Dentan, *The Knowledge of God in Ancient Israel*, p. xi.
53. Historical antecedents to the revival of the "genetic method" in the decade under discussion are found in the last century, particularly by the greatest name in OT theology in the second half of the 19th century, G. F. Oehler, *Prolegomena zur Theologie des AT* (Stuttgart, 1845); *Theologie des AT* (Tübingen, 1873), trans. *OT Theology* (New York, 1883).
54. C. K. Lehman, *Biblical Theology I: OT,* p. 38.
55. Ibid., p. 7.

and through Christ, all of which manifest the "organic being" of the Bible and Scripture's "own anatomy."[56] Here the influence of several scholars is at work[57] and also the developmental approach of "progressive revelation."[58]

Lehman divides his work into three major parts, which follow the division of the Hebrew canon. Part I treats God's revelation in creation and fall, from the fall through Abraham, and on through the patriarchs. This is followed by revelation and worship in the time of Moses, a section on Moses' final exposition of the law, and a topical section on sin and salvation in the Pentateuch. Part II deals with God's revelation through the (Former and Latter) Prophets with subsections on the rise, place, and nature of prophetism, the theology of the Former Prophets, God's revelation through the prophets of the Assyrian period, the theology of Isa. 40–66, and the theology of the prophets of the Chaldean (Neo-Babylonian), Exilic, and Persian periods. Part III discusses the theology of the Hagiographa in the sequence of Psalms, Proverbs, Ecclesiastes, Song of Songs, and Job.

This approach provides many valuable and important observations. The tripartite canonical structure, however, stands in seemingly irreconcilable tension with the genetic method of "historic progression," because the Hebrew canon does not give evidence of a consistent or even intended historical progression. Accordingly it cannot be said that the methodological proposal of Lehman found successful realization in his presentation of OT theology. His presentation reveals a mixture of tripartite canonical structure with a topical and/or book-by-book approach[59] *without* any consistent historical

56. Ibid., p. 38.
57. Lehman (pp. 7f., 26f., 35-38) makes a particular point regarding his indebtedness to his teacher Geerhardus Vos (*Biblical Theology: Old and New Testaments* [Grand Rapids, 1948]), to W. Eichrodt's *TOT,* and to G. F. Oehler.
58. Lehman, *Biblical Theology I: OT,* p. 12, where it is noted in M. S. Augsburger's introduction that Lehman sees the unfolding revelation with the NT at a higher level than the OT.
59. The topical approach is evident in presenting such topics as "the God of Israel," election, covenant, sin, etc. as manifested in various books of various periods. The book-by-book approach is carried through for Isa. 40–66

progression. Some books remain undated, totally outside a "historic progression" and genetically unrelated to the unfolding revelation.[60] One cannot help but conclude that this model of a genetic approach has not been very successful.

Without attempting to be unjust in any way, it appears that the well-known scholar R. E. Clements of Cambridge University belongs in a general sense to those who follow a broadly genetic method. Clements's tome, *OT Theology: A Fresh Approach* (1978), is a kind of preface or prolegomenon to OT theology and of great importance for the question of methodology.

Clements divides his monograph into eight chapters. Chapters 1 and 2 are a survey (at times not in great depth) with various questions on methodology and related issues. Chapters 3-6 deal with what Clements regards as the central themes in the OT. The theme of "The God of Israel" is treated under such aspects of the being, names, presence, and uniqueness of God; a historical-genetic flow of development is cautiously highlighted. This is manifested also in the chapter "The OT as Promise," in which the importance of this theme is shown without making it central to the OT (*pace* W. C. Kaiser).[61]

In contrast to many OT theologies, Clements correctly refuses to follow a center-oriented approach to OT theology with an organizing principle. For him the unity of the OT is not a single theme, center, organizing principle, or formula, but "it is the nature and being of God himself which establishes a unity in the Old Testament. . . ."[62] We have argued for the same direction independently.[63]

The chapter "The People of God" discusses the relationship

(ibid., pp. 304-328), Psalms (pp. 409-441), Proverbs (pp. 442-445), Ecclesiastes (pp. 446-450), Canticles (pp. 451-453), and Job (pp. 454-458).

60. The Hagiographa are treated in a separate part without any indication of a "historical progression." Are they ahistorical or is there an insurmountable flaw in the structure of Lehman's OT theology?

61. See below, pp. 52-54.

62. Clements, *OT Theology*, p. 23.

63. Hasel, "The Problem of the Center," pp. 65-82; and below, pp. 139-171.

of people and nation, the theology of election, and the theology of covenant. The chapter "The OT as Law" traces the meaning of *tôrāh* as applicable to the Pentateuch and its use in the prophetic writings and compares it to that of "law."

In contrast to other approaches to OT theology, Clements not only emphasizes the significance of the canon but argues with force that the canon of the Hebrew Scriptures, i.e., the OT, in itself and by itself is the authoritative norm for OT theology. "There is a real connection between the ideas of 'canon' and 'theology', for it is the status of these writings as a canon of sacred scripture that marks them out as containing a word of God that is still believed to be authoritative."[64] In a manner reflecting concerns similar to those of Yale University scholar B. S. Childs, we are reminded that "it is precisely the concept of canon that raises questions about the authority of the Old Testament, and its ability to present us with a theology which can still be meaningful in the twentieth century."[65] Clements thus refuses to conceive of OT theology as a purely descriptive exercise. The reason for rejecting such a "rigidly historicising approach" rests in the position that "the Old Testament does present us with a revelation of the eternal God."[66]

The insistence upon the canon of the OT as the boundary of OT theology is central in the contemporary discussion. The perennial question is one of dealing with the totality of writings in the canon of the OT. A typical test for the adequacy of a methodology for OT theology is the matter of integrating the complete OT in all its variety and richness. Virtually all OT theologies have had difficulties in dealing with the wisdom writings (Proverbs, Job, Ecclesiastes, Canticles). Typical examples are the approaches of G. von Rad, W. Zimmerli, and C. Westermann, who consider the wisdom literature of the OT in terms of Israel's answer to God. But hardly will one find

---

64. Clements, *OT Theology,* p. 15.
65. Ibid., p. 19.
66. Ibid.

such disregard of this part of the OT canon as is evident in
Clements's approach—he disregards it completely. This
means in effect that the canon of Clements consists of but the
Law and the Prophets, with a sprinkling of the Psalms.[67] Even
if this book grew out of a series of lectures,[68] it is a frustrating
lacuna to have wisdom literature so completely neglected.

The "fresh approach" of Clements also includes a new
look at "the Christian study of the Old Testament," which
involves "very full and careful attention . . . to the manner,
method and presuppositions of the interpretation of the Old
Testament in the New."[69] Among other things this involves
a rather welcome examination of "those key themes by which
the unity is set out in the Bible itself."[70] The significance of
this "fresh approach" can be more fully appreciated if we
keep in mind that one recent OT theology was written "as if
the New Testament did not exist"[71] and argued that the
relationship between the Testaments is not a major problem
in OT theology. That it is such a problem need no longer be
denied, as the studies of J. A. Sanders and J. Blenkinsopp
have amply demonstrated.[72] In sharp contrast to historical-
critical approaches to OT theology this "fresh approach"
affirms a wider starting-point for the discipline of OT theology. OT theology is not to be conceived of as a historical
and descriptive enterprise (so the Gabler-Wrede-Stendahl
school), but "instead of treating is as a subordinate branch
of the historical criticism of the Old Testament, it should be
regarded properly as a branch of theology."[73] Does this mean

67. See now the rich volume by H.-J. Kraus, *Theologie der Psalmen*
(Neukirchen-Vluyn, 1979), trans. *Theology of the Psalms* (Minneapolis, 1986).
68. "Talking Points from Books," *ExpTim*, 90 (1979), 194.
69. Clements, *OT Theology*, p. 185.
70. Ibid., p. 186.
71. McKenzie, *A Theology of the OT*, p. 319.
72. J. A. Sanders, *Torah and Canon* (2nd ed.; Philadelpia, 1974); idem,
"Hermeneutics," *IDB Supplement* (1976), pp. 402-407; J. Blenkinsopp, *Prophecy and Canon. A Contribution to the Study of Jewish Origins* (Notre Dame,
1977).
73. Clements, *OT Theology*, p. 191.

that it is a branch in the field of systematic theology where B. S. Childs would place Biblical theology, or does it mean that it remains part of the field of OT studies, but with a post-critical, post-historicist methodology? We shall return to this question later.

C. *The Cross-Section Method.* A major pioneer in OT theology and its methodology in this century is W. Eichrodt. In the 1930s he developed the cross-section approach.[74] He was able to achieve a cross-section through the world of OT thought by making the covenant the center of the OT. In this step he not only anticipated the revival of interest in the covenant under the impetus of G. Mendenhall,[75] which is presently in a heated debate,[76] but he stimulated others to follow him by producing their own cross-section theologies

---

74. W. Eichrodt, *TOT,* trans. from *Theologie des AT* (3 vols.; 5th ed.; Stuttgart, 1960, 1964). See also Dentan, *Preface to OT Theology,* pp. 66-68; Spriggs, *Two OT Theologies* (SBT, 2/30; Naperville, IL, 1974), pp. 11-33, who sees "Eichrodt's basic conception of the purpose and function of an OT Theology . . . more acceptable than von Rad's" (p. 97).

75. G. Mendenhall, *Law and Covenant in Israel and the Ancient Near East* (Pittsburgh, 1955); idem, "Covenant," *IDB,* I (1962), 714-723; idem, *The Tenth Generation* (Baltimore, 1973).

76. See, e.g., L. Perlitt, *Die Bundestheologie im AT* (WMANT, 36; Neukirchen Vluyn, 1969), and E. Kutsch, *Verheissung und Gesetz* (BZAW, 131; Berlin, 1972), for a late origin of the idea of covenant; the latter also that the OT knows no idea of covenant but only one of "obligation" *(Verpflichtung).* Among those strongly opposed to this new trend are D. J. McCarthy, *Treaty and Covenant* (2nd ed.; Rome, 1978); H. Lubsczyk, "Der Bund als Gemeinschaft mit Gott. Erwägungen zur Diskussion über den Begriff 'berit' im AT," in *Dienst der Vermittlung,* ed. W. Ernst, K. Feiereis, and F. Hoffmann (Leipzig, 1977), pp. 61-96; M. Weinfield, *"bᵉrîth,"* *TDOT,* II (1975), 253-279. For a general survey of selected issues see D. J. McCarthy, *OT Covenant* (London, 1972). Eichrodt defended his covenant concept in "Covenant and Law: Thoughts on Recent Discussion," *Interp,* 20 (1966), 302-321. He found support for making the Sinai covenant the center of the OT in Wright (*The OT and Theology,* pp. 57-62), but is criticized for neglecting altogether the Davidic covenant by F. C. Prussner ("The Covenant of David and the Problem of Unity in OT Theology," *Transitions in Biblical Scholarship,* ed. J. C. Rylaarsdam [Chicago, 1968], pp. 17-44) and the Davidic and Abrahamic covenants by D. G. Spriggs (*Two OT Theologies,* pp. 25-33). A clearly negative reaction to the use of the covenant as an organizing principle comes from N. K. Gottwald, "W. Eichrodt, Theology of the OT," in *Contemporary OT Theologians,* pp. 23-62, esp. 29-31.

of the OT. He has found a recent defender in D. G. Spriggs,[77] who produced a detailed comparative study of Eichrodt's and von Rad's OT theologies.

As early as 1929 Eichrodt called for a radical reorientation in methodology[78] in order to move beyond the impasse into which the application of a God-Man-Salvation principle had led the development of OT theology from Georg L. Bauer (1755-1806) to Emil Kautzsch (1911), under the influence of historicism.[79]

Eichrodt insists correctly that in every science there is a subjective element. Historians have come to take seriously that there is inevitably a subjective element in all historical research worthy of the name. The positivist errs when for the sake of objectivity he attempts to rid the individual sciences of philosophy. One cannot be a true historian if one ignores the philosophy of history. The historian will always be guided in his work by a principle of selection, which is certainly a subjective enterprise, and by a goal which gives perspective to his work, a goal which is equally subjective. Eichrodt admits the truth of the contention that history is unable to make an ultimate pronouncement on the truth or falsity of anything, on its validity or invalidity. He claims that while the OT theologian makes an existential judgment which, in part at least, determines the subjective element to be found in his account of OT religion, there is no weight to the charge that OT theology is unscientific in character.

77. Spriggs, *Two OT Theologies*, p. 101: "On the whole, I consider that Eichrodt's conception of an OT Theology is well able to withstand the shock-waves from von Rad's onslaught. His understanding of covenant certainly needs to be modified and I would not consider it the only organizing concept. As Eichrodt understands it—the God-Man relationship as revealed in the OT— it is both comprehensive enough and central enough to be useful."

78. W. Eichrodt, "Hat die alttestamentliche Theologie noch selbständige Bedeutung innerhalb der alttestamentlichen Wissenschaft?" *ZAW*, 47 (1929), 83-91. See Porteous, "OT Theology," pp. 317-324; O. Eissfeldt, "Israelitisch-jüdische Religionsgeschichte und alttestamentliche Theologie," *ZAW*, 44 (1926), 1-12, repr. in O. Eissfeldt, *Kleine Schriften*, I (Tübingen, 1962), 105-114.

79. Cf. Dentan, *Preface*, pp. 26-57; Kraus, *Biblische Theologie*, pp. 88-125.

Eichrodt's theology remains firmly historical and descriptive. He maintains that the OT theologian has to be guided by a principle of selection and a principle of congeniality. The great systematic task consists of making a cross-section through the historical process, laying bare the inner structure of religion. His aim is "to understand the realm of OT belief in its structural unity . . . [and] to illuminate its profoundest meaning."[80] Under the conviction that the "tyranny of historicism"[81] must be broken, he explains that "the irruption of the Kingship of God into this world and its establishment here" is "that which binds together indivisibly the two realms of the Old and New Testaments." But in addition to this historical movement from the OT to the NT "there is a current life flowing in reverse direction from the New Testament to the Old."[82] The principle of selection in Eichrodt's theology turns out to be the covenant concept, and the goal which provides perspective is found in the NT.

It is to Eichrodt's credit that he broke once and for all with the traditional God-Man-Salvation arrangement, taken over from dogmatics time and again by Biblical theologians.[83] His procedure for treating the realm of OT thought attempts to have "the historical principle operating side by side with the systematic in a complementary role."[84] The systematic principle Eichrodt finds in the covenant concept, which becomes the overriding and unifying category in his OT theology.[85] Out of the combination of the historical principle and the covenant principle grow Eichrodt's three major categories representing the basic structure of his *magnum opus*, namely God and the

80. *TOT,* I, 31.
81. Ibid.
82. Ibid., p. 26.
83. The OT theologies of E. König (Stuttgart, 1923), E. Sellin (Leipzig, 1933), and L. Köhler (Tübingen, 1935) were still to a larger or smaller degree dependent on the Theology-Anthropology-Soteriology arrangement of systematic theology that became dominant in the post-Gabler period in Biblical theology.
84. *TOT,* I, 17ff.
85. Ibid., p. 32.

people, God and the world, and God and man.[86] His systematic cross-section treatment is so executed as to exhibit the
development of thought and institution within his system.
The cross-section method, with Eichrodt's use of the covenant
concept as the means whereby unity is achieved, is to some
extent artificial, since the OT is less amenable to systematization than Eichrodt suggests.

Eichrodt's cross-section method has its serious problems.
Within his presentation one finds explications of "historical
developments"[87] in which the religio-historical view comes
through but hardly ever from the perspective of the NT. This
is especially surprising since he claims that there is a "two-
way relationship between the Old and New Testaments," and
contends that without this relationship "we do not find a
correct definition of the problem of OT theology."[88] In this
respect his work is hardly an improvement over the earlier
history-of-religions approaches. Furthermore, Eichrodt's systematic principle, i.e., the covenant concept, attempts to en-
close within its grasp the diversified thoughts of the OT. It is
here that the problem of the cross-section method lies. Is the
covenant concept, or Vriezen's community concept, or any
other single concept, sufficiently comprehensive to include
within it all variety of OT thoughts? In more general terms,
is the OT a world of thought or belief that can be systematized
in such a way?[89] Or does one lose the comprehensive per-

---

86. H. Schultz, *Alttestamentliche Theologie. Die Offenbarungsreligion in
ihrer vorchristlichen Entwicklungsstufe* (5th ed.; Leipzig, 1896), had already
anticipated Eichrodt in the systematic arrangement of the second part of his
OT theology. Eichrodt (*TOT,* I, 33 n. 1) confesses that he owes his three major
categories to the outline by Otto Procksch, *Theologie des AT* (Gütersloh, 1950),
pp. 420-713.

87. For example, the history of the covenant concept and the history of
the prophetic movement in *TOT,* I, 36ff., 309ff. The phrase "historical development" is used by Eichrodt himself, *TOT,* I, 32.

88. *TOT,* I, 26.

89. Inasmuch as Wright, *The OT and Theology,* p. 62, has recently given
support to the centrality of the covenant concept for the recitation of the acts
of God and thus to Eichrodt's methodology, one needs to call to mind also
his earlier strictures wth regard to the adequacy of the covenant concept.

spective of history with the compartmentalization of single thematic perspectives under a single common denominator? Is it not a basic inadequacy of the cross-section method as a tool of inquiry that it remains stretched in the tension of historical summary and theological pointer?

Th. C. Vriezen, the well-known Dutch scholar, follows largely the cross-section method and combines with it a squarely confessional interest.[90] Methodologically Vriezen is indebted to both O. Eissfeldt and W. Eichrodt.[91] He attempts to reconcile some aspects of the divergent approaches that emerged in the debate between Eissfeldt and Eichrodt in the 1920s. The basic position of Vriezen that "both as to its object and its method Old Testament theology is and must be a Christian theological science"[92] is indebted to Eissfeldt. But in the structural cross-section Vriezen follows the path of Eichrodt by insisting that he has "attempted to establish the 'communion' . . . as the center of all exposition."[93] In Vriezen's view this is "the best starting-point for a Biblical theology of the Old Testament, . . . [which must] be arranged with this aspect in view."[94] It should not be overlooked that this is a reaction against the diachronic traditio-historical approach pioneered by G. von Rad that insisted that there is no center and thus no unity.[95] Vriezen, as others after him, has reworked his whole OT theology in order to "stress more firmly the unity of the whole"[96] with the aid of the communion con-

---

Wright stated in *Studia biblica et Semitica*, p. 377: "It is improbable, however, that any one single theme is sufficiently comprehensive to include within it all variety." Cf. the critique of the cipher/symbol of covenant by Norman K. Gottwald, "W. Eichrodt, Theology of the OT," in *Contemporary OT Theologians*, pp. 53-56.

90. Vriezen, *Outline of OT Theology*, pp. 143-150.

91. See above, n. 78.

92. Vriezen, *Outline of OT Theology*, p. 147.

93. Ibid., p. 8. Vriezen, p. 351, maintains that the communion concept is preferred above that of the covenant because "we cannot be certain that the communion between God and the people was considered from the outset as a *covenantal* communion."

94. Ibid., p. 175.

95. *OTT*, I, 115-121; II, 412-415.

96. Vriezen, *Outline of OT Theology*, p. 8.

cept. The stimulation for this was von Rad's rejection of a conceptual unity of the OT. Let us raise a question at this point. Is there a single theme or concept that can serve as the center of the OT in order to unify the diversified materials and to organize them into a coherent structure of OT theology?

A clearly affirmative answer with detailed argumentation is provided by W. C. Kaiser, Jr. He believes that there is "an inductively derived theme, key, or organizing pattern which the successive writers of the Old Testament overtly recognized and consciously supplemented in the progressive revelation of the Old Testament text."[97] He argues that "the true and only centre or *Mitte* of an Old Testament theology"[98] is "the *Promise* theme."[99] Kaiser's 1978 monograph *Toward an OT Theology* is built upon these affirmations and argues strenuously for the existence of a "center" in the form of a "unifying but developing concept."[100] He suggests that it is known in the OT "under a constellation of such words as promise, oath, blessing, rest, seed" and "such formulas as the tripartite saying: 'I will be your God, you shall be my people, and I will dwell in the midst of you' or the redemptive self-assertion formula . . . 'I am the Lord your God who brought you up out of the land of Egypt.' It could also be seen as a divine plan in history which promised a universal blessing. . . ."[101] Kaiser conceives this "inner center or plan to which each writer consciously contributed" now as the "divine blessing-promise theme."[102] For

---

97. W. C. Kaiser, "The Centre of OT Theology: The Promise," *Themelios*, 10 (1974), 3. See also his earlier preparatory studies such as "The Eschatological Hermeneutics of 'Evangelicalism': Promise Theology," *JETS*, 13 (1970), 91-99; "The Old Promise and the New Covenant: Jeremiah 31:31-34," *JETS*, 15 (1972), 11-23; "The Promise Theme and the Theology of Rest," *BibSac*, 130 (1973), 135-150; "The Davidic Promise and the Inclusion of the Gentiles (Amos 9:9-15 and Acts 15:13-18): A Test Passage for Theological Systems," *JETS*, 20 (1977), 97-111; "Wisdom Theology and the Centre of OT Theology," *EvQ*, 50 (1978), 132-146.
98. Kaiser, "The Centre of OT Theology," p. 9.
99. Ibid., p. 3.
100. Kaiser, *Toward an OT Theology*, p. 23.
101. Ibid., pp. 12f.
102. Ibid., p. 11.

Kaiser the "blessing-promise" theme is a rather broad center of the Bible. It includes, as his exposition indicates, also what is normally understood as covenant and covenant theology. "Promise" is thus conceived to be a very broad if not all-inclusive umbrella under which all "variety of viewpoints" and "longitudinal themes" can be "harmonized."[103]

What does all of this mean when it comes to the structure of an OT theology? Kaiser affirms that in the promise of God "Scripture presents its own key of organization."[104] The shape of the organization follows a longitudinal sequence of historical eras. To each of these historical eras is assigned a chapter, eleven in all, which unfolds the growing "blessing-promise" theme under such catchwords as provisions, people, place, king, life, day, servant, renewal, kingdom, and triumph of the promise.

It seems that Kaiser has achieved another cross-section through the OT based on a broadly defined "blessing-promise" concept. This is another valiant effort to indicate the unity of the OT by means of a given theme. He is the first to use the "blessing-promise" theme as the key for an organization of OT theology. This is one way to do OT theology. But does it achieve what is claimed, namely, that the "blessing-promise" theme unites all of the OT, not to speak of the NT?

Kaiser himself was forced to admit that this basic theme involves a "principle of selectivity" and notes that certain pieces of OT information that bear on "religious history or practice" ought "to be relegated to other parts of the body of theology."[105] Among them are cultic and institutional studies. On what basis is the decision reached that some parts or aspects of the OT are "to be relegated to other parts of the body of theology"? If it is not a subjective decision, then it must be a decision reached on the basis of the supposedly all-inclusive center of the OT. If this is the case, how defensible is the claim that the "divine blessing-

103. Ibid., p. 65.
104. Ibid., p. 69.
105. Ibid., p. 15.

promise theme" includes all "variety of viewpoints" and "longitudinal themes"? For example, the creation theology of the OT has hardly any room in Kaiser's OT theology. H. H. Schmid argues forcefully that creation theology, i.e., "faith that God has created and maintains the world with its manifold orders, is not a marginal theme of biblical theology, but its basic theme as such."[106] Here the issue is not only whether Kaiser, Schmid, or someone else is correct as to the basic theme of Biblical theology, but the choice of *one* theme has inevitably led to making other themes marginal. The cult is certainly not marginal in the OT, but in Kaiser's OT theology it has not even a marginal status. It does not fit into the supposedly all-inclusive center of "blessing-promise." Even Kaiser's treatment of the covenant is unusual. It is often noted that Eichrodt's covenant center is one-sidedly built on the Sinaitic covenant. Kaiser seems to build one-sidedly on the Abrahamic-Davidic "promise," which is contrasted with the Sinaitic covenant[107] because the latter is obligatory instead of promissory. The exposition of the theology of the prophets is again oriented toward promise, salvation, and hope, at the expense of woe, doom, and judgment. In what "other parts of the body of theology," if not in OT theology, shall these and other matters of OT thought receive attention? Kaiser's cross-section by means of the "blessing-promise" theme or center does not seem to bring together the richness of OT themes and materials.

A comparison between Vriezen and Kaiser is difficult. There are several common elements. Both conceive of their subject as preparatory for the NT. The themes or centers chosen by both are to be valid for the whole OT and the NT as well. All in all Vriezen's approach turns out to be broader than Kaiser's. In both cases the respective centers inevitably lead to a principle of selectivity. The cross-section approach has this weakness as do seemingly all "centered" approaches. Is unity really found in one center of the OT? Or is the unity

---

106. Schmid, "Schöpfung, Gerechtigkeit und Heil. 'Schopfungstheologie' als Gesamthorizant biblischer Theologie," *ZTK*, 70 (1973), 15.

107. Kaiser, *Toward an OT Theology*, pp. 63, 233ff.

of the OT not found in the one God Yahweh whose variegated self-revelation in words and acts, in creation and re-creation, in judgment and salvation cannot be pressed into a single theme or a combination of themes? Does not God manifest himself in the variety and richness of all parts of the OT, all of which contribute to a knowledge of the divine purpose for Israel, the nations, and the universe?

The first OT theology ever published by an Italian appeared in 1981 from the pen of Anselmo Mattioli.[108] Although we list it in this section, his structure is a mixture of dogmatic and cross-section approaches. Part I is entitled "God and Man as Creator and Creature." It contains several chapters that include such topics as a genetic development of monotheism from patriarchal to later Israelite religion. Part II carries the title "The Origin and Religious Role of Evil." Part III is designated "The Most Important Saving Gifts of Yahweh," with chapters on "Israel as a Covenant People";[109] "Expectation of an Israel with Authentic Spirituality for the Future," which includes Messianic expectations of the OT; "Reception of Revelation among the Prophets"; "Holy Writings as Inspired Witness of Revelation," including the development of the OT canon, which in Mattioli's view was still concluded at Jamnia (ca. A.D. 90), a view that has to be abandoned;[110] and "Expec-

108. Anselmo Mattioli, *Dio e l'uomo nella Bibbia d'Israele. Theologia dell'Antico Testamento* (Casale Monferrato, 1891).

109. Mattioli is silent on the recent debate about an early covenant in ancient Israel. A kind of neo-Wellhausian position is taken up by L. Perlitt, *Die Bundestheologie im AT* (WMANT, 36; Neukirchen-Vluyn, 1969), and E. Kutsch, *Verheissung und Gesetz* (BZAW, 131; Berlin/New York, 1973), who argue for the exilic or postexilic origin of the OT covenant idea. See E. W. Nicholson's review of this entire development and debate in *God and His People: Covenant and Theology in the OT* (Oxford, 1986). Various recent studies argue forcefully for an early covenant in the OT, including those of Dennis J. McCarthy, *Treaty and Covenant* (2nd ed., AnBib, 21A; Rome, 1963), and various articles; Thomas E. McComiskey, *The Covenant of Promise: A Theology of OT Covenants* (Grand Rapids, 1985), and others.

110. Mattioli continues to build on the outdated concept of the fixing of the OT canon at the "council of Jamnia." He seems to be unaware of the definitive studies of, e.g., P. Schäfer in *Judaica*, 31 (1975), 54-64, 116-124; Jack P. Lewis, *JBR*, 32 (1964), 125-34; S. Z. Leiman, *The Canonization of the*

tations of Future Life after Death," a chapter that includes discussion of life after death in the Apocrypha and at Qumran. This tome contains a concluding part entitled "The True Yahweh Cult: Toward Liberation and Peace," with chapters on the Hebrew cult, on conversion, and on forgiveness.

Mattioli attempts to "present the major religious ideas which the Bible contains."[111] His OT theology is organized on the basis of these "ideas," ideas concerning God and man, which in the words of H. Graf Reventlow manifest the working of a "dogmatic principle."[112] While this seems to be sustained for the organization of the major parts of his volume, the individual chapters follow roughly a cross-section approach, since the various topics and themes selected from the OT follow more or less the support found for them throughout the OT. The chapter on the future life gives the impression of a genetic presentation. Thus it seems that Mattioli employs a mixture of approaches to accomplish his purposes.

John Goldingay had written several articles and a book on OT theology before his revised dissertation appeared as *Theological Diversity and the Authority of the OT*.[113] In his first book on OT interpretation he had made the point that one should not opt for an either/or approach as regards the descriptive over against the normative method for OT theology.[114] He opts for the position that "God's relationship with mankind

---

Hebrew Scriptures: The Talmudic and Midrashic Evidence (Hamden, CT, 1976); S. Talmon, "The OT Text," in Qumran and the History of the Biblical Text, ed. F. M. Cross and S. Talmon (Cambridge, MA, 1975), pp. 1-41. Each of these studies demonstrates in its own way that the OT canon was completed long before the NT came into existence.

111. Mattioli, p. 14.

112. H. Graf Reventlow, "Zur Theologie des AT," TRu, 52 (1987), 237.

113. John Goldingay, "The Study of OT Theology: Its Aim and Purpose," TynBul, 26 (1975), 34-52; idem, "The Chronicler as Theologian," BTB, 5 (1975), 99-126; idem, "The 'Salvation History' Perspective and the 'Wisdom' Perspective Within the Context of Biblical Theology," EvQ, 51 (1979), 194- 207; idem, "Diversity and Unity in OT Theology," VT, 34 (1984), 153-168; idem, Approaches to OT Interpretation (Downers Grove, IL, 1981); idem, Theological Diversity and the Authority of the OT (Grand Rapids, 1987).

114. Goldingay, Approaches, pp. 17-24.

(specifically with Israel) is the midpoint [center?] of OT faith rom which all other aspects of it should be examined."[115] But he warns immediately that "the search for the right structure of an OT theology, and for its right central concept from which to view OT faith as a whole, has been fruitless (or over-fruitful!)."[116] He opts for "a multiplicity of approaches [which] will lead to a multiplicity of insights."[117] He also notes that "the challenge to contemporary OT interpretation . . . arises from the twofold nature of these scriptures,"[118] namely, the word of God in the human word. "It is so to use the techniques appropriate to the study of the human words, that the divine word which they constitute may speak to us who live on this side of the coming of Christ."[119]

Goldingay's recent monograph on the *Theological Diversity and Authority of the OT* complements his earlier publications and deals penetratingly and perceptively with the hotly debated issues whether the diversity of the OT[120] is of such overwhelming weight that the scholar and theologian will simply give up and say no to OT theology.[121] It is also an alternative to the attempts of James Barr, particularly his recent book on the authority of Scripture.[122] Goldingay devotes the central part of his book to his own synthesis of the prob-

---

115. Ibid., p. 26.
116. Ibid., p. 27.
117. Ibid., p. 29.
118. Ibid., p. 155.
119. Ibid.
120. See the monograph of Paul D. Hanson, *The Diversity of Scripture: A Theological Interpretation* (OBT, 11; Philadelphia, 1982), in which the diversity of Scripture as posited by historical-critical research is seen in terms of dynamic polarities, such as "pragmatic/visionary" and "form/reform," as part of the interface of tradition and community.
121. This is exactly what R. N. Whybray, "OT Theology—A Non-existent Beast?," in *Scripture: Meaning and Method. Essays Presented to Anthony Tyrell Hanson for His Seventieth Birthday*, ed. B. P. Thompson (Pickering, North Yorkshire, 1987), pp. 168-180, has again suggested. He does not believe that the major attempts to unify the OT by means of a single theme, statement, or the like— whether dogmatic, philosophical, or psychological—will suffice.
122. James Barr, *Holy Scripture: Canon, Authority, Criticism* (Philadelphia, 1983).

lems facing OT theology and provides his own approach in this part, which is entitled "A Unifying or Constructive Approach."[123] Here he raises the question whether it is possible to "formulate one Old Testament theology."[124] This question has unique relevance, because voices from various quarters point out that the discipline is called OT theology but the OT has various and variegated theologies.[125]

Goldingay's proposals for OT theology are influenced by Eichrodt's cross-section approach and by directions beyond those of Eichrodt as outlined or hinted at by D. G. Spriggs.[126] He even goes beyond Spriggs and suggests in his recent reflections that there is no single center on which a theology of the OT can be based. "Many starting points, structures, and foci can illuminate the landscape of the OT; a multiplicity of approaches will lead to a multiplicity of insights."[127] Thus Goldingay opts for a "constructive approach." "OT theology is inevitably not merely a reconstructive task but a constructive one."[128] This means that "it is actually unrealistic to maintain that OT theology should be a purely descriptive discipline; it inevitably involves the contemporary explication of the biblical material."[129] Goldingay here departs from those

123. Goldingay, *Theological Diversity*, pp. 167-239.

124. Ibid., pp. 167-199.

125. See, e.g., Siegfried Wagner, "'Biblische Theologien' und 'Biblische Theologie,'" *TLZ*, 103 (1978), 785-798; S. E. McEvenue, "The OT, Scripture or Theology?," *Interp*, 35 (1981), 229-241; Rolf Rendtorff, "Zur Bedeutung des Kanons für eine Theologie des AT," in *"Wenn nicht jetzt, wann dann?" Aufsätze für Hans-Joachim Kraus zum 65. Geburtstag*, ed. H.-G. Geyer et al. (Neukirchen-Vluyn, 1983), pp. 3-11. Particularly important are also the essays by Manfred Oeming, "Unitas Scripturae? Eine Problemskizze," pp. 48-70; Ulrich Mauser, "*Eis Theos* und *Monos Theos* in Biblischer Theologie," pp. 71-87; and Peter Stuhlmacher, "Biblische Theologie als Weg der Erkenntnis Gottes. Zum Buch von Horst Seebass: Der Gott der ganzen Bibel," pp. 91-114, in *Einheit und Vielfalt Biblischer Theologie*, ed. I. Baldermann et al. (Jahrbuch für Biblische Theologie, 1; Neukirchen-Vluyn, 1986).

126. D. G. Spriggs, *Two OT Theologies* (SBT, 2/30; Naperville, IL, 1974), p. 89, as referred to by Goldingay, *Theological Diversity*, p. 181.

127. Goldingay, *Theological Diversity*, p. 115.

128. Ibid., p. 11.

129. Ibid., p. 185.

who limit OT theology to the descriptive task alone and sides with R. E. Clements and others who combine the descriptive with the theological tasks.[130] Here Goldingay separates himself from the "what is meant" (OT/biblical theology) and "what it means" (systematic theology) of Stendahl's program on the one hand and on the other reacts to the debate between O. Eissfeldt and W. Eichrodt in the 1930s by giving more credence to Eissfeldt than has been customary.[131]

There is a greater and greater recognition that no scholar works so isolated from his faith community or tradition that this does not, or should not, be taken into consideration. Goldingay insists, "Indeed, a Christian writing OT *theology* cannot avoid writing in the light of the NT, because he cannot make *theological* judgments without reference to the NT. Admittedly the converse is also true: he cannot make theological judgments on the NT in isolation from the OT."[132] Goldingay's

---

130. R. E. Clements, *OT Theology: A Fresh Approach* (Atlanta, 1978), pp. 10-11, 20, 155. Clements emphasizes repeatedly that OT theology is descriptive and theological in the sense that OT theology is "concerned with the theological significance which this literature possesses in the modern world" (p. 20). He insists that "Old Testament theology must more openly recognise that its function is to elucidate the role and authority of the Old Testament in those religions which use it as a sacred canon and regard it as a fundamental part of their heritage" (p. 155). Others who share similar concerns although in a variety of ways include Norman Porteous, *Living the Mystery: Collected Essays* (Oxford, 1967), pp. 22-24; Paul D. Hanson, "Theology, OT," in *Harper's Bible Dictionary*, ed. Paul Achtemeier (San Francisco, 1985), pp. 1057-1062; idem, *The People Called: The Growth of the Community in the Bible* (San Francisco, 1986); Joseph W. Groves, *Actualization and Interpretation in the OT* (SBLDS, 86; Atlanta, 1987), pp. 165-210, where he provides a penetrating criticism of G. von Rad's "chronological actualization" and outlines his own proposals.

131. See Otto Eissfeldt, "Israelitisch-jüdische Religionsgeschichte und alttestamentliche Theologie," *ZAW,* 44 (1926), 1-12, repr. in his *Kleine Schriften* (Tübingen, 1962), 1:105-114; trans. "History of Israelite-Jewish Religion and OT Theology," in *The Flowering of OT Theology: A Reader in Twentieth Century OT Theology,* ed. Ben C. Ollenburger, Elmer A. Martens, and Gerhard F. Hasel (Winona Lake, IN, 1991); Walther Eichrodt, "Hat die alttestamentliche Theologie noch selbständige Bedeutung innerhalb der alttestamentlichen Wissenschaft?," *ZAW,* 47 (1929), 83-91; trans. "Does OT Theology Still Have Independent Significance Within OT Scholarship," in *Flowering of OT Theology* (1991) .

132. Goldingay, *Theological Diversity,* pp. 186-187.

modified and enlarged "cross-section" method does not rule
out "theological constructions" that are based on "diachronic
approaches."[133] It remains unclear just how both "cross-
section" and "diachronic" approaches can function side by
side unless both are so transformed and redefined that they
are something new or something so different that the relationship with what has been so designated by either Eichrodt and
his followers or von Rad and his followers has undergone a
full transmutation. Goldingay challenges OT theology with
his formidable theological proposals and engages himself in
doing it.[134]

   D. *The Topical Method.* The topical method is distinguished
from the dogmatic-didactic method in its refusal to let outside
categories be superimposed as a grid through which the OT
materials and themes are read, ordered, and systematized. It
also steers away from the cross-section method and its synthesis of the OT world of thought. The topical method as
surveyed in this section is used either in combination with a
single or dual center of the OT or without an explicit thematic
center.

   John L. McKenzie has made an eloquent case for the topical
approach. In contrast to the vast majority of scholarly opinion
in the decade under review he is adamant in his emphasis
that he "wrote the theology of the Old Testament as if the New
Testament did not exist."[135] The significance of this position
is best recognized in contrast to the emphasis of B. S. Childs,
who pleads for a Biblical theology built on the Scriptural
canon,[136] and the American and European scholars who suggest a diachronic traditio-historical approach for Biblical theology. McKenzie sees himself standing close to A. von Har-

   133. Ibid., pp. 197-199.
   134. Ibid., pp. 200-239, where he engages in his "Unifying Approach to
'Creation' and 'Salvation' in the OT."
   135. J. L. McKenzie, *A Theology of the OT* (New York, 1974), p. 319.
   136. B. S. Childs, *Biblical Theology in Crisis;* idem, "The OT as Scripture
of the Church," *CTM,* 43 (1972), 709-722; idem, "The Canonical Shape of the
Prophetic Literature," *Interp,* 32 (1978), 46-55.

nack and R. Bultmann,[137] and we may add that he is close to F. Baumgärtel[138] in his affirmation that "the Old Testament is not a Christian book."[139] McKenzie's conception would never permit "a current of life flowing in reverse direction from the New Testament to the Old."[140]

The category of operation in McKenzie's OT theology is "the totality of experience"[141] expressed in the God-talk of the OT. Since "not every biblical experience of Yahweh, not every fragment of God-talk, is of equal profundity,"[142] the object of OT theology is to be governed by "the experience of the totality." McKenzie speaks of an "inner unity" of the OT without clearly designating it. It is linked with the "ways Israel . . . experienced Yahweh,"[143] and the totality of this experience "shows the reality of Yahweh with a clarity which particular books and passages do not have."[144] The structure of an OT theology, its categories or themes, will be based on that "totality of the experience" that admittedly "is an artificially unified analysis of a historic experience which has a different inner unity from the unity of logical discourse."[145]

On the basis of the quantitative totality of Israel's experience, McKenzie departs from all previous structures of OT theology[146] in placing the cult first.[147] This is followed by chapters on "Revelation," "History," "Nature," "Wisdom," and

137. McKenzie, *Theology of the OT,* p. 319.

138. F. Baumgärtel, "Erwägungen zur Darstellung der Theologie des AT," *TLZ,* 76 (1951), 257-272; "Gerhard von Rads Theologie des AT," *TLZ,* 86 (1961), 801-816, 895-908; "The Hermeneutical Problem of the OT," in *EOTH,* pp. 134-159. See also L. Schmidt, "Die Einheit zwischen Alten und Neuen Testament im Streit zwischen Friedrich Baumgärtel und Gerhard von Rad," *EvT,* 35 (1975), 119-139.

139. McKenzie, *Theology of the OT,* p. 319.

140. *TOT,* I, 26.

141. McKenzie, *Theology of the OT,* p. 35.

142. Ibid.

143. Ibid., p. 32.

144. Ibid., p. 35.

145. Ibid., pp. 34f.

146. Ibid., pp. 23-25.

147. Ibid., pp. 37-63.

"Political and Social Institutions," and concludes with a chapter entitled "The Future of Israel."

It is obvious that McKenzie has gone his own way and is to be credited with pioneering a new method—the topical method. As in the case of any other method, the pressing questions regard the principle of selectivity on the one hand and the principle of faithfulness to the proposed method on the other hand. The last point shall receive first consideration. In choosing a topical approach one would expect consistency. This does not seem to have been entirely achieved. McKenzie departs from his own path when it comes to the Writing Prophets within the chapter on "Revelation." The section entitled "The Message of the Prophets" provides "a very general summary of topics which can each be discussed on the scale of a book,"[148] i.e., a book-by-book approach in historical sequence and on the basis of literary-critical judgments. But even here there is no consistency. Joel and Zech. 9–14 are said to be treated in connection with apocalyptic in the last chapter, and Nahum and Obadiah are said to be discussed in the chapter on "History." In the case of Nahum and Obadiah their names are mentioned in connection with other oracles against the nations and that is all.[149] Joel and Zech. 9–14 fare slightly better; together they receive two pages of discussion.[150]

The principle of selectivity, namely, what is to be included or excluded in an OT theology, or, to use the words of McKenzie, what is "of equal profundity,"[151] is detected through the "most frequent manner in which the Israelite experienced Yahweh."[152] Evidently here the proper principle of selectivity is the quantitative frequency of experience. This is apparently the norm for both topical selection and topical sequence. This is the reason why the cult is given first place in McKenzie's OT theology. How defensible is the claim that the quantitative communal experience of Yahweh has priority

148. Ibid., p. 102.
149. Ibid., p. 171.
150. Ibid., pp. 302-304.
151. Ibid., p. 35.
152. Ibid., p. 32.

over a qualitative individual experience of Yahweh? One wonders whether there is "equal profundity" in regular cultic experience as compared to the single experience of a Moses, Isaiah, Jeremiah, Amos, Hosea, etc. One may inquire whether a quantitative "totality of experience" is an adequate means for selectivity and arrangement of topics. Departures from the quantitative principle to a qualitative one, as in the message of the prophets, may provide a clue to this problem.

At this place we want to turn our attention to two other famous scholars and their contributions to the subject of OT theology. Georg Fohrer presented his *Theologische Grundstrukturen des AT* (Basic Theological Structures of the OT) in 1972 after a number of preliminary studies[153] and a widely acclaimed *History of Israelite Religion*[154] was published. Fohrer affirms a center of the OT in the form of a "dual concept"[155] that consists of "the *rule* of God and the communion between God and man,"[156] but refrains from employing it as the principle for systematizing or organizing the OT materials into an OT theology. Fohrer's OT theology thus avoids the cross-section method, the genetic method, and the dogmatic method with its Theology-Anthropology-Soteriology structure. On the other hand, he is pioneering in OT theology by joining a topical approach that is descriptive in purpose with the meaning it carries for the present. In other words, he is attempting to bridge the gap between reconstruction and interpretation[157] or between "what it meant" and "what it means."[158]

---

153. Particularly important are the following studies: G. Fohrer, "Der Mittelpunkt einer Theologie des AT," *TZ*, 24 (1968), 161-172; "The Centre of a Theology of the OT," *Nederlands theologisch tijdschrift*, 7 (1966), 198-206; "Das AT und das Thema 'Christologie,'" *EvT*, 30 (1970), 281-298; *Studien zur alttestamentlichen Theologie und Geschichte (1949-1966)* (BZAW, 115; Berlin, 1969).

154. First published under the title *Geschichte der israelitischen Religion* (Berlin, 1969).

155. Fohrer, "Das AT und das Thema 'Christologie'," p. 295.

156. Fohrer, "Der Mittelpunkt einer Theologie des AT," p. 163.

157. See particularly O. Merk, *Biblische Theologie des NT in ihrer Anfangszeit* (Marburg, 1972), pp. 260-262.

158. K. Stendahl, "Biblical Theology, Contemporary," *IDB*, I (1962), 418-

An investigation of Fohrer's method[159] reveals that Chapter 4, "Unity in Manifoldness," is the heart of his book that elucidates the center of "the rule of God and the communion between God and man." The first three chapters, entitled respectively "Types of Interpreting the OT," "OT and Revelation," and "The Manifoldness of Attitudes of Existence," build toward Fohrer's central concern in Chapter 4. Chapter 5, "Power of Change and Capacity of Change," gives the impression of a kind of parenthesis within the total structure of his OT theology. It attempts to demonstrate how the influence of the theological center of the rulership of God and communion between God and man changed the faith of Israel and the conception of the theological center itself. The next chapter, "Developments," points back to what was developed, and the last chapter, "Applications," suggests the interpretation for modern man by elucidating "what it means."

It is necessary to linger a little longer with Fohrer because of certain innovative emphases. In Chapter 3 Fohrer discusses the diversity of man's attitudes of existence in terms of a "magic" attitude which is negatively evaluated and rejected. The second attitude of existence is the cultic one, which is "a transformation of the faith of the time of Moses"[160] primarily under the influence of magic. "The whole cult is geared to get something out of God."[161] Fohrer interprets the cult only in negative terms. Note the contrast to McKenzie, who gives it first place. In Fohrer's view the law "saves but in gaining God's favor and assuring his grace."[162] It too is negative.[163] Fohrer admits that "the faith in Israel's *election* through God is basic,"[164] but it too receives from him a negative evaluation.

---

432. On the varieties of meanings this distinction may carry, see Hasel, *NT Theology*, pp. 136-139.
   159. *TOT,* I, 26.
   160. Fohrer, *Theologische Grundstrukturen des AT,* p. 62.
   161. Ibid., p. 65.
   162. Ibid.
   163. Ibid., p. 67.
   164. Ibid., p. 69.

In contrast to Fohrer's negations of the attitudes of existence of magic, cult, law, and election, he suggests that the only attitude of existence that is to be seen positively is "the prophetic attitude of existence."[165] The dynamic prophetic attitude of existence also overcomes wisdom, because wisdom "is concerned with how one may best be the master of life."[166] In short, Fohrer depicts six attitudes of existence of which five—magic, cult, law, national election, and wisdom—are but temporal and thus negative attempts to secure existence,[167] whereas one—the prophetic attitude of existence—is supratemporal and thus positive. "In its core it is existence in believing submission and obedient service on account of a complete communion with God. Thus it has lasting meaning."[168]

At this point the criteria for the evaluations of the Israelite attitudes of existence are fully apparent. The attitudes of existence in which man attempts to be "the master of life" are considered temporal and negative. The attitude of existence that has a supratemporal quality and lasting meaning is characterized by "believing submission and obedient service." To what degree are these evaluations and assessments dependent on exegetical and theological conclusions? For example, not all experts in wisdom theology necessarily share Fohrer's position on OT wisdom.[169] Further research will have to address itself to these issues.

---

165. Ibid., pp. 71-86.
166. Ibid., p. 87.
167. Ibid., pp. 85, 93f.
168. Ibid., p. 94.
169. Wisdom literature and ideology has been reckoned as an "alien body" within the Israelite canon and biblical theology by H. D. Preuss, "Erwägungen zum theologischen Ort alttestamentlicher Weisheits Literatur," EvT, 30 (1970), 393-417; idem, "Alttestamentliche Weisheit in christlicher Theologie?" Bibliotheca ephemeridum theologicarum lovaniensium, 33 (1974), 165-181. For different assessments, see the literature cited by R. B. Y. Scott, "The Study of the Wisdom Literature," Interp, 24 (1970), 20-45; J. L. Crenshaw, "Wisdom," in OT Form Criticism, ed. J. H. Hayes (San Antonio, 1974), pp. 225-264; idem, ed., Studies in Ancient Israelite Wisdom (New York, 1975); idem, "Wisdom in the OT," IDB Supplement (1976), pp. 952-956.

Let us turn to Fohrer's discussion of six attitudes of existence and the issue of the center of the OT and OT theology.
Is the dual concept of "the rule of God and the communion
between God and man" for Fohrer typical of all six OT attitudes of existence, although Fohrer finds five inferior and
rejects them? C. Westermann understands Fohrer as deriving
his center from all six attitudes of existence and concludes
that he merges two originally independent methods in his OT
theology, namely, one built on the principle of attitudes of
existence and another built on the center of the OT.[170] I am
inclined to disagree with Westermann. Fohrer takes his center
from the one genuine attitude of existence and the traditions
that reflect it. Among them are some patriarchal experiences
and the purity of the Mosaic faith to which the prophetic
attitude of existence returns.[171] If our understanding of Fohrer
is correct, then he cannot be charged with a merging of
methods or with a methodological inconsistency at this point.
If we are correct another issue emerges, namely, the center of
OT theology is in this instance not identical with the totality
of the OT witness, and some parts of the Israelite experience
are not even marginal with reference to the center, but are
ruled out by the center. At this point, then, we are approaching
the idea of "a canon within the canon" and its concomitant
content criticism.

The issue of "a canon within the canon," or as the late G. E.
Wright called it, an "authoritative core" within the OT,[172] is
not a new problem in Biblical studies. It reaches back at least
to the Reformation,[173] and has exercised Biblical scholarship
ever since.[174] In the case of Fohrer, one has the impression
that the choice of his center is deeply involved with his

170. Westermann, "Zu zwei Theologien des AT," p. 100.
171. Fohrer seems to make the suggestion of his center on the basis of
materials that reflect the "prophetic" attitude of existence.
172. Wright, The OT and Theology, pp. 180-183.
173. I. Lönning, "Kanon im Kanon." Zum dogmatischen Grundlagenproblem des neutestamentlichen Kanon (Munich, 1972).
174. Representative bibliographies are provided in Hasel, NT Theology,
pp. 141 n. 1, 165 n. 139.

understanding of the OT prophets and his objections to a linking of the Israelite prophets and their message with the mainstream of Israelite traditions, as G. von Rad and other scholars have emphasized.[175] In any case, it remains to be seen what influence Fohrer's negative interpretation of the attitudes of existence of magic, cult, law,[176] wisdom, and election will have on subsequent scholarship. The matter of "a canon within the canon" as raised by Fohrer reminds us of the significant stirrings these days regarding the OT canon for Biblical theology in the studies of B. S. Childs, the "canonical criticism"[177] called for by James A. Sanders,[178] as well as Joseph Blenkinsopp's thesis that the Hebrew Bible is basically prophetic.[179]

Another giant of OT scholarship is W. Zimmerli, who has presented the ripe fruit of a lifetime of study[180] in *OT Theology in Outline.* It was released in English in 1978 and has largely

175. G. Fohrer, "Remarks on Modern Interpretation of the Prophets," *JBL*, 80 (1961), 309-319, esp. 316: "The prophets were neither mere reformers nor revolutionaries nor evolutionists. They were not dependent upon old traditions, did not create anything wholly new without basis in the religion of Israel, and did not complete a development already begun."

176. Fohrer's concept of law in connection with the attitude of existence apparently excludes the Decalogue, which is later in his exposition described in very positive ways (*Theologische Grundstrukturen des AT,* pp. 166-171). It is surprising that in the earlier section no hint is provided for excluding the Decalogue from the negative evaluation of law.

177. Childs ("The Canonical Shape of the Prophetic Literature," *Interp,* 32 [1978], 54) objects to this designation on the grounds that "it implies that the concern with canon is viewed as another historical-critical technique which can take its place alongside of source criticism, form criticism, rhetorical criticism, and the like."

178. J. A. Sanders, *Torah and Canon* (2nd ed.; Philadelphia, 1974); idem, "Hermeneutics," *IDB Supplement* (1976), pp. 402-407.

179. J. Blenkinsopp, *Prophecy and Canon. A Contribution to the Study of Jewish Origins* (Notre Dame, 1977).

180. W. Zimmerli, *Gottes Offenbarung. Gesammelte Aufsätze zum AT* (TBü, 19; Munich, 1963); *Der Mensch und seine Hoffnung im AT* (Göttingen, 1968), trans. *Man and His Hope in the OT* (SBT, 2/20; Naperville, IL, 1971); *The Law and the Prophets* (London, 1965); *Die Weltlichkeit des AT* (Göttingen, 1971), trans. *The OT and the World* (London, 1976). Among Zimmerli's many essays the following is particularly relevant: "Alttestamentliche Traditionsgeschichte und Theologie," in *Probleme biblischer Theologie,* pp. 632-647.

the same content as the German original published six years earlier. The dust jacket informs the reader that "the material is conveniently organized by topic" and "emphasizes theological themes." The topical-thematic approach is at the forefront.

The task of OT theology is conceived by Zimmerli as a descriptive one. OT theology must present "what the Old Testament says about God in a coherent whole."[181] Zimmerli denies that the "coherent whole" consists "merely in continuity of history, that is, the ongoing stream of historical sequence" (pace G. von Rad and followers).[182] Instead continuity is found "in the sameness of the God it [faith] knows by the name of Yahweh."[183]

Having linked continuity within evident change uniquely with the confession of the name of Yahweh as revealed to Moses and incorporated in the proclamation of the Decalogue (Ex. 20:2f.; Dt. 5:6f.),[184] Zimmerli sets out to present the theology of the OT in five major sections. Parts I-III treat OT theology under the headings "Fundamentals," "The Gifts Be-

181. Zimmerli, *OT Theology in Outline*, p. 12.
182. Ibid., p. 13.
183. Ibid., p. 14.
184. Earlier Zimmerli had argued that with the sentence "I am Yahweh, your God" (Ex. 20:2) "an actual foundation of everything following is given" ("Alttestamentliche Traditionsgeschichte und Theologie," p. 639) and that with the confessional response "You . . . Yahweh" has "come to view a center which is uniquely held onto in the entire OT history of tradition and interpretation" (ibid., p. 640). In later publications Zimmerli leaves the impression that he moves to a broader understanding of the center of the OT in his emphasis on the name of Yahweh. "If an OT theology proceeds from the name of Yahweh, which is the center of all OT speaking about God, then it will keep itself strictly to the self-interpretation of the OT and remain conscious that it meets in the name of Yahweh the one who speaks and who refuses to give up his freedom in such speaking" ("Erwägungen zur Gestalt einer alttestamentlichen Theologie," p. 84). It appears that in his article "Zum Problem der 'Mitte des AT,'" *EvT*, 35 (1975), 97-118, the center is Yahweh as Lord. If our observations are correct, then Zimmerli moves from a more narrowly defined conception of the center of the OT to a broader and more inclusive one which covers also the wisdom materials ("Zum Problem," pp. 104-109), which still pose special problems in his OT theology (*OT Theology in Outline*, pp. 155-166).

stowed by Yahweh," and "Yahweh's Commandment." The first of these parts is undoubtedly one of the two foci in Zimmerli's structure, because it sets out the "fundamentals" of Yahweh in the Pentateuch from the Mosaic era onward. This is similar to G. von Rad, whose first part deals with the theology of the Hexateuch, but von Rad includes the primeval history and the history of the patriarchs within this section.[185] The other focus in Zimmerli's tome is Part V, "Crisis and Hope," which is a kind of soteriology. It has a central emphasis in the message of the Writing Prophets that is summarized in book-by-book fashion. In other words, the Pentateuchal picture of Yahweh is the foundation; its crisis climaxes in OT prophecy.

Parts II and III are related to each other as gift and task *(Gabe-Aufgabe)*. Various themes are incorporated under the gifts of Yahweh: "war and victory," "the land and its blessings," "the gift of God's presence," and "charismata of leadership and instruction." The part on Yahweh's commandment puts an overemphasis on the first and second commandments of the Decalogue. Slight treatment is given to the laws of liturgical, ritual, and social import. The cult of Israel has first place in McKenzie, is written off as negative by Fohrer, and has hardly any place in Zimmerli's OT theology. The schemes of Zimmerli and Kaiser apparently do not lend themselves to inclusion of the Hebrew cultus within an OT theology.

Zimmerli entitles Part IV "Life before God" and thereby brings to mind von Rad's chapter "Israel before Yahweh"[186] in which Israel's response to Yahweh comes into view. Aside from the relationship in title, Zimmerli treats in this part the same topics as von Rad, but in much more compressed form, with only ten pages on wisdom theology,[187] the step-child in OT theology. It is high time that wisdom theology takes its own place in OT theology, and the attempt of S. Terrien[188] in this direction is overdue.

185. *OTT,* I, 136-279.
186. *OTT,* I, 355-459.
187. Zimmerli, *OT Theology in Outline,* pp. 155-165.
188. See below, pp. 86-88.

The methodological procedure of Zimmerli is in some respects unusual. Topics or themes are grouped together in some parts that raise the question of how they relate to each other. One would expect that the historical books be accorded a separate treatment that elucidates their theological emphases. Why should the theology of the prophets in book-by-book sequence be characterized as "judgment and salvation" and be part of a chapter on judgment and hope? Fohrer makes it the heart of his OT theology, and von Rad treats it extensively in the second volume of his OT theology, but Zimmerli tucks it away among other matters.

The OT theologies of McKenzie, Fohrer, and Zimmerli share more or less a topical approach but are methodologically so diverse that they can hardly be compared. The starting-points of each are radically different. McKenzie affirms an "inner unity" in the form of a quantitative experience of Yahweh. On this foundation the cult deserves first place. One would then assume that the topic that has last place, in McKenzie's case "The Future of Israel," is at the bottom of the quantitative scale. But this is hardly so and there is no logic in the sequence of themes.

Fohrer and Zimmerli proceed from explicit centers of the OT, but again each in his own way. Fohrer proceeds from a center which is apparently derived from the prophetic attitude of existence. In his view this is the only legitimate attitude of existence when compared to others such as magic, cult, law, election, and wisdom. It is from this prophetic attitude of existence that later "developments" and "applications" are elucidated. Zimmerli proceeds also from a center. It has its roots and origin squarely in the Pentateuch and particularly in the Mosaic era. The "crisis" forms the other pole and reaches from primeval history via some Pentateuchal traditions and the historical writings to the prophetic books. The three parts in between this arch are seen as gift, requirement, and response. Four of the five parts of Zimmerli are more or less topical, but the last part, which is the second major pole of his structure, gives way to a book-by-book approach in historical sequence. McKenzie also departs from the topical approach by inserting a book-by-book section on "The Message of the Prophets" in the chapter on "Revelation." In short, the three major representatives of the topical approach in this decade differ vastly in (1) starting-points, (2) structures of their materials, (3) selection of topics, (4) sequence of presentation, (5) centers of OT theology, (6) emphases and evaluations of OT materials, and (7) consistency in their own individual structures.

E. *The Diachronic Method.* The diachronic method for OT theology is dependent upon traditio-historical research which was developed in the 1930s.[189] Already then one of its founding fathers, G. von Rad, used it "in order to arrive at that which for him is theologically important."[190] In 1957 and 1961 he published the two volumes of his *OT Theology,* which stimulated fresh thought and research of unprecedented proportions together with a vigorous debate. Von Rad seeks to "retell" the kerygma or confession of the OT as uncovered by means of the diachronic traditio-historical method. The diachronic approach penetrates into the successive layers of the fixed text of the OT with the aim of unfolding "Israel's theological activity which is probably one of its most important and interesting ones, namely those ever new attempts to make the divine acts of salvation relevant for every new age and day— this ever new reaching-out to and avowal of God's acts which in the end made the old credal statements grow into such enormous masses of traditions."[191] Von Rad is the first and only scholar who has ever published a full-fledged diachronic OT theology of the historical traditions of Israel.

Von Rad's monumental *OT Theology*[192] needs to be under-

189. See D. A. Knight, *Rediscovering the Traditions of Israel* (SBLDS, 9; Missoula, 1973).

190. Ibid., p. 121.

191. *OTT,* I, vi.

192. Many important reviews are cited by G. Henton Davies, "Gerhard von Rad, OT Theology," in *Contemporary OT Theologians,* pp. 65-89. The following articles deal largely with the problems raised by von Rad: F. Hesse,

stood as the theology of the historical and prophetic traditions, fully using the diachronic method. He prefaces his
theology of the traditions with a sketch of the history of
Yahwism and Israelite sacral institutions as reconstructed by
the historical-critical method and states that "historical investigation searches for a critically assured minimum— the kerygmatic picture tends towards a theological maximum."[193]
This means for von Rad that an OT theology cannot do justice
to the content of the OT through a presentation of the minimum. The OT theologian must recognize that the "kerygmatic
picture" as painted by the faith of Israel is also "founded in
the actual history and has not been invented."[194] As a matter
of fact "Israel with her testimonies speaks from such a deep
level of historical experience which historical-critical research
is unable to reach."[195] Thus the subject of an OT theology is
above all "this world made up of testimonies" and not "a
systematic ordered world of faith" or thought.[196] This world
of "testimonies," i.e., "what Israel herself testified concerning
Jahweh,"[197] namely, "the word and deed of Jahweh in history,"[198] presents neither pure revelation from above nor pure

---

"Die Erforschung der Geschichte als theologische Aufgabe," *KuD,* 4 (1958),
1-19; idem, "Kerygma oder geschichtliche Wirklichkeit?" *ZTK,* 57 (1960),
17-26; idem, "Bewährt sich eine 'Theologie der Heilstatsachen' am AT? Zum
Verhältnis von Faktum und Deutung?" *ZTK,* 81 (1969), 1-17; V. Maag, "Historische und ausserhistorische Begründung alttestamentlicher Theologie,"
Schweizer Theologische Umschau, 29 (1959), 6-18; F. Baumgärtel, "Gerhard
von Rads Theologie des AT," *TLZ,* 86 (1961), 801-816, 895-908; Ch. Barth,
"Grundprobleme einer Theologie des AT," *EvT,* 23 (1963), 342-372;
M. Honecker, "Zum Verständnis der Geschichte in Gerhard von Rads Theologie des AT," *EvT,* 23 (1963), 143-168; H. Graf Reventlow, "Grundfragen einer
alttestamentlichen Theologie im Lichte der neueren deutschen Forschung,"
TZ, 17 (1961), 81ff.; Gerhard F. Hasel, "The Problem of History in OT Theology," *AUSS,* 8 (1970), 23-50; Harvey, *BTB,* 1 (1971), 9ff.
    193. *TAT,* I, 120; *OTT,* I, 108.
    194. Ibid.
    195. *TAT,* I, 120. Since *OTT,* I, was translated from the 2nd German
edition, it does not have this sentence.
    196. *TAT,* I, 124; *OTT,* I, 111. Here von Rad goes contrary to the approach
of Eichrodt.
    197. *TAT,* I, 118; *OTT,* I, 105.
    198. *TAT,* I, 127; *OTT,* I, 114.

perception and presentation from below, but is "drawn up by faith" and is accordingly "confessional in character."[199] It is these confessional statements of the "continuing activity of God in history"[200] that are the proper subject-matter of an OT theology. It is obvious that with von Rad kerygma theology has broken with full power into the field of OT studies.[201]

Von Rad emphasizes the more complete "kerygmatic picture" with the deeper dimensions of reality as the one which OT theology must explicate. But is not this kind of theologizing, which is based upon the confessional and thus kerygmatic testimonies of the OT, still very unrelated to the historical-critical reconstruction of Israel's history, because the latter does not coincide with the kerygmatic picture of OT faith and history? This is precisely the point von Rad likes to make. For him the historian's reconstructed picture of Israel's history is impoverished and therefore unable to be the basis for explicating the total reality contained in the OT testimonies, with which an OT theology must concern itself. Because of this he focuses in his theology on the OT interpretation, rather than basing his OT theology on the historical-critical interpretation of events whose historicity is not in question. At this point the sharp and incisive criticism of modern historiography's methods and presuppositions on the part of von Rad leads critical scholarship into self-critical introspection and evaluation of that which should have normative character. Although this is a step in the right direction, the history von Rad envisages too often falls short of the OT testimonies, because his history is history of tradition, or historical experiences influencing traditions. To this crucial point in his theological endeavor we need to return, because it raises the problem of the relation of *Traditionsgeschichte* to *Historie* and *Heilsgeschichte*.

199. *TAT,* I, 119; *OTT,* I, 107.
200. *TAT,* I, 118; *OTT,* I, 106.
201. *TOT,* I, 515. See also the interpretation of von Rad by O. Cullmann, *Salvation in History* (New York, 1967), pp. 54ff. On Cullmann's understanding and usage of von Rad, see Kraus, *Biblische Theologie,* pp. 186ff.

The matter of presenting OT theology is defined by von Rad in a new way. "Re-telling [*Nacherzählen*] remains the most legitimate form of theological discourse on the Old Testament."[202] What does von Rad understand by "re-telling"? How is the theologian or preacher to proceed? Is he just to relate, i.e., to tell again, what the OT has told without translating it theologically for modern man? Von Rad's notion of "re-telling" is ambiguous.

It appears that von Rad has chosen the notion of "retelling" because he refuses to construe a new system. In his view any system is alien to the nature of the OT. In this we might easily agree with him. Von Rad is also unable to find a "center [*Mitte*]"[203] in the OT. For these reasons he limits himself to narrating what the OT says about its own contents. He emphasizes that since Israel stated her kerygmatic-confessional testimonies in historical statements, we cannot state it in any other way except in "retelling," in a rehearsal of the narrative. The problem that this method produces for applied theology is immense.

With regard to this problem F. Baumgärtel asks how one can speak, e.g., in a theologically legitimate way about Hos. 1–3 when one merely retells what is stated there? How does this retelling proceed? In what way is it, whenever it takes place, the legitimate theological discourse on the OT?[204] One may surmise that the criticism concerning the ambiguous notion of "re-telling" caused von Rad to place less emphasis on it in more recent years.[205]

---

202. *TAT,* I, 135; *OTT,* I, 121. "Re-telling" as the most appropriate form of presenting the OT has been supported by Ch. Barth, *EvT,* 23 (1963), 346; H.-J. Stoebe, "Überlegungen zu Theologie des AT," in *Gottes Wort und Gottes Land. H.-W. Hertzberg zum 70. Geburtstag,* ed. H. Graf Reventlow (Göttingen, 1965), p. 206; F. Mildenberger *Die halbe Wahrheit oder die ganze Schrift* (Munich, 1967), pp. 79ff.

203. *TAT,* II, 376; *OTT,* II, 362; cf. Hasel, *AUSS,* 8 (1970), 25-29.

204. Baumgärtel, *TLZ,* 86 (1961), 903f.

205. In von Rad's important article "Offene Fragen im Umkreis einer Theologie des AT," *TLZ,* 88 (1963), 401-416, the notion of *Nacherzählen* recedes completely.

Despite the various criticisms that have been leveled against it in the early period, the whole issue pertaining to the matter of "re-telling" reveals nonetheless von Rad's interest to actualize the OT for modern man. In other words, the gap that the so-called scientific or historical-critical method of research has created between the past and the present remains the most intense issue for the Biblical scholar of today. How are Biblical texts to be applied today?[206] There are various uses of Scripture today, most of which are "functional" in approach, and it hardly matters whether the names are associated with liberalism in its more classical form or neo-orthodoxy in some shape or another.[207] Furthermore, the picture in modern Catholicism is not much different from that in Protestantism.[208]

It was the contribution of Gerhard von Rad to attempt the "actualization" *(Vergegenwärtigung)* in his OT theology. This term is chosen by Joseph W. Groves for the rubric of the methodological proposal "by which the Biblical text is contemporized."[209] "Actualization" is the most widely used hermeneutical method, which was developed and pioneered by von Rad and adopted and adapted by such OT theologians as C. Westermann (discussed later in this chapter), Norman Por-

206. One of the most penetrating analyses of the question of the religious application of Biblical texts for communities of faith today is the investigation of Hans W. Frei, *The Eclipse of Biblical Narrative: A Study in Eighteenth and Nineteenth Century Hermeneutics* (New Haven/London, 1974). Similar perspectives from a more recent vantage point are provided by Langdon Gilkey, *Naming the Whirlwind* (Indianapolis, 1969), pp. 91-106; and from a strictly evangelical point of view, Carl F. H. Henry, *God, Revelation, and Authority,* IV (Waco, 1979), 454-457.

207. See David H. Kelsey, *The Uses of Scripture in Recent Theology* (Philadelphia, 1975).

208. See Avery Dulles, "Scripture: Recent Protestant and Catholic Views," *TToday,* 37 (1980), 7-26; Joseph Cardinal Ratzinger, "Biblical Interpretation in Crisis: On the Question of the Foundations and Approaches of Exegesis Today," in *Biblical Interpretation in Crisis: The Ratzinger Conference on Bible and Church,* ed. Richard J. Neuhaus (Encounter Series, 9; Grand Rapids, 1989), pp. 1-23.

209. Joseph W. Groves, *Actualization and Interpretation in the OT* (SBLDS, 86; Atlanta, 1987), p. 5.

teous,[210] Peter Ackroyd,[211] Bernhard W. Anderson,[212] Walter
Brueggemann,[213] James A. Sanders,[214] and more, as mentioned by Groves.[215] Groves attains a careful analysis of
von Rad's thought, which he summarizes as regards "actualization" as follows: "Von Rad has presented the most complete
description of its [actualization] application to Old Testament
theology, but no one else has used the term in exactly the
same manner as he."[216] He explains, "While von Rad developed the concept of chronological actualization specifically
to describe the Old Testament's method of contemporizing old
traditions, neither he nor other scholars utilizing the concept
operate in a vacuum."[217] Groves goes on to show that as
regards the concepts of cult, history, and time the actualiza-
tions of von Rad, i.e., "the uniqueness of [von Rad's] chronological actualization remains an unproven assumption."[218]
Von Rad has built his case of the connection of the OT with
the NT on the foundation of the traditio-historical unity of
the Bible. Von Rad and the other proponents of actualization
attempt to bridge the gap between the past and the present
that the historical-critical method created[219] by appeal to "a

210. N. Porteous, "Actualization and the Prophetic Criticism of the Cult,"
in *Living the Mystery: Collected Essays* (Oxford, 1967), pp. 127-142.

211. Peter Ackroyd, *Studies in the Religious Tradition of the OT* (London,
1987).

212. Bernhard W. Anderson, "Mythopoeic and Theological Dimensions
of Biblical Creation Faith," in *Creation in the OT*, ed. B. W. Anderson (IRT, 6;
London/Philadelphia, 1984), pp. 1-24.

213. Walter Brueggemann, "Futures in OT Theology," *HBT*, 6 (1984), 1-11;
idem, "A Shape for OT Theology, I: Structure Legitimation," *CBQ*, 47 (1985),
28-46; idem, "A Shape for OT Theology, II: Embrace of Pain," *CBQ*, 47 (1985),
395-415.

214. James A. Sanders, *From Sacred Story to Sacred Text* (Philadelphia,
1987); idem, *Torah and Canon* (Philadelphia, 1972); idem, *Canon and Community: A Guide to Canonical Criticism* (Philadelphia, 1984).

215. Groves, *Actualization*, p. 5.

216. Ibid., pp. 104-105.

217. Ibid., p. 116.

218. Ibid., p. 129.

219. Wolfhart Pannenberg, *Basic Questions in Theology*, I (Philadelphia,
1970), p. 6, may serve as a reference point in his insightful analysis: "The
development of historical[-critical] research led to the dissolution of the

continuing series of witnesses, beginning with the earliest traditions of Israel, extending through God's revelation of Jesus Christ, and reaching to our present day."[220] Groves reveals with keen sensitivity the breaks in that continuous chain of chronological actualization in the OT and beyond.[221] In addition, the history of Christian exegesis flaws the overall design of the chronological actualization that is to link up with contemporary theology.[222] Groves's conclusions are revealing: "The traditio-historical method too often results in circular arguments, tenuous reconstructions, and fragmentation of the text, which make the critical method the master of the text and determinative for its interpretation. . . . In the final analysis the method is too weak to carry the weight of the tensions, omissions, and distortions of the modern methodologies which it uses to operate on the Old Testament. The goal of an inner-Biblical base for a theological-historical interpretation of the Old Testament is yet to be achieved."[223]

Thus the search for another basis for the theological meaning of the OT for Christian faith continues. What is said here for the "diachronic approach" has equal application for the "formation-of-tradition approach," which will be considered in the next section,[224] because it is built on the same methodology.

There are rumblings of readjustments in the reconstructed strata of the Pentateuch or Hexateuch (J, E, D, P).[225] Questions

---

Scripture principle in the form Protestant scholasticism had given it, and thereby brought on the crisis in the foundations of evangelical theology which has become more and more acute during the past century or so. . . . This distance [between the biblical texts and the present] has become the source of our most vexing theological problems."

220. Groves, *Actualization*, p. 129.
221. Ibid., pp. 129-141.
222. Ibid., p. 141.
223. Ibid., pp. 162-163.
224. Groves ended his penetrating study with his own beginnings of a "Redefinition of Actualization," ibid., pp. 165-210, which concludes that actualization is not the grand design for a theological and historical linkage (p. 210).
225. See R. E. Clements, "Pentateuchal Problems," in *Tradition and Interp. Essays by the Members of the Society for OT Study*, ed. G. W. Anderson (Oxford, 1979), pp. 96-124.

about the existence of the historical stratum E have been raised at various times by prominent scholars in the field (P. Volz, W. Rudolph, S. Mowinckel).[226] In the 1970s questions of a most serious nature were raised about the so-called strata of both J (Yahwist)[227] and P (Priestly Writers).[228] Various problems in the supposed P stratum[229] and in the so-called Deuteronomist (D stratum)[230] have been studied. New publications deal with various aspects of adaptations of source strata[231] or traditions[232] and assess the theological consequence of traditio-historical research.[233]

It is evident that current interest in traditio-historical research is focused largely on the theological formation of the material. A very recent trend in this area of research is a radical questioning regarding the early date of the so-called Yahwist in the tenth century and the unity of the "Yahwist"

226. See T. E. Fretheim, "Elohist," *IDB Supplement* (1976), pp. 259-263.
227. See below, n. 229.
228. B. A. Levine, "Priestly Writers," *IDB Supplement* (1976), pp. 683-687.
229. P. F. Ellis, *The Yahwist: The Bible's First Theologian* (Notre Dame, 1968); W. Brueggemann, "David and His Theologian," *CBQ*, 30 (1968), 156-181; idem, "Yahwist," *IDB Supplement* (1976), pp. 971-975, with literature; O. H. Steck, "Genesis 12, 1-3 und die Urgeschichte des Jahwisten," in *Probleme biblischer Theologie*, pp. 525-554; R. N. Whybray, *The Intellectual Tradition in the OT* (BZAW, 135; Berlin, 1974); C. Westermann, *Genesis* (Biblischer Kommentar: AT, I/10; Neukirchen-Vluyn, 1974), pp. 782-789, trans. *Genesis 1–11: A Commentary* (Minneapolis, 1984), pp. 594-599.
230. S. Loersch, *Das Deuteronomium und seine Deutungen* (Stuttgarter Bibelstudien, 22; Stuttgart, 1967); E. W. Nicholson, *Deuteronomy and Tradition* (Philadelphia, 1967); G. Seitz, *Redaktionsgeschichtliche Studien zum Deuteronomium* (Beiträge zur Wissenschaft vom Alten und Neuen Testament, 93; Stuttgart, 1971); R. P. Merendino, *Das deuteronomische Gesetz* (Bonner biblische Beiträge, 69; Bonn, 1969); M. Weinfeld, *Deuteronomy and the Deuteronomic School* (Oxford, 1972); N. Lohfink, "Deuteronomy," *IDB Supplement* (1976), pp. 229-232 with literature; D. N. Freedman, "Deuteronomic History," *IDB Supplement* (1976), pp. 226-228 with literature.
231. S. E. McEvenue, *The Narrative Style of the Priestly Writer* (AnBib, 50; Rome, 1971).
232. G. W. Coats and B. O. Long, eds., *Canon and Authority: Essays in OT Religion and Theology* (Philadelphia, 1977).
233. D. A. Knight, ed., *Tradition and Theology in the OT* (Philadelphia, 1977), with thirteen contributors of international standing.

with evidence for the proximity of the "Yahwist" with the Deuteronomic-Deuteronomistic formation of tradition, as emphasized by H. H. Schmid.[234] Already in 1974 some basic questions were raised by R. Rendtorff about the "Yahwist" as theologian, and he followed up those questions in a monograph on the traditio-historical problem of the Pentateuch.[235] Rendtorff's penetrating studies dismiss the idea of a Yahwist theology and give only restrained support to the notion of a "Priestly" theological stratum. He argues for the existence of "theologies" in the Pentateuch associated with Pentateuchal "themes" along the lines of M. Noth's studies. All of this has brought about a lively debate in which scholars such as R. N. Whybray, John van Seters, N. E. Wagner, G. W. Coats, and R. E. Clements are active participants[236] and in which even the whole traditio-historical method is under attack.[237] Whatever the final outcome of these movements may be, it is clear already that the essential consequences of these stirrings are ultimately immense for a diachronic traditio-historical theology of the OT.[238]

F. *The "Formation-of-Tradition" Method.* The continuous

234. H. H. Schmid, *Der sogenannte Jahwist. Beobachtungen und Fragen zur Pentateuchforschung* (Zurich, 1976).

235. R. Rendtorff, "Der 'Jahwist' als Theologe? Zum Dilemma der Pentateuchkritik," *VT Supplement*, 28 (1975), 158-166, trans. "The 'Yahwist' as Theologian? The Dilemma of Pentateuchal Criticism," *JSOT*, 3 (1977), 2-10; idem, *Das überlieferungsgeschichtliche Problem des Pentateuch* (BZAW, 147; Berlin, 1977).

236. R. N. Whybray, "Response to Professor Rendtorff," *JSOT*, 3 (1977), 11-14; J. van Seters, "The Yahwist as Theologian? A Response," *JSOT*, 3 (1977), 15-19; N. E. Wagner, "A Response to Professor Rolf Rendtorff," *JSOT*, 3 (1977), 20-27; G. W Coats, "The Yahwist as Theologian? A Critical Reflection," *JSOT*, 3 (1977), 28-32; R. E. Clements, "Review of R. Rendtorff, *Das überlieferungsgeschichtliche Problem des Pentateuch*," *JSOT*, 3 (1977), 46-56.

237. J. van Seters, *Abraham in History and Tradition* (New Haven, 1975), pp. 139-148; idem, "Form-Criticism in the Pentateuch: A Crisis in Methodology." Paper presented on Nov. 21, 1978, Annual Meeting of the Society of Biblical Literature, New Orleans, USA.

238. Schmid, *Der sogenannte Jahwist*, p. 174; idem, "In Search of New Approaches in Pentateuchal Research," *JSOT*, 3 (1977), 33-42; R. Rendtorff, "Pentateuchal Studies on the Move," *JSOT*, 3 (1977), 43-45.

discussion and stimulus of von Rad's diachronic method has
had another result in the development or continuation of an
aspect of the diachronic traditio-historical method.

In the wake of G. von Rad's OT theology and dependent upon
the traditio-historical method is the "formation-of-tradition"
method of the OT scholar Hartmut Gese[239] and following him
of the NT scholar Peter Stuhlmacher.[240] Gese insists that OT
theology "must be understood essentially as an historical
process of development. Only in this way does such a theology
achieve unity, and only then can the question of its relationship
to the New Testament be raised."[241] He characterizes his program in terms of "theology as formation of tradition" and claims
that "there is neither a Christian nor a Jewish theology of the
OT, but *one* theology of the OT realized by means of the OT
formation of tradition."[242]

Gese's programmatic thesis is that the NT forms the conclusion of the formation of tradition begun in the OT, so that
"the NT brings about the OT . . . [and thus] brings the so-
called OT to an end."[243] This means basically that Biblical
theology is built upon the unity of the tradition-building
process, or, as Gese puts it, the unity of the Testaments "exists
already because of tradition history."[244] It is evident that continuity between the Testaments and the unity of the Testaments is to be found neither in a center of each Testament

---

239. H. Gese, "Erwägungen zur Einheit der biblischen Theologie," *ZTK*,
67 (1970), 417-436, repr. in *Vom Sinai zum Zion. Alttestamentliche Beiträge
zur biblischen Theologie* (Munich, 1974), pp. 11-30; idem, *Zur biblischen
Theologie. Alttestamentliche Vorträge* (Munich, 1977); idem, "Tradition and
Biblical Theology," in *Tradition and Theology in the OT,* ed. D. A. Knight
(Philadelphia, 1977), pp. 301-326.

240. P. Stuhlmacher, *Schriftauslegung auf dem Wege zur biblischen Theologie* (Göttingen, 1975); idem, *Historical Criticism and Theological Interpretation of Scripture* (Philadelphia, 1977); idem, "Zum Thema: Biblische Theologie des NT," in *Biblische Theologie Heute,* ed. K. Haacker (Neukirchen-Vluyn,
1977), pp. 25-60.

241. Gese, "Tradition and Biblical Theology," p. 303.

242. Gese, *Vom Sinai zum Zion*, pp. 17f.

243. Gese, *Zur biblischen Theologie*, p. 11.

244. Gese, "Tradition and Biblical Theology," p. 322.

nor in a center common to both Testaments, but rather in the tradition process common to both Testaments. The NT is but an extension of the tradition-building process out of which the OT emerges, so that "the New Testament represents the goal and end, the *telos* of the path of biblical tradition."[245] In short, for Gese "only tradition history . . . can describe biblical theology. . . . Tradition history can become the method of biblical theology because it goes beyond historical facts and religious phenomena and describes the living process forming tradition."[246]

While Gese argues strongly *against* an approach to Biblical theology that is oriented and organized by a "center" *(Mitte)*, thus following his mentor G. von Rad, Stuhlmacher argues for a "center" as a key in his "synthetic biblical theology of the New Testament." For Stuhlmacher the "center" *(Mitte)* is "the gospel of the justification in Christ."[247] This does not mean that the basic traditio-historical orientation is abandoned. Stuhlmacher maintains that the OT is the framework of the NT formation of tradition.[248] "Old Testament and New Testament provide a united connection of tradition."[249] He shares with Gese the opinion of a late development of the OT canon. He even suggests that the development of the Masoretic canon was concluded only after the Bar Kochba revolt of A.D. 135.[250] Thus while both scholars disagree on the matter of the "center," they share a largely common view about the tradition-building process and the late closing of the OT canon, both of which are foundational for a "formation-of-tradition" theology.

The Gese-Stuhlmacher model of theology "as formation of

245. Ibid.
246. Ibid., p. 317.
247. P. Stuhlmacher, "Nachkritische Schriftauslegung," in *Was ist los mit der deutschen Theologie? Antworten auf eine Anfrage*, ed. H. N. Janowski and E. Stammler (Tübingen, 1978), pp. 59-65; idem, *Vom Verstehen des NT: Eine Hermeneutik* (Göttingen, 1979), pp. 228, 243f.
248. Ibid., p. 228.
249. Ibid., p. 244.
250. Ibid., pp. 228f.

tradition" has provoked a number of reactions[251] that have led
to lively interchanges. Stuhlmacher[252] is charged with soften-
ing a rigorous use of the historical-critical method and its
implications by E. Grässer[253] and for not going far enough in
his revision of historical criticism by H. Lindner, R. Sturm,
and G. Maier.[254] It is to be noted, however, that Stuhlmacher
does not consider his "synthetic biblical theology of the New
Testament" as simply a descriptive historical enterprise. He
notes emphatically that "the theology of the New Testament
as also the theology of the Old Testament is not simply an
historical discipline."[255] The rejection of the basic premise
that either OT theology or NT theology is but a historical
enterprise is also maintained recently by various scholars who
have entered the debate on the nature of OT theology, NT
theology, and Biblical theology.[256] Today the foundational dis-

---

251. Particularly important are those by H.-J. Kraus, "Probleme und
Perspektiven Biblischer Theologie," in *Biblische Theologie heute*, pp. 97-124;
idem, "Theologie als Traditionsbildung? Zu Hartmut Gese, 'Vom Sinai zum
Zion'," *EvT*, 36 (1976), 498-507; H. H. Schmid, "Unterwegs zu einer neuen
Biblischen Theologie? Anfragen an die von H. Gese und P. Stuhlmacher vorgetragenen Entwürfe Biblischer Theologie," in *Biblische Theologie heute*, pp.
75-95; W. Schmithals, "Schriftauslegung auf dem Wege zur Biblischen Theologie. Kritische Anmerkungen zu einem Buch von Peter Stuhlmacher," *Reformierte Kirchenzeitung*, 117 (1976), 282-285.

252. Stuhlmacher, *Historical Criticism and Theological Interpretation of
Scripture*, pp. 66-71; idem, *Vom Verstehen des NT*, pp. 216-218; idem,
"Biblische Theologie und kritische Exegese," *Theologische Beiträge*, 8 (1977),
88-90; idem, "Hauptprobleme und Chancen kirchlicher Schriftauslegung,"
Theologische Beiträge, 9 (1978), 53-69.

253. E. Grässer, "Offene Fragen im Umkreis einer Biblischen Theologie,"
ZTK, 77 (1980), 200-221; P. Stuhlmacher, ". . . in verrosteten Angeln," *ZTK*,
77 (1980), 222-238. Another reaction comes from A. H. J. Gunneweg, "'Theologie' des AT oder 'Biblische Theologie'?" in *Textgemäss*, ed. A. H. J. Gunneweg and O. Kaiser, pp. 38-46. See also W. Schmithals (above, n. 251).

254. G. Maier, "Einer biblischen Hermeneutik entgegen? Zum Gespräch
mit P. Stuhlmacher und H. Lindner," *Theologische Beiträge*, 8 (1977), 148-160;
H. Lindner, "Widerspruch oder Vermittlung?" *Theologische Beiträge*, 7 (1976),
185-197; R. Sturm, "Akzente zum Gespräch," *Theologische Beiträge*, 8 (1977),
37f.

255. Stuhlmacher, ". . . in verrosteten Angeln," p. 234.

256. Gunneweg, "'Theologie' des AT oder 'Biblische Theologie'?" p. 45;
Wagner, "'Biblische Theologien' und 'Biblische Theologie'," pp. 794ff. G. Siegwalt, "Biblische Theologie als Begriff und Vollzug," *KuD*, 11 (1979), 254-272.

tinction of the Gabler-Wrede-Stendahl approach of "what it meant" and "what it means" has been seriously, if not irreparably, eroded, and may actually be rejected. R. E. Clements calls now from perspectives of his own that OT theology should not be "a subordinate branch of the historical criticism of the Old Testament, it should be regarded properly as a branch of theology."[257] If this be the case, then serious questions are raised about the whole Gese-Stuhlmacher model of Biblical theology "as formation of tradition" within and between the Testaments.[258]

The "formation-of-tradition" model of OT theology as conceived by Gese (not by Stuhlmacher) seeks to overcome the issue of the "center" of the Testaments through a process of tradition common to both Testaments. This model is countered by all those who use a "center" approach to Biblical theology. More specifically it has been objected that Gese transforms "theology into a phenomenology of tradition history" built upon an entirely new ontology.[259] S. Wagner notes that the process of the formation of tradition is not identical in both Testaments and that it is therefore not appropriate to consider the Testaments as belonging together on the basis of the assumption of a unified process of tradition-building.[260] Douglas A. Knight states categorically that the *tradition-historical method cannot be used to explain the essential relationship between the Old Testament and the New Testament.* The reason for this is that within the OT "this growth process

257. Clements, *OT Theology*, p. 191.
258. H. Graf Reventlow, "Der Konflikt zwischen Exegese und Dogmatik. Wilhelm Vischers Ringen um den 'Christus im AT'," in *Textgemäss*, p. 122, notes incisively that the central task of a future Biblical theology is to work out the tension between exegesis and dogmatics, a tension which is seen as a basic and unresolved problem.
259. Kraus, "Theologie als Traditionsbildung?" in *Biblische Theologie heute*, pp. 67-73; also Schmid, "Unterwegs zu einer neuen Biblischen Theologie," in *Biblische Theologie heute*, p. 77.
260. Wagner, "'Biblische Theologien' und 'Biblische Theologie'," p. 793. See the decisive questions about the continuity of the tradition-building process claimed by Gese in the analysis of W. Zimmerli, "Von der Gültigkeit der 'Schrift' AT in der christlichen Predigt," in *Textgemäss*, pp. 193f.

reached an end in the various tradition complexes, books, and larger works; and in virtually this form they were eventually canonized."[261]

The approach of Gese has found at least one supporter in Horst Seebass.[262] His attempt to reach from the OT into the NT has caused some significant reactions.[263] It remains to be seen what directions the discussion will take and whether this new approach will remain strong enough to attract other supporters.

Manfred Oeming's dissertation, "Total Biblical Theologies of Today: The Relationship of the OT and NT in the Hermeneutical Discussion since Gerhard von Rad," is of great weight.[264] He indicated that Gese has deep roots in the program of von Rad and shows beyond this that Gese is heavily indebted as well to such philosophers as Hegel, the later Heidegger, and particularly H.-G. Gadamer.[265] Oeming reaches a conclusion identical to that of Groves on von Rad and others whom we have just discussed in relation to the "diachronic" methodology of von Rad in the previous pages. Oeming's analysis of the Gese approach has led him to state bluntly in his summary that "the alleged unity of the Biblical tradition claimed by Gese is historically unsupportable."[266] This is a tough judgment and raises many issues. Can such a sup-

---

261. Knight, *Rediscovering the Traditions of Israel,* p. 139.

262. See Horst Seebass, "Biblische Theologie," *Verkündigung und Forschung,* 27 (1982), 28-45, esp. 34-35; idem, *Der Gott der ganzen Bibel. Biblische Theologie zur Orientierung im Glauben* (Freiburg/Basel/Vienna, 1982), pp. 15-33.

263. See, e.g., P. Stuhlmacher, "Biblische Theologie als Weg der Erkenntnis Gottes," in *Einheit und Vielfalt Biblischer Theologie,* ed. I. Baldermann et al. (Neukirchen-Vluyn, 1986), pp. 91-114. Seebass responded under the title "Gerechtigkeit Gottes. Zum Dialog mit Peter Stuhlmacher," in *Einheit und Vielfalt Biblischer Theologie,* pp. 115-134.

264. Manfred Oeming, *Gesamtbiblische Theologien der Gegenwart: Das Verhältnis vom AT und NT in der hermeneutischen Diskussion seit Gerhard von Rad* (Stuttgart, 1985). See the critical review by H. Graf Reventlow, "Biblische Theologie auf historisch-kritischer Grundlage. Zu einem neuen Buch von Manfred Oeming," in *Einheit und Vielfalt Biblischer Theologie,* ed. I. Baldermann et al. (Neukirchen-Vluyn, 1986), pp. 201-209.

265. Oeming, *Gesamtbiblische Theologien,* pp. 108-110.

266. Ibid., p. 115.

posedly unsupportable historical basis be enough for a theology of the OT? Or can such a theology reach beyond the OT even into the present? The debate over this issue will not easily be exhausted in the near future.

Inasmuch as the Gese-Stuhlmacher proposals are dependent on the theory of the late closing of the OT canon at Jamnia (or later for Stuhlmacher) and the supposition of an extensive reduction of material in the process of canonization,[267] a period for the closing of the OT canon by the time of Christ[268] or earlier, even much earlier as argued by D. N. Freedman,[269] S. Z. Leiman,[270] and B. S. Childs,[271] decisively undercuts the central thesis of the Gese-Stuhlmacher traditio-historical Biblical theology program. Furthermore, it may be asked whether this approach is actually Biblical theology or theology of tradition-building. Can the tradition-building process claim to have at its various reconstructed stages canonical or Scriptural-Biblical status?[272] The designation OT or Biblical theology may be a misnomer. A more appropriate designation for the so-called formation-of-tradition theology would be a "history of tradition-building and its theology." A Biblical or OT theology turned into a phenomenology of tradition-building processes[273] is said to find continuity and unity no longer in the same God[274] but in a certain ontology of continuing processes of life.

---

267. Gese, "Tradition and Biblical Theology," p. 323; idem, "Zur biblischen Theologie," pp. 11-13; idem, *Vom Sinai zum Zion*, pp. 16f.; Stuhlmacher, *Vom Verstehen des NT*, p. 228.

268. Knight, *Rediscovering the Traditions of Israel*, p. 140.

269. D. N. Freedman, "Canon of the OT," *IDB Supplement* (1976), pp. 130-136.

270. S. Z. Leiman, *The Canonization of Hebrew Scripture* (Hamden, CT, 1976).

271. B. S. Childs, *Introduction to the OT as Scripture* (Philadelphia, 1979), pp. 62-67, 667-669.

272. A. H. J. Gunneweg, *Vom Verstehen des AT: Eine Hermeneutik* (Göttingen, 1977), pp. 163f., notes that in Gese's rejection of the Masoretic canon as binding for the Christian (Gese, "Erwägungen zur Einheit der biblischen Theologie," p. 16), Gese becomes "more canonical than the canon."

273. Kraus, "Theologie als Traditionsbildung?" p. 66.

274. See W. Zimmerli, "Alttestamentliche Traditionsgeschichte und

G. *The Thematic-Dialectical Method.* We have seen that the diachronic method and the subsequent "formation-of-tradition" method are closely related to each other. Both are deeply dependent upon the traditio-historical method, although each develops its own approach. The method now under discussion is a post-Eichrodt and equally a post-von Rad method. It surfaced only in the latter part of the 1970s but has found already an ardent supporter. W. Brueggemann[275] has suggested that there is a new convergence in recent OT theology that in his view points to a resolution of the methodological stalemate. This convergence is evident in approaches to OT (and Biblical) theology that use a dialectical and thematic relationship. He cites particularly the work of three prominent scholars: S. Terrien,[276] C. Westermann,[277] and Paul Hanson.[278] These three scholars suggest a governing dialectic of "ethic/aesthetic" (Terrien), "deliverance/blessing" (Westermann), and "teleological/cosmic" (Hanson). The convergence is evident in that each scholar uses a dialectic; the divergence is equally evident in that each one employs a different dialectic. Let us consider first the approach of S. Terrien.

The *magnum opus* of a lifetime of study by Terrien is based on the programmatic thesis that "the reality of the presence of God stands at the center of biblical faith."[279] He argues that

Theologie," in *Probleme biblischer Theologie*, pp. 631-647; idem, *OT Theology in Outline* (Atlanta, 1978), pp. 13-15; and above, n. 260.

275. W. Brueggemann, "A Convergence in Recent OT Theology," *JSOT*, 18 (1980), 2-18. A very similar essay in content by Brueggemann appeared as "Canon and Dialectic," in *God and His Temple. Reflections on Professor Samuel Terrien's The Elusive Presence: Toward a New Biblical Theology*, ed. L. E. Frizzell (S. Orange, NJ, 1981), pp. 20-29.

276. S. Terrien, *The Elusive Presence: Toward a New Biblical Theology* (New York, 1978).

277. C. Westermann, *Theologie des AT in Grundzügen* (Göttingen, 1978), trans. *Elements of OT Theology* (Atlanta, 1982).

278. Paul Hanson, *Dynamic Transcendence* (Philadelphia, 1978). See also Hanson's essay "The Responsibility of Biblical Theology to Communities of Faith," *TToday*, 37 (1980), 39-50. His book *The Diversity of Scripture: A Theological Interpretation* (OBT, 11; Philadelphia, 1982) continues to develop the twin polarities he sees in Scripture.

279. Terrien, *Elusive Presence*, p. xxvii.

"the motif of [divine] presence is primary"[280] and challenges
not only the primacy of the covenant motif, but also that of
the communion concept.[281] For Terrien "the rite and ideology
of covenant are dependent upon the prior reality of presence."[282] He puts it succinctly as follows: "It is the Hebraic
theology of presence . . . that constitutes the field of forces
which links . . . the fathers of Israel, the reforming prophets,
the priests of Jerusalem, the psalmists of Zion, the Jobian poet,
and the bearers of the gospel."[283] This means that the "motif
of divine presence" is seen as a dynamic "principle of coherence"[284] or of continuity and unity within the OT and between
the Testaments. The presence of God is certainly not static
and fixed, but "elusive and unpredictable"[285] and manifests
"growth and transformation."[286] He also conceives his "new
biblical theology" as "a prolegomenon to an ecumenical theology of the Bible," because the unifying and yet dynamic
principle of the presence of God "unites Hebraism and large
aspects of Judaism with nascent Christianity."[287]

Terrien has provided the first one-volume Biblical theology
in the post-von Rad era that moves from the OT directly on
to the NT. He has achieved a dialectic cross-section through
the NT in but sixty pages[288] whereas the theology of the OT
devours six times as much space. The theology of the patriarchal traditions about Abraham and Jacob are followed by
the Sinai theophanies and the presence in the temple. Then
follow chapters on the prophetic vision, the psalmody of
presence, and wisdom theology. The final epiphany covers
the Sabbath, the Day of Atonement, and the day of Yahweh.
Two chapters are devoted to the NT, treating "Presence as the

280. Ibid., p. 3.
281. Cf. Th. C. Vriezen, *Outline of OT Theology,* p. 351.
282. Terrien, *Elusive Presence,* p. 26.
283. Ibid., p. 31.
284. Ibid., p. 5.
285. Ibid., p. 27.
286. Ibid., p. 31.
287. Ibid., pp. 475f.
288. Ibid., pp. 410-470.

Word" with emphasis on annunciation, transfiguration, resurrection, and "The Name and the Glory."

Terrien's argument is forceful and his achievement is significant. He argues that the pursuit of the presence theme "will occupy biblical theologians for the next decade," because it is a "shift of emphasis from covenant to presence."[289] If one grants that the presence theme is a major Biblical motif, and few would wish to doubt it, one would still have to ask whether it is broad enough to encompass the richness and variety of all the expressions of faith in the OT and beyond that in the NT. That this question has to be raised is inevitable in view of the dialectical argument presented in *The Elusive Presence*, i.e., a dialectical dynamic which has been described as the dialectic of "ethical/aesthetic."[290] The "ethical" aspect of the dialectic is presented in the historical-covenantal materials and the "aesthetic" in the wisdom and psalmic materials. The latter are not so much concerned with demands, duty, and responsibility as they are with the emotional, mystical, and spiritual,[291] or simply with beauty. This field of forces is held together by the dynamic and unifying principle of the elusive presence of God.

The proposals of Terrien have found a forceful supporter in Walter Brueggemann,[292] who proposes the dialectic "of 'providence/election' which itself bespeaks an important tension."[293] This larger category, which is said to encompass the three former dialectical categories of Westermann, Terrien, and Hanson, reveals first of all that Terrien's dialectic and the theme of the elusive presence are too narrow. Indeed, Terrien admits to selectivity and of not being bound to be exhaus-

---

289. S. Terrien, "The Pursuit of a Theme," in *God and His Temple*, p. 72.

290. Brueggemann, "Canon and Dialectic," pp. 20-22; idem, "A Convergence in Recent OT Theology," pp. 4-6.

291. Terrien, *Elusive Presence*, pp. 278, 422, 449.

292. In addition to his essays already mentioned (see above, n. 275), see "The Crisis and Promise of Presence in Israel," *HBT*, 1 (1979), 47-86, and his review of *The Elusive Presence* in *JBL*, 99 (1980), 296-300, repr. in *God and His Temple*, pp. 30-34.

293. Brueggemann, "Canon and Dialectic," p. 25.

tive.[294] Second, no single dialectic is able to encompass the totality of the content of the Biblical writings. Thus while single-centered approaches to Biblical theology are inadequate, dual-dialectical approaches are helpful but unable to overcome the problem of the richness of the Biblical materials.

More recently Brueggemann seems to have altered the bipolar dialectic of "providence/election" in favor of a more comprehensive bipolar dialectic. In two articles published in 1985 he advances his new proposals for OT theology.[295] He continues to maintain as he did previously that the purely descriptive approach of a "what it meant" program for OT theology is inadequate.[296] His concept of bipolarity is to "reflect the central tension of the literature." At one pole is the tension of "how we got the text," which is linked to and part of *the process and character of the text."*[297] The emphasis is "in the fray" in the sense of how the social processes shaped the text. He is heavily dependent in this understanding on Norman Gottwald's sociological-literary approach to the OT.[298] To everyone's surprise, on the other pole Brueggemann seeks to be "above the fray" by following Brevard S. Childs, for whom the "canonical approach" is all- important, because the text that matters for theology is the one that has received canonical status. Brueggemann summarizes: "The *bi-polar*

294. Terrien, "The Pursuit of a Theme," p. 73.

295. Walter Brueggemann, "A Shape for OT Theology, I: Structure Legitimation," *CBQ,* 47 (1985), 28-46; idem, "A Shape for OT Theology, II: Embrace of Pain," *CBQ,* 47 (1985), 395-415. See also his earlier article, "Futures in OT Theology," *HBT,* 6 (1984), 1-11.

296. Brueggemann states unabashedly that the "meant" approach of K. Stendahl in the sense of historical description means that "this objectivity of historical description is too often found to be a mirror of the observer's hidden preunderstanding, and the adequacy of historical description is contingent on one generation's discoveries and postulates" (p. x in the Series Foreword in Paul Hanson, *The Diversity of Scripture* [OBT, 11; Philadelphia, 1982]).

297. Brueggemann, "A Shape, I," p. 30.

298. See particularly Norman Gottwald, *The Tribes of Yahweh* (Maryknoll, 1979), to which Brueggemann makes explicit reference. Now we can also take under consideration the more advanced work by Gottwald, *The Hebrew Bible: A Socio-Literary Introduction* (Philadelphia, 1985).

construct I suggest is that OT faith serves both *to legitimate structure* and *to embrace pain.*" He states his thesis in the following words: "OT theology fully partakes in 'the common theology' of its world and yet struggles to be free of that same theology."[299] The notion of "common theology" needs to be understood in the special sense in which it is used. Morton Smith has used this expression for the common theology of the entire ancient Near East of which the theology of ancient Israel was a (not unique) part.[300] Brueggemann takes the expression to mean (in dependence on Smith) a "set of standard assumptions and claims of religion that are pervasive in the ancient Near East and are shared in the literature of ancient Israel."[301] The concept of "in the fray" reflects the pole of social forces that are said to shape the Biblical text in the same way as any other text from the ancient world was shaped, and "above the fray" is the pole of the canonical form of the text which has theological meaning or is given theological meaning for modern communities of faith. The dual polarity of "in the fray" and "above the fray" seems to be a recasting of the polarity of "what it meant" and "what it means." Brueggemann sees the pole of "structure legitimation" in tension with the counterpole of "pain embracing." This tension is "an ongoing tension, unresolved and unresolvable," and it "must be kept alive in all faithful biblical theology."[302]

Brueggemann made this proposal before Brevard S. Childs published his own OT theology.[303] In this book Childs stated clearly that he sees his work in contradistinction to various approaches, including the one of Gottwald. Gottwald's sociological approach receives a remark that is worth pondering: "Gottwald's attempt to replace biblical theology with biblical

---

299. Brueggemann, "A Shape, I," pp. 30-31.

300. Morton Smith, "The Common Theology of the Ancient Near East," *JBL,* 71 (1952), 135-147.

301. Brueggemann, "A Shape, II," p. 395 n. 46.

302. Ibid., p. 414.

303. Brevard S. Childs, *OT Theology in a Canonical Context* (London, 1985; Philadelphia, 1986).

sociology by offering examples of his method of demythologizing the tradition only illustrates the high level of reductionism at work."[304] In Gottwald's approach, as Childs analyzes
it, there is no place for the traditional concept of revelation,
because Gottwald's hermeneutical stance "reads the biblical
text as a symbolic expression of certain underlying primary
social realities which he seeks to uncover by means of a
critical sociological analysis."[305] The Bible gives testimony to
the divine reality that breaks into human history in many and
varied ways, but a sociological reading of the texts "renders
the uniquely biblical witness mute," thus leading to a "massive theological reductionism."[306] The vertical dimension is
subsumed under the horizontal and thus "muted," but for
Childs "revelation is integral to the task of Old Testament
theology."[307] We will be able to investigate the "new Biblical
theology" method of Childs later in this chapter and need to
turn now to another giant of OT theology whose work employs
yet another bipolar dialectic.

The eminent University of Heidelberg professor C. Westermann published his long announced *Theologie des AT in
Grundzügen* in 1978 (translated as *Elements of OT Theology*
in 1982). Although it is not as extensive as the tomes of other
scholars such as W. Eichrodt, Th. C. Vriezen, G. von Rad, and
S. Terrien, it takes its place among these works.

Westermann's book is divided into six parts. The first one is
entitled "What Does the OT Say About God?" After a succinct
section on methodology, the topic is treated under the headings
of history *(Geschichte)*, word of God in the OT, the response of
man, and God's unity as possibility of interrelationship.

Westermann sees the task of OT theology as a summarizing
and a viewing together of what the whole OT has to say about
God. This means for him that it is illegitimate to elevate one

304. Ibid., p. 25.
305. Ibid., p. 24.
306. Ibid., p. 25.
307. Ibid.

part of the OT to a status of being most important or to interpret the whole on the basis of such concepts as covenant, election, or salvation. To raise the question of the center of the OT means also to go astray, because the OT does not manifest such a centering structure. In this respect it is different from the NT, which centers in the life, death, and resurrection of Christ.

It is argued that a presentation of what the OT has to say about God as a whole has to begin with the recognition that the OT narrates a history in the sense of happening *(Geschehen)*. Here Westermann follows explicitly G. von Rad and his traditio-historical approach,[308] but refuses to follow von Rad's principle of "re-telling" because the constant words of God that enter Israel's life bring about a human response or answer. Thus the OT functions in the dialectic of divine address manifested in manifold acts and words and man's response evidenced also in words and deeds. History *(Geschichte)* thus involves both God and man.

Westermann informs his readers that OT wisdom literature has no place in this basic structure of OT theology, "since it originally and in reality does not have as its object an occurrence between God and man."[309] The theological place of OT wisdom is to be seen in connection with the creation of man and his ability to understand and find his way in the world. Whereas von Rad viewed wisdom as part of Israel's answer to God, Westermann follows W. Zimmerli in arguing that the theological place of wisdom is within the framework of man's creation.[310] Thus Westermann shares with his German predecessors the problem of how to incorporate "wisdom" properly into an OT theology. As it stands Westermann has no real place for wisdom theology.

The second part discusses the God that saves and history,

---

308. Westermann, *Theologie des AT in Grundzügen* (Göttingen, 1978), p. 5; trans. *Elements of OT Theology* (Atlanta, 1982) and cited respectively as *TATG* and *EOTT.*

309. *TATG,* p. 7; *EOTT,* p. 11.

310. *TATG,* pp. 7, 85f.; *EOTT,* pp. 11f., 100-101.

which is presented under the rubrics of the meaning, process, and elements of God's saving activity. The third part deals with Creator and creation and also with blessing. This is followed by a fourth part in which the correlation of divine judgment and divine mercy, particularly in prophecy of both woe and weal, is expounded.

A brief section on apocalyptic deals with such texts as Isa. 24–27; Zech. 1–8; 12–14; Isa. 66; Joel 2–4; and the book of Daniel. Westermann states categorically, "The emergence of apocalyptic from wisdom is impossible."[311] He thus opposes outrightly the unilinear development of apocalyptic from wisdom for which G. von Rad had argued so forcefully. Apocalyptic receives "its theological aspect in its position within God's plan in which the history of humankind is predetermined."[312] In contrast to OT prophecy apocalyptic contains a conception of world history of cosmic dimensions which corresponds to primeval history.

The fifth part contains the human response side of the dialectic of divine address and human response. The response manifests itself in prayer, praise, and lamentation. Spoken response is followed by acted response in obedience to commandment and law, in worship and theological reflection, including the theological interpretation of history by the Yahwist, Deuteronomists, and the Priestly writing. Nothing is said about an Elohist or his theology.

The final part is entitled "The OT and Jesus Christ." This subject is divided into sections on historical books and Christ, prophetic proclamation and Christ, and Christ and the answer of God's people.

The concluding paragraphs raise the question of a Biblical theology. In contrast to earlier times of historical-critical research it is argued that "a biblical theology is a necessity for the incipient ecumenical era of the Christian churches."[313]

---

311. Ibid., p. 132.
312. Ibid., p. 133.
313. *TATG*, p. 205; *EOTT*, p. 232.

Westermann envisions such a Biblical theology as being presented along the lines of a historical structure correlated to the relationship between God and man. This means that the historical structure consists of testimonies about God in both the OT and NT. It is suggested that on this foundation a Biblical theology of both OT and NT can be produced.

It is evident that Westermann's approach is thoroughly form-critical and follows in one basic aspect the traditio-historical approach of G. von Rad. In the other basic aspect Westermann departs from von Rad's approach by emphasizing also a systematic aspect, which he recognizes in the OT's witness (speaking) about God. The latter is that which is constant in the OT, while the historical aspect provides variableness.

As we compare the works of Terrien and Westermann we note first of all that Terrien is the one who profoundly challenges the widespread and broadly supported theme of the covenant. It remains to be seen whether the presence theme will unseat the covenant theme as the dominant OT motif. Westermann, on the contrary, while following broadly the theme of blessing to which he had given attention in earlier studies[314] and seeing it in dialectic with deliverance, is "not singularly concerned with the development of the dialectic of blessing and deliverance."[315] Of the two books, one would be tempted to suggest that the one by Terrien is more successful.

H. *Recent "Critical" OT Theology Methods.* Some scholars have recently attempted not to write OT theologies but to reflect about the future of OT theology and argue for a renewal of "critical" approaches to OT theology. James Barr and John J. Collins, whose approaches will receive brief attention in what follows, share the perception that OT theology does not seem to have too bright a future.

James Barr is a major Biblical scholar with a keen and com-

314. See particularly C. Westermann, *Blessing in the Bible and the Life of the Church* (Philadelphia, 1978) and his English version of an aspect of his OT theology in somewhat different form under the title *What Does the OT Say About God?* (Atlanta, 1979).

315. Brueggemann, "Convergence in OT Theologies," p. 3.

prehensive perception of contemporary Biblical studies. Among his many writings about a dozen relate to various major issues of Biblical theology. His teaching career on two continents and his knowledge of major European languages has provided basic tools for his interest in interpretation, philology, semantics, canon, and biblical authority; he has even presented a biting attack on so-called fundamentalism.[316] Barr stands in the scholarly tradition of solid modern historical criticism, rejecting historical views of inspiration and biblical authority.

Barr has not provided as yet an all-inclusive presentation of his view of Biblical theology or OT theology and he is hardly expected to produce one. He is among those scholars who see a dim future for OT theology or Biblical theology. Barr recently stated that scholarship is moving away from OT theology, because the subject is too difficult to achieve and the new paradigms for the study of the OT or Bible, such as structuralism and literary approaches, are not "theological" in the expected sense. He is also concerned about the conception of a Jewish Biblical theology, the issue which we have discussed at the beginning of this chapter.

A number of previous essays and books describe various aspects of the modern Biblical theology and its advances over "the older biblical theology movement." Whereas Brevard Childs announced the latter's demise in 1970, Barr merely criticized the "older biblical theology" and spoke of "the healing of its wounds."[317] He argued for a "multiple approach,"[318]

---

316. James Barr, *Old and New in Interpretation: A Study of the Two Testaments* (London/New York, 1966); idem, *Comparative Philology and the Text of the OT* (London, 1968; rev. ed. 1987); idem, *The Semantics of Biblical Language* (London, 1961); idem, *Biblical Words for Time* (SBT, 1/33; London, 1962; rev. ed. 1969); idem, *The Scope and Authority of the Bible* (Philadelphia, 1983); idem, *Holy Scripture: Canon, Authority, Criticism* (Philadelphia, 1983); idem, *Fundamentalism* (London, 1977; 2nd ed. 1981); idem, *Beyond Fundamentalism* (Philadelphia, 1984). Note the incisive reaction of Donald Guthrie, "Biblical Authority and NT Scholarship," *Vox Evangelica*, 16 (1986), 7-23, esp. 12-18.

317. James Barr, *JR*, 56 (1976), 17.

318. James Barr, *Theology Digest*, 24 (1976), 271.

and insisted recently that "theology cannot simply be read off
from the [biblical] text as it stands: . . . theology *does* stand
'behind' the text."[319] He has engaged in an extensive attack[320]
against the "canonical approach" of Childs and in favor of the
traditio-historical approach (cf. G. von Rad, H. Gese) and a
literary understanding of the Bible as "story."

At the risk of oversimplification and in view of Barr's recent
doubts regarding the direction of OT theology, we may bring
together several points from his various writings in what we
may call his "synthetic modern biblical theology" (his designation). (1) It is to be descriptive and also theological without
being prescriptive or normative. (2) It is to be based on the
process of historical-critical exegesis, standing between exegesis and systematic theology. (3) It is to be done in solidarity
with the whole range of modern historical-critical Biblical
scholarship. (4) It is to be undertaken with a historical and
literary reading of the Bible which contains such categories
as myth, legend, allegory, story, etc. (5) Its sources are the
canonical books of the Bible, the traditions that lie behind
them, and the documents of Near Eastern religions and cul-
tures. (6) It is to be an amalgamation of history-of-religions,
literary, and theological approaches. (7) It is to be grounded
in the traditio-historical approach, finding its right proportion
also in relation to other adjacent disciplines. (8) It is to be

319. James Barr, "The Literal, the Allegorical, and Modern Biblical
Scholarship," *JSOT,* 44 (1989), 14.
320. His book *Holy Scripture: Canon, Authority, Criticism,* particularly
pp. 75-104, 130-171, is intended to be seen in that way. While it is based on
the James Sprunt Lectures of 1982 and was published in 1983 and thus cannot
reflect on the mature work of Childs as expressed in his *OT Theology in a
Canonical Context* (London, 1985; Philadelphia, 1986), it nevertheless is an
all-out refutation of Childs's proposals. Unfortunately, while Barr is aware of
some distinctions between Childs and James A. Sanders' "canonical criticism," he ascribes to Childs "canonical criticism," a designation which Childs
rejects for what he himself designates to be his "canonical approach." See
F. A. Spina, "Canonical Criticism: Childs versus Sanders," in *Interpreting
God's Word for Today: An Inquiry into Hermeneutics from a Biblical Theology
Perspective,* ed. J. E. Hartley and R. Larry Shelton (Wesleyan Theological
Perspectives, 2; Anderson, IN, 1982), pp. 165-194.

built on the recognition that the OT is basically "story" which may contain some history without being necessarily historical in the sense of "factual." (9) The distinctiveness of the religion of Israel is not God's action in history, but the idea of one God against other gods. (10) Biblical theology calls for a "multiple approach" because of the variety of perspectives to be incorporated and the disparity of theologies present in the OT (and NT). (11) The OT does not manifest a single "center" (with von Rad), but contains various "centers." (12) If Biblical theology is to thrive there must be "some theological flexibility and the need for free scholarly exploration of the Bible."[321] (12) "Theology cannot simply be read off from the [Biblical] text as it stands: . . . theology *does* stand 'behind' the text."[322]

This conspectus of what seem to be several of Barr's major ideas on the future of an OT "synthetic modern biblical theology" does not provide every nuance of his extensive argumentations. Paul R. Wells has suggested in his dissertation that Barr is a representative of a well-defined neo-liberalism.[323] Another dissertation recently argued that Barr's own perspectives actually do not allow him to construct a Biblical theology, and that a theology that has a basis in the Bible will carry the imprint of various aspects of the use of the Bible within the communities of faith.[324] Up to the present it appears that Barr is vehemently opposed to the latter aspect as being part of Biblical theology.

Various methods, movements, and scholarly directions have had a profound influence upon him. At one point he was sympathetic to the directions outlined by Childs, but in

321. See James Barr, "The Theological Case against Biblical Theology," in *Canon, Theology, and OT Interpretation: Essays in Honor of Brevard S. Childs*, ed. Gene M. Tucker, David L. Petersen, and Robert R. Wilson (Philadelphia, 1988), p. 17.

322. Barr, "The Literal, the Allegorical, and Modern Biblical Scholarship," p. 14.

323. Paul Ronald Wells, *James Barr and the Bible: Critique of a New Liberalism* (Phillipsburg, NJ, 1980).

324. Nathaniel S. Murrell, "James Barr's Critique of Biblical Theology: A Critical Analysis," unpublished Ph.D. dissertation, Drew University, 1988.

recent years he has leveled severe criticisms at him.[325] Barr
is dependent on modern linguistics in the form of French
structuralism (particularly Noam Chomsky), the study of the
Bible as literature (cf. Dietrich Ritschl and others), Paul Ricoeur in hermeneutical issues, etc. In recent lectures and
articles Barr moves in the direction of "natural theology" as
part of the biblical witness.[326] It remains to be seen in which
direction Barr will develop his thinking and whether this will
mean that he continues as a protagonist for a further move
away from OT theology and Biblical theology. For Barr a
full-fledged commitment to historical criticism remains essential in any enterprise.

John J. Collins has argued in a paper that OT and NT
theology are to be a part of a "critical biblical theology."[327] He
comes back to a theme that had occupied him already a few
years before[328] but now with greater intensity and reflection.
The adjective "critical" is particularly significant in this proposal. For Collins not only the "canonical approach" of
Brevard Childs, which we will discuss in the next section, but
also the approaches of G. E. Wright and even that of Gerhard
von Rad are still not critical enough. Both Wright and
von Rad, each in his own way, allowed "dogmatic convictions
to undercut its avowedly historical method."[329] Collins wishes
to ground his "critical biblical theology" in a radical histori-

---

325. Barr, *Holy Scriptures*, pp. 130-171. Barr is seconded in his criticisms
of the approach of Childs by John Barton, *Reading the OT: Method in Biblical
Study* (Philadelphia, 1984), pp. 79-103.

326. James Barr, "Mowinckel, the OT and the Question of Natural Theology: The Second Mowinckel Lecture—Oslo, 27 November 1987," *Studia
Theologica*, 42 (1988), 21-38.

327. John J. Collins, "Is a Critical Biblical Theology Possible?," in *The
Hebrew Bible and Its Interpreters*, ed. William Henry Propp, Baruch Halpern,
and David Noel Freedman (Winona Lake, IN, 1990), pp. 1-17. See also his
less reflective essay, "OT Theology," in *The Biblical Heritage in Modern
Catholic Scholarship*, ed. John J. Collins and John Dominic Crossan (Wilmington, 1986), pp. 11-33.

328. John J. Collins, "The 'Historical' Character of the OT in Recent
Biblical Theology," *CBQ*, 41 (1979), 185-204.

329. Collins, "Is a Critical Biblical Theology Possible?" p. 4.

cal-critical approach which has no room for a fourth principle, such as the Peter Stuhlmacher's "principle of consent."[330] Collins does not wish to be open to the "language of transcendence" which would qualify or hold in check an unmitigated functioning of the "principle of criticism" which he strongly defends. He does not seem to be bothered by the fact that the "principle of criticism," in the words of Edgar Krentz, "produces only probabilities, a conclusion which raises questions about the certainty of faith and its object in theology."[331]

Collins attempts to solve the issue of "facticity" and historicity through a paradigm shift to the literary notion of "story" along the lines of such literary critics as Robert Alter and Meir Sternberg. For Alter the sacred history of the Bible should be read as "prose fiction,"[332] and Sternberg claims that the Bible contains fiction writing from a literary point of view.[333] The introduction of the category of "story" into Biblical theology suggests that we are no longer interested in historical accuracy. The category of significance in such an approach is poetic imagination.[334] The implication of this shift from history to "story" means that "assertions about God or the supernatural [in Scripture] are most easily explained as rhetorical devices to motivate behavior," but they have nothing to do with binding or normative truth or the like.[335]

Among the essential elements of Collins's model of a "critical biblical theology" are the following: (1) It is based upon the presuppositions of the principles of criticism, analogy, and correlation essential for the functioning of the historical-

---

330. P. Stuhlmacher, *Historical Criticism and Theological Interpretation of Scripture* (Philadelphia, 1977), pp. 88-89; idem, *Vom Verstehen des NT. Eine Hermeneutik* (Göttingen, 1979), pp. 206-208.

331. Edgar Krentz, *The Historical-Critical Method* (Philadelphia, 1975), p. 57.

332. Robert Alter, *The Art of Biblical Narrative* (Princeton, 1980), pp. 23-40, as referred to by Collins, p. 10.

333. Meir Sternberg, *The Poetics of Biblical Narrative* (Bloomington, IN, 1987), p. 25.

334. Collins, "Is a Critical Biblical Theology Possible?" pp. 10-12.

335. Ibid., p. 14.

critical method.[336] (2) Any confessional aspect is to be denied
to a "critical biblical theology." (3) It is to function as a sub-
discipline of "historical theology."[337] (4) In another sense it is
part of a "narrative theology" or a "symbolic theology."[338] (5) It
is a functional theology in that it is to clarify "what claims
are being made, the basis on which they are made, and the
various functions they serve."[339] (6) It is "based on some
canon of scripture" without any "qualitative difference over
against other ancient literature but only a recognition of the
historical importance of these texts within the tradition."[340]

This model raises many questions. Why should this enterprise still be called "biblical theology"? Why retain the term
"biblical" when there is only appeal to "some canon of scripture" without any qualitative difference to any ancient literature? What does the word "some" in "some canon of scripture"
mean? For a Catholic scholar, is the "canon" the Roman
Catholic canon of Scripture, and for Jews and Protestants the
Jewish canon of Scripture, and for some others another canon?
If different communities of faith use different canons of Scripture, would this not introduce a "confessional" aspect into a
"critical" Biblical theology and produce a dogmatic conception? And this is what Collins wishes to avoid!

Furthermore, why should there be an appeal to "the historical importance of these texts within the tradition"? If such
an appeal is granted, then a "confessional" or "dogmatic" aspect does seem to function in this enterprise too. And if this
is so, on what basis is this function of "tradition" different
from that of, say, the "canon"? This functional and critical
model will be expected to be assessed by students of Scripture
and OT theology in relationship to its methodological foundations, i.e., its linkage to both historical criticism in its radical form and to literary paradigms, its functional intentional-
ity, and its faithfulness to the nature and purpose of Scripture.

336. Ibid., pp. 2-3.
337. Ibid., p. 9.
338. Ibid., p. 12.
339. Ibid., p. 13.
340. Ibid., p. 8.

Another "critical" approach to OT theology comes from the pen of Jesper Høgenhaven, whose concise book surveys some trends in OT theology before it outlines his own approach.[341] He perceives the OT as "the national literature of an ancient Near Eastern people."[342] This means that "historically, the OT must be interpreted within the context of the ancient Near Eastern culture to which it belongs. The contrasts [to that culture], which are certainly not to be overlooked, can from a historical point of view only be of a relative nature."[343] It is to be expected on this basis that the author will argue against a centered approach for organizing his proposed OT theology. Nevertheless, he suggests a "theological centre" which "cannot be vindicated by exegetical analysis." This "'centre' is in a certain sense the Christian gospel. Speaking in traditional terms, we may say that Jesus Christ is the 'scope' of the entire Holy Scripture."[344] This too cannot be validated exegetically.[345]

Høgenhaven's proposals may be briefly summarized as follows. (1) "Biblical theology . . . is a historical and descriptive discipline rather than a normative and prescriptive one."[346] No consideration is provided for the theological appropriation of the OT by communities of faith, whether Jewish or Christian. (2) The discipline of Biblical theology "should be regarded as an adjunct to biblical exegesis rather than dogmatics; and in this respect we are in agreement with the theological tradition that has developed since the Enlightenment."[347] It is "the indispensable, concluding part of biblical exegesis."[348] (3) Biblical or OT theology "belongs to the realm of historical theology, not to systematic theology."[349] This point has an affinity to the suggestion of Collins which we

341. Jesper Høgenhaven, *Problems and Prospects of OT Theology* (The Biblical Seminar; Sheffield, 1988).
342. Ibid., p. 88.
343. Ibid., p. 89.
344. Ibid., p. 91.
345. Ibid.
346. Ibid., p. 93.
347. Ibid.
348. Ibid., p. 94.
349. Ibid., p. 93.

have just reviewed. (4) "The characteristic feature of biblical theology is its interest in major religious motifs and decisive lines of religious development in so far as they are suggested in the biblical texts."[350] (5) OT theology is a part of this kind of Biblical theology and the latter has no concern whatsoever with the unity of the OT and NT.[351] (6) "The purpose of an 'Old Testament theology' is to present a summarizing description of the most important motifs, themes, and problems within the literature of the OT. . . . [As such it] is a historical undertaking, which presupposes . . . detailed exegesis . . . [and follows] a 'historical', diachronic, structure, rather than a 'systematic', or synchronic, cross-section."[352] (7) The literature of the OT is to be divided into its major categories (not according to a chronological order), such as wisdom, psalmic literature, narrative literature, law, and prophecy, and is to be treated according to form-critical and traditio-historical lines of research.[353] In general and in summary, Høgenhaven states that "as a historical discipline OT theology is dependent on the current state of historical and exegetical research."[354]

Høgenhaven's proposal evidently remains totally insensitive to the current interest in bridging the gap between the past and the present. It remains solidly indebted to the much-disputed "what it meant" (Biblical theology) and "what it means" (systematic theology) distinction advocated by the Gabler-Wrede-Stendahl model and actually revives it without any account of its current challenges, criticisms, and problems.[355] It is not a theological undertaking at all, because it

350. Ibid., p. 94.

351. Ibid., p. 95. Høgenhaven's suggestion that the unity issue is a matter for "systematic theology" is in sharpest contrast to the view of H. Graf Reventlow, *Problems of Biblical Theology in the Twentieth Century* (Philadelphia, 1986), pp. 10-144.

352. Ibid.

353. Ibid., pp. 96-98.

354. Ibid., p. 112.

355. See K. Stendahl, "Biblical Theology: A Program," in *IDB*, I (1962), pp. 418-432, repr. in K. Stendahl, *Meanings: The Bible as Document and as Guide* (Philadelphia, 1984), pp. 11-44. Among the reactions against the "what

remains historical and descriptive in its conception and design. Some may ask, Why is it called OT theology in the first place? Whatever one's response may be, and even if one were to think that hardly any new ground is broken here, this "critical" proposal reveals in its own way the divergence of current opinion on the nature, purpose, and function of OT theology.

I. *The "New Biblical Theology" Method.* We have noted time and again that scholars have attempted to reach beyond the OT to the NT. This is evidenced by Th. C. Vriezen, C. Lehman, R. E. Clements, S. Terrien, C. Westermann, H. Gese, and others. While none of these attempts is identical to another, there is nevertheless a strong trend, if not a slowly emerging consensus, that the question of the relationship of the OT to the NT is one of the most basic issues for Biblical scholarship and OT theology.[356]

Without doubt the one scholar who in our generation has pointed time and again to a "new Biblical theology" is Brevard Childs. He proposed a "new Biblical theology" that is to overcome the dichotomy of "what it meant" and "what it means"[357] so rigorously applied by modern criticism.[358] Childs' "new

---

it meant" and "what it means" distinction are those of W. Brueggemann, "Futures in OT Theology," *HBT,* 6 (1984), 1-2; David H. Kelsey, *The Uses of Scripture in Recent Theology* (Philadelphia, 1975), pp. 202 n. 8; Avery Dulles, "Response to Krister Stendahl's 'Method in the Study of Biblical Theology,'" in *The Bible in Modern Scholarship,* ed. J. P. Hyatt (Nashville, 1965), pp. 210-216; Ben C. Ollenburger, "What Krister Stendahl 'Meant'—A Normative Critique of 'Descriptive Biblical Theology,'" *HBT,* 8/1 (1986), 61-98.

356. See the valuable aspects pointed out by J. Goldingay, *Approaches to OT Interpretation* (Downers Grove, 1981), pp. 29-37. Goldingay affirms that "for a Christian everything of which the OT speaks has to be seen in the light of Christ. . . . But faith can only be Christian if it is built on the faith of the Hebrew scriptures" (p. 37). He further states that "for a Christian to interpret 'the OT' implies that he has a confessional stance in relation to it" (p. 33).

357. B. S. Childs, *Biblical Theology in Crisis* (Philadelphia, 1970), pp. 100, 141.

358. K. Stendahl, "Biblical Theology, Contemporary," *IDB,* I, 418-432; idem, "Method in the Study of Biblical Theology," in *The Bible in Modern Scholarship,* ed. J. P. Hyatt (Nashville, 1965), pp. 196-208. For an assessment, see Hasel, *NT Theology,* pp. 136-139.

Biblical theology" claims to take seriously the canon of Scripture as its context.[359] Precisely stated, it is Childs' "thesis that the canon of the Christian church is the most appropriate context from which to do Biblical Theology." A most significant corollary of this thesis is that inasmuch as the Biblical text in its canonical form is employed as the context for interpreting Scripture and doing Biblical theology, it amounts to "a rejection of the [historical-critical] method that would imprison the Bible within a context of the historical past."[360] This stricture is directed toward such methods as those of the history of religions and comparative religion as well as literary analysis,[361] by which is meant the whole enterprise of critical analysis leading up to and including the traditio-historical method.[362]

It is immediately evident that Childs' approach to Biblical theology and its definition is in strongest opposition to the diachronic method of G. von Rad and the "formation-of-tradition" method of H. Gese. The problem for Childs is that modern criticism "sets up an iron curtain between the past and the present, it is an inadequate method for studying the Bible as the church's Scripture."[363] "To do Biblical Theology within the context of the canon involves acknowledgement of the *normative* quality of the Biblical tradition."[364] Thus Childs provided a broad outline of his conception of a "new Biblical theology," pointing to a postcritical approach.

The idea of a Biblical Theology Movement as described by Childs and pronounced dead by the year 1963 has come under heavy attack, particularly by James D. Smart. Smart contests the existence of a cohesive Biblical theology movement in America and defines a "biblical theologian" broadly as "anyone who is seriously investigating the theological content of any part of

359. Childs, *Biblical Theology in Crisis*, pp. 99-106.
360. Ibid., pp. 99f.
361. Ibid., p. 98.
362. B. S. Childs, *Introduction to the OT as Scripture*, pp. 74f.
363. Childs, *Biblical Theology in Crisis*, pp. 141f.
364. Ibid., p. 100.

Scripture."[365] Thus "biblical theology" in the sense of concerning "itself with the theological contents of the Bible . . . must be
declared to be nonexistent in this century, and the complications
of scholarship having become so great in each of the Testaments,
[that] we are unlikely to find even on the horizon a scholar who
would dare to embark in one work the theological contents of
the whole of Scripture."[366] This statement was amazing even in
1979 when there were already a significant number of scholars,
from H. Gese and A. H. J. Gunneweg to B. S. Childs and S. Terrien, who called for, outlined, and attempted to present precisely
such a Biblical theology. Smart himself does indeed see a future
for Biblical theology, which remains a broad but ill-defined
concept, referring to anything that involves Biblical studies. He
thinks that this future is uncertain.[367]

Childs' breathtaking *Introduction to the OT as Scripture* has
been both highly praised and severely criticized.[368] Childs
informs us that after the publication of his earlier work in
1970 he came to realize "that the groundwork had not as yet
been carefully enough laid to support a [Biblical] theology of
both testaments." He remains convinced that a Biblical theology that covers both Testaments is virtually impossible as
long as the church's Scripture is separated into two airtight
compartments.[369]

Childs insists, against Gese[370] and others, that only the
canonical form of the Biblical text is normative for Biblical
theology.[371] Against those who hold that canonization is but

365. J. D. Smart, *The Past, Present, and Future of Biblical Theology*
(Philadelphia, 1979), p. 21.
366. Ibid., p. 20.
367. Ibid., pp. 145-157. See B. S. Childs' review of Smart's book in *JBL*,
100 (1981), 252f.
368. See, e.g., the extensive reviews and reactions of John F. Priest,
"Canon and Criticism: A Review Article," *JAAR*, 48 (1980), 259-271; W. Harrelson in *JBL*, 100 (1981), 99-103; and S. E. McEvenue, "The OT, Scripture
or Theology?" *Interp*, 35 (1981), 229-243.
369. B. S. Childs, "A Response," *HBT*, 2 (1980), 199f.
370. Gese, "Tradition and Biblical Theology," p. 317.
371. Childs, *Introduction*, pp. 76, 83.

a stage in the tradition-building process, as advocated in various ways by Robert Laurin,[372] James A. Sanders,[373] and S. E. McEvenue,[374] among others, Childs makes a sharp distinction "between a pre-history and a post-history of the [Biblical] literature,"[375] maintaining that the final form of the Biblical text is normative for Biblical theology.

The position which suggests that every stage in the tradition-building process has the same right to authority as does the canonical form because access to OT revelation is "through the tradition and the tradition process"[376] is countered by Childs. He writes, "This modern scholarly conviction was not shared by the editors of the biblical literature, nor by the subsequent Jewish and Christian communities of faith." Furthermore, "the whole intention in the formation of an authoritative canon was to pass theological judgments on the form and scope of the literature."[377] Childs also challenges forcefully the traditio-historical conceptions of revelation as the process of tradition-building.[378] He states, "It is only in the final form of the biblical text in which the normative history has reached an end that the full effect of this revelatory history can be perceived."[379] These claims reveal that we are in a battle arena of the nature of revelation and authority,[380] including the issue of

372. R. Laurin, "Tradition and Canon," in *Tradition and Theology in the OT,* ed. D. A. Knight (Philadelphia, 1977), p. 272.

373. J. A. Sanders, "Canonical Context and Canonical Criticism," *HBT,* 2 (1980), 193.

374. McEvenue, "The OT, Scripture or Theology?" *Interp,* 35 (1981), 236f., holds that "there is no single point of departure and no single final norm."

375. Childs, "A Response," p. 210.

376. D. A. Knight, "Revelation through Tradition," in *Tradition and Theology in the OT,* p. 162; idem, "Canon and the History of Tradition: A Critique of Brevard S. Childs' *Introduction to the OT as Scripture,*" *HBT,* 2 (1980), 127-149.

377. Childs, "A Response," p. 210.

378. Knight, "Revelation through Tradition," pp. 143-180.

379. Childs, *Introduction,* p. 76.

380. See R. Knierim, "Offenbarung im AT," in *Probleme biblischer Theologie,* pp. 206-235; Knight, "Revelation through Tradition," pp. 143-180; idem,

"levels of 'canonicity'."[381] For Childs, authority in the binding sense has its locus in the canonical form of Scripture.
The prehistory or posthistory of the text, the precanonical
or postcanonical developments, are not decisive as regards
the normative value of the Bible as Scripture, even though
they are not excluded from consideration. Thus for Childs
the canonical approach and accordingly his proposed "new
Biblical theology" assumes and is built upon "the normative
status of the final form of the text."[382] This means, of course,
that the historical context for interpreting the canonical
form of Scripture is replaced by the canonical context. This
is a most decisive shift. Since Childs holds that Biblical
theology is concerned with both Testaments,[383] it follows
that the whole Biblical canon of both Testaments is the
context for Biblical theology. This necessitates a rejection
of a "canon within the canon."[384] Does this mean too that
an approach to Biblical theology based upon a "center"
(Mitte) is out of the question? Is a cross-section approach
through the Testaments likewise ruled out? What about a
thematic-dialectical approach? Or, for that matter, what is
the proper approach and what organizational structure is to
be followed? It remains to be seen to what degree the proposals toward a Biblical theology made in his 1970 volume
remain valid for Childs.

It is within the purview of these questions that the relationship of OT theology and NT theology to Biblical theology
needs to be raised. Is OT theology a branch of Biblical theology? Is NT theology a branch of Biblical theology? If OT
theology and NT theology are historical and descriptive dis-

"Canon and the History of Tradition," pp. 144-146; G. W. Coats and B. O.
Long, eds., *Canon and Authority* (Philadelphia, 1977).

381. This expression is from Peter R. Ackroyd, "Original Text and
Canonical Text," *Union Seminary Quarterly Review*, 32 (1977), 166-173, esp.
171.

382. Childs, *Introduction*, p. 75.

383. Childs, "A Response," p. 199; idem, *Biblical Theology in Crisis*, pp.
101-103.

384. Childs, *Biblical Theology in Crisis*, p. 102.

ciplines where the historical and culturally conditioned context is determinative, as Childs seems to hold,[385] then he must deny them the status of Biblical theology. Childs appears to posit a radical hiatus between the disciplines of OT theology and NT theology and that of his "new Biblical theology." The former disciplines can function as theologies based on concerned non-Biblical, or better noncanonical, historical contexts and their respective methods which trace and describe the precanonical stages with their reconstructed processes of theological interpretation and historical forces. Contrary to this, the "new Biblical theology" method calls for a second stage which is confessional in the sense that it is canonical. The new context of the canon calls for a new method which overcomes the limitations, strictures, and inadequacies of historical criticism.

In our view the radical methodological wedge that Childs has driven between his "new Biblical theology" method, which is grounded in the context of the total Biblical canon, and the disciplines of OT and NT theology is artificial. Why should Biblical theology alone be normative and the theological enterprise and OT theology (and NT theology) be denied that status? If Eissfeldt put a wedge between OT theology, which is for him purely confessional, and the history of the religion of Israel, which is historical, descriptive, and objective, then Childs drives a wedge between Biblical theology, which is normative and theological, and OT theology (and NT theology), which is historical and nonnormative. Why should OT theology not become for Childs a history of the religion of Israel?

With the publication of Childs's own *OT Theology in a Canonical Context* in 1985/1986 additional matters were clarified for the first time. Now it is possible to see whether only Biblical theology was to be based on the "canonical approach" or whether OT theology was to be based on the same approach or on a purely descriptive historical method-

385. See Hasel, *NT Theology*, pp. 70f., where Childs' view is dealt with.

ology, as he had thought earlier. The "canonical approach" of Childs is not to be fused or confused with "canonical criticism" as advocated by James A. Sanders.[386] The "canonical approach" as a basis for OT theology means that "the object of theological reflection is the canonical writing of the Old Testament," which is consistent with "working within canonical categories."[387] The "canonical approach," in the words of Childs, "envisions the discipline of Old Testament theology as combining both descriptive and constructive features."[388] The "descriptive task" is one in which the OT text is correctly interpreted as "an ancient text which bears testimony to historic Israel's faith."[389] The "constructive task" envisions the discipline of OT theology to be "part of Christian theology, and . . . the Jewish scriptures as they have been appropriated by the Christian church within its own canon are the object of the discipline."[390] Childs puts himself here again into square opposition to the Gabler-Wrede-Stendahl dichotomy of "what it meant" and "what it means." Based on the combination of the "descriptive" and "constructive" tasks of OT theology, Childs maintains that "the heart of the canonical proposal is the conviction that the divine revelation of the Old Testament cannot be abstracted or removed from the form of the witness which the historical community of Israel gave it."[391] Here he is in full-fledged opposition to the approaches of von Rad and Gese, who engage in the diachronic tradition-historical or tradition-building approaches to OT theology which we have attempted to describe above.

386. See F. A. Spina, "Canonical Criticism: Childs versus Sanders," in *Interpreting God's Word for Today: An Inquiry into Hermeneutics from a Biblical Theological Perspective*, ed. J. E. Hartley and R. Larry Shelton (Anderson, IN, 1982), pp. 165-194. Note also the separation outlined by Sanders himself in his *From Sacred Story to Sacred Text* (Philadelphia, 1987), pp. 153-174.

387. B. S. Childs, *OT Theology in a Canonical Context* (London, 1985; Philadelphia, 1986), p. 6.

388. Ibid., p. 12.

389. Ibid.

390. Ibid., p. 7.

391. Ibid., pp. 11-12.

The "canonical approach" for OT theology as practiced by Childs refuses to employ a "center" as a structuring means for OT theology. He sides with von Rad on this issue. He also sides with von Rad on the matter of the polarity between "salvation history" *(Heilsgeschichte)* and scientific history *(Historie)*.[392] Thus it is not surprising that he disagrees with W. Pannenberg, who seeks to identify history with revelation.[393] The "issue of organizing" an OT theology cannot follow von Rad or Eichrodt, both of whom have attempted to organize their work from the point of view of a "closed body of material which is to be analysed descriptively."[394] For Childs there is no single answer to the structuring process for an OT theology.

Childs's *OT Theology in a Canonical Context* has 20 chapters. One can find some coherence in the presentation. After an introductory chapter, chapters 2-4 deal with the nature of revelation; chapters 5-8 have to do with the content of revelation in moral, ritual, and purity laws; chapter 9 handles the recipients of revelation both collective (Israel) and individual; chapters 10-13 treat community leaders such as Moses, judges, kings, prophets (true and false), and priests; chapters 14-15 deal with major cultic and secular institutions; chapters 16-17 treat the issues of anthropology; and chapters 18-20 turn to life in obedience and under threat and promise.

In summary, Childs has gone his own way. His presentation is innovative and challenging to others. It is methodologically at the end of a long pilgrimage that really began in 1964.[395] It is a mature statement of a scholar in full touch with the large range of historical-critical modern scholarship, which is challenged by various matters from within itself. Childs makes

392. Ibid., p. 16.
393. W. Pannenberg, *Revelation as History* (London, 1969); idem, *Basic Questions in Theology*, 2 vols. (Philadelphia, 1970, 1971). Cf. Childs, *OT Theology*, p. 16.
394. Childs, *OT Theology*, p. 15.
395. See B. S. Childs, "Interpretation in Faith: The Theological Responsibility of an OT Commentary," *Interp*, 18 (1964), 432-449.

a major effort to move beyond the impasse of scientific historical description and theological appropriation for the community of faith.[396] In distinction from other approaches that have the same interest in bridging the gap from the past to the present, which is the leading trend among both Jewish and Christian scholars, Childs refuses to use a philosophical system to "translate" the Biblical message to modern man. In this sense he refuses to engage in the task of systematic theology, which employs a philosophical system of one sort or another. He keeps the distinction between the Biblical theologian and systematic theologian in sharper focus than most other present proposals.

We shall not now engage in reflections of our own on Biblical theology,[397] but it is in order to summarize here our conception of OT theology that is outlined in greater detail in the last chapter of this book.

J. *Multiplex Canonical OT Theology.* In conclusion we list a number of essential proposals toward a canonical OT theology that follow a multiplex approach.

1. The content of OT theology is indicated beforehand inasmuch as this endeavor is a theology of the canonical OT. OT theology is not identical with the history of Israel. The fact that W. Eichrodt, Th. C. Vriezen, and G. Fohrer wrote separate volumes on the religion of Israel[398] is in itself an indication of distinction. The religion of Israel is seen as a part of or over

396. It is to be expected that particularly those who argue for a "critical" OT theology would be among the most ardent opponents of Childs. For example, James Barr, "Childs' *Introduction to the OT as Scripture,*" *JSOT,* 16 (1980), 13-23; idem, *Holy Scripture,* pp. 49-104; Collins, "Is a Critical Biblical Theology Possible?," pp. 5-7; John Barton, *Reading the OT* (Philadelphia, 1984), pp. 77-103.

397. See my essay "The Future of Biblical Theology," in *Perspectives on Evangelical Theology,* ed. K. S. Kantzer and S. N. Gundry (Grand Rapids, 1979), pp. 179-194; and "Biblical Theology: Then, Now, and Tomorrow," *HBT,* 4 (1982), 61-93.

398. W. Eichrodt, *Religionsgeschichte Israels* (Bern/Munich, 1969); Th. C. Vriezen, *The Religion of Ancient Israel* (London, 1967); G. Fohrer, *Geschichte der israelitischen Religion* (Berlin, 1969), trans. *History of Israelite Religion* (Nashville, 1972).

against the religions of the ancient Near East,[399] but OT theology as conceived here has a different content. OT theology is also a discipline separate from the history-of-religions approach, which emphasizes the relations of the Israelite religion with those of the surrounding world of religion.[400] Furthermore, OT theology is not a history of the transmission of tradition. We do not wish to argue the relative merits of all of these approaches to OT theology except to note that they are uninterested or unable to present the theology of the final form of the OT texts.

2. The task of OT theology consists of providing summary explanations and interpretations of the final form[401] of the individual OT writings or blocks of writings that let their various themes, motifs, and concepts emerge and reveal their relatedness to each other. It has been demonstrated that any attempt to elaborate on OT theology on the basis of a center, key concept, or focal point inevitably falls short of being a theology of the entire OT, because no such principle of unity has as yet emerged that gives full account of all the material in the Bible. The emphasis on the final or fixed form fits the emphasis of literary[402] and structuralist[403] approaches to the OT.

399. J. Barr ("Biblical Theology," *IDB Supplement* [1976], p. 110) would like to see a close relationship between the history of religion and OT theology.

400. An approach that conceives OT theology in terms of the history of religion should be called "history of Israelite religion." Zimmerli ("Erwägungen zur Gestalt einer alttestamentlichen Theologie," pp. 87-90) argues for a distinction of OT theology and a history of Israelite religion.

401. Kraus (*Biblische Theologie*, p. 365) insists that the "final form is in need of being presented by interpretation and summary" in fulfilling the actual task of Biblical theology. Blenkinsopp (*Prophecy and Canon*, p. 139) insists that "if biblical theology means a theology of the Bible it must take account of the Bible in its final form and what that form means for theology." From a different perspective Childs suggests that the final canonical form is the context for biblical theology (*Biblical Theology in Crisis*, pp. 99-122) and that "the significance of the final form of the biblical literature is that it alone bears witness to the full history of revelation" ("The Canonical Shape of the Prophetic Literature," p. 47).

402. In this case the emphasis on "close reading," namely, the meticulous, detailed anaysis of the verbal texture of the final text, is a part of the "new criticism" that a nonstructuralist literary approach requires. See also Hasel, *NT Theology*, pp. 214f. n. 41, for the insistence on the integrity of the finished piece of literature as a work of art.

403. Structuralism emphasizes also, at least at one pole, that it is the

3. The structure of OT theology follows the procedures of the multiplex approach. The multiplex approach refuses to follow the traditional "concepts-of-doctrine" *(Lehrbegriffe)* approach as well as the closely related dogmatic-didactic method with a Theology-Anthropology-Soteriology structure. These approaches succeed only by a *tour de force*, because the OT does not present its content in such systematized forms. The multiplex approach also avoids the pitfalls of the cross-section, genetic, and topical methods but accepts certain aspects of them. It avoids the pitfalls of structuring a theology of the OT by means of a center, theme, key concept, or focal point but allows the various motifs, themes, and concepts to emerge in all their variety and richness without elevating any of these longitudinal perspectives into a single structuring concept, whether it be communion, covenant, promise, kingdom of God, or something else. The multiplex approach allows aside from this and in the first instance that the theologies of the various OT books and blocks of writings emerge and stand next to each other in all their variety and richness. This procedure gives ample opportunity for the too often neglected theologies of certain OT writings to emerge in their own right and to stand side by side with other theologies. They make their own special contributions to OT theology on an equal basis with those more recognized ones.

4. The sequence of OT theology reflects the two-pronged emphasis of theologies of books-by-books, or blocks of writings, and the resulting themes, motifs, and concepts as they emerge. The presentation of the individual theologies of the OT books, or blocks of writings, will preferably not follow the sequence of the Hebrew canon or the Septuagint. The ordering of documents within them had apparently other than theological causes. It seems to be advisable to follow the historical sequence of the date of origin of the OT books, groups of

---

literary text as it meets the eye that must have attention. At the other pole is the "para-history" (Crossan's term) which allows the structuralist to move to the deep structures which have been coded in the text. Cf. D. Robertson, *Literary Criticism of the OT* (Philadelphia, 1977).

writings, or blocks of material, though admittedly a difficult task.

5. The presentation of the longitudinal themes of the OT as they emerged from the individual theologies of the books or blocks of writings follows next on the basis of a multitrack treatment. This procedure frees the theologian from the notion of the *tour de force* of a unilinear approach determined by a single structuring concept to which all OT testimonies are made to refer. The procedure here proposed seeks to avoid a superimposition of external points of view or presuppositions but urges that the OT themes, motifs, and concepts be formed by the Biblical materials themselves.

6. The final aim of the canonical approach to OT theology is to penetrate through the various theologies of the individual books and groups of writings and the various longitudinal themes to the dynamic unity that binds all theologies and themes together. A seemingly successful way to come to grips with the question of the unity is to take the various major longitudinal themes and explicate where and how the variegated theologies are intrinsically related to each other. In this way the underlying bond of the theology of the OT may be illuminated.

7. The Christian theologian understands OT theology as being part of a larger whole. The name "theology of the OT" distinguishes this discipline from a "theology of ancient Israel" and implies the larger whole of the entire Bible made up of both Testaments. An integral OT theology stands in a basic relationship to the NT. This relationship is polychromatic and can hardly be expected to be exhausted in a single pattern.

These proposals for a canonical OT theology seek to take seriously the rich theological variety of the OT texts in their final form without forcing the manifold witnesses into a single structure, unilinear point of view, or even a compound approach of a limited nature. It allows full sensitivity for both similarity and change as well as old and new, without in the least distorting the text.

III. The Question of History, History of Tradition, Salvation History, and Story

A cluster of questions connected with the proper understanding of history has come to the center of attention due especially to von Rad's theology.[1] He poses the problem in its acutest form through his sharp antithetical contrast of the two versions of Israel's history, namely that of "modern critical research and that which Israel's faith has built up."[2] We have already seen that the picture of Israel's history as reconstructed with the historical-critical method, in von Rad's terms, "searches for a critically assured minimum—the kerygmatic picture [of Israel's history as built up by its faith] tends toward a theological maximum."[3] Von Rad feels that the dichotomy of the two pictures of Israel's history is a "difficult historical problem."[4] But he emphatically asserts that the subject of a theology of the OT must deal with the "world made up of testimonies"[5] as built up by Israel's faith, i.e., with the kerygmatic picture of Israel's history, because in the OT "there are no *bruta facta* at all; we have history only in the form of interpretation, only in reflection."[6] It is crucial to von Rad's

1. See Hasel, *AUSS*, 8 (1970), 29-32, 36-46.
2. This phrase is found in the 1st ed. of *TAT*, I, 8, a section unfortunately not translated in *OTT*.
3. *TAT*, I, 120; *OTT*, I, 108.
4. *TAT*, I, 119; *OTT*, I, 106.
5. *TAT*, I, 124; *OTT*, I, 111.
6. This is the point made by von Rad, "Antwort auf Conzelmanns Fragen,"

argumentation that in the historical-critical picture of Israel's history no premises of faith or revelation are taken into account since the historical-critical method works without a God-hypothesis.[7] Israel, however, "could only understand her history as a road along which she travelled under Yahweh's guidance. For Israel, history existed only where Yahweh has revealed himself through acts and word."[8] Von Rad rejects the either-or choice of considering the kerygmatic picture as unhistorical and the historical-critical picture as historical. He contends that "the kerygmatic picture too . . . is founded in actual history and has not been invented." Nevertheless, he speaks of the "early historical experiences" of primeval history in terms of "historical poetry," "legend [Sage]," and "poetic stories"[9] containing "anachronisms."[10] The important thing for von Rad is not "that the historical kernel is overlaid with fiction" but that the experience of the horizon of the later narrator's own faith as read into the saga is "historical"[11] and results in a great enrichment of the saga's theological content. For von Rad the emphasis of the history of tradition method is again dominant.

Although the problem of the dichotomous pictures of Israel's history is not new,[12] von Rad's position has produced

---

EvT, 24 (1964), 393, in his dispute with the NT scholar Hans Conzelmann, "Fragen an Gerhard von Rad," EvT, 24 (1964), 113-125.

7. TLZ, 88 (1963), 408ff.; OTT, II, 417.

8. TLZ, 88 (1963), 409. The translation of these sentences in OTT, II, 418, does not reflect accurately the original emphasis. The problem of the relationship of word and event, word and acts, etc., is a subject of special discussion in Hasel, AUSS, 8 (1970), 32-36.

9. TAT, I, 120-122; OTT, I, 108f.

10. OTT, II, 421f.; TLZ, 88 (1963), 411f.

11. OTT, II, 421.

12. Toward the end of the 19th century, scholarship in general corrected the Biblical picture when it was felt that it was in conflict with historical knowledge without recognizing that it may contain a considerable theological problem. (Cf. C. Westermann, "Zur Auslegung des AT," in Vergegenwärtigung. Aufsätze zur Auslegung des AT [Berlin, 1955], p. 100.) Opponents to Wellhausenism recognized the deep rift. A. Köhler, Lehrbuch der Biblischen Geschichte AT (Erlangen, 1875), I, iv, distinguished between a secular and theological discipline of Biblical history, claiming that it is the theologian's

a lively and even spirited debate. Von Rad assumed that the two diverging pictures of Israel's history could "for the present"[13] simply stand next to each other with OT theology expounding the kerygmatic one and largely ignoring the historical-critical one. Franz Hesse, taking up von Rad's thesis that the OT "is a history book [*Geschichtsbuch*],"[14] promptly turns this thesis against him by arguing that unique theological relevance must be given to Israel's history as reconstructed by the historical-critical method.[15] This alone is theologically relevant.[16] Our faith needs to rest upon "that which has actually happened and not that which is confessed to have happened but about which we have to admit that it did not happen in that way."[17] Hesse turns against what he calls von Rad's "double tracking," namely, that the secular history is to deal with the history of Israel while the kerygmatic version is theologically meaningful.[18] He marks out the difference between the two pictures of Israel's history with designations such as "real" and "unreal" or "correct" and "incorrect." He maintains that the version of Israel's history as drawn up by historical-critical research is alone theologically relevant, because judged against the results of historical-critical research

---

task "to study and to retell the course of OT history as the authors of the OT understood it." Both pictures have to stand independently next to each other. J. Köberle, "Heilsgeschichtliche und religionsgeschichtliche Betrachtungsweise des AT," *Neue Kirchliche Zeitschrift*, 17 (1906), 200-222, to the contrary, wants to give theological validity only to the real history of Israel as reached by modern methodology. J. Hempel, "AT und Geschichte," in *Studien des apologetischen Seminars*, 27 (Gütersloh, 1930), pp. 80-83, believes that an objectively erroneous report about the past may not oppose the reality of divine revelation. It still remains that God has acted even if it is in question *how* he did it. G. E. Wright, *God Who Acts*, p. 115, makes the distinction between history and recital of history by faith where discrepancies, however, are only a "minor feature" (p. 126). Theology must deal with and communicate life, reason, and faith which are part of one whole.

13. *TAT*, I, 119; *OTT*, I, 107.
14. *TAT*, II, 370; *OTT*, II, 415.
15. *ZTK*, 57 (1960), 24f.; *ZAW*, 89 (1969), 3.
16. *ZAW*, 89 (1969), 6.
17. *ZTK*, 57 (1960), 26.
18. *KuD*, 4 (1958), 5-8.

the picture which Israel herself has drawn up is not only open to error but in very fact too often contains error. An OT theology must consist of "more than pure description of Old Testament tradition. . . . Our faith lives from that which happened in Old Testament times, not from that which is confessed as having happened. . . . Kerygma is not constitutive for our faith, but historical reality is."[19] Thus Hesse attempts to overcome the dichotomy of the two versions of Israel's history by closely identifying the historical-critical picture of Israel's history with salvation history.[20] He states: "In what the people of Israel in the centuries of its existence experienced, what it did and what it suffered, 'salvation history' is present. This [salvation history] does not run side by side with the history of Israel, it does not lie upon another 'higher' plane, but although it is not identical with the history of Israel it is nevertheless there; thus we can say that in, with, and beneath the history of Israel God leads his salvation history to the 'telos' Jesus Christ, that is to say, in, with, and beneath that which happens, which actually took place."[21] Hesse therefore contends that "a separation between the history of Israel and Old Testament salvation history is thus not possible," for "salvation history is present in hidden form in, with, and beneath the history of Israel."[22] From this it follows that the totality of "the history of the people of Israel with all its features is the subject of theological research. . . ."[23]

Hesse grounds saving history solely in the historical-critical version of Israel's history, insisting upon the "facticity of that which is reported," so that "the witness of Israel about its own history is not to concern us in as far as it wants to be witness of history, because it stands and falls with the historicity of that which is witnessed."[24] This seems to indicate that the

19. *ZTK*, 57 (1960), 24f.
20. See also Honecker, pp. 158f.
21. *KuD*, 4, 10.
22. P. 13.
23. P. 19.
24. *ZTK*, 57 (1960), 25f.

kerygma of the OT as well as the kerygmatic version of Israel's history is to be judged by the historicity of that which is witnessed by it.[25]

It is to be conceded that the historical-critical picture of Israel's history plays a historic role in modern times. But Hesse's one-sided emphasis is due to his unique confidence in modern historiography. He actually falls prey to historical positivism. He apparently does not recognize that the historical-critical version of Israel's history is also already interpreted history, namely, interpreted on the basis of historico-philosophical premises. Both von Rad[26] and F. Mildenberger[27] emphasize this point. Another serious stricture against Hesse's thesis concerns his seeking to attribute to the historical-critical picture of Israel's history a historic role in NT times. "God's history with Israel leading to the goal Jesus Christ is to be traced where history really happened. . . ."[28] But OT history as it is perceived today with the historical-critical method was unknown in NT times. On this point James M. Robinson adds that "to relate only this historical-critical history with the goal in Jesus Christ is to conceive of that history in an unhistoric way."[29] J. A. Soggin designates Hesse's attempt as an easy retreat behind modern historiography insofar as he seeks to get rid of the risk which the incarnate Word of God has taken upon itself.[30] Eva Osswald points out that Hesse seeks a purely historical solution to the problem and that therefore history as the scene of God's action

25. *KuD*, 4, 17-19.

26. Von Rad points out that the version of Israel's history given by modern historiography is already interpreted history; *TAT*, II, 9: "Auch das Bild der modernen Historie ist gedeutete Geschichte und zwar von geschichts-philosophischen Prämissen aus, die für das Handeln Gottes in der Geschichte keinerlei Wahrnehmungsmöglichkeiten ergeben, weil hier notorisch nur der Mensch als der Schöpfer seiner Geschichte verstanden wird."

27. *Gottes Tat im Wort* (Gütersloh, 1964), p. 31 n. 37.

28. *KuD*, 4, 11.

29. "The Historicality of Biblical Language," *OTCF*, p. 126.

30. "Alttestamentliche Glaubenszeugnisse und geschichtliche Wirklichkeit," *TZ*, 17 (1960), 388; idem, "Geschichte, Historie und Heilsgeschichte," *TLZ*, 89 (1964), 721ff.

recedes into the background.[31] In my opinion it is methodologically not possible to abstract an actual event or fact from
the confessional-kerygmatic tradition of Israel with the historical-critical method, and then to designate this "factual
happening" as the action of God, thereby making it theologically relevant.[32]

In connection with Hesse's approach it is significant that the
historical-critical picture of Israel's history is by no means a
unified picture. We should remind ourselves that the historical-
critical method has produced two versions of the proto-history,
namely the version of the school of Alt-Noth on the one hand
and that of the school of Albright-Wright-Bright[33] on the other,
not to speak of the views of Mendenhall.[34] In addition there are
a host of unsolved problems in the later period according to
these historical-critical pictures of Israel's history, so that it is
an illusion to speak of *a* or *the* scientific picture of Israel's
history, for such a picture is just not available.[35] Thus the
attempt to ground theology solely on the so-called historical-
critical picture of Israel's history falls short on account of
decisive and insurmountable shortcomings.

Walther Eichrodt also objects vehemently to von Rad's establishing such a dualism between the two pictures of Israel's
history. He feels that the rift between the two pictures of

31. "Geschehene und geglaubte Geschichte," *Wissenschaftliche Zeitschrift der Universität Jena,* 14 (1965), 707.

32. See here Mildenberger's incisive criticism of Hesse, in *Gottes Tat im
Wort,* p. 42 n. 67. In view of these observations it is difficult to conceive how
J. M. Robinson, "Heilsgeschichte und Lichtungsgeschichte," *EvT,* 22 (1962),
118, can speak of a "basic strength of Hesse's position" over against that of
von Rad.

33. See especially M. Weippert, *Die Landnahme der israelitischen
Stämme in der neueren wissenschaftlichen Diskussion* (FRLANT, 92; Göttingen, 1967), pp. 14-140; R. de Vaux, *Die Patriarchenerzählungen und ihre
Religion* (2nd ed.; Stuttgart, 1968), pp. 126-167; idem, "Method in the Study
of Early Hebrew History," in *The Bible in Modern Scholarship,* pp. 15-29; and
the response by G. E. Mendenhall, pp. 30-36.

34. "The Hebrew Conquest of Palestine," *Biblical Archaeologist,* 25
(1962), 66-87. Note the critical discussion by one belonging to the Alt-Noth
school, Weippert, *Die Landnahme,* pp. 66-69.

35. Soggin, *TZ,* 17 (1961), 385-387.

Israel's history "is wrenched apart with such violence . . . that it seems impossible henceforth to restore an inner coherence between the aspects of Israel's history." Von Rad dissolved the "true history of Israel" into "religious poetry"; even worse, it is drawn up by Israel "in flat contradiction of the facts."[36] It seems that Eichrodt's negative reaction is centered in his distinction of the "external facts" of saving history in the OT from the "decisive inward event," namely, "the interior over-mastering of the human spirit by God's personal invasion."[37] Here, in the creation and development of God's people, in the realization of the covenant relationship, the "decisive" event takes place "without which all external facts must become myth."[38] Here, then, is the "point of origin for all further relation in history, here is the possibility and norm for all statements about God's speech and deed."[39] In reality, however, the faith of Israel is "founded on facts of history" and only in this way can this faith have "any kind of binding authority."[40] Thus it appears that a reconciliation of both versions of Israel's history is in Eichrodt's thinking not only possible, but in the interest of the trustworthiness of the biblical witness absolutely necessary.[41]

Friedrich Baumgärtel sees the weakness of von Rad's starting-point not so much in the question concerning the meaning of Israel's confession for Christian faith. This question cannot be answered by historical research but must be an-

---

36. *TOT,* I, 512f.

37. *TOT,* I, 15.

38. *TOT,* I, 15f.; also Eichrodt, *Theologie des AT,* II/III (4th ed.; Göttingen, 1961), p. XII. It is to be regretted that much of the important discussion contained in the introductory section of the German edition is omitted in English.

39. *Theologie des AT,* II/III, p. VIII.

40. *TOT,* I, 517.

41. *TOT,* I, 516: ". . . It is realized that in the OT we are dealing not with an anti-historical transformation of the course of history into fairy tale or poem, but with an interpretation of real events. . . . Such interpretation is able, by means of a one-sided rendering, or one exaggerated in a particular direction, to grasp and represent the true meaning of the event more correctly than could an unobjectionable chronicle of the actual course of history."

swered theologically.[42] His criticism is directed against von Rad's attempt to solve the theological question concerning the meaning of the OT for Christian faith phenomenologically with the aid of traditio-historical interpretation. For Baumgärtel neither of the two versions of Israel's history possesses theological relevance for Christian faith. Why? Because the problem is that the whole OT is "witness out of a non-Christian religion."[43] "Viewed historically it has another place than the Christian religion."[44] Thus according to Baumgärtel, von Rad's error lies in assuming that Israel's witness to God's actions in history can be taken at face value and as relevant for the Christian church. The apt reply of another OT theologian, Claus Westermann, is hardly an overstatement: "Ultimately he [Baumgärtel] admits, then, that the church could also live without the Old Testament."[45] The essential weakness of Baumgärtel's criticism of von Rad at this point lies in his ultimate denial of the relevance of the OT for Christian faith.

Another solution to the problem is sought by Johannes Hempel and Eva Osswald. The former maintains that even an "objectively mistaken report about the past, which has part in the lack of trustworthiness of human tradition,"[46] can be a witness about the activity of God, even if it is only a broken witness. According to Hempel it remains established that God has acted in history even if it is an open question how he acted. The investigation of the "how" is according to Hempel also part of the historian's task.[47] Osswald is not able to follow Hempel.

42. "Gerhard von Rads 'Theologie des AT'," *TLZ*, 86 (1961), 805.

43. "Das hermeneutische Problem des AT," *TLZ*, 79 (1954), 200; "The Hermeneutical Problem of the OT," in *EOTH*, ed. C. Westermann (Richmond, VA, 1963), p. 135.

44. *EOTH*, p. 145.

45. "Remarks on the Theses of Bultmann and Baumgärtel," in *EOTH*, p. 133.

46. *Studien des apologetischen Seminars*, 27, pp. 80f.

47. *Geschichten und Geschichte im AT bis zur persischen Zeit* (Gütersloh, 1964), p. 38: "[The] historian [has] a twofold task in dealing with the historical material of the OT: He has to ask for the events which have given rise to Israel's faith in the historical activity of her God which shaped it, and have modified it during the course of centuries. This means that he has to inves-

She believes that "one cannot always in a clear manner answer
how Yahweh has acted with Israel. Thus the only witness that
remains is *that* Yahweh has acted with Israel."[48] The distinction
between the "thatness" and the "howness,"[49] not unfamiliar
from NT studies,[50] can hardly be considered to provide the
solution to the problem, because in the final analysis it finds its
absolute claim to truth solely in modern historiography. But
modern historiography is unable to speak about God's acts.[51]
This Osswald concedes. "With the aid of the critical science [of
historiography] one is certainly not able to make statements
about God, for there is no path that leads from the objectifying
science of historiography to a particular theological statement."[52] Thus one is forced to ask whether an event is not
grasped in a basically deeper dimension in the given Biblical
testimony which sees and presents reality in relationship to a
history in which God brings about the salvation of his people.[53]

---

tigate whether or not the distinct claim which is made for the facticity of
these expressions can be verified. He has to ask for Israel's thoughts of faith
which have been active in the formation of her historical tradition, but also
already in the perception of the particular events."

48. Osswald, p. 709.

49. M. Sekine, "Vom Verstehen der Heilsgeschichte. Das Grundproblem
der alttestamentlichen Theologie," *ZAW*, 75 (1963), 145-154, follows Hempel
in distinguishing *dicta*, i.e., Biblical statements, from *facta*, historical facts.
The former are always based upon the latter; both are inseparable in the
Bible. Therefore the object of a Biblical theology is *facta dicta*, declared facts
which make up salvation history. Up to the present some have placed either
a one-sided emphasis upon the *facta* (e.g., Hesse, Eichrodt) or upon the *dicta*
(von Rad, Rendtorff). Attempts to bridge the disparity between the two have
so far been unsuccessful. In the OT existential thought connects *facta* and
dicta with typology. Thus structural typology is a relevant method. One must
ask critically whether this constitutes a superimposing upon the material of
something that is alien to the material itself.

50. Typical of its dilemma is the debate about the "new quest" of the
historical Jesus.

51. A. Weiser, "Vom Verstehen des AT," *ZAW*, 61 (1945/48), 23f., explains
that the rational cognition of history is limited to the temporal-spatial dimension, and that the dimension of the knowledge of God can be gained only
through the cogntion of faith. Cf. Osswald, p. 711: "Faith is not directed upon
single historical events, but upon God as the Lord of history."

52. Osswald, p. 711.

53. This is the point made by W. Beyerlin, "Geschichte und 'heilsge-

Here the question has been raised whether or not it is materially pertinent to stress either the historical facts or the confessional kerygma, which is of course also based on facts. A. Weiser and Hempel[54] have recognized that historical reality and kerygmatic expression, i.e., fact and interpretation, form a unity in the OT.[55] Georg Fohrer holds that if there is an essential unity between fact and interpretation, event and word, then we should not pitch one against the other, because the OT authors used traditions that they considered "historical."[56] Hempel shows that the Biblical narrators do not know the tension between report and event which exists for modern man. This had no importance for them at all because they were convinced about the facticity of what had happened.[57] Osswald believes that the facticity of what had happened is binding only for the ancient author, however, and not for modern man, who has raised many doubts by means of modern historiogra-

---

schichtliche' Traditionsbildung im AT," VT, 13 (1963), 25, with regard to the Gideon tradition and its historical reality.

54. A. Weiser, Glaube und Geschichte im AT und andere ausgewählte Schriften (München, 1961), pp. 2, 22; J. Hempel, "Die Faktizität der Geschichte im biblischen Denken," in Biblical Studies in Memory of H. C. Alleman (Locus Valley, NY, 1960), pp. 67ff.; idem, Geschichten und Geschichte, p. 11ff. Note also R. H. Pfeiffer, "Facts and Faith in Biblical History," JBL, 70 (1951), 1-14; J. C. Rylaarsdam, "The Problem of Faith and History in Biblical Interpretation," JBL, 77 (1958), 26-32; C. Blackman, "Is History Irrelevant for the Christian Kerygma?" Interp, 21 (1967); 435-446; C. E. Braaten, History and Hermeneutics (Philadelphia, 1966); idem, "The Current Controversy on Revelation: Pannenberg and His Critics," JR, 45 (1965), 225-237; J. Barr, "Revelation Through History in the OT and in Modern Theology," Interp, 17 (1963), 193-205.

55. W. Pannenberg, "The Revelation of God in Jesus Christ," in Theology as History (New Frontiers in Theology, III; New York, 1967), p. 127, proposes also that "we must reinstate today the original unity of facts and their meaning." That is to say that "in principle, every event has its original meaning within the context of occurrence and tradition in which it took place. . . ." He says further, "the knowledge of history on which faith is grounded has to do with the truth and reliability of that on which faith depends. . . . Such knowledge . . . assures faith about its basis" (p. 269).

56. "Tradition und Interpretation im AT," ZAW, 73 (1961), 18.

57. Hempel, Biblical Studies, pp. 67ff.; idem, "Faktum und Gesetz im alttestamentlichen Geschichtsdenken," TLZ, 85 (1960), 823ff.; idem, Geschichten und Geschichte, pp. 11ff.

phy.[58] We are thrown back upon the question of what measuring rod is applied to establish "facticity." In view of the Biblical testimony the historical-critical method working without a God-hypothesis of which Scripture testifies brings with it a crisis of objectivity and facticity. The question arises whether we do not need to develop, in order to overcome the present dilemma, a new set of concepts[59] which is more appropriate to the dynamic nature and full reality of the texts that admittedly encompass the unity of *facta* and *dicta*, fact and interpretation, event and word, happening and meaning.

An attempt of major proportions to come to grips with the problem of the two pictures of Israel's history and salvation history *(Heilsgeschichte)* has been undertaken by Wolfhart Pannenberg, now professor of systematic theology at Munich, who has presented a forceful criticism of current theological positions from the viewpoint, derived from the OT, that "history is the most comprehensive horizon of Christian theology."[60] Pan-

58. Osswald, p. 710.

59. Von Rad, *TAT,* I, 120, focuses our attention on the observation "that Israel's expression derives from a layer of depth of historical experience which historical-critical investigation is unable to fathom."

60. This sentence opens the essay "Heilsgeschehen und Geschichte," *KuD,* 5 (1959), 218-237, 259-288, whose first part is translated as "Redemptive Event and History," in *EOTH,* 314-335. Significant for our discussion are the following contributions of Pannenberg: "Kerygma und Geschichte," in *Studien zur Theologie der alttestamentlichen Überlieferungen,* ed. R. Rendtorff und K. Koch (Neukirchen, 1961), pp. 129-140 (hereafter cited as *Studien*); Pannenberg, ed., *OaG* (2nd ed.; Göttingen, 1963), trans. *Revelation as History* (New York, 1968); Pannenberg, *Jesus—God and Man* (Philadelphia, 1968); idem, *Grundfragen systematischer Theologie* (Göttingen, 1968). Noteworthy critiques of Pannenberg and his group are by Hans-Georg Geyer, "Geschichte als theologisches Problem," *EvT,* 22 (1962), 92-104; Lothar Steiger, "Offenbarungsgeschichte und theologische Vernunft," *ZTK,* 59 (1962), 88-113; Günther Klein, "OaG?" *Monatsschrift für Pastoraltheologie,* 51 (1962), 65-88, to which Pannenberg replied in the "Postscript" of the 2nd ed. of *OaG,* pp. 132-148; Klein, *Theologie des Wortes Gottes und die Hypothese der Universalgeschichte. Zur Auseinandersetzung mit Wolfhart Pannenberg (Beiträge zur Evangelischen Theologie,* 37; Munich, 1964); Hesse, "Wolfhart Pannenberg und das AT," *Neue Zeitschrift für systematische Theologie und Religionswissenschaft,* 7 (1965), 174-199; Gerhard Sauter, *Zukunft und Verheissung, Das Problem der Zukunft in der gegenwärtigen theologischen und philosophischen*

nenberg's presupposition for his entire theological program
seems to lie in his understanding of history as "reality in its
totality."[61] History is encompassing man's past and present reality.[62] He traces the development of this concept of history as
"reality in its totality" from ancient Israel to the present. Pannenberg argues against the common distinction between historical facts and their meaning, evaluation, and interpretation
by man. He feels that this common procedure in modern historiography is a result of the influence of positivism and neo-
Kantianism. Pannenberg proposes that against such an artificial
distinction "we must reinstate today the original unity of facts
and their meaning."[63] That is to say that "in principle, every
event has its original meaning within the context of occurrence
and tradition in which it took place. . . ."[64] Pannenberg's objective, in light of this analysis, is to create a situation in which faith
can rest on historically proven fact in order to be saved from
subjectivity, self-redemption, and self-deception.[65]

Pannenberg emphasizes the thesis of "revelation as history."[66] The goal of "Yahweh's action in history is that he be
known—revelation. His action . . . aims at the goal that
Yahweh will be revealed in his action as he fulfills his vow."[67]

Diskussion (Zürich/Stuttgart, 1965), pp. 239-251; R. L. Wilken, "Who Is
Wolfhart Pannenberg?" *Dialogue*, 4 (1965), 140-142; D. P. Fuller, "A New German Theological Movement," *SJT*, 19 (1966), 160-175; G. G. O'Collins, "Revelation as History," *Heythrop Journal*, 7 (1966), 394-406; R. T. Osborn, "Pannenberg's Programme," *CJT*, 13 (1967), 109-122; H. Obayashi, "Pannenberg
and Troeltsch: History and Religion," *JAAR*, 38 (1970), 401-419.

61. *EOTH*, p. 319.

62. Pannenberg, *Grundfragen systematischer Theologie*, p. 391.

63. *Supra*, n. 55.

64. Pannenberg, *Theology as History*, p. 127.

65. P. 269: "The knowledge of history on which faith is grounded has
to do with the truth and reliability of that on which faith depends; these are
presupposed in the act of trusting, and thus logically precede the act of faith
in respect to its perceived content. But that does not mean that the subjective
accomplishment of such knowledge would be in any way a condition for
participating in salvation, but rather it assures faith about its basis."

66. This is the title of the collection of programmatic essays in *Revelation
as History* (New York, 1968).

67. *EOTH*, p. 317.

The connection between the Testaments is constituted by the one history, namely universal history, "which is itself grounded in the unity of the God who works here as well as there and remains true to his promises."[68] In universal history "the destiny of mankind, from creation onward, is seen to be unfolding according to a plan of God."[69] Thus he broadens salvation history *(Heilsgeschichte)* and makes it identical with universal history.[70] When "reality in its totality"[71] is conceived as universal history there would be nothing that can be excluded from this totality. Thus God's revelation is the inherent meaning of history, not something that is super-added to history.[72]

Whereas von Rad leaves open the relation of salvation history to history, Pannenberg, in his unified view of universal history, draws salvation history into his large category of universal history. Thus it seems impossible to maintain a radical disjunction between the two pictures of Israel's history, or between the past and the present or the present and the future. Thus Pannenberg enlarges the modern concept of history to incorporate the totality of reality into the historical-critical method, which by definition had limited itself. Pannenberg's whole theology seems to fly away from radical historicalness of the present to contemplation of the whole. H. Obayashi says that Pannenberg's understanding of history as the totality of reality, despite its allegedly historical character, takes "off from the classical ontological question and settles it in an ontological end of time."[73] "If *Heilsgeschichte* theology had fled from history to some safe harbor, Pannenberg departed from that harbor and re-entered history only to find in the nature of history, which is immense and inexhaustible, a

68. P. 329.
69. Pannenberg, *Revelation as History*, p. 132.
70. P. 133.
71. *EOTH*, p. 319.
72. *Revelation as History*, p. 136.
73. Obayashi, p. 405; cf. W. Hamilton, "Character of Pannenberg's Theology," in *Theology as History*, p. 178.

self-contained totality in which the end plays an overwhelming role that immunizes the significance of the present."[74]

On the positive side it must be emphasized that Pannenberg
seeks to take a firm stand on the transcendent reality which
E. Troeltsch held in abeyance and relegated to personal
choice.[75] For Pannenberg a transcendent reality is presupposed
in man's openness and structure of existence.[76] Pannenberg's
critique of Troeltsch's historical method, in which the principle
of analogy is based upon a one-sided anthropocentric presupposition, is to the point.[77] Pannenberg works with a synthetic
historical-critical method which emphasizes the original unity
of facts and their meaning and a methodological anthropocentrism which is said to be capable of including the realm
of the transcendent within its own presupposition.[78]

Rolf Rendtorff,[79] a member of Pannenberg's "working
circle" with Ulrich Wilckens[80] and Dietrich Rössler,[81] proposes to relate salvation history to the historical-critical picture of Israel's history. He would combine what is currently
separated into "history of Israel," "history of tradition," and
"OT theology" into one new genre of scholarly research. Since

74. P. 413.
75. E. Troeltsch, *Gesammelte Schriften* (Tübingen, 1922), III, 657ff.
76. *Grundfragen systematischer Theologie*, pp. 283f.
77. Pannenberg, "Heilsgeschehen und Geschichte," in *Grundfragen systematischer Theologie*, pp. 46-54; cf. Obayashi, pp. 407f.
78. *Grundfragen systematischer Theologie*, p. 54.
79. Rendtorff is the OT theologian of the group, of whose writings the
following are important for the issue at hand: "Hermeneutik des AT als Frage
nach der Geschichte," *ZTK*, 57 (1960), 27-40; idem, "Die Offenbarungsvorstellungen im alten Israel," *OaG*, pp. 21-41; idem, "Die Entstehung der israelitischen Religion als religionsgeschichtliches und theologisches Problem,"
TLZ, 88 (1963), cols. 735-746; idem, "Alttestamentliche Theologie und israelitisch-jüdische Religionsgeschichte," in *Zwischenstation. Festschrift für Karl
Kupisch zum 60. Geburtstag*, ed. Helmut Gollwitzer and J. Hoppe (Munich,
1963), pp. 208-222. Noteworthy also is the critique of Rendtorff by Arnold
Gamper, "Offenbarung in Geschichte," *ZTK*, 86 (1964), 180-196.
80. "Das Offenbarungsverständnis in der Geschichte des Urchristen-
tums," *OaG*, pp. 42-90.
81. D. Rössler, *Gesetz und Geschichte. Untersuchungen zur Theologie der
jüdischen Apokalyptik und der pharisäischen Orthodoxie* (WMANT, 3; 2nd
ed.; Neukirchen, 1962).

this is all united in the tradition, he elevates the term "tradition" to the center of his discussion. He explains that "Israel's history takes place in the external events which are commonly the subject of historical-critical research of history *and* in the manifold and stratified inner events, which we have gathered under the term tradition."[82] Therefore, the historical-critical method is to be transformed and extended so as to be able to verify at the same time God's revelation in history. It is not surprising that Rendtorff has much to say about the relation of word and event. He is of the conviction that "word has an essential part in the event of revelation." But this should not be understood to mean that word has priority over event. Quite on the contrary, the word does not need to be the mediator between the event and the one who experiences the event, because "the event itself can and should bring about a recognition of Yahweh in the one who sees it and understands it to be the act of Yahweh."[83]

But apart from employing the term "tradition" in his comprehensive horizon, Rendtorff's attempt does not go beyond von Rad, who even used it in the subtitles of his two volumes on OT theology. It needs to be asked what kind of relevance one can expect of the tradition history. Undoubtedly the history of tradition is able to further Biblical-theological expounding and interpretation, but the question remains whether or not this method, even in a broadened perspective, can be made the "canon" of Biblical-theological understanding. H.-J. Kraus remarks critically that "the strange optimism, believing that with the wonder word 'history of tradition' both faith and history can be handled, leads of necessity to the security of the program 'revelation as history'."[84]

---

82. Rendtorff, *Studien*, p. 84.

83. *OaG*, p. 40. Zimmerli countered Rendtorff in " 'Offenbarung' im AT," *EvT,* 22 (1962), 15-31, to which Rendtorff replied with "Geschichte und Wort im AT," *EvT,* 22 (1962), 621-649. A summary of the debate is given by Robinson, "Revelation as Word and as History," in *Theology as History,* pp. 42-62.

84. *Biblische Theologie,* p. 370.

In view of this situation Kraus has correctly pointed out that "one of the most difficult questions of the laying hold of and presenting of 'Biblical theology' is that of the starting-point, the meaning and function of historical-critical research."[85] Von Rad's theology is in its starting-point definitely a historical-critical undertaking, as is evident in that his theology is a theology of traditions. This approach contains many questions. One crucial problem area is the relationship of history of tradition and salvation history. Let me illustrate what I mean. The prophets of Israel actualized the ancient traditions; the old was made new. Among them "a critical way of thinking sprang up which learned how to select, combine, and even reject, data from the wealth of tradition. . . ."[86] This whole process von Rad calls a "charismatic-eclectic process."[87] What about this "process" out of which a "linear course of history"[88] was constructed which in turn produced new historical events? The question that arises is whether or not the Biblical event is traditio-historical event. Or to express it differently, Is the horizontal structural framework of the traditions the decisive "process" which an OT theology has to adopt and to explicate? Is the theology of the history of traditions properly OT theology? The aim of these critical questions is not to minimize the right and meaning of traditio-historical research. Yet one cannot shirk the responsibility to come to grips with the question whether or not OT theology has its methodological starting-point in the traditio-historical method. To speak with Kraus, it seems that OT theology is only theology of the OT[89] in that it "accepts the given textual context as contained in the canon as *historical truth* whose final form is in need of explanation and interpretation in a summary presen-

85. P. 363.
86. *TAT,* II, 118; *OTT,* II, 108.
87. *TAT,* II, 345. Cf. Baumgärtel, *TLZ,* 12 (1961), 901-903.
88. *TAT,* II, 118; *OTT,* II, 108.
89. Ebeling, *Word and Faith,* pp. 79f., points up the ambiguity of the term Biblical theology, which can mean either the theology contained in the Bible or the theology that has Biblical character and accords with the Bible. The same distinction is applicable to OT theology. OT theology means the theology contained in the OT, and this theology has also normative claims.

tation."[90] If this is the proper task of OT theology, then it is not to be considered a "history of revelation," "history of religion," or "history of tradition" as the case may be.[91]

In the present writer's opinion it seems feasible neither to ground "salvation history" in the historical-critical method (Hesse) nor to enlarge the historical-critical method to such an extent that the totality of reality can come to expression through it (Pannenberg, Rendtorff), because the major presuppositional and philosophical adjustments to be made would so radically change this method that its historical-critical nature as commonly understood at present would be obliterated. Nevertheless, no matter how we evaluate the way in which Pannenberg and his group worked out their theologies, Pannenberg's proposal that "we must reinstate today the original unity of facts and their meaning"[92] calls for serious consideration as a new starting-point for overcoming the modern dichotomy by which historiography has wrenched apart the history of Israel under such outmoded and questionable influences as positivism and neo-Kantianism.[93] Faith would thus not be established by the "language of facts"[94] nor by any proof of events on the basis of the historical-critical method, but by the fact of language, which brings both event and word as a central original unity to the hearer. Thus when we speak of God's acts in Israel's history, there is no reason to confine this activity to a few bare events, *bruta facta,* that the schema of historical criticism can verify by cross-checking with other

90. *Biblische Theologie,* p. 364.

91. Vriezen, *An Outline of OT Theology*[2], pp. 146f.; and also Kraus, *Biblische Theologie,* pp. 364f. Kraus goes on to explain that this is not a new Biblicism but a part of the critical theological task to continue to test and explain methodological procedures.

92. Pannenberg, *Theology as History,* p. 127.

93. The OT theologian Christoph Barth argues in "Grundprobleme einer Theologie des AT," *EvT,* 23 (1963), 368, against a critical methodology that declares every "suprahuman and supranatural causality" unhistorical, as well as against a "rational-objective method" that believes itself able to distinguish without great difficulty between "real" and "interpreted" history.

94. Pannenberg, *OaG,* pp. 100, 112.

historical evidences. Nor is it adequate and appropriate to employ the hermeneutical schema of von Rad, because with neither schema has scholarship been able to reach a fully acceptable understanding of historical reality, due to serious methodological, historical, and theological limitations, restrictions, and inadequacies. God's acts are with the totality of Israel's career in history, including the highly complex and diverse ways in which she developed and transmitted her confessions. Thus we must work with a method that takes account of the totality of that history under the recognition of the original unity of facts and their meaning and an adequate concept of total reality.

By the 1970s the historical-critical paradigm which had been built on modern, rationalistic principles of historiography, as we have seen in our discusssion so far, was still in the grip of subordinating literary questions to the reconstructions of history and religion. This remained true also in form criticism and in the tradition-historical method.[95] Hans Frei most effectively and insightfully described this whole development in his pregnant work *The Eclipse of Biblical Narrative* (New Haven, 1974).[96] It would go too far beyond our range to describe the change in the study of the Bible from the historical paradigm to the literary paradigm at this point. It is noteworthy nevertheless that this change is conditioned not only by the inadequacies of the historical-critical method or its failure to free the Bible from the past but also by a shift that was

95. For a concise survey of the emergence of new literary (and also social science) approaches to Biblical study, see Norman Gottwald, *The Hebrew Bible: A Socio-Literary Introduction* (Philadelphia, 1985), pp. 20-34; John Barton, *Reading the OT: Method in Biblical Study* (Philadelphia, 1984), pp. 104-179; Robert Morgan with John Barton, *Biblical Interpretation* (Oxford/New York, 1988), pp. 203-268; see also from another perspective Edgar V. McKnight, *Post-Modern Use of the Bible: The Emergence of Reader-Oriented Criticism* (Nashville, 1988).

96. Cf. also the reaction and criticisms by E. M. Klaaaren, "A Critical Appreciation of Hans Frei's *Eclipse of Biblical Narrative*," *Union Seminary Quarterly Review*, 37 (1982), 283-297; C. West, "On Frei's *Eclipse of Biblical Narrative*," *Union Seminary Quarterly Review*, 37 (1982), 299-302.

taking place in the USA particularly from the seminary to the (nonprivate) university as the latter developed departments of religious studies, where the Bible was not to be studied as Scripture—from a theological tradition or in a confessional way as canon—but as "source" for the various traditions of both Jewish and Christian religions or with thoroughly comparative and anthropological approaches.[97] Accordingly, much work on the Bible as literature, using various literary approaches, aside from social, anthropological, and comparative approaches, has been done by persons associated with the university. That this has in turn influenced the study of the Bible at the seminary is self-evident.[98]

At one point, fairly early in the discussion, James Barr entered the fray by suggesting that the "historical" model for Biblical (and OT) theology be replaced with the "story" model.[99] Before him John Wharton had already argued in a long essay that the category "story" is to replace that of history, since the latter is of fairly recent origin in Western culture and is not the "proper starting point for OT exegesis and theology."[100] After providing a study of the concept "story," Wharton explains that "story" is what Israel "remembered in

97. Note the provocative title of the book by Robert A. Oden, Jr., *The Bible Without Theology: The Theological Tradition and Alternatives to It* (San Francisco, 1987). This volume is a masterly *tour de force* in the attempt to show that at the secular university in North America the Bible should be studied in a context outside that of theology (p. 159) and that a "thoroughly comparative and anthropological approach offers us a clear set of alternatives to the theological tradition. Further, these departures from the long dominant tradition [of theology] are more in keeping with methods employed elsewhere in the modern university, a setting in which the study of religion has only recently been invited and in which it still sits somewhat unsurely" (pp. 161-162).

98. This is evident everywhere. See the contributors to various journals, and also, e.g., *Semeia: An Experimental Journal for Biblical Criticism*, 48, ed. Edgar V. McKnight (1989).

99. James Barr, "Story and History in Biblical Theology," *JR*, 56 (1976), 11-17; repr. in James Barr, *Scope and Authority of the Bible* (London, 1980), pp. 1-17.

100. John Wharton, "The Occasion of the Word of God: An Unguarded Essay on the Character of the OT as the Memory of God's Story with Israel," *Austin Seminary Bulletin*, 84 (Sept. 1968), 5-54, esp. p. 20.

an astonishing variety of modes reaching out to embrace most aspects of human life."[101] The "story" model is able to communicate with modern man.[102]

For Barr the OT became in the course of time a "completed story."[103] Dietrich Ritschl speaks of a "meta-story" as regards the OT, which is made up of different "detail-stories." The "meta-story" is the overarching expression of Israel's identity.[104] Barr's programmatic view of the "story" paradigm means that "ultimately 'history' [in its modern usage as a science developed since the Enlightenment], when used as an organizing and classifying bracket, is *not* a biblical category."[105] "Story" is a more appropriate way of describing the materials in the Bible. If this were granted, what about the revelation of God in the literary form "story"? Barr states, "Just as there is variation in the degree of approximation of stories to 'history,' so we may consider that there is a great deal of variation in the degree to which God 'reveals himself' in the stories."[106] The "story" concept is one of understanding the Bible as literature. This mode of viewing the Bible comes in one sense as a reaction to seeing it purely or solely in terms of "history." Whichever direction it would be taken, the mode of seeing the Bible and Biblical materials as "story" puts the Bible into the framework of reading it as literature, and that is a different reading from its predominant paradigm of reading it in the historical mode.

Krister Stendahl emphasized that it will not do merely to read the Bible as "story." He insists on the Bible's "normative" nature. The Bible as "classic" literature does not have any

---

101. Ibid., p. 22.

102. Ibid., pp. 29, 53.

103. Barr, *Scope and Authority*, p. 15.

104. Dietrich Ritschl, "'Story' als Rohmaterial der Theologie," in D. Ritschl and H. O. Jones, *"Story" als Rohmaterial der Theologie* (Munich, 1976), pp. 22-24; D. Ritschl, *The Logic of Theology* (London, 1986). See also H. O. Jones, "Das Story-Konzept in der Theologie," in *"Story" als Rohmaterial der Theologie*, pp. 42-68; J. Licht, *Storytelling in the Bible* (Jerusalem, 1978).

105. James Barr, *Old and New in Interpretation* (New York, 1966), p. 69.

106. Ibid., p. 70.

more claim on anyone than any other classic literature. In his presidential address before the Society of Biblical Literature, he insists that "it may be worth noting that the more recent preoccupation with 'story' tends to obscure exactly the normative dimension [of the Bible as Scripture based on the canon]."[107]

Modern literary studies received a new turn in the 1940s when the study of literature moved into what became known as "New Criticism."[108] John Barton depicts the three major theses of the New Criticism: (1) The literary text is an "artefact"; (2) "intentionalism" is a fallacy; and (3) "the meaning of a text is a function of its place in a literary canon."[109] The New Criticism won independence from the traditional philological and historical emphasis in the study of classical literature over a 200-year period. As it was begun by I. A. Richards and T. S. Eliot in the 1920s, New Criticism insisted on the autonomy of the individual work of literary art. Each work had and needed to be seen as a unit with its own aesthetic value. It reacted against the emphasis on history and reached its high point in the early 1960s. It was known for its emphasis on the "close reading" of the text.

The Israeli scholar Meir Weiss is possibly the best representative of the "close reading" mode for the Hebrew Bible and his stated dependence on the New Criticism.[110] Here is again a conscious attempt to break loose from the paradigm of scientific history with all its limitations and problems.[111] Here is also the claim that B. S. Childs' "canonical approach"

107. Krister Stendahl, "The Bible as a Classic and the Bible as Holy Scripture," *JBL*, 103 (1984), 3-10, quotation from p. 8.

108. For a history of developments in literary studies, see R. Wellek and A. Warren, *Theory of Literature* (3rd ed.; New York, 1977); F. Lentrieccha, *After the New Criticism* (London, 1980).

109. John Barton, *Reading the OT*, p. 144. In what follows I remain heavily dependent on his excellent survey.

110. Meir Weiss, *The Bible From Within: The Method of Total Interpretation* (Jerusalem, 1984), pp. 1-46.

111. See the helpful book by Tremper Longman III, *Literary Approaches to Biblical Interpretation* (Foundations of Contemporary Interpretation, 3; Grand Rapids, 1987), pp. 25-45.

depends on the New Criticism,[112] though Childs himself insists that he has no such conscious dependence.[113] Against the interpretation and association of his "canonical approach" as a part of the New Criticism or the like, Childs emphatically maintains that this "is a misunderstanding"[114] on the part of John Barton. For Childs, in contrast to a literary reading of the Bible, "the initial point to be made is that the canonical approach to Old Testament theology is unequivocal in asserting that the object of theological reflection is the canonical writing of the Old Testament."[115] The object for theological reflection is not the OT as literature but the OT as canonical Scripture! In this instance Childs would side with Stendahl's emphasis that while the Bible may be seen as a literary classic of some special sort, the Bible belongs "to the genre of Holy Scripture,"[116] "because what makes the Bible the Bible is the canon."[117] In its normative nature the Bible "is different from Shakespeare or from the way one now reads Homer."[118]

It is on this point that Wesley A. Kort reflects, in his sensitive book *Story, Text, and Scripture*, that a literary paradigm and its "literary interests in biblical narrative require or imply a new concept of scripture."[119] This "new concept" is that "the concept of scripture . . . has a literary base before it has a theological consequence."[120] This means that if the "Bible reveals something about religion and about God, it does so in and through narrativity and textuality."[121] Stendahl, Childs, and hosts of others will demur and insist that the normativity

112. Barton, *Reading the OT,* pp. 153-156.

113. This is stated by John Barton, "Classifying Biblical Criticism," *JSOT,* 29 (1984), 27-28.

114. B. S. Childs, *OT Theology,* p. 6.

115. Ibid., p. 6.

116. Stendahl, "Bible as a Classic," p. 8.

117. Ibid., p. 6.

118. Ibid., p. 8.

119. Wesley A. Kort, *Story, Text, and Scripture: Literary Interests in Biblical Narrative* (University Park, PA/London, 1987), p. 1.

120. Ibid., p. 3.

121. Ibid.

of the Bible is rooted in its canonicity and not in its literary nature of textuality and narrativity. Childs also maintains the notion of revelation as a vertical dimension in addition to the horizontal dimension of canon in which the normativity of the Bible is manifested.[122] To ground authority and truth in a piece of literature that is a "classic," which David Tracy[123] proposed as a main category for Scripture, is highly prolematical for both Stendahl and Childs. Furthermore, the view that the canon of Scripture "does not necessarily imply a qualitative difference over against other ancient literature but only a recognition of the historical importance of these texts within the tradition"[124] diminishes the normativity of Scripture in a most significant way for the process of OT (and Biblical) theology.

The issues regarding "story" and also "narrative,"[125] another major category of literature which has diversified into numerous types[126]—a subject of breadth that deserves a separate treatment—will continue to exercise exegetes, literary

122. Childs, *OT Theology*, pp. 20-26.
123. David Tracy, *The Analogical Imagination: Christian Theology and the Culture of Pluralism* (New York, 1981), pp. 102, 114, 119.
124. John J. Collins, "Is a Critical Biblical Theology Possible?," p. 8.
125. See, e.g., Edgar V. McKnight, *Meaning in Texts: The Historical Shaping of Narrative Hermeneutics* (Philadelphia, 1978); Robert Alter, *The Art of Biblical Narrative* (New York, 1981); idem, *The Art of Biblical Poetry* (New York, 1985); George W. Stroup, *The Promise of Narrative Theology* (Atlanta, 1981); Michael Goldberg, *Theology and Narrative: A Critical Introduction* (Nashville, 1982); Adele Berlin, *Poetics and Interpretation of Biblical Narrative* (Sheffield, 1983); F. McConnell, ed., *The Bible and the Narrative Tradition* (New York, 1986); Meir Sternberg, *The Poetics of Biblical Narrative* (Bloomington, IN, 1987). The collected "classical" essays edited by Stanley Hauerwas and L. Gregory Jones, *Why Narrative? Readings in Narrative Theology* (Grand Rapids, 1990), are first-class reading on the subject from those who are at the forefront of narrative theology. See also Carl F. H. Henry, "Narrative Theology: An Evangelical Appraisal," *Trinity Journal*, NS 8 (1987), 3-19, and the rejoinder by Hans Frei, "Response to 'Narrative Theology: An Evangelical Appraisal,'" *Trinity Journal*, NS 8 (1987), 21-24. Of great interest is also Kevin J. Vanhoozer, "A Lamp in the Labyrinth: The Hermeneutics of 'Asthetic' Theology," *Trinity Journal*, NS 8 (1987), 25-56.
126. See Gabriel Fackre, "Narrative Theology: An Overview," *Interp*, 37 (1983), 340-352.

critics, and theologians alike. The very shift from the paradigm of history to that of literature for a new critical theology
of the Bible will need to bring about new reflections with
regard to OT theology and Biblical theology. Among these will
be the new understanding of truth,[127] the understanding that
the Biblical narrative is "history-like" (H. W. Frei),[128] or "myth"
(R. A. Oden),[129] or "prose fiction" (R. Alter),[130] or generally
that the Biblical materials are imaginative construals that are
not necessarily factual. For the Bible, perceived as literature
with "imaginative construals" of Scripture, this means in the
words of Collins that "their value for theology lies in their
function as myth or story rather than in their historical accuracy."[131] The literary paradigm with "story" or "narrative"
works with totally different sets of references and contexts
than the historical-critical paradigm but shares with the latter
new understandings of the nature, function, and purpose of
the Bible as compared with the traditional mode of seeing and
understanding it as the Word of God that is self-sufficient and
inspired. These limited pointers to some of the new aspects
related to the "story" paradigm hopefully indicate where some
of the intricacies and complexities rest that will occupy the
student of the Bible for some time to come.

127. See David Robertson, *The OT and the Literary Critic* (Philadelphia,
1977), pp. 11-13; and the extensive section in Sternberg, *Poetics of Biblical
Narrative*, pp. 23-35.
128. Frei, *Eclipse of Biblical Narrative*, p. 258.
129. Oden, *Bible Without Theology*, pp. 57-91.
130. Alter, *Art of Biblical Narrative*, pp. 23-24.
131. Collins, "Is a Critical Biblical Theology Possible?," p. 11.

IV. The Center of the OT and OT Theology

The question whether the OT has something that can be considered its center (German *Mitte*) is of considerable importance for its understanding and for doing OT theology. The matter of the center plays an important and at times even decisive role for presentations of OT theology.

It is not necessary to survey the development of this question during the last two centuries in which rather divergent presentations of Biblical theology were brought forth.[1] With the publication of Eichrodt's theology this question has come into new focus. For him the "central concept" and "covenient symbol"[2] for securing the unity of Biblical faith is the "covenant." "The concept of the covenant," explains Eichrodt, "was given this central position in the religious thinking of the OT so that, by working outward from it, the structural unity of the OT message might be made more readily visible."[3] He does not consider it a "doctrinal concept, with the help of which a complete corpus of dogma can be worked out, but the characteristic *description of a living process,* which was begun at a particular time and at a particular place, in order to reveal a divine reality unique in the whole history of re-

---

1. We would like to draw attention to the short recent study of the subject by R. Smend, *Die Mitte des AT* (Zürich, 1970), pp. 7, 27-33.
2. *TOT,* I, 13f.
3. *TOT,* I, 17.

ligion."[4] Thus Eichrodt's theology represents one of the most impressive attempts to understand the OT as a whole not only from a center but from the unifying concept "covenant."

It appears that the discoveries of the legal background of the Mosaic covenant as particularly stimulated by G. E. Mendenhall[5] further undergird Eichrodt's emphasis. The ensuing discussion, however, has somewhat dampened the early enthusiasm.[6] Now G. Fohrer even thinks that the covenant between Yahweh and Israel played no role at all in Israel between the end of the 13th and the end of the 7th century B.C.,[7] a point to which Eichrodt has responded[8] and in which Fohrer may see things from a too limited perspective. The importance of the covenant motif in the OT is not to be denied, but the crucial question remains: Is the covenant concept broad

---

4. *TOT*, I, 14. The centrality of the covenant for OT religion has found supporters long before Eichrodt: August Kayser, *Die Theologie des AT in ihrer geschichtlichen Entwicklung dargestellt* (Strassburg, 1886), p. 74: "The overriding thought of the prophets, the anchor and support of OT religion in general, is the idea of theocracy, or to use the expression employed in the OT itself, the idea of covenant." G. F. Oehler, *Theologie des AT* (Tübingen, 1873), I, 69: "The foundation of OT religion is the covenant through which God has entered the chosen tribe for the purpose of realizing his saving purpose."

5. *Law and Covenant in Israel and the Ancient East* (Pittsburgh, 1955); idem, "Covenant," *IDB*, I, 714-723.

6. For a summary of the discussion, see D. J. McCarthy, "Covenant in the OT: The Present State of Inquiry," *CBQ*, 27 (1965), 217-240; idem, *Der Gottesbund im AT* (2nd ed.; Stuttgart, 1967); trans. *The OT Covenant* (Oxford, 1972). The latter contains a comprehensive bibliography.

7. "AT — 'Amphiktyonie' und 'Bund'?" *TLZ*, 91 (1966), 893-904; idem, "Der Mittelpunkt einer Theologie des AT," *TZ*, 24 (1968), 162f. L. Perlitt, *Bundestheologie im AT* (WMANT, 36; Neukirchen-Vluyn, 1971), believes that the covenant theology in the OT is a late fruit of Israelite belief which is due to the theological creativity of the Deuteronomistic movement and epoch. This then explains the "covenant silence" in the prophets of the 8th century.

8. W. Eichrodt, "Prophet and Covenant: Observations on the Exegesis of Isaiah," in *Proclamation and Presence: OT Essays in Honor of G. Henton Davies*, ed. J. I. Durham and J. R. Porter (Richmond, 1970), pp. 167-188, maintains that the original covenant of Yahweh with Israel is not mentioned by Isaiah because the prophet did not wish to argue about a concept that was so important in his own faith. On the whole question, see R. E. Clements, *Prophecy and Covenant* (SBT, 1/43; London, 1965).

enough to include adequately within its grasp the totality of OT reality? One cannot but give a negative answer to the question. The problem remains whether or not any single concept should or can be employed for bringing about a "structural unity of the OT message" when the OT message resists from within such systematization.

Various scholars have felt that the OT has other centers. E. Sellin chooses as the central idea to guide him in his exposition of OT theology the holiness of God. "It is that which characterizes the deepest and innermost nature of the OT God."[9] Sellin makes the point that his OT theology is interested "only in the single great line which has found its completion in the Gospel, the word of the eternal God in the OT writings."[10] Whereas the national-cultic religion of popular belief looks mainly to the past and present, the ethical and universal religion of the prophets looks to the future, to the coming of the Holy One in judgment and salvation both of which arise out of the holiness of God.[11]

Like Eichrodt and Sellin, Ludwig Köhler has his own favorite central concept, namely that of God as the Lord.[12] For Köhler the fundamental and determining assertion of OT theology should be that God is the Lord. "This statement is the backbone of Old Testament theology."[13] The rulership and kingship of God are merely corollaries to God's lordship.[14]

Hans Wildberger suggests that "the central concept of the OT is Israel's election as the people of God."[15] Horst Seebass stresses the "rulership of Cod."[16] Günther Klein argues for the

9. *Theologie des AT* (2nd ed.; Leipzig, 1936), p. 19.

10. P. 1.

11. Pp. 21-23.

12. *OT Theology*, trans. A. S. Todd (Philadelphia, 1957), p. 30.

13. P. 35.

14. P. 31.

15. "Auf dem Wege zu einer biblischen Theologie," *EvT*, 19 (1959), 77f.

16. "Der Beitrag des AT zum Entwurf einer biblischen Theologie," *WuD*, 8 (1965), 34-42.

"kingdom of God as a central concept"[17] in both OT and NT. Georg Fohrer answers the question of the OT "from which it can proceed and around which everything can be grouped"[18] with a "dual concept,"[19] "namely the *rule* of God and the *communion* between God and man."[20] These two poles belong together as the two foci of an ellipse.[21] They "constitute the unifying element in the manifoldedness"[22] of the theological expressions and movements in the OT from which a Biblical theology of both OT and NT can be constructed. The OT and NT are then not to be correlated in terms of promise and fulfillment or failure and realization, but "in the relationship of beginning and continuation [*Beginn und Fortsetzung*]."[23] With the aid of this dual center and on the basis of this twofold relationship the OT does not need to be devaluated or reinterpreted but it can be taken seriously in its own uniqueness.

The thoroughly revised and rewritten new edition of Vriezen's theology is related at least in one key aspect to the views of Fohrer. Although Vriezen explicitly affirms that God "is the *focal point* of all the Old Testament writings" and stoutly maintains that "Old Testament theology must *centre* upon Israel's God as the God of the Old Testament in His relations to the people, man, and the world. . . ,"[24] one must clearly understand that the central element for his structure of OT theology is the concept of "communion."[25] Vriezen calls

17. " 'Reich Gottes' als biblischer Zentralbegriff," *EvT,* 30 (1970), 642-670.

18. "The Centre of a Theology of the OT," *Nederduitse Gereformeerde Teologiese Tydskrif,* 7 (1966), 198; the same article appeared in German, with footnotes, under the title, "Der Mittelpunkt einer Theologie des AT," *TZ,* 24 (1968), 161.

19. "Das AT und das Thema 'Christologie'," *EvT,* 30 (1970), 295: "In the quest for the center of OT theology appears the dual concept of the rule of God and the communion between God and man."

20. *TZ,* 24 (1968), 163.

21. *EvT,* 30 (1970), 295.

22. *TZ,* 24 (1968), 163; *EvT,* 30 (1970), 295.

23. *TZ,* 24 (1968), 163.

24. *An Outline of OT Theology*[2], p. 150 (italics mine).

25. P. 8, where Vriezen writes that the main part of his book (chs. 6-11) has undergone an important transformation in form since he "attempted to establish the 'communion' . . . as the centre of all the expositions."

the communion concept the "underlying idea," "essential root idea,"[26] "fundamental idea,"[27] or "keystone"[28] of the message of the OT. Why does he prefer the communion concept to the covenant concept as used by Eichrodt? Vriezen believes that the covenant did not bring the two covenant partners "into contract-relation, but into a communion, with God. . . ."[29] He adds that "we cannot be certain that the communion between God and the people was considered from the outset as a *covenantal* communion."[30] Since the NT is in Vriezen's view, shared also by Fohrer,[31] in complete agreement with the OT in that communion is the "fundamental point of faith," it follows for Vriezen that the fundamental idea of "communion between God and man is the best starting-point for a Biblical theology of the Old Testament," which must "be arranged with this aspect in view."[32] Thus it turns out that Vriezen's newest attempt is a combination of the cross-section and his confessional methods. The similarity between Eichrodt's OT theology and that of Vriezen is that both work with complementary methodologies. The difference between the two scholars lies in that Eichrodt employs his type of cross-section method with the use of the covenant concept but remaining with both feet planted in history. Eichrodt is thus more descriptive and Vriezen more confessional. The latter achieves structural unity with the aid of the single communion concept.

Rudolf Smend's recent study on the center of the OT revives Wellhausen's formula, "Yahweh the God of Israel, Israel the people of Yahweh."[33] If this particularistic formula is ac-

---

26. P. 160.
27. P. 170.
28. P. 164.
29. P. 169.
30. P. 351.
31. *EvT,* 30 (1970), 296-298.
32. *An Outline of OT Theology*[2], p. 175.
33. *Die Mitte des AT,* pp. 49, 55. J. Wellhausen, *Israelitisch-jüdische Religion. Die Kultur der Gegenwart I/4:1* (Leipzig, 1905), p. 8, states that the sentence "Yahweh the God of Israel and Israel the people of Yahweh" has

cepted, argues Smend, then the tension between God and Israel can come to expression in an OT theology. At this point it is significant to note that Smend, as Fohrer before him, recognizes that a single concept is unable to do justice to the manifold and multiform testimony of the OT. He would, therefore, choose this formula rather than a single concept because with this formula one is able to come to grips with a significant tension in the OT. But Smend himself admits that this formula does not express the center of the whole OT and is decidedly of limited value with regard to the Christian Scriptural canon of OT and NT.[34] Aside from the latter point, however, this formula would seem too particularistic, for within the tension between Yahweh and his people with which this formula is concerned one is unable to expound the universalistic emphasis of the OT, i.e., Yahweh's action with the world and the world vis-à-vis Yahweh. Yahweh is not only the God of Israel but also the Lord of the world.[35]

Smend argues that the OT should be studied on the basis of its center.[36] Against this principle there is hardly any sound objection to be advanced. But one needs to be on guard that one does not yield to the temptation to make a single concept or a certain formula into an abstract divining-rod with which all OT expressions and testimonies are combined into a unified system. Though Smend is aware of this danger, he nevertheless makes such a definite use of his particularistic

---

"been for all times the short essence of the Israelite religion." Bernhard Duhm, *Die Theologie der Propheten* (Leipzig, 1875), p. 96, has argued that in the dual formula "Israel, Yahweh's people and Yahweh, Israel's God" the "whole content of prophetic religion has come fully to expression." B. Stade, *Biblische Theologie des AT* (2nd ed.; Tübingen, 1905), I, 31, holds that "Yahweh, Israel's God" is "the basic idea of the religion of Israel." Martin Noth, *Die israelitischen Personennamen im Rahmen der gemeinsemitischen Namengebung* (2nd ed.; Hildesheim, 1966), p. 81, believes that in the "sentence, that expresses that Yahweh is Israel's God and Israel is Yahweh's people" comes to expression the "characteristic nature" of Israelite religion.

34. *Die Mitte des AT,* pp. 55-58.
35. Seebass, *WuD,* 8 (1965), 38-41, speaks of Yahweh as a "Weltherrschergott."
36. *Die Mitte des AT,* p. 49.

formula that it turns out to serve as *the* key for the systematic ordering of the OT materials, subjects, themes, and motifs.[37] This goes beyond the limits that must be imposed upon the usage and significance of a center of the OT, whatever it may be. One must always be on guard not to overstep the boundaries inherent in any kind of center. K. H. Miskotte has correctly warned that we should not consider a center as establishing "the timeless, usable content of the Old Testament."[38] Each of the suggestions so far described has undoubtedly much in its favor. At the same time every one of them seems to be wanting. They fall short because they try to grasp the OT in terms of a single basic concept or limited formula through which the OT message in its manifoldness and variety, its continuity and discontinuity, is ordered, arranged, and systematized when the multiplex and multiform nature of the OT resists such handling of its materials and thoughts.

Here Gerhard von Rad's absolute No to the question of the center of the OT in its relation to the doing of OT theology has a unique significance. Von Rad's position merits a more detailed analysis, since he claims unequivocally that "on the basis of the Old Testament itself, it is truly difficult to answer the question of the unity of that Testament, for it has no focalpoint [*Mitte*] as is found in the New Testament."[39] Whereas

---

37. Pp. 54f.

38. *When the Gods Are Silent* (New York, 1967), p. 119.

39. *TAT,* II, 376; *OTT,* II, 362. Earlier von Rad, "Kritische Vorarbeiten zu einer Theologie des AT," in *Theologie und Liturgie,* ed. L. Hennig (Munich, 1952), p. 30, stated the following: "Therefore we have to be confronted still more consciously and consistently with the mysterious phenomenon of the lack of a center in the OT. The place of the center is the way or, as Isaiah formulated it for the entire OT, the 'work' of Yahweh (Isa. 5:19; 10:12; 22:12)." *TLZ,* 88 (1963), col. 405 n. 3a: "What is actually intended by the almost universal question of the 'unity,' the 'center' of the OT? Is it so self-evident, that its appearance belongs to the *conditio sine qua non* of an OT theology? And in what sphere shall this unity (accepted from the beginning as present) be demonstrated, in the area of Israel's historical experiences or in her world of thoughts? Or is this postulate less a concern of historical or theological knowledge and more a speculative-philosophical principle which becomes active as a conscious premise?"

the NT has Jesus Christ as its center, the OT lacks such a center.[40] Yahweh as the center of the OT "would not be sufficient."[41] Why? "Unlike the revelation in Christ, the revelation of Jahweh in the Old Testament is divided up over a long series of separate acts of revelation which are very different in content. It seems to be without a centre which determines everything and which could give to the various separate acts both an interpretation and their proper theological connection with one another."[42] The later von Rad is less rigid in his denial of a center of the OT. He actually admits that "one can say, Yahweh is the center of the Old Testament."[43] "God stood at the center," says von Rad, "of the (theologically rather flexible) conception of history of the writers of ancient Israelite history."[44] Nevertheless this is where the question begins for von Rad: "What kind of Yahweh after all is this?"[45] Is it one who hides himself more and more in every act of self-revelation? This question can be answered best by von Rad's own methodological procedure.

Von Rad proceeds from a kind of secret center, which reveals itself in his basic thesis, namely that the establishment of God's self-revelation takes place in his acts in history: "History is the place in which God reveals the secret of his person."[46] With this thesis von Rad has won a "heuristic

40. *TAT,* II, 376f.; *OTT,* II, 362.

41. *OTT,* II, 362f.

42. *TAT,* I, 128; *OTT,* I, 115. On the other hand, on the same page we find that von Rad claims that OT theology has "its starting point and its centre . . [in] Jahweh's action in revelation."

43. *TLZ,* 88 (1963), 406. Vriezen, *An Outline of OT Theology*[2], p. 150 n. 4, seems to go astray when he implies that von Rad may make Christ the center of the OT.

44. *TLZ,* 88 (1963), 409.

45. Col. 406.

46. I have supplied my own translation of this key sentence from *TAT,* II, 349: "Der Ort, an dem Gott sein Personengeheimnis offenbart, ist die Geschichte." In the translation of *OTT,* II, 338, part of its significance is lost: ". . that it is in history that God reveals the secret of his person." Von Rad does not follow the usual distinction made in German between *Historie* and *Geschichte.* He employs the term *Geschichte* almost to the complete exclusion of *Historie,* which according to the index is used only once, *TAT,* II, 8.

measuring rod"[47] with which all statements, all witnesses of faith of the OT, are measured as to their theological relevance and legitimacy.

Von Rad is very emphatic to point out that the OT is not a book that gives an account of historical facts as they "really happened." He states: "The Old Testament is a history book [*Geschichtsbuch*]; it tells of God's history with Israel, with the nations, and with the world, from the creation of the world down to the last things, that is to say, down to the time when dominion over the world is given to the Son of Man (Dan. VII.13f.)."[48] Already the earliest confessions (the Credo of Deut. 26) were historically determined, i.e., "they connect the name of this God with some statement about an action in history." Von Rad explains, "This history can be described as saving history [*Heilsgeschichte*] because, as it is presented, creation itself is understood as a saving act of God and because, according to what the prophets foretold, God's will to save is, in spite of many acts of judgment, to achieve its goal."[49] As a result of this view the Psalms and Wisdom literature of the OT are accorded the position of "Israel's answer"[50] to the early experiences of Israel with Yahweh. The OT prophets, on the other hand, are not reformers with a message of an entirely new kind. "Instead, they regarded themselves as the spokesmen of old and well-known sacral traditions which they reinterpreted for their own day and age."[51] Thus it becomes apparent that von Rad employs his understanding of OT history as a hermeneutical schema for interpreting the OT. The type of history of which von Rad speaks finds its clearest formulation in the Deuteronomist, whose view of history is described in the following way: "The history of Israel is a course of events [*Zeitablauf*] which re-

---

47. This phrase stems from Martin Honecker, "Zum Verständnis der Geschichte in Gerhard von Rads Theologie des AT," *EvT,* 23 (1963), 145.
48. *TAT,* II, 370; *OTT,* II, 415.
49. *TAT,* II, 370f.; *OTT,* II, 357f.
50. *TAT,* I, 366ff.; *OTT,* I, 355ff.
51. *TAT,* II, 185; *OTT,* II, 175.

ceived its own peculiar dramatic quality from the tension
between constantly promulgated prophecies and their corresponding fulfilment."[52] This explains why in von Rad's OT
theology cultic and wisdom elements recede,[53] for his view
of history is interested neither in secular history nor in the
history of faith and cult, but is concerned solely "with the
problem of how the word of Jahweh functioned in history."[54]
Fundamentally expressed, this means that the "Deuteronomistic theology of history was the first which clearly formulated
the phenomenon of saving history, that is, of a course of
history which was shaped and led to a fulfilment by a word
of judgment and salvation continually injected into it."[55]

The prophetic message is by von Rad likewise interpreted
from this center, namely the Deuteronomistic theology of history.[56] Accordingly, one of the greatest achievements of prophecy "was to recapture for faith the dimension in which Jahweh
had revealed himself par excellence, that of history and
politics."[57] The essential step of the prophets beyond the
tradition of salvation history handed down to them, which
was oriented in the past, consists in their opening the future
as the place of the action of God.[58] This projection of God's
acts to the future, which is felt to be an "eschatologizing of
concepts of history,"[59] takes up the old confessional traditions
and places them with the help of "creative interpretation"[60]

52. *TAT,* I, 352; *OTT,* I, 340.
53. Honecker, p. 146.
54. *TAT,* I, 354; *OTT,* I, 343.
55. *TAT,* I, 356; *OTT,* I, 344.
56. The problem of this one-sided interpretation of prophecy is apparently known to von Rad, since he points to the question of how far the
prophet was "a spiritual man who stood in direct religious relationship to
God" and a proclaimer of "the universal moral order." "In all probability, the
questions considered by earlier criticism will one day require to be taken up
again, though under different theological presuppositions" (*TAT,* II, 311; *OTT,*
II, 298).
57. *TAT,* II, 192; *OTT,* II, 182.
58. *TAT,* II, 129ff.; *OTT,* II, 115ff.
59. *TAT,* II, 125ff.; *OTT,* II, 112ff.
60. *TAT,* II, 313; *OTT,* II, 300.

within the horizon of a new saving event. "Projecting the old traditions into the future was the only possible way open to the prophets of making material statements about a future which involved God."[61] The eschatological character of the prophetic message consists of a negation of the old historical bases of salvation, and in that it does not remain with past historical acts, it "suddenly shifted the basis of salvation to a future action of God."[62] The kerygma of the prophets thus takes place within tensions created by three factors: "the new eschatological word with which Jahweh addresses Israel, the old election tradition, and the personal situation, be it one which incurred penalty or one which needed comfort, of the people addressed by the prophet."[63]

In short, von Rad gains his understanding of history from the Deuteronomistic theology of history according to which salvation history is led to its goal, its fulfillment, by means of the word of Yahweh. This seems surprising if one considers that von Rad's research had its starting-point in the Hexateuch, from which it moved to the prophets as the closing interpreters of the transmitted events of salvation. The eschatologizing thought of prophecy is, however, interpreted by von Rad on the basis of the center as found in the Deuteronomistic theology of history and in this way it is bound to the primitive *heilsgeschichtliche* confession. Thus von Rad introduces into OT theology not only a historico-relational concept but also a certain historico-theological center, that of the theology of history of the Deuteronomistic historian, as a determinative hermeneutical schema.

Parenthetically, we may point out that a complete discussion of von Rad's center as found in history should include a treatment of his exposition of salvation history as it moves in the tension between promise and fulfillment to be finally fully consummated in the Christ-event. This would carry us,

61. *TAT*, II, 312; *OTT*, II, 299.
62. *TAT*, II, 131; *OTT*, II, 118.
63. *TAT*, II, 140; *OTT*, II, 130.

however, beyond the immediate scope of the question at hand. For our purpose it will suffice to point out that what is at work here is the interrelatedness of a twofold methodology: first, the "structural analogy," which consists of the "peculiar interconnexion of revelation by word and revelation by event";[64] and, secondly, "typological thinking," which is based not "on myth and speculation, but on history and eschatology."[65] The questions that are raised by such a twofold methodology cannot be treated at this point.[66] In short, we must say that von Rad arrives at the crowning consummation of salvation history in the Christ-event as a result of the combination of three conceptions: the center of Deuteronomistic history; the predominance of event over word; and the interpretation of history from the movement along the line of tension between promise and fulfillment.

As we have seen above, von Rad believes he has found the center from which to unlock the OT in the Deuteronomistic theology of history. This, in fact, is his hermeneutical schema for the interpretation of the entire OT. He has, however, failed to justify the right to use such a center as a hermeneutical key; i.e., he has been satisfied with the phenomenological utilization of his center as a method for doing OT theology. One must ask whether with the same right one could not use the so-called Priestly schema for interpreting the OT or the apocalyptic universalism of history of the Pannenberg group.[67]

---

64. *TAT,* II, 376; *OTT,* II, 363; cf. the discussion of Hasel, "The Problem of History in OT Theology," *AUSS,* 8 (1970), 32-35.

65. *TAT,* II, 378; *OTT,* II, 365.

66. For these questions see Hans Walter Wolff, "Zur Hermeneutik des AT," *EvT,* 16 (1956), 337-370, trans. "The Hermeneutics of the OT," in *EOTH,* pp. 160-199; idem, "Das Geschichtsverständnis der alttestamentlichen Prophetie," *EvT,* 20 (1960), 218-235, trans. "The Understanding of History in the OT Prophets," in *EOTH,* pp. 336-355; Walther Eichrodt, "Ist die typologische Exegese sachgemässe Exegese?" *VT Supplement,* IV (1957), 161-180, trans. "Is Typological Exegesis an Appropriate Method?" in *EOTH,* pp. 224-245; Jürgen Moltmann, "Exegese und Eschatologie in der Geschichte," *EvT,* 22 (1962), 61 n. 75.

67. Pannenberg speaks of the concept of the apocalyptic universalism of history in terms of an "universalgeschichtliche Konzeption" and an "uni-

In a twofold way von Rad admits inadvertently to a center in the OT. On the one hand, he himself operates on the basis of a center, namely the Deuteronomistic theology of history, and on the other, he concedes more recently that it is right to say that "God stood at the center of the (theologically rather flexible) conception of history of the writers of ancient Israelite history."[68] Thus it appears that von Rad's initial No to the question of the center of the OT is not so much directed against a center as such but against making such a center "a speculative-philosophical principle, which becomes operative as a conscious premise"[69] in the doing of OT theology. Here von Rad's caution is to be taken seriously even though he himself is in the last analysis unfaithful to his own warning cries. Nevertheless we are indebted to von Rad for inviting us to look for a center anew and to redefine its function more strictly. We should neither return to a stage of discussion before von Rad[70] nor should we bypass him, but we should go beyond him.

So far we have restricted our discussion primarily to attempts which put forth a single concept, theme, motif, or idea as the center of the OT as a unifying principle on the basis of which the diversified OT materials can be organized into a systematized OT theology. It is now also necessary to refer to a number of recent approaches which do not fit into the above pattern but still speak to the problem of the center and unity of the OT. W. H. Schmidt published a concise study on the first commandment in which he expressed his conviction that due to "the claim [at exclusiveness and uniqueness of Yahweh

---

versalgeschichtliches Schema," in *KuD*, 5 (1959), 237, and in his "Geschichts-verständnis der Apokalyptik," in *OaG*, p. 107; cf. U. Wilckens, *OaG*, pp. 53f.; and Rössler, *Gesetz und Geschichte*, pp. 111ff. For a critique of Rössler, see Phillipp Vielhauer, "Apocalypses and Related Studies: Introduction," in Edgar Hennecke, *NT Apocrypha*, ed. Wilhelm Schneemelcher, trans. R. McL. Wilson (Philadelphia, 1965), pp. 581-607, esp. 593.

68. Von Rad, *TLZ*, 88 (1963), 409.

69. Col. 405 n. 3a.

70. This seems to be the case with Smend, *Die Mitte des AT,* pp. 49-55, in his revival of the formula of Wellhausen.

in] . . . the first commandment, it . . . can be used as a connecting link between an earlier and later time and can at the
same time provide an answer to the old question concerning
the 'unity' or 'center' of the Old Testament in the manifoldedness of its testimonies."[71] On this basis one should be able to
develop an OT theology from the center of the exclusiveness
of God as expressed in the first commandment.[72] This "basic
commandment [Grundgebot]"[73] supports history and vice
versa.[74] Therefore this commandment and its later influence
do not aim at a timeless Being or a definite structure, but
remain related to history.[75] Schmidt supports the single concept approach referred to above as providing an organizing
principle whereby the OT materials can be systematized into
a "certain kind of . . . structure."[76] His approach differs from

---

71. W. H. Schmidt, *Das erste Gebot. Seine Bedeutung für das AT* (Munich,
1969), p. 11. The claim of the first commandment's link between an earlier
and later time, namely on a chronological basis, rests upon Schmidt's position
that this commandment was formulated only after the taking of Canaan
during a time when Israel was in controversy with neighboring religions
(p. 13; cf. R. Knierim, "Das erste Gebot," *ZAW*, 77 [1965], 20-39; H. Schulz,
Das Todesrecht im AT [Berlin, 1969], pp. 58ff.). A grave difficulty for Schmidt's
"chronological" center of the first commandment arises, if one dates this
commandment with the majority of scholars at the time of Moses (cf. F. Baumgärtel, "Das Offenbarungszeugnis des AT im Lichte der religionsgeschichtlich-
vergleichenden Forschung," *ZTK*, 64 [1967], 398; S. Herrmann, "Mose," *EvT,*
28 [1968], 322; idem, *Israels Aufenthalt in Agypten;* W. Harrelson, "Ten Commandments," *IDB*, IV, 572; W. Zimmerli, *Der Mensch und seine Hoffnung im
AT* [Göttingen, 1968], p. 67; G. Fohrer, *Geschichte der israelitischen Religion*
[Berlin, 1969], p. 74; J. J. Stamm and M. E. Andrew, *The Ten Commandments
in Recent Research* [SBT, 2/2; London, 1967], pp. 22ff.; Th. C. Vriezen, *The
Religion of Ancient Israel* [Philadelphia, 1967], p. 143; W. F. Albright, *Yahweh
and the Gods of Canaan* [Garden City, NY, 1968], pp. 173, 174; etc.).
72. Schmidt, *Gebot*, pp. 49-55.
73. P. 51.
74. Pp. 50f.: "Therefore the total presentation [of an OT theology] gains
in a certain sense a common thread when one develops the history of the OT
as a history of the first commandment in that one questions the individual
literary productions where and how much the first commandment is brought
out in them. In this way historical and systematic methods can meet each
other."
75. P. 50.
76. Ibid.

the others in that he looks for something "specific [and] special,"[77] something that is exclusive and without any analogy in the ancient Near East and thus " 'genuinely' Israelite."[78]

Closely related to Schmidt's proposed center is that of Walther Zimmerli as outlined in the latest von Rad *Festschrift*[79] and worked out in his recent OT theology.[80] Zimmerli also believes that with the sentence "I am Yahweh, your God" (Ex. 20:2) "an actual foundation of everything following is given."[81] It is the call to which Israel answers in her responding praise "You . . . Yahweh" (Dt. 26:1). In this responding praise has "come to view a center which is uniquely held on to in the entire OT history of tradition and interpretation." According to Zimmerli "the task committed to the theological work on the OT is to describe the 'theology of the OT' with an inquiry for this Lord who is at work as the only Lord of the world and Israel according to the testimony of this first part of the Bible from the creation of the world . . . to the post exilic time."[82] Whereas Schmidt places emphasis on the "I . . . Yahweh" of Exodus 20, Zimmerli stresses the confessional response "You . . . Yahweh," of Deuteronomy 26 which has its basis in the prior "I . . . Yahweh."[83] Both Schmidt and Zimmerli emphasize the manifoldness of tradition history in its witness to the name of the Lord.[84] They also agree that this recognition does not provide a way for constructing a lifeless body of doctrine.[85]

---

77. P. 51.

78. P. 50.

79. W. Zimmeri, "Alttestamentliche Traditionsgeschichte und Theologie," in *Probleme biblischer Theologie. Gerhard von Rad zum 70. Geburtstag,* ed. Hans Walter Wolff (Munich, 1971), pp. 632-647.

80. Zimmerli, *Grundriss der alttestamentlichen Theologie,* pp. 10f. See the reaction by C. Westermann, "Zu zwei Theologien des AT," *EvT,* 30 (1974), 102-110.

81. Zimmerli, in *Probleme,* p. 639.

82. P. 640.

83. Pp. 639, 641.

84. Pp. 641-647; Schmidt, *Gebot,* pp. 50f.

85. Zimmerli in *Probleme,* p. 640; Schmidt, *Gebot,* pp. 50-52.

The first question concerning the centers proposed by Schmidt and Zimmerli is the justification of the choice of this particular commandment over any other. Why should it be the first commandment and not the second or another? Schmidt argues in favor of his proposed center on the basis of its lack of analogy in ancient Near Eastern religion and thought.[86] But for that matter, does not the lack of analogy hold true for other commandments as well? On this basis one could possibly argue with equal vigor for the Sabbath commandment as the center of the OT. It also knows unique aspects of Yahweh. He is the Creator of heaven, earth, and sea (Ex. 20:8-11); he gave this day as a day of rest by resting himself; he endowed it with special blessing and made it holy by separating it from the rest of time (Gen. 2:2-3); he is Yahweh, their God, whose interest goes beyond Israel's welfare to that of the slaves, foreigners, and animals (Ex. 20:8-11; Dt. 5:12-15). This commandment has likewise no analogy in the ancient Near East. The point is that this kind of argument in support of a center of the OT has seemingly insurmountable deficiencies. Furthermore, if one were able to inquire of the authors of the various OT books whether or not it was their purpose in writing their testimonies to prove Yahweh's exclusiveness, it may be doubted, on the basis of what we have available, that their response would be in the affirmative. This is not to deny that the first commandment or the response by Israel had an important function and history in Israel. But this is an inadequate qualification for making it *the* center of the OT.

Let us pause for a moment for certain basic considerations. Those to whom we have referred so far primarily agree on the matter that a single Scriptural concept, theme, motif, or idea can be made into a center which can serve as an organizing principle for a sort of systematic structure of an OT theology. This is done on the basis of an unspoken presupposition which has its roots in philosophical premises going back to scholastic theology of medieval times. It appears that the doing of OT theology is at this point in the grip of a philo-

86. Schmidt, *Gebot*, p. 50.

sophical-speculative presupposition which claims that the multiform and multiplex OT materials in all their rich manifoldness will fit into and can be systematically ordered and arranged by means of a center. A basic and in my view one of the most crucial and decisive hermeneutical questions arises at this point, namely whether or not a single central concept, though taken from the biblical material, is sufficient and adequate in bringing about an organization of the OT materials in terms of a systematized "structural unity."[87] Surprisingly a negative answer to this hermeneutical question is given even by some of those who actually argue for and have adopted a center as an organizing principle.[88] G. E. Wright has frankly stated: "It must be admitted that no single theme is sufficiently comprehensive to include within it all variety of viewpoint."[89] Such a recognition and the inconsistency in application indicate the force of the philosophical premise under which much of OT theology is done. It is evident that even the most carefully worked out single center or formula will prove itself finally to be one-sided, inadequate, and insufficient, if not outrightly erroneous, and therefore will lead to misconceptions.[90] The phenomenon of constantly increasing numbers of new suggestions at what constitutes the center of the OT and how they contribute to systematized structures of the variegated and manifold testimonies is in itself a telling witness to the evident inefficiency of a single concept, theme, motif, or idea for the task at hand.

On the basis of undeniable inadequacies of a single con-

---

87. Eichrodt, *TOT,* I, 31. Zimmerli speaks again of this issue in "Erwägungen zur Gestalt einer alttestamentlichen Theologie," *TLZ,* 98 (1973), 81-98.

88. Among the opponents of a "structural unity" of the basic ideas of the OT are the following: Artur Weiser, *Glaube und Geschichte im AT* (Munich, 1961), pp. 196f.; Barth, *EvT,* 23 (1963), 350ff.; Honecker, *EvT,* 23 (1963), 144ff.; von Rad, *OTT,* II, 362; idem, "Kritische Vorarbeiten zur einer Theologie des AT," in *Theologie und Liturgie,* ed. L. Hennig (Munich, 1952), p. 30; Kraus, *Biblische Theologie,* p. 128.

89. Wright, *Interpreter's One-Volume Commentary on the Bible,* p. 983. Köhler, *OT Theology,* p. 9, writes: "The Old Testament itself does not offer any scheme for that compilation we call its theology."

90. Barth, *EvT,* 23 (1963), 351.

cept, theme, motif, or idea as constituting the center on the basis of which the diversified OT materials could be organized into a systematized structure some scholars have suggested and worked out systems with the aid of broader conceptions. It is here that G. Fohrer's "dual concept" of "the *rule* of God and the *communion* between God and man,"[91] which is said to even "constitute the unifying element in the manifold-ness"[92] of both Testaments, seeks to make its contribution. Since Fohrer has now published his OT theology, *Theologische Grundstrukturen des AT* (1972), it is possible to evaluate whether or not his "dual concept" is adequate. Unfortunately Fohrer's attempt does not seem successful, although he points in the right direction. His correlation of God and man is still too narrow. Fohrer was unable to structure his OT theology on the basis of his proposal. OT eschatology is undervalued.[93] Wisdom theology is treated all too briefly *before* the major divisions of his structure! The OT is too variegated and manifold to be handled properly with a "dual concept."[94]

S. Herrmann seems to have chosen a broader basis by his suggestion that the book of Deuteronomy presents itself "as the center of biblical theology."[95] This seems to have been inspired by von Rad's view that Deuteronomy needs to be designated "in every respect as the center of the OT Testament."[96] An OT theology, says Herrmann, has to have its center in Deuteronomy because there the "basic issues of OT theology are concentrated *in nuce.*"[97] In Deuteronomy such single "central thoughts"[98] and "structural elements"[99] as "cult

---

91. Fohrer, *TZ,* 24 (1968), 161f.
92. Fohrer, *EvT,* 30 (1970), 295.
93. Fohrer, *Theologische Grundstrukturen des AT,* pp. 262-273.
94. See now especially C. Westermann, "Zu zwei Theologien des AT," *EvT,* 30 (1974), 96-102.
95. S. Herrmann, "Die konstruktive Restauration. Das Deuteronomium als Mitte biblischer Theologie," in *Probleme biblischer Theologie,* pp. 155-170.
96. *Studies in Deuteronomy* (SBT, 1/9; Chicago, 1953).
97. Herrmann in *Probleme,* p. 156.
98. P. 160.
99. P. 162.

unity" and "cult purity" (cf. A. Alt), exclusive worship of Yahweh, unity of Israel, election and covenant, possession of the land, etc. have been combined into a "unified and rounded Israelite order for people and life" and "are the keys for the understanding of Israel's historical traditions, for the structure of the Pentateuch in its combination of history and law. Still more these are the starting-points for the post-Josianic development of Israel and developing Judaism."[100] This concentration of OT thought in Deuteronomy is "finally the point of orientation"[101] for any OT theology no matter how differentiated it may turn out. Thus Herrmann emerges with the broadest conception of a center for the OT. This is a move in the right direction, but does it go far enough? Not all theologies and conceptions of the OT come to expression in Deuteronomy. We believe that even Deuteronomy as a center is insufficient and too narrow. Furthermore, we must be cautious over against the particular orientation on Deuteronomy by Herrmann as well as von Rad, Zimmerli, and Smend. It may turn out in the course of time that Deuteronomy may have to yield its present supremacy to another emphasis as it happened in an earlier period of OT research when the orientation centering around the Tetrateuch had to be given up.[102]

Where do we go from here? A brief sketch must suffice for pointing out the direction in which a fruitful solution may be found. The great number of suggestions as to what constitutes the center of the OT indicates not only the difficulty and acuteness of the problem,[103] but also the subjective nature of the undertaking. Philosophical-speculative premises that claim that the diverse and manifold OT testimonies can be organized into a systematized structure by means of a single or dual center should be radically questioned. In other words,

100. P. 166.
101. P. 167.
102. Smend, *Die Mitte des AT,* p. 13.
103. Dentan's statement (*Preface to OT Theology,* p. 117) is still pertinent, namely that "no question is more vexing to writers on OT theology" than "the question of a unifying principle."

the event-centered and word-centered[104] character and manner of God's revelation cannot be systematized in such a way.
Will not any center which is to serve as an organizing principle
for the entire OT world of revelation and experience always
turn out to be a *tour de force?* "The static unity of a systematization cannot define the dynamic unity of that growth and
outgrowing of Old Testament faith and worship."[105] Those
who would systematize on the basis of a particular center
obviously have to superimpose that center upon the diverse
and manifold encounters between God and man over so long
a period and are able to deal adequately only with those parts
of the rich Biblical witness that fit into the framework of that
center, no matter what it is. Would it be sound methodologically, adequate hermeneutically, and proper theologically
to lose sight of, neglect, or totally disregard theological insights, aspects, and emphases because they do not fit the
framework of a particular center that is chosen as a unifying
element?

Biblical theologians who opted for systematizing the Biblical
materials with the God-Man-Salvation (Theology-Anthropology-Soteriology) scheme borrowed from systematic (dogmatic) theology[106] have employed an *external* structure based

104. Among others Wright, *The Interpreter's One-Volume Commentary
on the Bible*, p. 984, stresses exclusively the "event-centered" nature of God's
revelation. But this is one-sided and must be complemented by a recognition
that much in the OT is at the same time "word-centered." Zimmerli, *VT*, 13
(1963), 108f., rightly emphasizes this aspect: "The single word of the prophet
contains not only a word of God, but is the Word of God" (p. 109). J. Barr,
Old and New in Interpretation (New York, 1966), pp. 15-23, discusses the
"word" and "act" (event) relationship in the OT, concluding that "the 'word'
emphasis might deserve to have priority" (p. 23). On this problem, see Hasel,
"The Problem of History in OT Theology," *AUSS*, 8 (1970), 32-35, 41-46, and
above, Chapter III.

105. P. Fannon, "A Theology of the OT—Is it Possible?" *Scripture*, 19
(1967), 52.

106. Among those who chose the systematic theology scheme in one
way or another are: Sellin, *Theologie des AT* (Leipzig, 1938; Köhler, *OT Theology* (1957); O. Baab, *The Theology of the OT* (Nashville, 1949); E. Jacob,
Theology of the OT (London, 1958); G. A. F. Knight, *A Christian Theology of
the OT* (London, 1959); P. van Imschoot, *Théologie de l'AT*, 2 vols. (Tournai,

upon categories of thought alien to Biblical theology. The approach to the Bible that searches for an *internal* key, one that grows out of the Biblical materials themselves, can alone be expected to be adequate and proper for a theology or theologies which is or are present in the Bible itself. Accordingly, the quest for the center of the OT (and the NT) which is based on the inner Biblical witnesses is not only justified but must be carried on with utmost vigor. Such single concepts, themes, ideas, or motifs as "covenant,"[107] "election,"[108] "communion,"[109] "promise,"[110] "the kingdom of God,"[111] "the rulership of God,"[112] "holiness" of God,[113] "experience" of God,[114] "God is Lord,"[115] and others have shown that they are too narrow a basis on which to construct an OT (or Biblical) theology which does not relegate essential aspects of the OT (or Biblical) faith to an inferior and unimportant position. Therefore, twin concepts in

---

1954-56) of which Vol. 1 is translated *Theology of the OT* (New York, 1965); J. B. Payne, *The Theology of the Older Testament* (Grand Rapids, 1962); R. C. Dentan, *The Knowledge of God in Ancient Israel* (New York, 1968).

107. So Eichrodt and following him Wright, *The OT and Theology*, p. 62; F. C. Prussner, "The Covenant of David and the Problem of Unity in OT Theology," in *Transitions in Biblical Scholarship*, ed. J. C. Rylaarsdam (Chicago, 1968), pp. 17-44, supplements the idea of the Sinai covenant as the center of OT theology with that of the Davidic covenant. The covenant's supreme position in the OT as a whole is argued from a structuralist perspective by P. Beauchamp, "Propositions sur l'alliance de l'AT, comme structure centrale," *RSR*, 58 (1970), 161-194. F. C. Fensham, "The Covenant as Giving Expression to the Relationship between OT and NT," *TynBul*, 22 (1971), 82-94, claims the covenant as the center that binds OT and NT together.

108. Wildberger, *EvT*, 19 (1959), 77f.

109. Vriezen, *An Outline of OT Theology*[2], p. 8 and ch. 4.

110. W. C. Kaiser, "The Centre of OT Theology: The Promise," *Themelios*, 10 (1974), 1-10; idem, "The Promise Theme and the Theology of Rest," *BibSac*, 130 (1973), 135-150. Kaiser fails to demonstrate that the "promise theme" is superior to other OT themes and overcomes any of the pitfalls associated with the choice of a single unifying concept.

111. So now Klein, *EvT*, 30 (1970), 642-670, and long before him H. Schultz, *OT Theology* (Edinburgh, 1892), I, 56.

112. Seebass, *WuD*, 8 (1965), 34-42.

113. J. Hänel, *Die Religion der Heiligkeit* (Gütersloh, 1931), p. iii, and Sellin, *Theologie des AT*, p. 19.

114. Baab, *Theology of the OT*, p. 22.

115. Köhler, *OT Theology*, p. 30.

the form of "the *rule* of God and the *communion* between God and man,"[116] "Yahweh the God of Israel, Israel the people of God,"[117] and covenant-kingdom[118] have been suggested, hoping that these broader conceptions give more room for the total OT (or Biblical) witness. Among these broadened suggestions are also the positions which hold that the entire book of Deuteronomy[119] or "creation faith"[120] provides the total horizon of OT (or Biblical) theology.

Our survey has indicated (1) that there two major positions on the issue of the "center" of the OT and (2) that the issue of the center involves such matters as (a) the unity of the OT, (b) the organizing principle for the writing of an OT theology, and (c) the affirmation that the OT has indeed a center but that it is "theological" and not organizational.[121] The first major position is that the OT does not have a center. As we have seen, this was argued most forcefully for the first time by Gerhard von Rad and has received support from various other scholars. P. Fannon follows von Rad and thus even questions the possibility of an OT theology.[122] Similarly, R. N. Whybray holds that in contrast to NT theology and Biblical theology "only in the case of Old Testament theology is there a problem of coherence, of a 'centre.'"[123] In the mind of

116. Fohrer, *TZ*, 24 (1968), 163.

117. Smend, *Die Mitte des AT*, pp. 49, 55.

118. R. Schnackenburg, *NT Theology Today* (New York, 1965).

119. Herrmann in *Probleme*, pp. 155ff.

120. H. H. Schmid, "Schöpfung, Gerechtigkeit und Heil, 'Schöpfungstheologie' als Gesamthorizont biblischer Theologe," *ZTK*, 70 (1973), 1-19, esp. p. 15: "Creation faith, namely faith that God has created and sustains the world in its manifold orders, is not a marginal theme of biblical theology, but its basic theme as such."

121. Jesper Høgenhaven, *Problems and Prospects of OT Theology* (The Biblical Seminar; Sheffield, 1988), pp. 38-44, speaks of a "historical" level for establishing a center as "a sort of common denominator for all the documents in the OT 'anthology' [which] can hardly be regarded a very meaningful enterprise in itself" (p. 44). Nevertheless, "theologically, the idea of a 'centre' of the OT may indeed have a certain justification" (ibid.).

122. P. Fannon, "A Theology of the OT—Is it Possible?" *Scriptorium*, 19/46 (1967), 46-53.

123. R. N. Whybray, "OT Theology—A Non-existent Beast?," in *Scrip-*

Whybray even the usage of the idea of God as a center in the sense of being the lowest or highest common denominator will be insufficient because "God was perceived very differently at different times and by different worshippers."[124]

The concern for the lack of a center is also most dominant in Claus Westermann. At the beginning of his book on OT theology he states, "The New Testament clearly has its center in the suffering, death, and resurrection of Christ, to which the Gospels are directed and which the Epistles take as their starting point. The Old Testament, however, bears no similarity at all to this structure, and it is thus not posssible to transfer the question of a theological center from the New to the Old Testament."[125] Westermann is in genuine disagreement with Whybray and others who see such a divergency in the various understandings of God in the OT that they rule out an OT theology. For Westermann, "It is the task of a theology of the Old Testament to describe and view together what the Old Testament as a whole, in all its sections, says about God."[126] D. L. Baker feels that "God may legitimately be considered the centre of the Old Testament in the sense that he is its origin and focus, though obviously not part of it."[127]

---

ture: Meaning and Method. Essays Presented to Anthony Tyrrell Hanson on His Seventieth Birthday, ed. Barry T. Thompson (Pickering, North Yorkshire, 1987), p. 169.

124. Ibid., p. 176.

125. Claus Westermann, Elements of OT Theology (Atlanta, 1982), p. 9. The German original Theologie des AT in Grundzügen (Göttingen, 1978), p. 5, reads, "Es ist daher unmöglich die Frage nach der Mitte vom Neuen Testament auf das Alte Testament zu übertragen." In the German there is no statement of a "theological center" as in the English translation. It is not entirely clear whether the adjective "theological" here comes from the translator or from Westermann himself. But Westermann's lectures on OT theology published in What Does the OT Say About God? (Atlanta, 1979), p. 12, contain the same sentence: "It is therefore not possible to translate the problem of the theological center from the New to the Old Testament."

126. Westermann, What Does the OT Say About God?, p. 11.

127. D. L. Baker, Two Testaments, One Bible (Downers Grove, IL, 1977), pp. 384-385. We should not overlook, however, that Baker does not follow a single center. He states, "There is indeed a unity in the Old Testament but it cannot be expressed by a single concept" (p. 386).

In the recent view of Werner H. Schmidt, who is concerned regarding the religio-historical approach toward the formulation of an OT theology and who wishes to refrain from using a "center" for the task of structuring such an enterprise, there is "a common denominator [in the search for unity] of the Old Testament in spite of its changing history and diverse literature, as well as that which binds it to the New Testament and even to the subsequent history of theology, [and that] is the first commandment."[128] Schmidt insists on the "exclusiveness" of Yahweh over against all other gods in the OT and the ancient Near East.[129] Zimmerli had already pointed out that one cannot overlook the "obvious inclination toward unity in OT pronouncements that, throughout history, never recognized a multiplicity of gods but only the *one* God."[130] Zimmerli states thetically, "The right and necessity to presuppose a 'center' of the OT arises out of the OT literature itself."[131] He provides a sustained argument why this is so and supports his earlier contention that the center is the name of Yahweh.[123]

A. H. J. Gunneweg questions what theological quality such an inner OT center would have in view of a Christian theological understanding, and thus his implied skepticism regarding a center of the OT.[133] But Zimmerli, Schmidt, and

128. Werner H. Schmidt, "The Problem of the 'Centre' of the OT in the Perspective of the Relationship Between History of Religion and Theology," in *OT Essays*, 4 (1986), 46-64, quote on p. 49, which is an enlargement of his "Die Frage der 'Mitte' des AT im Spannungsfeld der Religionsgeschichte und Theologie," in *Gott loben das ist unser Amt. Festschrift für D. J. Schmidt*, ed. K. Jürgensen et al. (Kiel, 1984), pp. 55-65.

129. Schmidt, "The Problem of the 'Centre,'" pp. 49-55.

130. W. Zimmerli, *Studien zur alttestamentlichen Theologie und Prophetie* (TBü, 51; Munich, 1974), p. 38.

131. W. Zimmerli, "Biblische Theologie I, Altes Testament," in *Theologische Realenzyklopädie*, ed. G. Krause and G. Müller (Berlin/New York, 1980), VI:445.

132. Ibid., pp. 445-455.

133. A. H. J. Gunneweg, *Vom Verstehen des AT: Eine Hermeneutik* (Göttingen, 1977), p. 79, trans. *Understanding the OT* (Philadelphia, 1978), p. 89; idem, "'Theologie' des AT oder 'Biblische Theologie,'" in *Textgemäss. Aufsätze und Beiträge zum AT. Festschrift für Ernst Würthwein zum 70. Geburtstag*, ed. A. H. J. Gunneweg and O. Kaiser (Göttingen, 1979), pp. 39-46.

others have adequately answered the reservations and hesitations of Gunneweg and those like him. For example, Horst Seebass sees Biblical theology as the way to the knowledge of God.[134] He maintains that there is one God for the whole Bible of the two Testaments. These and other scholars have responded to the various objections for a center of the OT. The OT has a center indeed. And it is a *theological* center, as we shall see, but not an organizational center on the basis of which the OT can be systematized.

Bruce Birch expressed himself on the issue of the center as an organizing principle and not a theological principle. He speaks of "multi-valent" approaches in the future as regards the structuring of an OT theology. "No single understanding of the mode of God's working (salvation history, von Rad) nor a single, central theme (covenant, Eichrodt) is capable of doing justice to the multi-faceted witness of the Old Testament. This does not mean that one should cease the effort to find meaningful ways of organizing and describing the various witnesses of Old Testament faith. It does mean that future, viable approaches to Old Testament theology are likely to be multi-valent, and will have to suggest ways of understanding the tensions and complementarities which exist between the different perspectives present in the pages of the Old Testament."[135]

Rolf Knierim suggests one such "multi-valent" approach in a programmatic essay on the task of OT theology.[136] It has had responses from several scholars.[137] Among the most pressing issues in this debate is Knierim's position that an OT theology is to be systematic in nature based on priorities which are

---

134. Horst Seebass, *Der Gott der ganzen Bibel. Biblische Theologie zur Orientierung im Glauben* (Freiburg/Basel/Vienna, 1982), pp. 212-218.

135. Bruce C. Birch, "OT Theology: Its Task and Future," *HBT,* 6/1 (1984), vi.

136. Rolf Knierim, "The Task of OT Theology," *HBT,* 6/1 (1984), 25-57.

137. In the same issue of *HBT,* see Walter Harrelson, "The Limited Task of OT Theology," pp. 59-64; Roland E. Murphy, "A Response to 'The Task of OT Theology,'" pp. 65-71; W. Sibley Towner, "Is OT Theology Equal to Its Task? A Response to a Paper by Rolf P. Knierim," pp. 73-80.

intrinsic to the OT itself. If it is to be systematic in nature, what principle, center, or theological priority is to be used? Knierim has proposed as his central organizing rubric, or what he calls the "ultimate vantage point" from which to view the plurality of theologies in the OT, "the universal dominion of Yahweh in justice and righteousness."[138] This principle of systematization is said to cut "across the three essential realms to which the Lord is related: the natural world, human corporate existence (including that of Israel), and individual human existence."[139]

W. Sibley Towner has pressed Knierim on his "ultimate vantage point" by asking, or actually suggesting, that "the universal dominion of Yahweh in justice and righteousness" may not be faithful in recognizing this as a vantage point which is claimed by Knierim to be "intrinsic" to the OT; it is actually relativized or conditioned by modern concerns and questions such as the ecological crisis, the feminist issue, and the like.[140] Towner suggests further that this "ultimate vantage point" would be quite legitimate, even though it may be subjective. Towner believes that it may be valid to bring in or to write from a subjective vantage point. Roland E. Murphy levels the charge against Knierim of introducing a "post-biblical" criterion for systematization, one borrowed from systematic theology, and "while the criterion . . . is derived from the Bible, its *use* is foreign to the Bible itself."[141] Murphy does not deny continuities in the OT, but insists, "A biblical theology that aspires to be systematic goes counter to the ongoing development within the Bible. The most one can do is to recognize what might be called systems or better, biblical categories of thought, which are in themselves diverse and were never conceived or recorded from the vantage point of sytematization."[142] Murphy concludes, "I would say that I

138. Knierim, "The Task of OT Theology," p. 43.
139. Murphy, "Response to 'The Task,'" p. 65.
140. Towner, "Is OT Theology Equal to Its Task?," pp. 75-79.
141. Murphy, "Response to 'The Task,'" p. 67.
142. Ibid., p. 69.

doubt if Rolf Knierim's program will work, or at least that I
do not think it is a tragedy if this or any other sytematization
of the Old Testament fails."[143]

Where does this debate on systematization of an OT theology take us? Knierim gives an extensive and spirited response to his critics.[144] This is not the place to recite the
variety of arguments used by Knierim. The largest area of his
rejoinder deals with the issue of systematization.[145] In contrast to Murphy and others he insists that the OT provides
examples of systematization, that the Tanakh in its three parts
of the OT canon provides some type of systematization and
hierarchy, and all of this invites us to follow what has been
started in the OT and those who put the OT together in its
canonical form. It seems that Knierim admits that the selection of his "vantage point" or his criterion may not be all-
inclusive. While he defends it over against the questions
raised, he still does not indicate why his choice is better, more
inclusive, or has higher value than other suggestions made by
different scholars.

In this connection it may be interesting to refer to another
suggestion made since Knierim's essays were written. Walter
Dietrich of the University of Berne published his inaugural
lecture, "The Red Thread in the OT."[146] His opening paragraph
sets out the problem: "The OT is not a book, but a library
which has not one but innumerable authors. It was not written
in one sitting, but over the course of a thousand years in
ever-new interpretations and expansions. It does not follow
one theme or one intention, but of both there are immense
numbers. Inevitably the question is raised concerning the
unity in diversity, for that which is maintained, which lasts—
even until today."[147] Dietrich argues that the category which

---

143. Ibid., p. 70.
144. Rolf Knierim, "On the Task of OT Theology," *HBT,* 6/2 (1984),
91-128.
145. Ibid., pp. 108-128.
146. Walter Dietrich, "Der rote Faden im AT," *EvT,* 49 (1989), 232-250.
147. Ibid., p. 232.

fulfills this criterion that goes through the whole OT as a red
thread and reaches to the present, thus forming its center, is
"righteousness."[148] He develops further what H. Seebass suggested in 1986.[149] He shows how extensively "righteousness"
manifests itself in all major types of OT literature.[150] Dietrich
agrees with Rudolf Smend that a "center" does not need to
encompass the entire OT.[151] It has the advantage to continue
throughout the NT and thus serves as a bridge between the
two Testaments.[152] "The entire Pauline doctrine of righteousness is prefigured in the OT, since Paul has developed
it from the OT, not against it [the OT], and not against the
Jews."[153]

This is an exciting concept, but it raises the question why
for Knierim the center is "righteousness and justice" but for
Dietrich only "righteousness." In contradistinction to Knierim
Dietrich does not make it into a category for the systematization of an OT theology. For Knierim this is the essential point.
The concept of righteousness is certainly a key theme of the
OT and beyond. But is it really the one center of the OT that
reaches beyond? Can one not immediately think of a number
of other centers that also reach beyond the OT?[154] The issue
is, Why should this one be elevated to a hierarchical status
above any of the other proposals? What warrant is there really
for it in the OT? What in the OT makes it evident on intrinsic
grounds that it is so? Few scholars will be satisfied to use the

148. Ibid., p. 232, where he entitles the first section " 'Gerechtigkeit' als
Mitte des AT."
149. H. Seebass, "Gerechtigkeit Gottes, Zum Dialog mit Peter
Stuhlmacher," in *Einheit und Vielfalt Biblischer Theologie*, ed. I. Baldermann
et al. *(Jahrbuch für Biblische Theologie*, 1; Neukirchen-Vluyn, 1986), pp.
115-134.
150. Ibid., pp. 237-246.
151. Ibid., p. 247 n. 70.
152. Ibid., pp. 248-249.
153. Ibid., p. 248, with reference to O. Hofius, " 'Rechtfertigung der
Gottlosen' als Thema biblischer Theologie," in *Jahrbuch für Biblische Theologie*, 2 (Neukirchen-Vluyn, 1987), pp. 95-105.
154. See, e.g., F. F. Bruce, *NT Development of OT Themes* (Grand Rapids,
1973).

statistical approach and count in the concordance how often a term is used and in what literature of the OT it appears. This is not to question the legitimacy of such an enterprise by itself. Nonetheless, all students of the OT know that a concept or theme can be spoken about without ever invoking its key term or terms. Sometimes it is made fairly clear that a particular center is selected for its alleged higher hierarchical status. In this case the selecting agent involves *Sachkritik* (content criticism) in some form or another. Since this is the case in some instances, the criteria for such content criticism may not be intrinsic to the OT at all. It may derive from other sources such as scholarly conventions, modern concerns, ecclesiastical interests, NT evaluations, community-of-faith decisions, and the like. This is not to deny that such concerns carry validity, but it needs to be stated forthrightly what criteria for selectivity are involved.

Can the various proposals and the richness of themes of the OT not be recognized for what they are, expressions of the OT that manifest in one respect or another the richness and multiplicity of ways in which God has communicated with humanity and Israel in all his relations with them? It is inevitable that one reflects on the conclusion of D. L. Baker's insightful study on the center of the OT: "There is indeed a unity in the Old Testament but it cannot be expressed by a single concept."[155] This may be the case because the unique God manifested in the OT cannot be grasped in any single way.

It is evident that the search and the suggestions made for the "center" of the OT have not created any consensus in the previous century and much less in this century, despite the variety of suggestions made. This debate has, however, led to at least two major insights. One is that such a rich variety of suggestions—which have gained in numbers in recent years regardless of whether these are single, dual, or multiple centers—that this smorgasbord of centers seems to demonstrate

155. Baker, *Two Testaments, One Bible,* p. 386.

its own inherent limitation. The centers as organizing or systematizing criteria are rooted in the OT *and* in the OT theologian's choice, but hardly in the former alone. Despite all efforts by its supporters, the case for any center intrinsic to the OT and based on that criteria alone still lacks the power to convince those who have made other suggestions for such a center. In our view the OT is so rich that it does not yield a center for the systematization or organization of an OT theology. The other insight is that there may be a center in the OT that functions as a unifying aspect despite its richness and variety, but it is not capable of being used as an organizing or systematizing principle or criterion for writing an OT theology. For convenience' sake this may be called a "theological" center.

It is highly significant that virtually all proposals for a center have God or an aspect of God and/or his activity for the world and humankind as a common denominator. This points inadvertently to the fact that the OT is *theo*centric,[156] as the NT is *christo*centric. In short, God/Yahweh is the dynamic, unifying center of the OT.[157]

156. J. Lindblom, *The Bible: A Modern Understanding* (Philadelphia, 1973), p. 168, states, "From the first page [of the Bible] to the last God stands in the center." He sees "theocentricity" as the "chief characteristic" of the Bible.

157. Among those who take God/Yahweh as the center of the OT are P. R. Ackroyd, *Continuity: A Contribution to the Study of the OT Religious Tradition* (Oxford, 1962), p. 31; F. Baumgärtel, "Gerhard von Rads Theologie des AT," *TLZ*, 86 (1961), 896; A. Deissler, *Die Grundbotschaft des AT* (Freiburg/Basel/Vienna, 1972), p. 153; idem, "Der Gott des AT," in *Die Frage nach Gott*, ed. J. Ratzinger (2nd ed.; Freiburg, 1973), pp. 45-58; E. Jacob, *Grundfragen alttestamentlicher Theologie* (Stuttgart, 1970), pp. 18-24; A. Jepsen, "Theologien des AT. Wandlungen der Formen und Ziele," in *Bericht von der Theologie*, ed. G. Kulicke et al. (Berlin, 1971), pp. 15-32, esp. 24-26; Abraham J. Heschel, *Man Is Not Alone* (New York, 1951), p. 129; Lindblom, *The Bible: A Modern Understanding*, p. 166; C. R. North, "OT Theology and the History of Hebrew Religion," *SJT*, 2 (1949), 122-23; K. H. Miskotte, *When the Gods Are Silent* (New York, 1967), pp. 193-194; Reventlow, *Problems of OT Theology*, pp. 131-133 with literature; H.-J. Stoebe, "Überlegungen zur Theologie des AT," in *Gottes Wort und Gottes Land. H.-W. Hertzberg zum 70. Geburtstag*, ed. H. Graf Reventlow (Göttingen, 1965), p. 208; S. Wagner, " 'Biblische Theologien' und 'Biblische Theologie,' " *TLZ*, 103 (1978), 794;

In affirming God as the dynamic, unifying center of the OT, one must be reminded that the OT (or the NT) does not speak of the existence, nature, and activity of God in an abstract manner.[158] Yet, "God is the beginning, center, and end of the Old Testament."[159] God's existence is not only assumed but proven in the manifoldness of his self-revelation. The manner of God's self-disclosure takes the form of the revelation of his nature in actions as they relate to the world and man. The OT speaks of God with regard to his deed and word as they relate to men and nations in creation,[160] nature, and history. God introduces and identifies himself by great events in deeds and words, and it is around them that Israel responds in praise and worship, and that Biblical literature originates. God is shown as the God of the world[161] and of Israel in that he bound himself to humankind and Israel in a special manner through election and covenant. But God has also bound himself in a special way to humankind, for man is created in the image of God, indicating among other things the token of man's intimate relation with his Maker.

At every juncture in the OT God shows himself as active. His activity has broad aspects and wide relations. Nevertheless a most fundamental OT claim for God is his saving activity.[162] Quantitatively God's saving activity for Israel is attested from the gracious redemption from Egyptian bondage through the time of the judges and kings and receiving new impetus in the salvation from Babylonian exile. But God's

---

E. Zenger, "Die Mitte der alttestamentlichen Glaubensgeschichte," *Katechetische Blätter*, 101 (1976), 3-16.

158. Fohrer, *TZ*, 24 (1968), 161.

159. Jacob, *Grundfragen alttestamentlicher Theologie*, p. 18.

160. Schmid, *ZTK*, 70 (1973), 1-19, seems to go too far in his claim that "creation" faith and theology is the "basic theme" of the OT as such. His contribution rests in the fact that he points to a painfully neglected aspect of the total witness and reality of the OT.

161. R. Knierim, "Offenbarung im AT," in *Probleme biblischer Theologie*, pp. 228f., shows that the experience of OT reality includes Yahweh's revelation in the world of nature which led to a recognition of Yahweh as the God of the world.

162. This is barely touched on by Zimmerli, *Grundriss der alttestamentlichen Theologie*, p. 19. Cf. Westermann, *EvT*, 30 (1974), 105f.

saving action is not restricted to Israel's national entity alone, because in the Psalms the salvation of the individual is predominant. The historical books make their own contribution to the notion of individual salvation. Furthermore, God's saving and redeeming activity is not restricted to Israel alone. God saved Noah from the destruction of the flood. The divine saving purpose reaches out to all nations and all men (Jonah; Isa. 40–66; Ezek.; etc.). The divine "I" appears again[163] with regard to the world and Israel, to believer *and* unbeliever, in both judgment *and* salvation, as the self-disclosure and revelation of the God who leads and guides men on their way in history toward a promising future. Yahweh promises his guiding presence.[164] Faith in God leads to right action in the present and to confidence in the future since it rests on trusting in the experience of God's power in the past. The profound testimonies of the OT witness to God's concern for man, to his words and deeds in Israel and among the nations, to the purpose of God in bridging the gulf between himself and fallen man, and to the restoration of communion and harmony between himself and man and between man and his fellow-man. So man is led constantly forward into the future. This history as the "way" of Yahweh[165] leads to an ever deepening and more complete knowledge of God and an increasing expectation of an as yet outstanding final revelation of God.

An OT theology which recognizes God as the dynamic unifying center is not forced into making this center a static organizing principle.[166] With God as the dynamic unifying

---

163. F. Baumgärtel, "Die Formel *ne'um jahwe,*" *ZAW,* 73 (1961), 277-290; H. W. Wolff, *Dodekapropheton-Amos* (Neukirchen-Vluyn, 1967), pp. 123f., 165f., 169f. The "I am"-formula by which God announced Himself is also of significance (cf. K. Koch, *The Growth of the Biblical Tradition* [New York, 1969], pp. 10, 21, 31). On the whole see the valuable summary by H. D. Preuss, *Jahweglaube und Zukunftserwartung* (Stuttgart, 1968), pp. 19ff.

164. See here the motif of the presence of God as it comes to expression in the phrase ". . . I will be with you." Cf. H. D. Preuss, ". . . ich will mit dir sein!" *ZAW,* 80 (1968), 139-173.

165. Preuss, *Jahweglaube und Zukunftserwartung,* pp. 71-108.

166. G. F. Hasel, "The Problem of the Center in the OT Theology Debate," *ZAW,* 86 (1974), 65-82.

center, the OT allows the Biblical writings or blocks of writings to speak for themselves in that their individual theologies are allowed to emerge. Wisdom theology, creation theology, and others are not forced to fit into a unilinear and limiting center, concept, theme, or motif at the expense of relegating large portions to an inferior status or to neglect them altogether.

An OT theology which recognizes God as the dynamic, unifying center provides the possibility to describe the rich and variegated theologies and to present the various longitudinal themes, motifs, and ideas. In affirming God as the dynamic, unifying center of the OT we also affirm that this center cannot be forced into a static organizing principle on the basis of which an OT theology can be structured. Although this affirmation means that we have anticipated what we later describe as the emergence of the "hidden inner unity,"[167] we must allow the individual Biblical writings or blocks of writings to present their own theologies. Accordingly, wisdom theology, creation theology, etc. are permitted to take their rightful place and are not relegated to an inferior status or completely left out of consideration.

The question of the center of the OT touches most basically on the nature of the unity and continuity of the OT. With the recognition that God is the dynamic, unifying center of the OT one can speak of the unity and continuity of the OT in its most fundamental sense. Unity and continuity has its source in God, in the manifoldness of His self-revelation in acts and words. The OT shows itself at the same time as an "open book" which points beyond itself. The NT also witnesses to the centrality of God and His judging *and* saving work for Israel and the world. As these common aspects of both Testaments come into focus we must break off. The next chapter discusses major aspects of the relationship between the OT and NT in the current debate.

---

167. Below, Chapter VI, §6.

V. The Relationship between the Testaments

For every Christian theologian OT theology is and must remain a part of Biblical theology. Separate treatments of the theology of the OT and NT were produced ever since the year 1797 when the first *Theologie des Alten Testaments* was published by Georg Lorenz Bauer. We are reminded anew by G. Ebeling that the Biblical theologian has to study the interconnection between the Testaments and "has to give an account of his understanding of the Bible as a whole, i.e. above all of the theological problems that come of inquiring into the inner unity of the manifold testimony of the Bible."[1] This raises the questions of continuity and discontinuity, of whether one reads uniquely from the OT to the NT or from the NT back into the OT, or reciprocally from the OT to the NT and the NT to the OT. Basic to the whole question is not merely an articulation of the theological problem of the interrelatedness between the two Testaments but also an inquiry into the nature of this unity and disunity, whether it is one of language, thought-forms, or content. It is not necessary at this point to present a comprehensive sketch of the positions scholars take currently on these problems.[2] We may limit

1. *Word and Faith*, p. 96.
2. The following studies are especially concerned with this problem: A. A. van Ruler, *The Christian Church and the OT*, trans. G. W. Bromiley (Grand Rapids, 1971); S. Amsler, *L'AT dans l'église* (Neuchâtel, 1960); J. D. Smart, *The Interpretation of Scripture* (Philadelphia, 1961); P. Grelot, *Sens*

ourselves to significant recent attempts which mirror the major positions.

Some scholars have posited the problem of the relationship between the Testaments by designating the OT in fact as a book of a non-Christian religion. It is the merit of Rudolf Bultmann to seek the connection between the Testaments in the factual course of Israel's history.[3] But Bultmann determines this connection in such a way that OT history is a history of failure. The application of the Lutheran law/gospel distinction[4] and a modern type of Christomonism[5] leads him to view the OT as a "miscarriage [*Scheitern*] of history" which only through this failure turns into a kind of promise.[6] "To the Christian faith the Old Testament is no longer revelation as it has been, and still is, for the Jews." To the Christian "the history of Israel is not history of revelation."[7] "Thus the Old Testament is the presupposition of the New"[8] and nothing more nor anything less. Bultmann argues for the complete theological discontinuity between the OT and NT. The rela-

---

chrétien de l'AT (Tournai, 1962); OTCF; C. Westermann, The OT and Jesus Christ (Minneapolis, 1970); R. E. Murphy, "The Relationship Between the Testaments," CBQ, 26 (1964), 349-359; idem, "Christian Understanding of the OT," Theology Digest, 18 (1970), 321f.; F. Hesse, Das AT als Buch der Kirche (Gütersloh, 1966); K. Schwarzwäller, Das AT in Christus (Zürich, 1966); idem, "Das Verhältnis AT-NT im Lichte der gegenwärtigen Bestimmungen," EvT, 29 (1969), 281-307; P. Benoit and R. E. Murphy, eds., How Does the Christian Confront the OT? (New York, 1967); A. H. J. Gunneweg, "Über die Prädika-bilität alttestamentlicher Texte," ZTK, 65 (1968), 389-413; N. Lohfink, The Christian Meaning of the OT (Milwaukee, 1968); H.-D. Preuss, "Das AT in der Verkündigung der Kirche," Deutsches Pfarrerblatt, 63 (1968), 73-79; Kraus, Biblische Theologie, pp. 193-305. Additional bibliography can be derived from all these studies.

3. Cf. Bultmann, in EOTH, pp. 50-75, and in OTCF, pp. 8-35.

4. OTCF, pp. 22-30.

5. On this the critique of Wright, The OT and Theology, pp. 30-38, is especially relevant.

6. Bultmann, EOTH, p. 73: ". . . the miscarriage of history actually amounts to a promise." See on this Barr, Old and New in Interpretation, pp. 162f.; "The OT and the New Crisis of Biblical Authority," Interp, 25 (1971), 30-32.

7. Bultmann, EOTH, p. 31.

8. OTCF, p. 14.

tionship between the two Testaments "is not theologically relevant at all."[9] Nonetheless this history has according to him a promissory character precisely because in the failure of the hopes centered around the covenant concept, in the failure of the rule of God and his people, it becomes clear that "the situation of the justified man arises only on the basis of this miscarriage [*Scheitern*]."[10] In answer to this position, Walther Zimmerli has rightly asked whether for the NT "the hopes and history of Israel are really only shattered." "Is there not fulfillment here, even in the midst of the shattering?" He recognizes clearly that the concept of failure or shattering becomes the means by which Bultmann is able "to elevate the Christ-message purely out of history in existential interpretation. . . ." Zimmerli suggests not without reason that the concept of a pure brokenness of Israel's history must of necessity lead to an unhistorical conception of the Christ-event, namely a "new Christ-myth."[11] He points out that an aspect of shattering is present even in the OT, where the prophets themselves bear witness to the freedom of Yahweh to "legitimately interpret his promise through his fulfillment, and the interpretation [by Yahweh] can be full of surprises even for the prophet himself."[12] W. Pannenberg notes that the reason Bultmann finds no continuity between the Testaments "is certainly connected with the fact that he does not begin with the promises and their structure which for Israel were the foundation of history, . . . promises which thus endure precisely in change."[13]

The conviction of Friedrich Baumgärtel shares with Bultmann the emphasis of the discontinuity between the Testaments.[14] But Baumgärtel is not able to follow Bultmann's thesis

---

9. P. 13. Cf. Westermann's critique in *EOTH*, pp. 124-128.

10. Bultmann, *EOTH*, p. 75.

11. "Promise and Fulfillment," *EOTH*, pp. 118-120.

12. P. 107.

13. Pannenberg, "Redemptive Event and History," *EOTH*, pp. 325f.

14. F. Baumgärtel, *Verheissung. Zur Frage des evangelischen Verständnisses des AT* (Gütersloh, 1952), p. 92.

of a total failure. He assumes an enduring "basic-promise [*Grundverheissung*]."[15] All the OT promises *(promissiones)* "really have no relevance for us"[16] except the timeless basic-promise *(promissum)* "I am the Lord your God."[17] He completely abandons the proof from prophecy as unacceptable to our historical consciousness. Beyond this Baumgärtel sees the meaning of the OT only in that its frustrated "salvation-disaster history" exemplifies the way of man under law. As such the OT contains a "witness of a religion outside the Gospel."[18] "Viewed historically it has another place than the Christian religion,"[19] for the OT "is a witness out of a non-Christian religion."[20] Here Baumgärtel comes close to the position of Bultmann in relating the Testaments to each other in terms of the Lutheran law/gospel dichotomy. Baumgärtel, therefore, maintains that the historicity of Jesus Christ is not grounded in the OT but solely in the Incarnation.[21] One comes to recognize how in such an approach "the historicity of Jesus Christ falls when the history of Israel falls."[22] C. Westermann points out that Baumgärtel ultimately admits "that the church could also live without the Old Testament."[23] Von Rad attacks the unhistorical concept of "basic-promise" by characterizing the separation of such a single promise from particular historically realized promises and prophecies as a "presumptuous encroachment."[24]

Baumgärtel's former student Franz Hesse makes the same basic reduction of the manifold promises to the single basic-

---

15. F. Baumgärtel, "The Hermeneutical Problem of the OT," *EOTH*, p. 151.

16. P. 132.

17. P. 151.

18. P. 156.

19. P. 135; cf. *TLZ*, 806.

20. *EOTH*, p. 145.

21. P. 156.

22. Pannenberg, *EOTH*, p. 326.

23. "Remarks on the theses of Bultmann and Baumgärtel," *EOTH*, p. 133.

24. "Verheissung," *EvT*, 13 (1953), 410. See also the incisive criticism against Baumgärtel by Gunneweg, *ZTK*, 65 (1968), 398-400.

promise.[25] In the OT the promises failed. This is due to the
chastening hand of God that made Israel harden their hearts.
By turning God's word into its opposite, it is a warning and
a dialectical witness to God's activity in Israel which culmi-
nates in Christ's cross.[26] Hesse pronounces the sharpest theological strictures on the OT on the ground that certain historical data supposedly do not fit the facts.[27] Therefore the
OT can have meaning for the Christian only in pointing him
toward the salvation which is found in the NT.[28] The criticisms against Baumgärtel apply also to Hesse. It will not do,
as it happened again and again in the case of F. D. E. Schleiermacher[29] and still happens with Baumgärtel[30] and Hesse,[31] to
discuss the NT arguments of fulfillment of prophecy as nothing but an anti-Jewish apologetic, relevant only to the NT
period.[32] It is a mistake to believe, as Bultmann does, that the
meaning of the "proof from Scripture" has as its purpose to
"prove" what can only be grasped by faith, or to approach and
criticize the NT's method of quotation from the point of view
of modern literary criticism.[33] Over against this limited position one must maintain that the NT quotations presuppose
the unity of tradition and indicate keywords and major motifs
and concepts in order to recall a larger context within the OT.

In direct contrast to the position just described are those
attempts that place primary emphasis on the OT by making
it all-important theologically. Wilhelm Vischer wants the exegesis of the OT to be dominated by the NT, thereby making
the OT all-important.[34] "Strictly speaking only the Old Testa-

25. *Das AT als Buch der Kirche*, p. 82.
26. "The Evaluation and Authority of the OT Texts," in *EOTH*, pp.
308-313.
27. Pp. 293-299.
28. P. 313.
29. *The Christian Faith* (2 vols.; New York, 1963).
30. *Verheissung*, p. 75ff.
31. *Das AT als Buch der Kirche*, pp. 82ff.
32. Pannenberg, *EOTH*, p. 324.
33. Bultmann, *EOTH*, pp. 50-55, 72-75.
34. *Das Christuszeugnis des AT. Das Gesetz* (7th ed.; Zollikon, 1946);
trans. *The Witness of the OT to Christ* (London, 1949).

ment is 'The Scripture,' while the New Testament brings the good news that now the meaning of these writings, the import of all their words, their Lord and fulfiller, has appeared incarnate."[35] In very similar terms A. A. van Ruler explains that "the Old Testament is and remains the true Bible."[36] The NT is but "its explanatory glossary [Wörterverzeichnis]."[37] In strict dialectic "The New Testament interprets the Old Testament as well as the Old the New."[38] The central concern in the whole Bible is not reconciliation and redemption but the kingdom of God. For this the OT is of special importance, namely it brings its legitimization, foundation, interpretation, illustration, historicization, and eschatologization.[39] Van Ruler thereby reduces the relationship between the Testaments to the single spiritual denominator of the kingdom of God, reading the NT very one-sidedly without recognizing the distinction between theocracy and eschatology.[40]

Klaus Schwarzwäller's position should be briefly mentioned here. His thesis is that the OT relates to the NT in terms of the formula of "course of proof and result."[41] The OT can be understood only from Christ because it points forward to him. "The Christ event presupposes the history of the old covenant and points back into its testimonies."[42] His position has so far found little response.

On the whole it must be said that the Christological-theocratic approaches to the unity of the Testaments pose special difficulties because they telescope and virtually eliminate the varieties of the Biblical testimonies. They suffer from a reductionism of the multiplicity of OT thought, which

35. *Witness*, pp. 7-8. Cf. Schwarzwäller, *EvT*, 29 (1969), 281-285, for a sympathetic evaluation of Vischer's importance in contemporary theology.

36. Van Ruler, *The Christian Church and the OT*, p. 72.

37. P. 74 n. 45.

38. P. 82.

39. Pp. 75-98.

40. A very incisive critique of van Ruler's position has been given by Th. C. Vriezen, "Theocracy and Soteriology," *EOTH*, pp. 221-223.

41. *Das AT in Christus*, pp. 51-56.

42. *EvT*, 29 (1969), 305.

merely becomes a pale reflection of the Messiah to come. Here the somewhat shrill cry of "Christomonism"[43] has a point. With G. E. Wright, J. Barr, and R. E. Murphy[44] it seems that the lines of a Trinitarian approach better meet the needs of delineating the relationship between the Testaments. This approach preserves the *sensus litteralis* of the OT testimony and avoids the development of a hermeneutical method based merely on the NT usage of OT texts. Once the true meaning of Christ is grasped within the context of the Trinity, then one can say that Christ is the destination and at the same time the guide to the true understanding of the OT. W. Vischer once posed the question that remains crucial: "Is the interpretation which sees in the whole of the Old Testament a testimony to Jesus the Messiah correct, or is it a violent distortion of the Old Testament scriptures?"[45]

A recent major approach to delineate the relationship between the Testaments is by reverting to typology. W. Eichrodt[46] and G. von Rad[47] have been staunch supporters. Eichrodt uses

43. Wright, *The OT and Theology,* pp. 13-38. He protests against resolving the tension between the OT and NT in terms of a "new kind of monotheism based on Christ" ("Historical Knowledge and Revelation," in *Understanding and Translating the OT,* p. 302).

44. Wright, *Understanding and Translating the OT,* pp. 301-303; Barr, *Old and New in Interpretation,* pp. 151-154; Murphy, *Theology Digest* (1970), 327.

45. *Witness,* p. 27. Of course, Vischer gives an affirmative answer to the question. He designates Jesus as the "hidden meaning of the Old Testament scripture" (p. 28). In his book *Die Bedeutung des AT für das christliche Leben* (Zürich, 1947), p. 5, he writes: "All movements of life of which the OT reports move from him [Jesus] and towards him. The life-stories of all these men are part of his life-story. Therefore they are written with so little biographical interest for the individual persons. What is written about them is actually written as a part of the biography of the One through whom and towards whom they live." This would mean that we can reconstruct a biography of Jesus from the OT. If Vischer's position were correct it is difficult to perceive why the OT speaks in the first place about Abraham and Moses. Why does it not speak right away about Jesus, and why does it speak of him only in such "hidden" form?

46. "Is Typological Exegesis an Appropriate Method?," in *EOTH,* pp. 224-245.

47. "Typological Interpretation of the OT," in *EOTH,* pp. 17-39; *OTT,* II, 364-374.

typology "as the designation for a peculiar way of looking at history." The types "are persons, institutions, and events of the Old Testament which are regarded as divinely established models or prerepresentations of corresponding realities in the New Testament salvation history."[48] His exposition appears to agree with the traditional views of earlier Christianity. But he differs from the views of von Rad, whose basic premise it is that "The Old Testament is a history book."[49] It is the history of God's people, and the institutions and prophecies within it, that provide prototypes to the antitypes of the NT within the whole realm of history and eschatology.[50] Von Rad is very broadly based, as can be gathered from his relating Joseph to Christ as type to antitype.[51]

Some scholars reject the typological approach completely.[52] However, the importance of the typological approach is not to be denied, if it is not developed into a hermeneutic method which is applied to all texts like a divining-rod. Typological correspondence must be rigidly controlled on the basis of direct relationship between various OT elements and their NT counterparts in order that arbitrary and fortuitous personal views may not creep into exegesis.[53] One should be cautious enough not to be trapped into applying typology as *the* single definite theological ground-plan whereby the unity of the

48. *EOTH*, p. 225.
49. *EOTH*, p. 25; cf. *OTT*, II, 357.
50. *OTT*, II, 365.
51. *OTT*, II, 372.
52. F. Baumgärtel, *TLZ*, 86 (1961), 809, 897, 901-906. R. Lucas, "Considerations of Method in OT Hermeneutics," *The Dunwoodie Review*, 6 (1966), 35: "Typology lacks that criterion which would establish both its limitation and validity. . . . It is a theology of biblical texts. It leaves the Old Testament behind, in the last analysis, and discovers its significance outside and beyond its historical testimony." Murphy, *Theology Digest*, 18 (1970), 324, believes that typology is not creative enough for the possibilities of theology and in comparison to the early Church "it is simply less appealing to the modern temper." See also Barr, *Old and New in Interpretation*, pp. 103-148, who is not willing to separate typology from allegory.
53. See also, with regard to a proper usage of typology, the remarks by H. W. Wolff, "The Hermeneutics of the OT," in *EOTH*, pp. 181-186; and Vriezen, *An Outline of OT Theology²*, pp. 97, 136f.

Testaments is established. The advocacy of typological unity
between the Testaments is not primarily concerned to find a
unity of historical facts between the OT prefiguration and its
NT counterpart,[54] though this is not to be denied altogether;
it is more concerned to recognize the connection in terms of
a structural similarity between type and antitype. It is undeniable that the typological analogy begins with a relationship
which takes place in history. For example, the typological
analogy between Moses and Christ in 2 Cor. 3:7ff. and Heb.
3:1-6 begins with a relationship that takes place in history;
but the concern is not with all the details of the life and service
of Moses, but primarily with his "ministry" and "glory" in the
former passage and with his "faithfulness" as leader and mediator in the divine dispensation in the second passage. It is
equally true that the NT antitype goes beyond the OT type.[55]
Even if it is correct, at least to some degree, that the course
of history which unites type and antitype emphasizes the
distinction between them, while the connection is primarily
discovered in its structural analogy and correspondence, this
should not be used as an argument against typology unless
typology is seen only in terms of a historical process.[56] The
conceptual means of the typological correspondence has its

54. Von Rad, however, *EOTH*, pp. 17-19, advocates that the typological
approach seeks to "regain reference to the facts attested in the New Testament," i.e., to discover the connection in the historical process.

55. Eichrodt, *EOTH*, pp. 225f.

56. This is where Pannenberg, *EOTH*, p. 327, goes astray. For him the
only analogy that has any value is the historical one. Pannenberg adopts the
"promise and fulfillment" schema without realizing that this "structure"
(p. 325), as he repeatedly calls it, functons in his own presentation as another
instance of a timeless principle being employed to replace history. Pannenberg
emphasizes that freeness, creativeness, and unpredictability are central in
history, but he finds this central aspect of history preserved only in that the
fulfillment often involves the "breaking down" of the prophecy as a "legitimate interpretation," a "transformation of the content of prophecy," which is
"fulfilled otherwise" than the original recipients of the prophetic word expected (p. 326). Here Pannenberg has unconsciously conceded the incompati-
bility between history and its structure. Thus even in Pannenberg's position,
structure and construction tend to replace history and render his use of the
promise-fulfillment structure unhistorical.

distinct place in its expression of the qualification of the Christ-event, but it is in itself not able to express fully the Christ-event in terms of OT history. Therefore additional approaches will need to complement the typological one. The Bible is too rich in relations between God and man for it to be confined to one special connection. Whereas we must not hesitate to accept typological references in definite cases, every attempt to view the whole from a single point of view must beware of wishing to explain every detail in terms of this one aspect and to impose an overall picture upon the variety of possible relations. While the OT context must be preserved in its prefiguration so that NT meanings are not read into the OT texts, it seems that a clear NT indication is necessary so that subjective imaginative fancies and arbitrary typological analogies can be avoided. That is to say that the question of the *a posteriori* character of the typological approach should not be suppressed.

A prominent approach for coming to grips with the extremely complex question of the relationship between the OT and the NT is by way of the promise-fulfillment schema, as developed by C. Westermann, W. Zimmerli, G. von Rad, and others.[57] This approach maintains that the OT contains a "history of promise which comes to fruition in the NT."[58] This does *not* mean that the OT describes what was promised and the NT what has been fulfilled.[59] The OT already knows promise and fulfillment. W. Zimmerli makes the point that the promise,

57. C. Westermann, "The Way of Promise through the OT," in *OTCF,* pp. 200-224; idem, *The OT and Jesus Christ* (Minneapolis, 1970); W. Zimmerli, "Promise and Fulfillment," in *EOTH,* pp. 89-122; G. von Rad, "Verheissung," *EvT,* 13 (1953), 406-413; R. E. Murphy, "The Relationship Between the Testaments," *CBQ,* 26 (1964), 349-359; idem, "Christian Understanding of the OT," *Theology Digest,* 18 (1970), 321-332.

58. Murphy, *Theology Digest,* 18 (1970), 328.

59. This is obviously the way in which Fohrer, *TZ,* 24 (1968), 171f., understands the category of promise-fulfillment. If this mistake is avoided, then there is no conflict between the promise-fulfillment category and Fohrer's beginning-continuation category. Both formulae essentially agree but place emphasis on slightly different aspects.

when it receives the character of fulfillment in history through Yahweh's guidance and word, receives again a new character of promise.[60] In this way the fulfillment has an open end, looking on to the future.[61] This eschatological aspect is present in both Testaments. Westermann remarks: "Promise and fulfillment constitute an integral event which is reported in both the Old and New Testaments of the Bible." In view of the multiplex character of the relationship between the Testaments, Westermann admits that under the single idea of promise-fulfillment "it is not possible to sum up everything in the relation of the Old Testament to Christ."[62] On a more comprehensive scale, we must admit that the promise-fulfillment schema does not sum up everything in the relation between the Testaments. As fundamental and fruitful as the promise-fulfillment approach is, it is not by itself able to describe the multiplex nature of the relationship between the Testaments.

If we raise the question how the OT can be related adequately and properly to the NT, then we have admittedly decided on an *a priori* basis that both are related to each other in some way. We must be conscious of this decision, which always has a bearing on our questioning of the OT materials. This prior decision does not come easily. This is true especially when the OT is viewed in the way in which von Rad looks at it, namely that "the Old Testament can only be read as a book of ever increasing anticipation."[63] This claim presupposes a particular understanding of the OT history of tradition, i.e., one which is from the beginning focusing upon the transition to the NT. Von Rad's view finds its justification only in terms of a direct line of connection that moves from the testimony of the initial action of God toward

60. "Promise and Fulfillment," *EOTH*, p. 112.

61. This tension between promise and fulfillment is a dynamic characteristic of the OT. Since this is a basic kind of interpreted history which the OT and NT themselves present to us, J. M. Robinson's attempt (*OTCF*, p. 129) to dismiss the category of promise-fulfillment as a structure imposed on Biblical history from without is abortive.

62. *The OT and Jesus Christ*, p. 78.

63. *TAT*, II, 331; *OTT*, II, 319.

judgment and on to the expectation of God's renewed action in which God yet proves his divine character. It is amazing to see how Israel never allowed a promise to come to nothing, how she thus swelled Yahweh's promise to an infinity, and how, placing absolutely no limit on God's power yet to fulfill, she transmitted the promises still unfulfilled to generations to come. Thus we must ask with von Rad, "does not the way in which comparative religion takes hold of the Old Testament in abstraction, as an object which can be adequately interpreted without reference to the New Testament, turn out to be fictitious from the Christian point of view?"[64] On the other hand, there is nothing mysterious about coming to grips with the question of the relationship between the Testaments. Initially, therefore, we do not begin from the NT and its manifold references to the OT. This method has often been adopted, most recently again by B. S. Childs, as we have noted above. It has also led all too often to contrasting the Testaments with a sharpness that does not do justice to the great hermeneutical flexibility of the relationship between them. A proper method will then initially be an attempt to show characteristic ways in which the OT leads forward to the NT. The NT can then on the basis of this initial approach also enlighten the content of the OT.

In view of these considerations, it would seem that the only adequate way to come to grips with the multiplex nature of the relationship between the Testaments is to opt for a multiplex approach, which makes a guarded and circumspect use of typology, employs the idea of promise-fulfillment, and also uses in a careful way the approach of *Heilsgeschichte*.[65] Such a multiplex approach leaves room for indicating the variety

64. *TAT*, II, 333; *OTT*, II, 321.
65. We cannot go into the manifold ramifications of the salvation history approach, its weak and strong points as well as its varied use among past and present theologians. Yet this approach should not be dismissed too easily. For a recent exposition of this approach, see O. Cullmann, *Salvation in History* (New York, 1967). A critique is given by D. Braun, "Heil als Geschichte," *EvT*, 27 (1967), 57-76. See also the appreciative evaluation of this approach by Kraus, *Biblische Theologie*, pp. 185-187.

of connections between the Testaments and avoids, at the same time, the temptation to explain the manifold testimonies in every detail by one single point of view or approach and so to impose a single structure upon testimonies that witness to something else. A multiplex approach will lead to a recognition of similarity and dissimilarity, old and new, continuity and discontinuity, etc., without in the least distorting the original historical witness and literal sense nor falling short in the larger kerygmatic intention and context to which the OT itself testifies.

It is not surprising that in the recent debate about the complex nature of the relationship between the Testaments the question of the proper context has become crucial. Von Rad himself speaks of "the larger context to which a specific Old Testament phenomenon belongs. . . ."[66] He reflects the concern of H. W. Wolff, who maintains that "in the New Testament is found the context of the Old, which, as its historical goal, reveals the total meaning of the Old Testament. . . ."[67] The systematic theologian Hermann Diem expresses himself to the extent that "for the modern interpretation of Scripture it can be no question needing judgment whether the interpretation will follow the apostolic witness and read the OT with their eyes or whether it will read presuppositionless, which would mean to read it as a phenomenon of general history of religion. . . ."[68] In a similar vein Kurt Frör maintains that "the canon forms the given and compulsory context for all single texts and single books of both Testaments."[69] The idea of "context" should not be limited to the nearest relationship of a pericope, not even to the connection within a book or historical work. With regard to the larger connections the canon as a given fact receives hermeneutic relevance. "The first step on the path of the continuation of the self-interpreta-

66. *OTT,* II, 369.
67. *EOTH,* p. 181.
68. H. Diem, *Theologie als kirchliche Wissenschaft* (Gütersloh, 1951), I, 75; cf. his *Was heisst schriftgemäss?* (Gütersloh, 1958), pp. 38f.
69. *Biblische Hermeneutik* (3rd ed.; Munich, 1967), p. 65.

tion of the text is to give ear to the remaining Scriptural witnesses."[70] Hans-Joachim Kraus has sensed what Eichrodt meant when the latter emphasized that "only where this two-way relationship between the Old and New Testaments is understood do we find a correct definition of the problem of OT theology and of the method by which it is possible to solve it."[71] As regards Kraus, his assessment of the matter of the context shows that "the question of the *context* is decisive for the connection of texts and themes. This means for the OT undertaking of Biblical-theological exegesis: How do the Old and New Testaments refer to certain kerygmatic intentions apparent in a text?"[72]

In this connection it is of great importance to explicate what it means that OT theology—and also NT theology—is bound to the given connections of the texts in the canon. Alfred Jepsen writes "that the interpretation of the Old Testament, being the interpretation of the church's canon, is determined by its connection with the New Testament and by the questions that follow from it."[73] If properly conceived, no violence is done to the message of the OT, for what the interpreter receives from the side of the NT is primarily the question, the point of view. To have the right question means to be able to find the right answers. This approach is not a return to a new type of Biblicism. Rather we need to emphasize strongly that Biblical events and meanings must not be looked for behind, beneath, or above the texts,[74] but *in* the texts, because the divine deeds and words have received form and found expression in them. Biblical-theological interpretation attempts to study a passage within its own original historical context,

70. Diem, *Was heisst schriftgemäss?*, p. 38.
71. Eichrodt, *TOT,* I, 26.
72. Kraus, *Biblische Theologie*, p. 381.
73. "The Scientific Study of the OT," in *EOTH*, p. 265.
74. This is the way in which Hesse, *KuD*, 4 (1958), 13, seeks to secure a reality that he feels is not there. F. Mildenberger, *Gottes Tat im Wort* (Gütersloh, 1964), pp. 93ff., argues for the unity of the canon as a rule of understanding but revives a new kind of pneumatic exegesis.

the *Sitz im Leben* of the situation into which a word was spoken or an action took place, and also the life-settings and contextual relations and connections in the later traditions as well as the *Sitz im Leben* in the given context of the book in which it is preserved and the larger kerygmatic intention. In all of this the given context of the two Testaments has a bearing on interpretation.[75] Thus the matter of the given context in the nearest and more removed relationships within both Testaments will always have a decisive bearing for Biblical-theological interpretation and for the Biblical theologian's task of doing OT theology.[76]

There are several major trends in the discussion of the relationship between the Testaments. The tendency toward Marcionism with its low estimate of the OT is present in full-fledged form in A. Harnack who called for the dismissal of the OT, and in Friedrich Delitzsch for whom the OT was an unchristian book.[77] An attenuated Marcionist strain is manifested by E. Hirsch for whom the Testaments stand in "antithetical tension" to each other,[78] and to a lesser extent

75. Childs, *Biblical Theology in Crisis*, pp. 99ff., has developed the relevance of the "larger canonical context" as the appropriate horizon for Biblical theology and applied it to his own methodological approach.

76. Despite von Rad's emphasis on a charismatic-kerygmatic interpretation, his approach goes along the lines of *Heilsgeschichte*. Von Rad's emphasis on typology (*OTT*, II, 323ff.) presupposes a wider salvation-historical framework and connects two points on this background, as is true of the current revival of typological interpretation. On the relationship between typology and salvation history see Cullmann, *Salvation in History*, pp. 132-135. G. Fohrer's negative reaction against the notion of salvation history ("Prophetie und Geschichte," *TLZ*, 89 [1964], 481ff.) comes on the basis that both salvation and doom are part of salvation history. To a great extent the history of salvation is a history of disaster. Yet even here the continuity is preserved in that later the proclamation of salvation is taken up without the preaching of the message of judgment disappearing. Fohrer's thesis, that the aim of God's action is the rule of God over the world and nature, is not opposed to salvation history but a characteristic part of it.

77. A. Harnack, *Marcion: Das Evangelium vom fremden Gott* (Leipzig, 1924; 2nd ed.; Darmstadt, 1960); F. Delitzsch, *Die grosse Täuschung*, 2 vols. (Stuttgart, 1920-21).

78. E. Hirsch, *Das AT und die Predigt des Evangeliums* (Tübingen, 1936), pp. 27, 59, 83.

by Bultmann, Baumgärtel, and Hesse.[79] The opposite extreme makes the OT all-important historically and theologically for the Christian. It appears in a variety of forms in van Ruler, Miskotte, and Vischer.[80] In other words, on one side of the spectrum are those who stress diversity between the Testaments to such a degree that there is total disunity and complete discontinuity between OT and NT, while on the other side are those who emphasize unity without any room for diversity whatsoever. There is, however, a degree of diversity between the Testaments which must not be denied. The truth of the matter seems to be that there is unity in diversity.[81]

Among most recent discussions divergent emphases continue to appear on the question of the relationship between

79. The following studies criticize this position from rather different perspectives: U. Mauser, *Gottesbild und Menschwerdung. Eine Untersuchung zur Einheit des Alten und Neuen Testaments* (Tübingen, 1971); G. Siegwalt, *La Loi, chemin du Salut. Étude sur la signification de la loi de l'AT* (Neuchâtel, 1971); W. Zimmerli, *The OT and the World* (Atlanta, 1976); J. D. Smart, *The Strange Silence of the Bible in the Church* (London, 1970); J. Bright, *The Authority of the OT* (Nashville, 1967), pp. 58-79.

80. K. H. Miskotte, *When the Gods Are Silent* (London, 1967); W. Vischer, *The Witness of the OT to Christ* (London, 1949).

81. In addition to the studies by Amsler, Grelot, Smart, Westermann, Murphy, Schwarzwäller, Lohfink, Preuss, Kraus, Mauser, Siegwalt, Zimmerli, and Bright mentioned in footnotes 2 and 79 of this chapter, the following recent items are of special significance: A. J. B. Higgins, *The Christian Significance of the OT* (London, 1949); P. Auvray et al., *L'AT et les chrétiens* (Paris, 1951); F. V. Filson, "The Unity of the OT and the NT: A Bibliographical Survey," *Interp*, 5 (1951), 134-152; H. H. Rowley, *The Unity of the Bible* (London, 1953); E. O'Doherty, "The Unity of the Bible," *The Bible Today*, 1 (1962), 53-57; D. E. Nineham, ed., *The Church's Use of the Bible* (London, 1963); H. Seebass, "Der Beitrag des AT zum Entwurf einer biblischen Theologie," *WuD*, 8 (1965), 20-49; H. Cazelles, "The Unity of the Bible and the People of God," *Scripture*, 18 (1966), 1-10; F. N. Jasper, "The Relation of the OT to the New," *ExpTim*, 78 (1967/68), 228-232, 267-270; F. Lang, "Christuszeugnis und Biblische Theologie," *EvT*, 29 (1969), 523-534; A. H. van Zyl, "The Relation between OT and NT," *Hermeneutica* (1970), 9-22; M. Kuske, *Das AT als Buch vom Christus* (Göttingen, 1971); S. Siedl, "Das Alte und das NT. Ihre Verschiedenheit und Einheit," *Tübinger Praktische Quartalschrift*, 119 (1971), 314-324; J. Wenham, *Christ and the Bible* (Chicago, 1972); F. F. Bruce, *The NT Development of OT Themes* (Grand Rapids, 1973); H. Gese, *Vom Sinai zum Sion. Alttest. Beitrage zur biblischen Theologie* (Munich, 1974), pp. 11-30; Harrington, *The Path of Biblical Theology* (Dublin, 1974), pp. 260-336.

the Testaments. B. S. Childs emphasizes the "canonical context" as decisive for OT theology and suggests that "the theological issue at stake is whether there is such a thing as a canonical context, which has been the claim of the church." He points out that the "historical-critical approach" to the Bible has fallen into its "own type of dogmatism in laying exclusive claim to the correct interpretation of the Bible."[82] It is certain that the question of the proper context is the root problem of Biblical interpretation. H.-J. Kraus elaborates that "in the relation of texts and themes the question of *context* is decisive."[83] He argues that the Biblical context has a decisive bearing on the meaning of a given theme or subject.[84]

OT theologians have had sharply divergent views on this. The self-assessment of J. L. McKenzie is that "I wrote it [theology of the OT] as if the New Testament did not exist."[85] His justification for this procedure is the fact that the books of the OT were written when the NT did not yet exist. On the basis of this criterion one would expect that for the sake of consistency the respective OT books would be questioned for their theologies independent of OT books written later. This is, however, not the procedure chosen by McKenzie. There seems to be a methodological inconsistency here, especially when out of Christian faith judgments are made on OT writers!

For Fohrer "understanding the OT does not require faith."[86] The interpreter does not enter from within but from without. The NT has no bearing on the understanding of the OT.[87] This does not mean, however, that the interpreter enters from a particular philosophical system but by means of the historical-critical method. The OT is to be investigated and explained in terms identical to that of any other literature.[88] Is

82. B. S. Childs, "The OT as Scripture of the Church," *CTM*, 43 (1972), 713. See also his *Biblical Theology in Crisis*, pp. 99-107.
83. Kraus, *Biblische Theologie*, p. 381.
84. Pp. 367-371.
85. McKenzie, *A Theology of the OT*, p. 319.
86. Fohrer, *Theologische Grundstrukturen des AT*, p. 31.
87. P. 29.
88. P. 31.

it here that Childs' cry of the historical-critical method's "own type of dogmatism in laying exclusive claim to the correct interpretation of the Bible" applies? Nevertheless Fohrer explicates the relationship between the Testaments with the principle of "beginning [OT] and continuation [NT]."[89] Contrary to the positions of Eichrodt, Westermann, Childs, Kraus, and others, Fohrer does not allow any current of life flowing from the NT to the OT. There is no reciprocal relationship between the Testaments; there is only a one-way road from the OT to the NT in terms of "beginning and continuation." The decidedly positive contribution of this position is its denial of considering the relationship in terms of opposites such as shadow and reality, law and gospel, letter and spirit, darkness and light. However, the principle of "beginning and continuation" can only function on the basis of the "prophetic attitude of existence" which "continues into and permeates the NT."[90] What is at work here is a reductionism of the OT for which the "prophetic attitude of existence" is raised to a supreme principle of OT faith. Westermann rightly points out that such a reductionism does injustice to the multiplex nature of OT faith and therefore leads to a one-sided principle by which the Testaments are related to each other.[91]

The impressive OT theology of Zimmerli contains a strange silence regarding the matter of the relationship between the Testaments. In earlier publication he has been a strong supporter of the "promise and fulfillment" scheme.[92] Von Rad explicates that the NT fulfillment far surpasses the OT promise, and among those who strongly support the category of promise and fulfillment as explicating the interrelatedness of the Testaments are R. E. Murphy, C. Westermann, H. H. Rowley, J. D. Smart, and W. J. Harrington.[93]

89. Pp. 274-276.
90. P. 274.
91. Westermann, *EvT,* 34 (1974), 102.
92. *EOTH,* pp. 89-122. In his *OT Theology in Outline,* pp. 27-32, he deals with the promise theme but restricts his discussion to the OT.
93. R. E. Murphy, "The Relationship between the Testaments," *CBQ,* 26 (1964), 349-359; Westermann, *EOTH,* pp. 17-39; J. D. Smart, *The Interpretation*

Two great turning-points in the development of Biblical theology centered on the freeing of Biblical theology from the fetters of dogmatics (systematic theology) in the time of Gabler and the separation of OT theology from the fetters of the history-of-religions approach during the beginning of this century.[94] One of the great turning-points in today's interest in OT theology is the reflection on the interrelationship between the Testaments. Fruitful beginnings may be seen in various attempts that point in forceful ways to the fact that the Testaments witness to multiple interrelationships. W. Eichrodt has pointed out that there is a reciprocal relationship between the Testaments, namely "in addition to this historical movement from the Old Testament to the New there is a current of life flowing in reverse direction from the New Testament to the Old. This reverse relationship also elucidates the full significance of the realm of OT thought." Then follows the striking claim that "only where this two-fold relationship between the Old and New Testaments is understood do we find a correct definition of the problem of OT theology and of the method by which it is possible to solve it."[95] G. von Rad's emphasis on the larger Biblical context of the OT[96] is seconded by H. W. Wolff,[97] H.-J. Kraus,[98] B. S. Childs,[99] and others who strive toward a Biblical theology.[100]

---

of Scripture (London, 1961), pp. 82-84; H. H. Rowley, The Unity of the Bible (London, 1953), pp. 9-121; Harrington, The Path of Biblical Theology, pp. 334-336, 346.

94. See especially C. Steuernagel, "Alttestamentliche Theologie und alttestamentliche Religionsgeschichte," Festschrift für K. Marti (BZAW, 41; 1925), p. 269.

95. Eichrodt, TOT, I, 26.

96. Von Rad, OTT, II, 320-335.

97. Wolff, EOTH, p. 181: "In the New Testament is found the context of the Old, which, as its historical goal, reveals the total meaning of the Old Testament."

98. Kraus, Biblische Theologie, pp. 33-36, 279-281, 344-347, 380-387.

99. Above, note 82.

100. In both Protestant and Catholic scholarship there is a marked increase of voices asking for a Biblical theology: F. V. Filson, "Biblische Theologie in Amerika," TLZ, 75 (1950), 71-80; M. Burrows, An Outline of Biblical Theology (Philadelphia, 1946); G. Vos, Biblical Theology (Grand Rapids, 1948);

The complex nature of the interrelationship between the Testaments requires a multiplex approach. No single category, concept, or scheme can be expected to exhaust the varieties of interrelationships.[101] Among the patterns of historical and theological relationships between the Testaments are the following: (1) A common mark of both Testaments is the continuous history of God's people and the picture of God's dealings with mankind.[102] (2) New emphasis has been put upon the connection between the Testaments on the basis of Scriptural quotations.[103] (3) Among the interrelationships between the Testaments appears the common use of theological key terms.[104] "Almost every key theological word of the New Testament is derived from some Hebrew word that had a long history of use and development in the Old Testament."[105] As among the other connecting links, unity does not mean uniformity, even when one speaks of "Greek words and their Hebrew meanings."[106] (4) The interrelationship between the

---

C. Spicq, "L'avènement de la Théologie Biblique," *Revue biblique*, 35 (1951), 561-574; F. M. Braun, "La Théologie Biblique," *Revue Thomiste*, 61 (1953), 221-253; R. de Vaux, "A propos de la Théologie Biblique," *ZAW*, 68 (1956), 225-227; O. P. Robertson, "The Outlook for Biblical Theology," in *Toward a Theology for the Future*, ed. D. P. Wells and C. H. Pinnock (Carol Stream, IL, 1971), pp. 65-91; Harrington, *The Path of Biblical Theology*, pp. 260-335, 371-377.

101. In this respect we agree with W. H. Schmidt, " 'Theologie des AT' vor und nach Gerhard von Rad," in *Verkündigung und Forschung* (Beiheft zur *EvT*, 17; Munich, 1972), p. 24.

102. F. V. Filson, "The Unity Between the Testaments," *The Interpreter's One-Volume Commentary on the Bible* (Nashville, 1971), p. 992.

103. Childs, *Biblical Theology in Crisis*, pp. 114-118; P. A. Verhoef, "The Relationship Between the Old and New Testaments," in *New Perspectives on the OT*, ed. J. B. Payne (Waco, Texas, 1970), p. 282; R. H. Gundry, *The Use of the OT in St. Matthew's Gospel* (Leiden, 1967); R. T. France, *Jesus and the OT* (London, 1971).

104. So H. Haag in *Mysterium Salutis. Grundriss heilsgeschichtlicher Dogmatik*, ed. J. Feiner and M. Lohr (1965), I, 440-457.

105. J. L. McKenzie, "Aspects of OT Thought," *The Jerome Biblical Commentary* (Englewood Cliffs, NJ, 1968), p. 767.

106. D. Hill, *Greek Words and Hebrew Meanings: Studies in the Semantics of Soteriological Terms* (London, 1967); cf. J. Barr, *The Semantics of Biblical Language* (Oxford, 1961).

Testaments comes also to expression through the essential unity of major themes. "Each of the major themes of the Old [Testament] has its correspondent in the New, and is in some way resumed and answered there."[107] Such themes as rulership of God, people of God, exodus experience, election and covenant, judgment and salvation, bondage and redemption, life and death, creation and new creation, etc., present themselves for immediate consideration. (5) A guarded and circumspect use of typology is indispensable for an adequate methodology that attempts to come to grips with the historical context of the OT and its relationship to the NT.[108] Typology must be sharply separated from allegory,[109] because it is essentially a historical and theological category between OT and NT events. Allegory has little concern with the historical character of the OT. (6) The category of promise/prediction and fulfillment elucidates another aspect of the interrelatedness of the Testaments.[110] This interrelationship is fundamental and decisive not only for inner OT unity and the understanding of the relationship of the OT to Jesus Christ but also for the interrelationship between the Testaments.[111] As important as this category is, it is not exhaustive of the total relationship of OT to NT. (7) Last but not least is the concept

---

107. J. Bright, *The Authority of the OT* (Nashville, 1967), p. 211. Cf. F. F. Bruce, *The NT Development of OT Themes* (Grand Rapids, 1973).

108. L. Goppelt, *Typos: The Typological Interpretation of the OT in the New* (Grand Rapids, 1982); idem, "Typos," *TDNT*, VIII (1972), 246-259; France, *Jesus and the OT*, pp. 38-80; G. W. H. Lampe and K. J. Woollcombe, *Essays on Typology* (SBT, 1/22; London, 1957); Wolff, *EOTH*, pp. 181-190; G. von Rad, "Typological Interpretation of the OT," *Interp*, 15 (1961), 174-192; John H. Stek, "Biblical Typology Yesterday and Today," *Calvin Theological Journal*, 5 (1970), 133-162.

109. This basic interpretation has been attacked by Barr, *Old and New in Interpretation*, pp. 103-111, but rightly defended by Eichrodt, *EOTH*, pp. 227f.; Lampe, *Essays on Typology*, pp. 30-35; and France, *Jesus and the OT*, pp. 40f.

110. This is supported in recent years by H. H. Rowley; C. H. Dodd; G. von Rad; H. W. Wolff, "The OT in Controversy; Interpretive Principles and Illustration," *Interp*, 12 (1958), 281-291; idem, *EOTH*, pp. 160-199; Zimmerli, *EOTH*, pp. 89-122; Westermann, *The OT and Jesus Christ*; and others.

111. Westermann, *The OT and Jesus Christ*, p. 78.

of salvation history that links the two Testaments together.[112] Secular history and salvation history are not to be conceived as two separate realities. Particular historical events have a deeper significance, perceived through divine revelation; such events are divine acts in human history. The course of salvation history was inaugurated for man after the fall and moved from Adam and all mankind through Abraham to Christ, and from him it moves to the goal of history, the final future consummation in glory.[113]

If properly conceived, these multiple interrelationships between the Testaments may be considered to elucidate the unity of the Testaments without forcing a uniformity upon the diverse Biblical witnesses. There is unity in diversity.

112. See here especially O. Cullmann, *Christ and Time* (2nd ed.; London, 1962); idem, *Salvation in History* (London, 1967); P. Grelot, *Sens Chrétien de l'AT* (Tournai, 1962), Ch. 5.

113. See the emphasis by Vriezen, *An Outline of OT Theology,* p. 123; Rowley, *The Unity of the Bible,* pp. 109f.; Zimmerli, *EOTH,* p. 114; Verhoef, *New Perspectives on the OT,* p. 293.

VI. Basic Proposals
for Doing OT Theology

Our attempt to focus on unresolved crucial problems which are at the center of the current crisis in OT theology has revealed that there are basic inadequacies in the current methodologies and approaches. The inevitable question that has arisen is, Where do we go from here? Our strictures with regard to the paths trodden by Biblical theologians have indicated that a basically new approach must be worked out. A productive way to proceed from here on appears to have to rest upon the following basic proposals for doing OT theology.

(1) Biblical theology must be understood to be a historical-theological discipline. This is to say that the Biblical theologian engaged in doing either Old or New Testament theology must claim as his task both to discover and describe what the text meant and also to explicate what it means for today. The Biblical theologian attempts to "get back there,"[1] i.e., he wants to do away with the temporal gap by bridging the time span between his day and that of the Biblical witnesses, by means of the historical study of the Biblical documents. The nature of the Biblical documents, however, inasmuch as they are themselves witnesses of the eternal purpose of God for Israel and for the world as manifested through divine acts and words

---

1. This phrase comes from G. E. Wright, "The Theological Study of the Bible," *The Interpreter's One-Volume Commentary on the Bible* (Nashville, 1971), p. 983.

of judgment and salvation in history, requires a movement from the level of the historical investigation of the Bible to the theological one. The Biblical witnesses are themselves not only historical witnesses in the sense that they originated at particular times and particular places; they are, at the same time theological witnesses in the sense that they testify as the word of God to the divine reality and activity as it impinges on the historicality of man. Thus the task of the Biblical theologian is to interpret the Scriptures meaningfully, with the careful use of the tools of historical and philological research, attempting to understand and describe in "getting back there" what the Biblical testimony meant; and to explicate the meaning of the Biblical testimony for modern man in his own particular historical situation.

The Biblical theologian neither takes the place of nor competes with the systematic theologian or dogmatician. The latter has and always will have to fulfill his own task in that he endeavors to use current philosophies as the basis for his primary categories or themes. For the systematic theologian it is indeed appropriate to operate with philosophical categories, because his foundations are on a base different from that of the Biblical theologian. The Biblical theologian draws his categories, themes, motifs, and concepts from the Biblical text itself. The Biblical theologian stands in danger of surreptitiously introducing contemporary philosophy into his discipline.[2] But he must carefully guard himself against this temptation. Therefore, it must be emphasized that the Biblical and systematic theologians do not compete with each other. Their function is complementary. Both need to work side by side, profiting from each other. The Biblical theologian is to present the Biblical categories, themes, motifs, and concepts, which

2. A. Dulles (*The Bible in Modern Scholarship*, p. 215) states not incorrectly that "any number of supposedly biblical theologies in our day are so heavily infected with contemporary personalist, existential, or historical thinking as to render their biblical basis highly suspect." In this respect Karl Barth and Rudolf Bultmann have often been accused of finding too many of their own favorite philosophical ideas in the Scripture.

in contrast to the "clear and distinct ideas" of the systematic theologian are often less clear and distinct. All too often the Biblical categories are more suggestive and dynamic ones for expressing the rich revelation of the deep mystery of God. As a result Biblical theology is able to say something to modern man that systematic theology cannot say, and vice versa.

(2) If Biblical theology is understood to be a historical-theological discipline, it follows that its proper method must be both historical *and* theological from the starting-point. A theology of the OT presupposes exegesis based upon sound principles and procedures. Exegesis, in turn, is in need of OT theology. Without OT theology the work of exegetical interpretation may easily become endangered by isolating individual texts from the whole. For example, if one is on the basis of OT theology acquainted with the motif of the remnant in the period prior to and contemporary with the writing prophets, one will not overlook that Amos' use of the remnant motif is to some extent one-sided among the pre-exilic prophets. And if one knows Amos' remnant theology, one will not likely misunderstand the remnant theology as a whole merely as an expression of the positive aspect of a holy remnant saved from eschatological judgment or as an expression of an insignificant and meaningless remainder of God's chosen people.[2a] On the other hand, a careful, clear-sighted, and sound exegesis will always be able to check critically OT theology.

At this point we must pause to note H.-J. Kraus' reminder that "one of the most difficult questions confronting Biblical theology today is that of the starting-point, the meaning and function of historical-critical research."[3] Von Rad has sensed

---

2a. See the writer's monograph, *The Remnant. The History and Theology of the Remnant Idea from Genesis to Isaiah* (2nd ed.; Andrews University Monographs, V; Berrien Springs, MI, 1975), pp. 173-371.

3. Kraus, *Biblische Theologie*, p. 363; cf. p. 377. On this point Childs (*Biblical Theology in Crisis*, pp. 141f.) writes: "The historico-critical method is an inadequate method for studying the Bible as the Scriptures of the church because it does not work from the needed context. . . . When seen from the context of the canon both the question of what the text meant and what it

more keenly than his predecessors who produced OT theologies in this century that the Biblical theologian cannot move on the pathway of a "critically assured minimum," if he actually attempts to grasp "the layers of depth of historical experience, which historical-critical research is unable to fathom."[4] The reason for the inability of the historical-critical method to grasp all layers of depth of historical experience, i.e., the inner unity of happening and meaning based upon the inbreaking of transcendence into history as *the* final reality to which the Biblical text testifies, rests upon its limitation to study history on the basis of its own presuppositions.

The historical-critical method, which came out of the Enlightenment,[5] views history as a closed continuum, an unbroken series of causes and effects in which there is no room for transcendence.[6] "The historian cannot presuppose supernatural intervention in the causal nexus as the basis for his work."[7]

---

means are inseparably linked and both belong to the task of interpretation of the Bible as Scripture. To the extent that the use of the critical method sets up an iron curtain between the past and the present, it is an inadequate method for studying the Bible as the church's Scripture." For the inadequacy of the historical-critical method with regard to the new quest of the historical Jesus, see G. E. Ladd, "The Search for Perspective," *Interp*, 26 (1971), 41-62.

4. *TAT*, I, 120; cf. *OTT*, I, 108.

5. This must be clearly seen, if one does not want to confuse the issues. Ebeling, *Word and Faith*, p. 42: "The critical historical method first arose out of the intellectual revolution of modern times." On this whole point see U. Wilckens, "Über die Bedeutung historischer Kritik in der modernen Bibelexegese," in *Was heisst Auslegung der Heiligen Schrift?* (Regensburg, 1966), pp. 85-133. A critique of the adequacy of the historical-critical method for theological research is provided by E. Reisner, "Hermeneutik und historische Vernunft," *ZTK*, 49 (1952), 223-238, and a defense by E. Käsemann, "Vom theologischen Recht historisch-kritischer Exegese," *ZTK*, 64 (1967), 259-281; idem, *Der Ruf der Freiheit* (3rd ed.; Munich, 1968).

6. *OTT*, II, 418: "For Israel, history consisted only of Jahweh's self-revelation by word and action. And on this point conflict with the modern view of history was sooner or later inevitable, for the latter finds it perfectly possible to construct a picture of history without God. It finds it very hard to assume that there is divine action in history. God has no natural place in its schema."

7. R. W. Funk, "The Hermeneutical Problem and Historical Criticism,"

Accordingly, historical events must be capable of being explained by antecedent historical causes and understood in terms of analogy to other historical experiences. The method which prides itself of its scientific nature and objectivity turns out to be in the grip of its own dogmatic presuppositions and philosophical premises about the nature of history. C. E. Braaten sees the problem as follows: "The historian often begins by claiming that he conducts his research purely objectively, without presuppositions, and ends by surreptitiously introducing a set of presuppositions whose roots lie deeply embedded in an anti-Christian *Weltanschauung*."[8] A Biblical theology which rests upon a view of history that is based on an unbroken continuum of causes and effects cannot do justice to the Biblical view of history and revelation nor to the Scripture's claim to truth.[9] Von Rad has come to recognize that "a consistently applied historico-critical method could [not] really do justice to the Old Testament scripture's claim to truth."[10] What needs to be emphatically stressed is that there is a transcendent or divine dimension in Biblical history which the historical-critical method is unable to deal with. "If all historical events must by definition be explained by sufficient historical causes, then there is no room for the acts of God in history, for God is not a historical character."[11] If one's view of history is such that one cannot acknowledge a divine intervention in history through deed and word, then one is unable to deal adequately and properly with the testimony of Scripture. We are, therefore, led to conclude that the crisis respecting history in Biblical theology is not so much a result of the scientific study of the evidences, but stems from

in *The New Hermeneutic*, ed. J. M. Robinson and J. B. Cobb, Jr. (New York, 1964), p. 185.

8. C. E. Braaten, "Revelation, History, and Faith in Martin Kähler," in M. Kähler, *The So-called Historical Jesus and the Historic Biblical Christ* (Philadelphia, 1964), p. 22.

9. Wallace, *TZ*, 19 (1963), 90; cf. J. Barr, "Revelation through History in the OT and in Modern Theology," *Interp*, 17 (1963), 201f.

10. *OTT*, II, 417.

11. Ladd, *Interp*, 26 (1971), 50.

the historical-critical method's inadequacy to deal with the role of transcendence in history due to its philosophical presuppositions about the nature of history.[12] If the reality of the Biblical text testifies to a supra-historical dimension which transcends the self-imposed limitations of the historical-critical method, then one must employ a method that can account for this dimension and can probe into all the layers of depth of historical experience and deal adequately and properly with the Scripture's claim to truth.[13]

We have stated that the proper method for Biblical theology is to be both historical *and* theological from the beginning. Too often it is assumed that exegesis has the historical-critical function to work out the meaning of *single* texts, and Biblical theology the task to join these single aspects into a theological *whole*, namely a sequential procedure. H.-J. Kraus has rightly called for a "Biblical-theological process of interpretation" in which exegesis is from its starting-point Biblical-theological in orientation.[14] If we add to this aspect that a proper and adequate method of research dealing with the Biblical text needs to take into account the reality of God and his inbreaking into history,[15] because the Biblical text testifies to the transcendent dimension in historical reality,[16] then we have

12. Von Rad, *TAT,* II, 9: "The historical method opens up for us only one aspect in the many-layered phenomenon of history, and at that one which cannot say anything about the relationship between history and God."

13. Von Rad, *TAT,* I, 120; *OTT,* I, 108. Osswald, *Wissenschaftliche Zeitschrift der Universität Jena,* 14 (1965), 711: "With the aid of critical science one can certainly make no statement about God, because there is no path that leads from the objectifying science of history to a real theological expression. The rational process of knowing history remains limited to the spatial-temporal dimension. . . ."

14. *Biblische Theologie,* p. 377.

15. This point is also made by Floyd V. Filson, "How I Interpret the Bible," *Interp,* 4 (1950), 186: "I work with the conviction that the only really objective method of study takes the reality of God and his working into account and that any other point of view is loaded with presuppositions which actually, even if subtly, contain an implicit denial of the full Christian faith."

16. One presupposition of the historical-critical method is the consistent application of the principle of analogy. E. Troeltsch writes, "The means by

a basis upon which historical *and* theological interpretation can go hand in hand from the start without needing to be artificially separated into sequential processes.[17] On this basis one is able to "get back there" into the world of the Biblical writer by bridging the temporal and cultural gap, and can attempt to understand historically and theologically what the text meant. It is then possible to express more adequately and comprehensively what the text means for man in the modern world and historical situation.

This methodological procedure does not seek to skip history in favor of theology. The Biblical theologian working with the method that is both historical and theological recognizes fully the relativity of human objectivity.[18] Accordingly he is aware that he must never let his faith cause him to modernize his materials on the basis of the tradition and community of faith in which he stands. He must ask questions of the Biblical text on its own terms; he makes room that his tradition and the content of his faith may be challenged, guided, enlivened, and enriched by his finds. He recognizes also that a purely philological, linguistic, and historical approach is never enough to disclose the full and complete meaning of a historical text. One can apply all the exegetical instruments avail-

---

which criticism [with the historical-critical method] is at all possible is the application of analogy. . . . But the omnipotence of analogy implies that all historical events are identical in principle" (quoted by von Rad, *OTT,* I, 107). Von Rad states in *TAT,* II, 9, that also the course of history as built up by the historical-critical method "is interpreted history on the basis of historical-philosophical presuppositions, which do not allow any possible recognition of God's action in history, because only man is notoriously considered to be the creator of history." Mildenberger, *Gottes Tat im Wort,* p. 31 n. 37, agrees with von Rad and adds that historical criticism "presupposes a closed relation of reality which cannot grant 'supernatural' causes."

17. On this point von Rad, *TAT,* II, 12, has made the following observation: "The theological interpretation of OT texts does not actually begin when the exegete, trained in literary criticism and history (either this or that!), has done his job, as if we had two exegetical processes, first a historical-critical one and then a 'theological one.' A theological interpretation that seeks to grasp a statement about God in the text is active from the very beginning of the process of understanding."

18. So also Stendahl, *IDB,* I, 422.

able from historical, linguistic, and philological research and never reach the heart of the matter unless one yields to the basic experience out of which the Biblical writers speak, namely faith. Without so yielding, one will never come to a recognition of the full reality that finds expression in the Biblical testimony. We do not wish to turn faith into a method, nor do we intend to disregard the demand of the Biblical books, as documents from the past, to translate them as objectively as possible by careful employment of the respective and proper methods of interpretation. But we mean that the interpretation of Scripture is to become part of our own real experience, as should all interpretation.[19] The historical-theological interpretation is to be at the service of faith, if it is to fathom all layers of depth of historical experience and to penetrate into the full meaning of the text and the reality expressed in it. We must, therefore, affirm that when interpretation seeks to grasp statements and testimonies witnessing to God's self-disclosure as the Lord of time and event, who had chosen to reveal himself in actual datable happenings of human history through acts and words of judgment and salvation, then the process of understanding such statements and testimonies must be from the start both historical *and* theological in nature in order to comprehend fully the complete reality that has come to expression.

(3) The Biblical theologian engaged in OT theology has his subject indicated beforehand inasmuch as his endeavor is a theology of the *Old* Testament. It is founded exclusively on materials taken from the OT. The OT comes to him through the Christian church as part of the inspired Scriptures. Introduction to the OT seeks to throw light on the pre-literary and literary stages and forms of the OT books by tracing their

19. To confine oneself to philology, linguistics, and history when studying the Gilgamesh Epic or the Assyrian annals, without ever giving oneself over to the thought of the authors of these documents, without ever trying to share in the experiences of the authors that came to expression in these documents, would mean to miss forever the concept of reality which these men discovered and which made up their very life and thought.

history of transmission and formation as well as the text-forms
and the canonization of the OT. The history of Israel is studied
in the context of the history of antiquity with special emphasis
on the ancient Near East, where archeology has been invalu-
able in providing the historical, cultural, and social setting for
the Bible. Exegesis has the task to disclose the full meaning
of the individual texts.

Old Testament theology questions the various books or
blocks of writings of the OT as to their theology.[20] For the OT
is composed of writings whose origin, content, forms, intentions, and meaning are very diverse. The nature of these
matters makes it imperative to look at the material at hand in
light of the context which is primary to us, namely the form
in which we meet it first, as a verbal structure of an integral
part of a literary whole.[21] Viewed in this way an OT theology
will neither become a "history of religion,"[22] "history of the

20. This has been stressed for NT theology especially by Heinrich Schlier
("The Meaning and Function of a Theology of the NT," *Dogmatic vs. Biblical
Theology*, ed. H. Vorgrimler [Baltimore, 1964], pp. 88-90); for OT theology by
Kraus (*Biblische Theologie*, p. 364), by D. J. McCarthy ("The Theology of
Leadership in Joshua 1-9," *Bib*, 52 [1971], 166), and with his own emphasis
by Childs (*Biblical Theology in Crisis*, pp. 99-107).

21. Contemporary (non-Biblical) literary critics place special emphasis
upon the "new criticism," which the Germans call *Werkinterpretation*. Cf.
W. Kayser, *Das sprachliche Kunstwerk* (10th ed.; Bern-Munich, 1964); Emil
Staiger, *Die Kunst der Interpretation* (4th ed.; Zürich, 1963); Horst Enders, ed.,
Die Werkinterpretation (Darmstadt, 1967). The primary concern according to
the practitioners of the "new criticism" is to occupy oneself with the study
of a finished piece of literature. The "new criticism" insists on the formal
integrity of the literary piece as a work of art, the *Kunstwerk*. Such a work
must be appreciated in its totality; to look behind it in an attempt at discovering its history of origin is irrelevant. The emphasis is on the finished literary
product *qua* work of art. An increasing number of OT scholars have taken
up the emphasis of the "new criticism." Among them are: Z. Adar, *The Biblical
Narrative* (Jerusalem, 1959); S. Talmon, " 'Wisdom' in the Book of Esther," *VT,*
13 (1963), 419-455; M. Weiss, "Wege der neueren Dichtungswissenschaft in
ihrer Anwendung auf die Psalmenforschung," *Bib*, 42 (1961), 225-302; idem,
"Einiges über die Bauformen des Erzählens in der Bibel," *VT,* 13 (1963),
455-475; idem, "Weiteres über die Bauformen des Erzählens in der Bibel,"
Bib, 46 (1965), 181-206; idem, *The Bible from Within: The Method of Total
Interpretation* (Jerusalem, 1984).

22. One should refrain from designating a book like H. Ringgren's

transmission of tradition," or "history of revelation,"[23] nor will
it turn into a "theology of redaction criticism" or something
of that sort. A theology of the OT is first of all a summary
interpretation and explanation of the OT writings or blocks
of writings. This does not imply that there is no value in
capturing the theology of particular traditions; it simply views
this to be part of another endeavor. The procedure of explicating the theology of the OT books or blocks of writings in
the final form[24] as verbal structures of literary wholes has the
distinct advantage of recognizing the similarities *and* differ-
ences between the various books or blocks of writings. This
means, for example, that the theologies of the individual prophetic writings will be able to stand independently next to
each other. Each voice can be heard in its testimony to the
activity of God and the divine self-disclosure. Another advantage of this approach, one that is crucial for the whole enterprise of OT theology, is that no systematic scheme, pattern of
thought, or extrapolated abstraction is superimposed upon the
Biblical materials. Since no single theme, scheme, or motif is
sufficiently comprehensive to include within it all varieties
of OT viewpoints, one must refrain from using a particular
concept, formula, basic idea, etc., as the center of the OT

Israelite Religion (Philadelphia, 1966) as an OT theology. Ringgren himself
states that "the reader will not find in this book a theology of the Old
Testament but a history of Israelite religion. . . . Theologians will also miss
points of view based on *Heilsgeschichte;* these points of view have their place,
but only within a theological presentation" (p. v).

23. Kraus, *Biblische Theologie*, p. 365: " 'Biblical theology' should be
biblical theology in that it accepts the canon in the given textual connections
as *the historical truth* which is in need of explanation, whose final form is in
need of being presented by interpretation and summary. This should be the
actual task of Biblical theology. Every attempt at a different procedure would
not be Biblical theology, but 'history of revelation,' 'history of religion,' or
even 'history of tradition.' "

24. An emphasis on the "final form" even for the exegetical task is
supported by M. Noth, *Exodus: A Commentary* (Philadelphia, 1962), p. 18;
Landes, *Union Seminary Quarterly Review*, 26 (1971), 273ff. Barr, *The Bible
in the Modern World*, pp. 163ff., points out quite correctly that the "final form
of the text has the first importance, and this is likely to be still more widely
accepted with the influence both of 'redaction criticism' and structuralism."

whereby a systematization of the manifold and variegated OT testimonies is achieved. On the other hand, we must affirm that God is the center of the OT as its central subject. By saying that God is the center of the OT we have stated that the OT Scripture has a central content without falling into the trap of organizing the event-centered character and manner of God's self-disclosing revelation into a system. It is refraining to systematize that which cannot be systematized without losing its essential nature.

(4) The presentation of the theologies of the OT books, or groups of writings, will preferably not follow the order of the books in the canonical sequence, for this order, whether in the Hebrew canon or the LXX, etc., had apparently other than theological causes. Though admittedly difficult to fix, the date of origin of the books, groups of writings, or blocks of material within these writings may provide a guide for establishing the order of presentation of the various theologies.

(5) An OT theology not only seeks to know the theology of the various books, or groups of writings; it also attempts to draw together and present the major themes of the OT. To live up to its name, OT theology must allow its themes, motifs, and concepts to be formed for it by the OT itself. The range of OT themes, motifs, and concepts will always impose itself on the theologian insofar as they silence his own, once the theological perspectives of the OT are really grasped. On principle, a theology of the OT must tend toward themes, motifs, and concepts and must be presented with all the variety and all the limitations imposed on them by the OT itself.

For example, the election themes as reflected in God's call to Abraham and his promises to him and the fathers of Israel, God's deliverance of enslaved Israel in the exodus experience with Israel's establishment in the Promised Land, and God's choice of and promises to David with Zion/Jerusalem as the holy mountain and divine dwelling-place, are in need of being presented in an OT theology in their variety of appearances and usages in the individual books or blocks of material. This would be equally true with regard to so central a concept as the Mosaic covenant. The utterly gracious action of the Giver of the covenant drew from the recipients a response, and created the special and unique relationship between them and their God. The covenant concept furnishes major elements for worship and cult as well as for the proclamation of the prophets and the theology of the historical books. Inherent in these and other OT concepts, motifs, and themes is a basic future expectation, namely the outstanding blessing for all nations, the new Exodus, the second David, the new Jerusalem, the new covenant, which reveals that Israelite faith needs to be viewed as intensely directed toward the future. Special motifs in the wisdom theology stress man's life and responsibility in the here and now. It is beyond our purpose to list the variety of major concepts, themes, and motifs.

The presentation of these longitudinal perspectives of the OT testimonies can be achieved only on the basis of a multi-track treatment. The richness of the OT testimonies can be grasped by such a multiplex approach as is commensurate with the nature of the OT. This multiplex approach with the multitrack treatment of longitudinal themes frees the Biblical theologian from the notion of an artificial and forced unilinear approach determined by a single structuring concept, whether it is covenant, communion, kingdom of God, or something else, to which all OT testimonies, thoughts, and concepts are made to refer or are forced to fit.

(6) As the OT is interrogated for its theology, it answers first of all by yielding various theologies, namely those of the individual books and groups of writings, and then by yielding the theologies of the various longitudinal themes. But the name of our discipline as *theology* of the OT is not only concerned to present and explicate the variety of different theologies. The concept foreshadowed by the name of the discipline has *one* theology in view, namely *the* theology of the OT.

The final aim of OT theology is to demonstrate whether or not there is an inner unity that binds together the various theologies and longitudinal themes, concepts, and motifs. This is an extremely difficult undertaking which contains many dangers. If there is behind the experience of those who left us the OT Scriptures a unique divine reality, then it would seem that behind all variegation and diversity of theological reflection there is a hidden inner unity which has also drawn together the OT writings. The ultimate object of a theology is then to draw the hidden inner unity out of its concealment as much as possible and to make it transparent.

The task to achieve this objective must not be performed too hastily. The constant temptation to find unity in a single structuring theme or concept must be avoided. Here misgivings should arise not only because OT theology would be reduced to a cross-sectional or some other development of a single theme or concept, but the real task would be lost sight of, which is precisely not to overlook or pass by the variegated and diverse theologies while at the same time to search for and articulate the inner unity which seemingly binds together in a concealed way the divergent and manifold OT testimonies. One can indeed speak of such a unity in which ultimately the divergent theological utterances and testimonies are intrinsically related to each other from the theological viewpoint on the basis of a presupposition that derives from the inspiration and canonicity of the OT as Scripture.

A seemingly successful way to come to grips with the question of unity is to take the various major longitudinal themes and concepts and explicate whether and how the variegated theologies are intrinsically related to each other. In this way the underlying bond of the one theology of the OT may be illuminated. In the quest to find and explicate the inner unity one must refrain from making the theology of one book or group of books the norm of what is OT theology. For example, one must not make a particular theology of history the norm of OT theology.[25] The often neglected theologies, among them especially those of the wisdom materials of the OT, must be allowed to stand side by side with other theolo-

---

25. This has been the case even in von Rad's approach. He has chosen a particular theology of history, that of the Deuteronomist, as the main norm for his exposition of OT theology. Thus the wisdom traditions are forced to recede into the background.

gies. They make their own special contributions to OT theology on equal basis with those more recognized ones, because they too are expressions of OT realities. The question of unity implies tension, but tension does not of necessity mean contradiction. It would appear that where conceptual unity seems impossible the creative tension thereby produced will turn out to be a most fruitful one for OT theology.

(7) The Biblical theologian understands OT theology as being more than the "theology of the Hebrew Bible." The name "theology of the Old Testament" implies the larger context of the Bible of which the New Testament is the other part. An integral OT theology must demonstrate its basic relationship to the NT or to NT theology. For the Christian theologian the OT has the character of Scripture on the basis of its relation to the other Testament.

As noted earlier, the multiplex question and complex nature of the relationship between the Testaments and its implication for OT theology make it necessary to opt for a multiplex approach.[26] A multiplex approach leaves room for indicating the variety of connections between the Testaments and avoids an explication of the manifold testimonies through a single structure or unilinear point of view. The multiplex approach has the advantage of remaining faithful to both similarity and dissimilarity as well as old and new without in the least distorting the original historical witness of the text in its literal sense and its larger kerygmatic intention nor falling short in the recognition of the larger context to which the OT belongs. Thus both Testaments will finally shed light upon each other and aid mutually in a more comprehensive understanding of their theologies.

*   *   *   *   *

On the basis of these proposals outlining a new approach to OT theology, one is in a position to work out a theology of

26. *Supra*, pp. 139-149.

the OT that may avoid the pitfalls and blind alleys that have precipitated the current crisis in OT theology. At the same time one may be a crucial step closer in bringing about a much hoped for and talked about Biblical theology of both the Old and New Testaments.

Selected Bibliography

Note: With the help of my doctoral student Reinaldo Siqueira, I have enlarged this "selected bibliography" over the one in the previous edition—more than doubling its entries—by including books and articles on OT theology which are representative of the discipline in its various shapes from its beginning, with an emphasis on the period since 1950.

Abramowski, Rudolf. "Vom Streit um das Alte Testament," *TRu,* 9 (1937), 65-93.

Achtemeier, Elizabeth. "The Relevance of the Old Testament for Christian Preaching." In *A Light Unto My Path: Old Testament Studies in Honor of Jacob M. Myers.* Ed. H. Bream, R. Heim, and C. Moore. Philadelphia, 1974. Pp. 3-24.

Ackroyd, Peter. "Recent Biblical Theologies: VII. G. A. F. Knight's 'A Christian Theology of the Old Testament,'" *ExpTim,* 73 (1961-1962), 164-168.

————. *Continuity: A Contribution to the Study of the Old Testament Religious Tradition.* Oxford, 1962.

————. "The Vitality of the Word of God in the Old Testament," *ASTI,* 1 (1962), 7-23.

————. *Studies in the Religious Tradition of the Old Testament.* London, 1987.

Addinall, Peter. "What is Meant by a Theology of the Old Testament?" *ExpTim,* 97/11 (1986), 332-336.

Albertz, R. *Weltschöpfung und Menschschöpfung.* Calwer Theologische Monographien, 3. Stuttgart, 1974.

Albrektson, Bertil. "Främreorientaliska och gammaltestamentliga föreställlingar om uppenbarelse i historien. Några preliminäre synpunkter," *Teologinen aikakauskirja,* 71 (1966), 13-34.

————. *History and the Gods: An Essay on the Idea of Historical Events as Divine Manifestations in the Ancient Near East and in Israel.* Coniectanea Biblica: Old Testament Series, 1. Lund, 1967.

Albright, William F. "Return to Biblical Theology," *Christian Century,* 75 (1958), 1328-1331.

Allen, E. L. "On Demythologizing the Old Testament," *JBR*, 22 (1954), 236-241.

———. "The Limits of Biblical Theology," *JBR*, 25 (1957), 13-18.

Alonso-Schökel, L. "Biblische Theologie des AT," *Stimme der Zeit*, 172 (1962-1963), 34-51.

———. "Old Testament Theology." In *Sacramentum Mundi: An Encyclopedia of Theology*. Ed. K. Rahner. London, 1969. IV, 286-290.

Alter, Robert. *The Art of Biblical Narrative*. New York, 1980.

———. *The Art of Biblical Poetry*. New York, 1985.

Ammon, Christoph F. von. *Biblische Theologie*. 3 vols. 2nd ed. Erlangen, 1801-1802.

Anderson, A. A. "Old Testament Theology and Its Methods." In *Promise and Fulfilment: Essays Presented to Professor S. H. Hook*. Ed. F. F. Bruce. Edinburgh, 1963. Pp. 7-19.

Anderson, Bernhard W. *Creation Versus Chaos: The Reinterpretation of Mythical Symbolism in the Bible*. New York, 1967.

———. "The Crisis of Biblical Theology," *TToday*, 28 (1971), 321-332.

———. "Mythopoeic and Theological Dimensions of Biblical Creation Faith." In *Creation in the Old Testament*. Ed. Bernhard W. Anderson. IRT, 6. London / Philadelphia, 1984. Pp. 1-24.

———. "Biblical Theology and Sociological Interpretation," *TToday*, 42 (1985), 292-306.

———. "Response to Matitahu Tsevat 'Theology of the Old Testament—A Jewish View,'" *HBT*, 8/2 (1986), 55.

Anderson, Bernhard W., ed. *OTCF*. New York, 1963.

Anderson, G. W. "Recent Biblical Theologies: V. Th. C. Vriezen's 'Outline of Old Testament Theology,'" *ExpTim*, 73 (1961-1962), 113-116.

———. "Israel's Creed: Sung, Not Signed," *SJT*, 16 (1963), 277-285.

Aubert, R. "Discussions récentes autour de la Théologie de l'Histoire," *Collectanea Mechliniensia*, 18 (1948), 129-149.

Auvray, P., et al. *L'AT et les chrétiens*. Paris, 1951.

Baab, Otto J. "Old Testament Theology: Its Possibility." In *The Study of the Bible Today and Tomorrow*. Ed. H. R. Willoughby. Chicago, 1947. Pp. 401-418.

———. *The Theology of the Old Testament*. Nashville, 1949.

Baker, D. L. *Two Testaments, One Bible: A Study of Some Modern Solutions to the Theological Problem of the Relationship Between the Old and New Testaments*. Downers Grove, 1977.

Baker, L. "The Construction of an Old Testament Theology," *Theology*, 58 (1955), 252-257.

Barnett, T. A. "Trends in Old Testament Theology," *CJT*, 6 (1960), 91-101.

Barr, J. "The Problem of Old Testament Theology and the History of Religion," *CJT*, 3 (1957), 141-149.

———. *The Semantics of Biblical Language*. Oxford, 1961.

———. "Recent Biblical Theologies: VI. Gerhard von Rad's Theologie des AT," *ExpTim*, 73 (1962), 142-146.

————. *Biblical Words for Time.* SBT, 1 / 33. London, 1962. Rev. ed. 1969.

————. "Revelation Through History in the Old Testament and in Modern Theology," *Interp,* 17 (1963), 193-205.

————. *Old and New in Biblical Interpretation.* New York, 1966.

————. *Comparative Philology and the Text of the Old Testament.* London, 1968. Rev. ed. 1987.

————. "Le Judaîsme postbiblique et la théologie de l'Ancien Testament," *Revue de Théologie et de Philosophie,* 3/18 (1968), 209-217.

————. "The Old Testament and the New Crisis of Biblical Theology," *Interp,* 25 (1971), 24-40.

————. "Semantics and Biblical Theology — A Contribution to the Discussion." In *Congress Volume: Uppsala, 1971. Supplements to VT,* 22. Leiden, 1972. Pp. 11-19.

————. *The Bible in the Modern World.* London, 1973.

————. "Trends and Prospects in Biblical Theology," *Journal of Theological Studies,* 25 (1974), 265-282.

————. "Revelation in History." In *IDB Supplement.* Nashville, 1976. Pp. 746-749.

————. "Story and History in Biblical Theology," *JR,* 56 (1976), 1-17.

————. "Biblical Theology." In *IDB Supplement.* Nashville, 1976. Pp. 104-111.

————. *Fundamentalism.* London, 1977. 2nd ed. 1981.

————. *Does Biblical Study Still Belong to Theology?* Oxford, 1978.

————. "Childs' *Introduction to the Old Testament as Scripture,"* *JSOT,* 16 (1980), 12-23.

————. *Holy Scripture: Canon, Authority, Criticism.* Philadelphia, 1983.

————. *The Scope and Authority of the Bible.* Philadelphia, 1983.

————. *Beyond Fundamentalism.* Philadelphia, 1984.

————. "Biblische Theologie." In *Evangelisches Kirchenlexikon,* 1/2 (1985), 488-494.

————. "Mowinckel, the Old Testament and the Question of Natural Theology: The Second Mowinckel Lecture — Oslo, 27 November 1987," *Studia Theologica,* 42 (1988), 21-38.

————. "The Theological Case against Biblical Theology." In *Canon, Theology, and Old Testament Interpretation: Essays in Honor of Brevard S. Childs.* Ed. G. M. Tucker, D. L. Petersen, and R. R. Wilson. Philadelphia, 1988. Pp. 3-19.

————. "Are We Moving Toward an Old Testament Theology, or Away From It?" Paper read at the Society of Biblical Literature, Nov. 1989. Abstract printed in *Abstracts: American Academy of Religion, Society of Biblical Literature, 1989.* Ed. J. B. Wiggins and D. J. Lull. Atlanta, 1989. P. 20.

Barrois, G. A. *The Face of Christ in the Old Testament.* New York, 1974.

Barstad, Hans M. "The Historical-Critical Method and the Problem of Old Testament Theology: A Few Marginal Remarks," *Svensk Exegetisk Årsbok,* 45 (1980), 7-18.

Barth, C. "Grundprobleme einer Theologie des AT," *EvT,* 23 (1963), 342-362.

Barth, M. "Whither Biblical Theology," *Interp,* 25 (1971), 350-354.

Barthelemy, D. *Dieu et son Image. Ébauche d'une Théologie biblique.* Paris, 1964.

Barton, John. "Old Testament Theology." In *Beginning Old Testament Study.* Ed. J. Rogerson. London, 1983. Pp. 90-112.

————. "Classifying Biblical Criticism," *JSOT,* 29 (1984), 27-28.

————. *Reading the Old Testament: Method in Biblical Study.* Philadelphia, 1984.

Bauer, Georg Lorenz. *Theologie des Alten Testaments oder Abriss der religiösen Begriffe der alten Hebräer. Von den ältesten Zeiten bis auf den Anfang der christlichen Epoche. Zum Gebrauch akademischer Vorlesungen.* Leipzig, 1796.

————. *Biblische Theologie des Alten und Neuen Testaments.* Leipzig, 1796-1802.

Baumgärtel, Friedrich. *Die Bedeutung des Alten Testaments für den Christen.* Schwerin, 1925.

————. "Erwägungen zur Darstellung der Theologie des AT," *TLZ,* 76 (1951), 257-272.

————. *Verheissung. Zur Frage des evangelischen Verständnisses des Alten Testaments.* Gütersloh, 1952.

————. "Ohne Schlüssel vor der Tür des Wortes Gottes?" *EvT,* 13 (1953), 413-421.

————. "Das alttestamentliche Geschehen als 'heilgeschichtliches' Geschehen." In *Geschichte und Altes Testament. Aufsätze von W. F. Albright et al.* Beiträge zur historischen Theologie, 16. Tübingen, 1953. Pp. 13-28.

————. "Das hermeneutische Problem des Alten Testaments," *TLZ,* 79 (1954), 199-211. Trans. "The Hermeneutical Problem of the Old Testament." In C. Westermann, ed., *EOTH.* Richmond, 1963. Pp. 134-159.

————. "Der Dissensus im Verständnis des Alten Testaments," *EvT,* 14 (1954), 298-313.

————. "Gerhard von Rads Theologie des AT," *TLZ,* 86 (1961), 801-816, 895-908.

————. "Der Tod des Religionsstifters," *KuD,* 9 (1963), 223-233.

Baumgarten-Crusius, F. L. O. *Grundzüge der biblischen Theologie.* Jena, 1828.

Baumgartner, Walter. "Die Auslegung des Alten Testament im Streit der Gegenwart," *Schweizerische Theologische Umschau,* 11 (1941), 17-38.

Beauchamp, P. "Propositions sur l'alliance de l'AT comme structure centrale," *RSR,* 58 (1970), 161-194.

————. *L'un et l'autre Testament. Essai de lecture.* Paris, 1976.

Beisser, F. "Irrwege und Wege der historisch-kritischen Bibelwissenschaft," *Neue Zeitschrift für systematische Theologie,* 15 (1973), 192-214.

Beker, J. Christiaan. "Biblical Theology Today," *Princeton Seminary Bulletin,* 6 (1968), 13-19.

————. "Biblical Theology in a Time of Confusion," *TToday,* 25 (1968), 185-194.

————. "Reflections on Biblical Theology," *Interp,* 24 (1970), 303-320.

Benoit, P. "Exégèse et Théologie Biblique." In *Exégèse et Théologie*. Paris, 1968. III, 1-13.

Berlin, Adele. *Poetics and Interpretation of Biblical Narrative*. Sheffield, 1983.

Betti, Emilio. "Hermeneutics as the General Science of *Geisteswissenschaften*." In *Contemporary Hermeneutics: Hermeneutics as Method, Philosophy, and Critique*. Ed. Josef Bleicher. London, 1980. Pp. 51-94.

Betz, Otto. "Biblical Theology, History of." In *IDB*, I, 432-437.

Bikerland, H. "Israelitisk-jødisk religionshistorie og gammeltestamentlig bibelteologie," *Norsk Teologisk Tidsskrift*, 37 (1936), 1-19.

Birch, B. C. "Tradition, Canon and Biblical Theology," *HBT*, 2 (1980), 113-125.

———. "Old Testament Theology: Its Task and Future," *HBT*, 6 / 1 (1984), vi.

Bjørdalen, A. J. "Det Gamle Testaments Teologi, Metodiske haved problemer," *Tidsskrift for Teologi og Kirke*, 30 (1959), 92-116.

Blenkinsopp, J. A. *Sketchbook of Biblical Theology*. London, 1968.

———. *Prophecy and Canon: A Contribution to the Study of Jewish Origins*. Notre Dame, IN, 1977.

———. *Wisdom and Law in the Old Testament*. Oxford, 1983.

Bodenstein, W. "Verheissung im Alten und Neuen Testament," *Zum Beispiel*, 6 (1971), 90-97.

Boman, Thorleif. *Hebrew Thought Compared with Greek*. London, 1960.

Bormann, C. von. "Die Zweideutigkeit der hermeneutischen Erfahrung." In *Hermeneutik und Ideologiekritik*. Frankfurt, 1971. Pp. 83-119.

Bormann, C. von, and Holzhey, H. "Kritik." In *Historisches Wörterbuch der Philosophie*, IV, 1249-1282.

Borowitz, Eugene B. "The Problem of the Form of a Jewish Theology," *Hebrew Union College Annual*, 40-41 (1969-1970), 391-408.

Boschi, B. G. "Per una teologia dell'Antico Testamento," *Sacra Dottrina*, 21 (1976), 147-174.

Braaten, C. F. *History and Hermeneutics*. Philadelphia, 1966.

Branton, J. R., R. A. Brown, M. Burrows, and J. D. Smart, "Our Present Situation in Biblical Theology," *Religion in Life*, 26 (1956-57), 5-39.

Braun, F. M. "La Théologie Biblique," *Revue Thomiste*, 61 (1953), 221-253.

Braun, Roddy L. "Chronicles, Ezra and Nehemiah: Theology and Literary History." In *Studies in the Historical Books of the Old Testament*. Ed. J. A. Emerton. *Supplements to VT*, 30. Leiden, 1979. Pp. 52-64.

Brecht, M. "Johann Albrecht Bengels Theologie der Schrift," *ZTK*, 64 (1967), 99-120.

Brekelmans, C., ed. *Questions disputées d'Ancien Testament: Méthode et théologie*. Bibliotheca Ephemeridum Theologicarum Lovaniensium, 33. Louvain, 1974.

Brettler, Marc. "Canon: How the Books of the Hebrew Bible Were Chosen," *Bible Review*, 5/4 (1989), 12-13.

Bright, John. "Recent Biblical Theologies: VIII. Edmond Jacob's 'Theology of the Old Testament,'" *ExpTim*, 73 (1961-1962), 304-308.

———. *The Authority of the Old Testament*. Nashville, 1967.

Brown, R. E. "The Contribution of Historical Biblical Criticism to Ecumenical Church Discussion." In *Biblical Interpretation in Crisis: The Ratzinger Conference on Bible and Church.* Ed. Richard J. Neuhaus. Encounter Series, 9. Grand Rapids, 1989. Pp. 24-49.

Brown, R. M. "Story and Theology." In *Philosophy of Religion and Theology: Proceedings of the American Academy of Religion.* Ed. J. W. McClennon, Jr. Missoula, 1974. Pp. 55-72.

Bruce, F. F. *The New Testament Development of Old Testament Themes.* Grand Rapids, 1973.

Brueggemann, W. *Tradition for Crisis: A Study in Hosea.* Richmond, 1968.

———. "The Kerygma of the Priestly Writers," *ZAW,* 84 (1972), 397-413.

———. "Yahwist." In *IDB Supplement.* Nashville, 1976. Pp. 971-975.

———. "A Convergence in Recent Old Testament Theologies," *JSOT,* 18 (1980), 2-18.

———. "A Shape for Old Testament Theology, I: Structure Legitimation," *CBQ,* 47 (1985), 28-46.

———. "Canon and Dialectic." In *God and His Temple.* Ed. L. E. Frizzell. S. Orange, NJ, 1981. Pp. 20-29.

———. "A Shape for Old Testament Theology, II: Embrace of Pain," *CBQ,* 47 (1985), 395-415.

———. "Futures in Old Testament Theology," *HBT,* 6 (1984), 1-11.

Brueggemann, W., and Wolff, H. W. *The Vitality of Old Testament Traditions.* 2nd ed. Atlanta, 1982.

Bultmann, Rudolf. "Die Bedeutung des Alten Testament für den christlichen Glauben." In *Glauben und Verstehen,* I. 5th. ed. Tübingen, 1964. 1st ed. 1933. Pp. 313-336. Trans. "The Significance of the Old Testament for the Christian Faith." In *OTCF: A Theological Discussion.* Ed. Bernhard W. Anderson. London, 1964. Pp. 8-35.

———. "Weissagung und Erfüllung," *Studia Theologica,* 2 (1948), 21-44 (= *ZTK,* 47 [1950], 360-383; = R. Bultmann, *Glauben und Verstehen,* II. 3rd. ed. Tübingen, 1961. Pp. 162-186). Trans. "Prophecy and Fulfillment." In *Essays Philosophical and Theological.* London, 1955. Pp. 182-208.

Burden, J. J. "Methods of Old Testament Theology: Past, Present and Future," *Theologia Evangelica,* 10 (1977), 14-33.

Burrows, M. "The Task of Biblical Theology," *JBR,* 14 (1946), 13-15.

———. *An Outline of Biblical Theology.* Philadelphia, 1946.

Buss, Martin. "The Meaning of History." In *Theology as History.* Ed. J. M. Robinson and J. B. Cobb. New Frontiers in Theology, 3. New York, 1967. Pp. 135-154.

Calull, P. J. "The Unity of the Bible," *Biblica,* 65 (1984), 404-411.

Campos, José da Silva. "História da Salvação e Teologia Bíblica," *Revista de cultura bíblica,* 17 (1970), 72-88.

Cancik, H. *Mythische und historische Wahrheit. Interpretationen zu Texten der hethitischen, biblischen und griechischen Historiographie.* Stuttgarter Bibelstudien, 48. Stuttgart, 1970.

Carroll, R. P. "Canonical Criticism: A Recent Trend in Biblical Studies," *Exp-Tim*, 92 (1980), 73-78.

Cazelles, H. "The Unity of the Bible and the People of God," *Scripture*, 18 (1966), 1-10.

————. *Le Messie de la Bible. Christologie de l'Ancien Testament.* Jésus et Jésus Christ, 7. Paris, 1978.

————. "The Canonical Approach to Torah and Prophets," *JSOT*, 16 (1980), 28-31.

Childs, B. S. "Prophecy and Fulfillment," *Interp*, 12 (1958), 259-271.

————. "Interpretation in Faith: The Theological Responsibility of an Old Testament Commentary," *Interp*, 18 (1964), 432-449.

————. *Biblical Theology in Crisis.* Philadelphia: Westminster, 1970.

————. "The Old Testament as Scripture of the Church," *CTM*, 43 (1972), 709-722.

————. "The Canonical Shape of the Prophetic Literature," *Interp*, 33 (1978), 46-55.

————. "The Exegetical Significance of Canon for the Study of the Old Testament." In *Congress Volume, Göttingen, 1977. Supplements to VT*, 24. Leiden, 1978. Pp. 66-80.

————. *Introduction to the Old Testament as Scripture.* Philadelphia, 1979.

————. "Response to Reviewers of *Introduction to the Old Testament as Scripture*," *JSOT*, 16 (1980), 52-60.

————. "A Response," *HBT*, 2 (1980), 199-211.

————. "Differenzen in der Exegese. Biblische Theologie in Amerika," *Evangelische Kommentare*, 14 (1981), 405-406.

————. "Some Reflections on the Search for a Biblical Theology," *HBT*, 4 (1982), 1-12.

————. *The New Testament as Canon: An Introduction.* London, 1984; Philadelphia, 1985.

————. *Old Testament Theology in a Canonical Context.* London, 1985; Philadelphia, 1986.

Clavier, H. *Les variétés de la pensée biblique et le problème de son unité.* New Testament Studies, 43. Leiden, 1976.

Clements, R. E. "The Problem of Old Testament Theology," *London Quarterly and Holborn Review* (Jan. 1965), 11-17.

————. "Theodorus C. Vriezen, An Outline of Old Testament Theology." In *Contemporary Old Testament Theologians.* Ed. Robert B. Laurin. Valley Forge, 1970. Pp. 121-140.

————. *One Hundred Years of Old Testament Interpretation.* Philadelphia, 1976.

————. "Recent Developments in Old Testament Theology," *Epworth Review*, 3 (1976), 99-107.

————. "Pentateuchal Problems." In *Tradition and Interpretation: Essays by Members of the Society for Old Testament Study.* Ed. G. W. Anderson. Oxford, 1977. Pp. 96-124.

——. *Old Testament Theology: A Fresh Approach.* Atlanta: Knox, 1978.

——. "History and Theology in Biblical Narrative," *HBT,* 4-5 (1982-1983), 45-60.

Coats, George W. "Theology of the Hebrew Bible." In *The Hebrew Bible and Its Modern Interpreters.* Ed. Douglas A. Knight and Gene M. Tucker. Philadelphia / Chico, CA, 1985. Pp. 239-262.

Coats, G. W., and Long, B. O., eds. *Canon and Authority: Essays in Old Testament Religion and Theology.* Philadelphia, 1977.

Coggins, R. J. "History and Story in Old Testament Study," *JSOT,* 11 (1979), 36-46.

Collins, J. J. "The Biblical Precedent for Natural Theology," *JAAR Supplement,* 45 (1977), 35-62.

——. "The 'Historical Character' of the Old Testament in Recent Biblical Theology," *CBQ,* 41 (1979), 185-204.

——. "Is a Critical Biblical Theology Possible?" In *The Hebrew Bible and Its Interpreters.* Ed. William Henry Propp, Baruch Halpern, and David Noel Freedman. Winona Lake, IN, 1990. Pp. 1-17.

——. "Old Testament Theology." In *The Biblical Heritage in Modern Catholic Scholarship.* Ed. J. J. Collins and J. D. Crossan. Wilmington, 1986. Pp. 11-33.

Cölln, D. G. C. von. *Die biblische Theologie des Alten Testaments; Die biblische Theologie des Neuen Testaments.* Ed. D. Schultz. 2 vols. Leipzig, 1836.

Conzelmann, Hans. "Fragen an Gerhard von Rad," *EvT,* 24 (1964), 113-125.

Cordero, M. G. *Theologia de la Biblia I. Antiguo Testamento.* Madrid, 1970.

Craig, Clarence Trucker. "Biblical Theology and the Rise of Historicism," *JBL,* 62 (1943), 281-294.

Crenshaw, James L. *Gerhard von Rad.* Waco, 1979.

Crenshaw, James L., ed. *Studies in Ancient Israelite Wisdom.* New York, 1976.

Crites, S. "The Narrative Quality of Experience," *JAAR,* 39 (1971), 291-311.

Crönert, H. "Plädoyer für den Ketzer Markion," *Deutsches Pfarrerblatt,* 81 (1981), 562-564.

Cullmann, O. *Christ and Time.* 2nd ed. London, 1962.

——. *Salvation in History.* London, 1967.

Curtis, J. B. "A Suggested Interpretation of the Biblical Philosophy of History," *Hebrew Union College Annual,* 34 (1963), 115-123.

Cwiekowski, Frederick J. "Biblical Theology as Historical Theology," *CBQ,* 24 (1962), 404- 410.

Davey, F. N. "Biblical Theology," *Theology,* 38 (1939), 166-176.

Davidson, A. B. *The Theology of the Old Testament.* Ed. S. D. F. Salmond. Edinburgh, 1904.

Davidson, R. "Faith and History in the Old Testament," *ExpTim,* 77 (1965 / 66), 100-104.

——. "The Theology of the Old Testament." In R. Davidson and A. R. C. Leaney, *Biblical Criticism.* Pelican Guides to Modern Theology, 3. London, 1970. Pp. 138-165.

SELECTED BIBLIOGRAPHY 217

————. "The Old Testament—A Question of Theological Relevance." In *Biblical Studies: Essays in Honour of William Barclay*. Ed. J. R. McKay and J. F. Miller. London, 1976. Pp. 43-56.

Davies, G. Henton. "Gerhard von Rad, Old Testament Theology." In *Contemporary Old Testament Theologians*. Ed. Robert B. Laurin. Valley Forge, 1970. Pp. 63-90.

de Wette, W. M. L. *Biblische Dogmatik Alten und Neuen Testaments. Oder kritische Darstellung der Religionslehre des Hebraismus, des Judenthums und Urchristenthums. Zum Gebrauch akademischer Vorlesungen.* Berlin, 1813.

Deissler, A. *Die Grundbotschaft des Alten Testaments*. Freiburg: Herder, 1972.

————. "Der Gott des AT." In *Die Frage nach Gott*. Ed. J. Ratzinger. 2nd ed. Freiburg i. Br., 1973. Pp. 45-58.

Dentan, R. C. "The Old Testament and a Theology for Today," *Anglican Theological Review*, 27 (1945), 17-27.

————. "The Nature and Function of Old Testament Theology," *JBR*, 14 (1946), 16-21.

————. "The Unity of the Old Testament," *Interp*, 5 (1951), 153-173.

————. *Preface to Old Testament Theology*. 2nd ed. New York, 1963.

————. *A First Reader in Biblical Theology*. New York, 1965.

————. *The Knowledge of God in Ancient Israel*. New York, 1965.

Deutschmann, J. *Theologia Biblica*. 1710.

Dever, William G. "Biblical Theology and Biblical Archaeology: An Appreciation of G. Ernest Wright," *Harvard Theological Review*, 73 (1980), 1-16.

DeVries, Simon J. *Yesterday, Today and Tomorrow: Time and History in the Old Testament*. Grand Rapids, 1975.

Dibelius, Martin. "Biblical Theology and the History of Biblical Religion." In *Twentieth Century Theology in the Making, I*. Ed. J. Pelikan. New York, 1971. Pp. 23-31.

Dickerhoff, Heinrich. *Wege ins Alte Testament—und zurück. Vom Sinn und den Möglichkeiten einer 'Theologie mit dem Alten Testament' in der Arbeit mit Erwachsenen*. Europäische Hochschulschriften, 23 / 211. Frankfurt / Bern / New York, 1983.

Diem, H. *Theologie als kirchliche Wissenschaft*. Gütersloh, 1951.

Diest, Henricus A. *Theologia biblica, Praeter succinctam Locorum communium delineationem exhibens Testimonia Scripturae, Ad singulos locos, locorumque singula capita, capitumque singula membra, pertinentia*. Daventria, 1643.

Dietrich, W. "Rache. Erwägungen zu einem alttestamentlichen Thema," *EvT*, 36 (1976), 450-472.

————. "Der rote Faden im Alten Testament," *EvT*, 49 (1989), 232-250.

Dilley, F. B. "Does the 'God Who Acts' Really Act?" *Anglican Theological Review*, 47 (1965), 66-80.

Dillmann, A. *Handbuch der alttestamentlichen Theologie*. Ed. R. Kittel. Leipzig, 1895.

218 OLD TESTAMENT THEOLOGY

Dirksen, P. B. "Die mogelijkheid van een theologie van het Oude Testament," *Nederlands(ch)e theologisch Tijdschrift*, 36 (1982), 279-290.

Dreyfus, F. "L'Actualisation à l'interieur de la Bible," *Revue Biblique*, 83 (1976), 161-202.

Duhm, Bernhard. *Die Theologie der Propheten.* Leipzig, 1875.

Dulles, Avery. "Response to Krister Stendahl's 'Method in the Study of Biblical Theology.' " In *The Bible in Modern Scholarship.* Ed. J. P. Hyatt. Nashville, 1965. Pp. 210-219.

———. "Scripture: Recent Protestant and Catholic Views," *TToday*, 37 (1980), 7-26.

Dunn, J. D. G. "Levels of Canonical Authority," *HBT*, 4 (1982), 13-60.

Dyrness, W. *Themes in Old Testament Theology.* Downers Grove, IL, 1979.

Eakin, F. E. "Wisdom, Creation and Covenant," *Perspectives in Religious Studies*, 4 (1977), 225-239.

Ebeling, G. "Die Bedeutung der historisch-kritischen Methode für die protestantische Theologie und Kirche," *ZTK*, 47 (1950), 1-46. Trans. "The Significance of the Critical Historical Method for Church and Theology in Protestantism." In G. Ebeling, *Word and Faith.* London, 1963. Pp. 17-61.

———. "Die Anfänge von Luthers Hermeneutik," *ZTK*, 48 (1951), 172-230.

———. "The Meaning of 'Biblical Theology.' " In G. Ebeling, *Word and Faith.* London, 1963. Pp. 79-97.

———. *Einführung in die theologische Sprachlehre.* Tübingen, 1971.

———. *Studium der Theologie. Eine enzyklopädische Orientierung.* Tübingen, 1975.

Ehlen, J. A. "Old Testament Theology as Heilsgeschichte," *CTM*, 35 (1964), 517-544.

Eichrodt, Walther. "Hat die alttestamentliche Theologie noch selbständige Bedeutung innerhalb der alttestamentlichen Wissenschaft?" *ZAW*, 47 (1929), 83-91. Trans. "Does Old Testament Theology Still Have Independent Significance Within Old Testament Scholarship." In *The Flowering of Old Testament Theology: A Reader in Twentieth Century Old Testament Theology.* Ed. B. C. Ollenburger, E. A. Martens, and G. F. Hasel. Winona Lake, IN, 1991.

———. *Theologie des AT.* 3 vols. Leipzig, 1933, 1935, 1939. Trans. *TOT.* 2 vols. Philadelphia, 1961, 1967.

———. "Offenbarung und Geschichte im Alten Testament," *TZ*, 4 (1948), 321ff.

———. "Ist typologische Exegese sachgemässe Exegese?" Repr. in *Probleme alttestamentlicher Hermeneutik.* Ed. C. Westermann. TBü, 11. Munich, 1960. Pp. 205-226. Trans. "Is Typological Exegesis an Appropriate Method?" In *EOTH.* Pp. 224-245.

———. "Darf man heute noch von einem Gottesbund mit Israel reden?" *TZ*, 30 (1974), 193-206.

Eissfeldt, Otto. "Israelitisch-jüdische Religionsgeschichte und alttestamentliche Theologie," *ZAW*, 44 (1926), 1-12. Reprinted in *Kleine Schriften*, I. Tübingen, 1962. Pp. 105-114. Trans. "History of Israelite-Jewish Religion and Old Testament Theology." In *The Flowering of Old Testament Theology:*

A Reader in Twentieth Century Old Testament Theology. Ed. B. C. Ollenburger, E. A. Martens, and G. F. Hasel. Winona Lake, IN, 1991.

————. "Geschichtliches und Übergeschichtliches im Alten Testaments: Volk und 'Kirche' in Alten Testament," *Theologische Studien und Kritiken,* 109 (1947), 9-23.

Ellis, P. F. *The Yahwist: The Bible's First Theologian.* Notre Dame, 1968.

Evans, M. J. "The Old Testament as Christian Scripture," *Vox Evangelica,* 16 (1986), 25-32.

Fackre, Gabriel. "Narrative Theology: An Overview," *Interp,* 37 (1983), 340-352.

Fannon, Patrick. "A Theology of the Old Testament—Is it Possible?" *Scriptorium,* 19 / 46 (1967), 46-53.

Fensham, F. C. "The Covenant as Giving Expression to the Relationship between Old Testament and New Testament," *TynBul,* 22 (1971), 82-94.

————. "Die vorhoudingstheologie as 'n moontlike oplossing vir 'n theologie van die Ou Testament," *Nederduitse Gereformeerde Teologiese Tydskrif,* 26 (1985), 246-249.

Festorazzi, F. "Rassegna di teologia dell'AT," *Rivista Biblica,* 10 (1962), 297-316; 12 (1964), 27-48.

Filson, Floyd V. "A New Testament Student's Approach to Biblical Theology," *JBR,* 14 (1946), 22-28.

————. "Biblische Theologie in Amerika," *TLZ,* 75 (1950), 71-80.

————. "The Unity of the Old and the New Testaments: A Bibliographical Survey," *Interp,* 5 (1951), 134-152.

————. "The Unity Between the Testaments." In *The Interpreter's One-Volume Commentary on the Bible.* Nashville, 1971. Pp. 989-993.

Flückiger, F. *Theologie der Geschichte. Die biblische Rede von Gott und die neuere Geschichtstheologie.* Wuppertal, 1970.

Fohrer, G. "Der Mittelpunkt einer Theologie des AT," *TZ,* 24 (1968), 161-172. Trans. "The Centre of a Theology of the Old Testament," *Nederduitse Gereformeerde Teologiese Tydskrif,* 7 (1966), 198-206.

————. *Theologische Grundstrukturen des Alten Testaments.* Theologische Bibliothek Töpelmann, 24. Berlin, 1972.

Ford, David. *Barth and God's Story: Biblical Narrative and the Theological Method of Karl Barth in the "Church Dogmatics."* Frankfurt / Bern, 1981.

France, R. *Jesus and the Old Testament.* London, 1971.

Freedman, David Noel. "The Biblical Idea of History," *Interp,* 21 (1967), 32-49.

Frei, Hans. *The Eclipse of Biblical Narrative: A Study in Eighteenth and Nineteenth Century Hermeneutics.* New Haven, 1974.

————. "Response to 'Narrative Theology: An Evangelical Appraisal,'" *Trinity Journal,* NS 8 (1987), 21-24.

Fretheim, T. E. "Elohist." In *IDB Supplement.* Nashville, 1976. Pp. 259-263.

Fridrichsen, A. et al. *The Root of the Vine: Essays in Biblical Theology.* Westminster / New York, 1953.

Fritsch, Charles T. "New Trends in Old Testament Theology," *BibSac,* 103 (1946), 293-305.

————. "Biblical Theology II: The Bible as Redemptive History," *BibSac,* 103 (1946), 418-430.

Frizzell, L. E., ed. *God and His Temple: Reflections on Professor Samuel Terrien's The Elusive Presence: Toward a New Biblical Theology.* S. Orange, NJ, 1981.

Fruchon, P. "Sur l'herméneutique de Gerhard von Rad," *RSPT,* 55 (1971), 4-32.

————. "Herméneutique, language et ontologie. Un discernement du platonisme chez H.-G. Gadamer," *Archives de Philosophie,* 36 (1973), 529-568; 37 (1974), 223-242, 353-375, 533-571.

Fuchs, E. "Theologie oder Ideologie," *TLZ,* 88 (1963), 257-260.

————. *Marburger Hermeneutik.* Hermeneutische Untersuchungen zur Theologie, 9. Tübingen, 1968.

Gabler, J. P. "De iusto discrimine theologiae biblicae et dogmaticae regundisque recte utriusque finibus." In *Opuscula academica, Kleinere theologische Schriften,* II. Ulm, 1831. Pp. 179-198. Trans. "On the Proper Distinction Between Biblical and Dogmatic Theology and the Specific Objectives of Each." In J. Sandys-Wunsch and L. Eldredge. "J. P. Gabler and the Distinction Between Biblical and Dogmatic Theology: Translation, Commentary, and Discussion of His Originality," *SJT,* 33 (1980), 134-144.

Gadamer, Hans-Georg. *Truth and Method.* New York, 1975. 2nd ed. 1989.

Gaffin, Richard B. "Systematic Theology and Biblical Theology," *Westminster Theological Journal,* 38 (1976), 281-299.

Gamble, Connolly. "The Nature of Biblical Theology," *Interp,* 5 (1951), 462-467.

————. "The Literature of Biblical Theology: A Bibliographical Study," *Interp,* 7 (1953), 466-480.

Gélin, A. *Les idées maîtresses de l'Ancien Testament.* Paris, 1948.

Gese, H. "The Idea of History in the Ancient Near East and the Old Testament," *Journal of Theology and the Church,* 1 (1965), 49-64.

————. "Erwägungen zur Einheit der biblischen Theologie," *ZTK,* 67 (1970), 417-436.

————. *Vom Sinai zum Zion. Alttestamentliche Beiträge zur biblischen Theologie.* Beiträge zur evangelischen Theologie, 64. Munich, 1974.

————. "Tradition and Biblical Theology." In *Tradition and Theology in the Old Testament.* Ed. D. A. Knight. Philadelphia, 1977. Pp. 301-326.

————. *Zur biblische Theologie. Alttestamentliche Vorträge.* Munich, 1977. Trans. *Essays on Biblical Theology.* Minneapolis, 1981.

————. "Wisdom, Son of Man, and the Origins of Christology: The Consistent Development of Biblical Theology," *HBT,* 3 (1981), 23-57.

Geyer, Hans-Georg. "Geschichte als theologisches Problem," *EvT,* 22 (1962), 92-104.

————. "Zur Frage der Notwendigkeit des Alten Testaments," *EvT,* 25 (1965), 207-237.

Gilkey, L. B. "Cosmology, Ontology, and the Travail of Biblical Language," *JR,* 41 (1961), 194-205.

Goldberg, Michael. *Theology and Narrative: A Critical Introduction.* Nashville, 1982.

Goldingay, John. " 'That You May Know That Yahweh Is God': A Study in the Relationship Between Theology and Historical Truth in the Old Testament," *TynBul*, 23 (1972), 58-93.

———. "The Chronicler as Theologian," *BTB*, 5 (1975), 99-126.

———. "The Study of Old Testament Theology: Its Aims and Purpose," *TynBul*, 26 (1975), 34-52.

———. "The 'Salvation History' Perspective and the 'Wisdom' Perspective Within the Context of Biblical Theology," *EvQ*, 51 (1979), 194-207.

———. *Approaches to Old Testament Interpretation*. Downers Grove, 1981.

———. "Diversity and Unity in Old Testament Theology," *VT*, 34 (1984), 152-168.

———. *Theological Diversity and the Authority of the Old Testament*. Grand Rapids, 1987.

Goossens, G. "La philosophie de l'histoire dans l'Ancient Orient," *Sacra pagina*, 1 (1959), 242-252.

Goppelt, L. *Typos: Die Typologische Bedeutung des AT im Neuen*. 2nd ed. Darmstadt, 1966. Trans. *Typos: The Typological Interpretation of the Old Testament in the New*. Grand Rapids, 1982.

———. "Typos." In *TDNT*, VII. Grand Rapids, 1972. Pp. 246-259.

Goshen-Gottstein, M. H. "Tanakh Theology: The Religion of the Old Testament and the Place of Jewish Biblical Theology." In *Ancient Israelite Religion: Essays in Honor of Frank Moore Cross*. Ed. P. D. Miller, P. D. Hanson, and S. D. McBride. Philadelphia, 1987. Pp. 617-644.

Gottwald, N. K. "Recent Biblical Theologies: IX. Walther Eichrodt's 'Theology of the Old Testament,' " *ExpTim*, 74 (1963), 209-212.

Gottwald, N. K. *The Tribes of Yahweh*. Maryknoll, 1979.

———. *The Hebrew Bible: A Socio-Literary Introduction*. Philadelphia, 1985.

Grass, H. *Christliche Glaubenslehre*. Stuttgart, 1974.

Grässer, Erich. "Die Politische Herausforderung an die biblische Theologie," *EvT*, 30 (1970), 228-254.

———. "Antijudaismus bei Bultmann? Eine Erwiderung," *Wissenschaft und Praxis in Kirche und Gesellschaft*, 67 (1978), 419-429.

———. "Offene Fragen im Umkreis einer Biblischen Theologie," *ZTK*, 77 (1980), 200-221.

Greig, Joseph. "Geschichte and Heilsgeschichte in Old Testament Interpretation with Special Reference to Gerhard von Rad." Unpublished Ph.D. dissertation, University of Edinburgh, 1974.

———. "Some Formative Aspects in the Development of Gerhard von Rad's Idea of History," *AUSS*, 16 (1978), 313-331.

Grelot, P. *Sens Chrétien de l'AT*. Tournai, 1962.

———. "La lecture chrétienne de l'AT." In *Où en sont les études bibliques?* Ed. J. J. Weber and J. Schmitt. Paris, 1968. Pp. 29-50.

Gross, Heinrich. "Was ist alttestamentliche Theologie?" *TZ* (Trier), 67 (1958), 355-363.

Gross, W. and F. Mussner, "Die Einheit von Alte und Neuem Testament," *Internationale Katholische Zeitschrift*, 3 (1974), 544-555.

Groves, Joseph W. *Actualization and Interpretation in the Old Testament.* SBLDS, 86. Atlanta, 1987.

Gunkel, Hermann. "Biblische Theologie und biblische Religionsgeschichte, I. des Alten Testaments." In *Die Religion in Geschichte und Gegenwart.* 2nd ed. Tübingen, 1927. I, 1089-1091.

————. *What Remains of the Old Testament and Other Essays.* New York, 1928.

————. *The Legends of Genesis: The Biblical Saga and History.* New York, 1965.

Gunneweg, A. H. J. *Vom Verstehen des Alten Testaments: Eine Hermeneutik.* Göttingen, 1977. Trans. *Understanding the Old Testament.* Old Testament Library. London / Philadelphia, 1978.

————. " 'Theologie' des Alten Testaments oder 'Biblische Theologie'?" In *Textgemäss. Aufsätze und Beitäge zur Hermeneutik des Alten Testaments. Festschrift für Ernst Würthwein zum 70. Geburtstag.* Ed. A. H. J. Gunneweg and O. Kaiser. Göttingen, 1979. Pp. 38-46.

————. *Sola Scriptura. Beiträge zu Exegese und Hermenutik des Alten Testaments.* Göttingen, 1983.

————. "Altes Testament und existentiale Interpretation." In *Rudolf Bultmanns Werk und Wirkung.* Ed. B. Jasper. Darmstadt, 1984. Pp. 332-347.

Gunneweg, A. H. J., and Kaiser, O., eds. *Textgemäss. Aufsätze und Beitäge zur hermeneutik des Alten Testaments. Festschrift für Ernst Würthwein zum 70. Geburtstag.* Göttingen, 1979.

Guthrie, Donald. "Biblical Authority and New Testament Scholarship," *Vox Evangelica,* 16 (1986), 7-23.

Guthrie, H. H., Jr. *God and History in the Old Testament.* London, 1961.

Haacker, K. "Die Fragestellung der Biblischen Theologie als exegetische Aufgabe." In K. Haacker et al., *Biblische Theologie heute.* Biblisch-theologische Studien, 1. Neukirchen-Vluyn, 1977. Pp. 9-23.

Haacker, K., ed. *Biblische Theologie heute.* Biblisch-theologische Studien, 1. Neukirchen-Vluyn, 1977.

Haag, H. "Biblische Theologie," *Mysterium Salutis,* I (Einsiedeln / Zürich / Köln, 1965), 440-459.

————. *Das Buch des Bundes. Aufsätze zur Bibel und zu ihrer Welt.* Düsseldorf, 1980.

————. "Vom Eigenwert des Alten Testaments," *Theologische Quartalschrift,* 160 (1980), 2-16.

Hahn, F. "Probleme historischer Kritik," *Zeitschrift für die neutestamentliche Wissenschaft,* 63 (1972), 1-17.

————. "Exegese und Fundamentaltheologie," *Theologische Quartalschrift,* 155 (1975), 262-280.

————. "Provokative Thesen zu einem provokativen Buch," *EvT,* 83 (1983), 178-184.

Halbe, Jorn. " 'Altorientalisches Weltordnungsdenken' und alttestamentliche Theologie: Zur Kritik eines Ideologems am Beispiel des Israelitischen Rechts," *ZTK,* 76 (1979), 381-418.

Halperin, J. "Les dimensions juives de l'histoire," *Revue de théologie et de philosophie*, 98 (1965), 222-240.

Hamp, V. "Neuere Theologien des Alten Testaments," *Biblische Zeitschrift*, 2 (1958), 303-313.

———. "Geschichtsschreibung im Alten Testament." In *Speculum Historiale. Festschrift für J. Spörl*. Fribourg / Munich, 1965. Pp. 134-142.

Hanson, P. *Dynamic Transcendence: The Correlation of a Confessional Heritage and Contemporary Experience in a Biblical Model of Divine Activity.* Philadelphia, 1978.

———. *The Diversity of Scripture: A Theological Interpretation.* OBT, 11. Philadelphia, 1982.

———. "Theology, Old Testament." In *Harper's Bible Dictionary*. Ed. Paul Achtemeier. San Francisco, 1985. Pp. 1057-1062.

———. *The People Called: The Growth of Community in the Bible*. San Francisco, 1986.

Haroutunian, J. "Recent Theology and the Biblical Mind," *JBR*, 8 (1940), 18-23.

Harrelson, Walter. "The Limited Task of Old Testament Theology," *HBT*, 6 / 1 (1984), 65-71.

Harrington, Wilfrid J. *The Path of Biblical Theology*. Dublin, 1973.

Hartlich, C. "Historisch-kritische Methode in ihrer Anwendung auf Geschehnisaussagen der Hl. Schrift," *ZTK*, 75 (1978), 467-484.

Hartlich, C. and W. Sachs. *Der Ursprung des Mythosbegriffes in der modernen Bibelwissenschaft*. Tübingen, 1952.

Harvey, J. "Symbolique et théologie biblique," *Sciences ecclésiastiques*, 9 (1957), 141-157.

———. "The New Diachronic Biblical Theology of the Old Testament (1960-1970)," *BTB*, 1 (1971), 5-29.

———. "Wisdom Literature and Biblical Theology, I," *BTB*, 1 (1971), 308-319.

Harvey, Van A. *The Historian and the Believer*. New York, 1966.

Hasel, G. F. "The Problem of History in Old Testament Theology Debate," *AUSS*, 8 (1970), 32-35, 41-46.

———. "Capito, Schwenckfeld and Crautwald or Sabbatarian Anabaptist Theology," *Mennonite Quarterly Review*, 46 (1972), 41-57.

———. *The Remnant: The History and Theology of the Remnant Idea from Genesis to Isaiah*. Andrews University Monographs, 5; Berrien Springs, MI, 1972. 2nd ed. 1975.

———. "The Problem of the Center in the OT Theology Debate," *ZAW*, 86 (1974), 65-82.

———. *New Testament Theology: Basic Issues in the Current Debate*. Grand Rapids, 1978.

———. "The Future of Biblical Theology." In *Perspectives on Evangelical Theology*. Ed. K. S. Kantzer and S. N. Gundry. Grand Rapids, 1979. Pp. 179-194.

———. "A Decade of Old Testament Biblical Theology: Retrospect and Prospect," *ZAW*, 93 (1981), 165-184.

————. "Biblical Theology: Then, Now and Tomorrow," *HBT,* 4 (1982), 61-93.

————. "Biblical Theology Movement." In *Evangelical Dictionary of Theology.* Ed. Walter A. Elwell. Grand Rapids, 1984. Pp. 149-152.

————. "The Relationship Between Biblical Theology and Systematic Theology," *Trinity Journal,* NS 5 (1984), 113-127.

————. "Major Recent Issues in Old Testament Theology 1978-1983," *JSOT,* 31 (1985), 31-53.

————. "Old Testament Theology from 1978-1987," *AUSS,* 26 / 2 (1988), 133-157.

————. "Biblical Theology: Current Issues and Future Prospects," *Catalyst,* 16 / 1 (Jan. 1990), 6-8.

————. "The Future of Old Testament Theology." In *The Flowering of Old Testament Theology: A Reader in Twentieth Century Old Testament Theology.* Ed. B. C. Ollenburger, E. A. Martens, and G. F. Hasel. Winona Lake, IN, 1991.

Hauerwas, Stanley and L. Gregory Jones, eds. *Why Narrative? Readings in Narrative Theology.* Grand Rapids, 1990.

Hausmann, G. "Biblische Theologie und kirchliches Bekenntnis." In *Lebendiger Umgang mit Schrift und Bekenntnis: Theologische Beiträge zur Beziehung von Schrift und Bekenntnis und zu ihrer Bedeutung für das Leben der Kirche.* Ed. J. Track. Stuttgart, 1980. Pp. 41-61.

Hayes, John H. and Frederick Prussner. *Old Testament Theology: Its History and Development.* Atlanta, 1985.

Haymann, Carl. *Biblische Theologie.* Leipzig, 1708.

Heinisch, P. *Theologie des AT.* Bonn, 1940. Trans. *Theology of the Old Testament.* Collegeville, MN, 1950.

Hellbart, Hans. "Die Auslegung des Alten Testament als theologische Disziplin," *TBl,* 16 (1937), 140ff.

Hempel, J. "Alttestamentliche Theologie in protestantischer Sich heute," *Bibliotheca Orientalis,* 15 (1958), 206-214.

————. "Die Faktizität der Geschichte im biblischen Denken." In *Biblical Studies in Memory of H. C. Alleman.* Locust Valley, NY, 1960. Pp. 67-88.

————. *Geschichten und Geschichte im AT bis zur persischen Zeit.* Gütersloh, 1964.

Hengel, M. "Historische Methoden und theologische Auslegung des Neuen Testaments," *KuD,* 19 (1973), 85-90.

Henry, Carl F. H. *God, Revelation, and Authority.* 6 vols. Waco, TX, 1976-1983.

————. "Narrative Theology: An Evangelical Appraisal," *Trinity Journal,* NS 8 (1987), 3-19.

Herberg, W. "Biblical Faith as 'Heilsgeschichte,'" *Christian Scholar,* 39 (1956), 25-31.

Herbert, Arthur S. "Is there a Theology of the Old Testament?" *ExpTim,* 12 (1950), 361-363.

Hermisson, Hans-Jürgen. "Observations on the Creation Theology in Wisdom." In *Israelite Wisdom: Theological and Literary Essays in Honor of Samuel Terrien.* Ed. John G. Gammie et al. Missoula, 1978. Pp. 43-57.

Herms, E. and J. Ringleben, eds. *Vergessene Theologen des 19. und frühen 20. Jahrhunderts*. Göttingen, 1984.

Herrmann, S. "Die Konstruktive Restauration. Das Deuteronomium als Mitte biblischer Theologie." In *Probleme biblischer Theologie. Gerhard von Rad zum 70. Geburtstag*. ed. H. W. Wolff. Munich, 1970. Pp. 155-170.

Heschel, Abraham J. *Man Is Not Alone*. New York, 1951.

Hesse, F. "Die Erforschung der Geschichte als theologische Aufgabe," *KuD*, 4 (1958), 1-19.

————. "Kerygma oder geschichtliche Wirklichkeit?" *ZTK*, 57 (1960), 17-26.

————. "Zur Frage der Wertung und der Geltung alttestamentlicher Texte." In *Probleme alttestamentlicher Hermeneutik*. Ed. C. Westermann. 1960. Pp. 266-294. Trans. "The Evaluation and Authority of Old Testament Texts." In *EOTH*. Pp. 285-313.

————. "Wolfhart Pannenberg und das AT," *Neue Zeitschrift für systematische Theologie und Religionswissenschaft*, 7 (1965), 174-199.

————. *Das Alte Testament als Buch der Kirche*. Gütersloh, 1966.

————. "Bewährt sich eine 'Theologie der Heilstatsachen' am AT? Zum Verhältnis von Faktum und Deutung?" *ZTK*, 81 (1969), 1-17.

————. *Abschied von der Heilsgeschichte*. Theologischer Studien, 108. Zurich, 1971.

————. "Zur Profanität der Geschichte Israels," *ZTK*, 71 (1974), 262- 290.

————. "Die Israelfrage in neueren Entwürfen Biblischer Theologie," *KuD*, 27 (1981), 180-197.

Hessen, J. *Griechische oder Biblische Theologie*. Leipzig, 1956.

Hessler, R. "De Theologiae Biblicae Veteris Testamenti Problemate," *Anton*, 25 (1950), 407-424.

Hicks, R. L. "G. Ernest Wright and Old Testament Theology," *Anglican Theological Review*, 55 (1976), 158-178.

Hicks, R. L. "Present-day Trends in Biblical Theology," *Anglican Theological Review*, 32 (1950), 136-153.

Higgins, A. J. B. *The Christian Significance of the Old Testament*. London, 1949.

Hinson, D. F. *The Theology of the Old Testament*. London, 1976.

Hirsch, E. *Das AT und die Predigt des Evangeliums*. Tübingen, 1936.

Hirsch, E. D. *Validity in Interpretation*. New Haven, 1967.

————. *The Aims of Interpretation*. Chicago, 1976.

Hitzig, F. *Vorlesungen über biblische Theologie und messianische Weissagungen des Alten Testaments*. Ed. J. J. Kneucker. Karlsruhe, 1880.

Hofius, O. " 'Rechtfertigung der Gottlosen' als Thema biblischer Theologie," *Jahrbuch für Biblische Theologie*, 2 (Neukirchen-Vluyn, 1987), 95-105.

Hofmann, Johann Christian Konrad von. *Weissagung und Erfüllung im Alten und in Neuen Testaments*. Nördlingen, 1841.

————. *Interpreting the Bible*. Minneapolis, 1959.

Høgenhaven, Jesper. *Problems and Prospects of Old Testament Theology*. The Biblical Seminar. Sheffield, 1988.

Hohmann, M. *Die Korrelation von Altem und Neuem Bund. Innerbiblische Korrelation statt Kontrastrelation*. Berlin, 1978.

Holman, J. C. M. "Twintig jaar theologie van het Oude Testament," *Twintig jaar ontwikkelingen in de theologie* (Logister, 1987), 35-44.

Honecker, M. "Zum Verständnis der Geschichte in Gerhard von Rads Theologie des AT," *EvT,* 23 (1963), 143-168.

Hübner, H. "Das Gesetz als elementares Thema einer Biblischen Theologie?" *KuD,* 22 (1976), 250-276.

――――. "Biblische Theologie und Theologie des Neuen Testaments," *KuD,* 27 (1981), 2-19.

――――. "Rudolf Bultmann und das Alte Testament," *KuD,* 30 (1984), 250-272.

Hufnagel, W. F. *Handbuch der biblischen Theologie,* I-II / 1. Erlangen, 1785, 1789.

Hummel, Horace D. "Christological Interpretation of the Old Testament," *Dialog,* 2 (1963), 108-117.

Imschoot, P. van. *Théologie de l'Ancien Testament.* Vol. I, *Dieu;* Vol. II, *L'homme.* Tournai, 1954, 1956. Vol. I trans. *Theology of the Old Testament.* New York, 1965.

Irwin, William A. "The Reviving Theology of the Old Testament," *JR,* 25 (1945), 235-246.

――――. "Trends in Old Testament Theology," *JBR,* 19 (1951), 183-190.

Jacob, Edmond. "Possibilités et limits d'une théologie biblique," *RHPR,* 46 (1951), 116-130.

――――. *Les thèmes essentiels d'une théologie de l'Ancien Testament.* Neuchâtel, 1955.

――――. *Théologie de l'Ancien Testament.* Neuchâtel, 1955. Trans. *Theology of the Old Testament.* London, 1958.

――――. "Possibilités et limites d'une théologie biblique," *RHPR,* 46 (1966), 116-130.

――――. "La théologie de l'Ancien Testament," *Ephemerides theologicae lovanienses,* 44 (1969), 420-432.

――――. *Grundfragen alttestamentlichen Theologie.* Stuttgart, 1970.

――――. "Principe canonique et formation de l'Ancien Testament." In *Congress Volume, Edinburgh, 1974. Supplements to VT,* 28. Leiden, 1975. Pp. 101-122.

――――. "De la théologie de l'Ancien Testament à la théologie biblique," *RHPR,* 57 (1977), 513-518.

――――. "Orientations actuelles de la théologie de l'Ancien Testament," *RHPR,* 67 (1987), 193-198.

――――. "L'Ancien Testament et la Théologie," *ZAW,* 100 (1988 Supplement), 268-78.

Janzen, J. Gerald. "The Old Testament in 'Process' Perspective." In *Magnalia Dei: The Mighty Acts of God: Essays on the Bible and Archaeology in Memory of G. Ernest Wright.* Ed. Frank Moore Cross et al. Garden City, NY, 1976. Pp. 480-509.

Jasper, F. N. "The Relation of the Old Testament to the New," *ExpTim,* 78 (1967/68), 228-232, 267-270.

Jensen, Jørgen I. "Literaturkritische Herausforderungen an die Theologie. Biblische Formprobleme," *EvT,* 41 (1981), 377-401.

Jepsen, A. "Die Botschaft des Alten Testaments: Überlegungen zum Aufbau einer alttestamentliche Theologie." In *Dienst unter dem Wort. Festschrift für H. Schreiner.* Gütersloh, 1953. Pp. 149-163.

―――. "Probleme der Auslegung des Alten Testaments," *Zeitschrift für systematische Theologie,* 23 (1954), 373- 386.

―――. "Theologie des AT." Wandlungen der Formen und Ziele." In *Bericht von der Theologie.* Ed. G. Kulicke, K. Matthiae, and P. P. Sänger. Berlin, 1971. Pp. 15-32.

Jones, H. O. "Das Story-Konzept in der Theologie." In D. Ristchl and H. O. Jones, *"Story" als Rohmaterial der Theologie.* Theologische Existenz heute, 192. Munich, 1976. Pp. 42-68.

Jüngel, E. "Metaphorische Wahrheit. Erwägungen zur theologischen Relevanz der Metapher als Beitrag zur Hermeneutik einer narrativen Theologie." In *Metapher.* Sonderheft to *EvT.* Munich, 1974. Pp. 71-122.

Kähler, Martin. "Biblische Theologie." In *Realenzyklopädie für protestantische Theologie und Kirche,* III. Leipzig, 1893-1913. Pp. 192-200.

Kaiser, Gottlob Philipp Christian. *Die biblische Theologie oder Judaismus und Christianismus nach der grammatisch-historischen Interpretation und nach einer freymüthigen Stellung in die kritisch-vergleichende Universalgeschichte der Religion und die universale Religion.* Erlangen, 1813-1821.

Kaiser, O. *Der Mensch unter dem Schicksal. Studien zur Geschichte, Theologie und Gegenwartsbedeutung der Weisheit.* Beiträge zur ZAW. Berlin, 1984.

Kaiser, W. C. "The Promise Theme and the Theology of Rest," *BibSac,* 130 (1973), 135-150.

―――. "The Centre of Old Testament Theology: The Promise," *Themelios,* 10 (1974), 1-10.

―――. *Toward an Old Testament Theology.* Grand Rapids, 1978.

―――. "Wisdom Theology and the Center of Old Testament Theology," *EvQ,* 50 (1978), 132-146.

Kantzer, K. S., and Gundry, S. N., eds. *Perspectives on Evangelical Theology.* Grand Rapids, 1979.

Kapelrud, A. S. "Die Theologie der Schöpfung im Alten Testament," *ZAW,* 91 (1979), 159-170.

Käsemann, Ernst. *Das Neue Testament als Kanon. Dokumentation und Kritische Analyse zur gegenwärtigen Diskussion.* Göttingen, 1970.

Katz, Peter. "The Old Testament Canon in Palestine and Alexandria." In *An Introduction to the Canon and Masorah of the Hebrew Bible.* Ed. Sid Z. Leiman. New York, 1971. Pp. 72-98.

Kautzsch, Emil F. *Die bleibende Bedeutung des Alten Testaments.* Tübingen, 1902.

―――. *Biblische Theologie des AT.* Tübingen, 1911.

Kayser, A. *Die Theologie des AT in ihrer geschichtlichen Entwicklung dargestellt.* Strassburg, 1886.

Keller, Carl A. "Gerhard von Rad, Theologie des Alten Testament," *TZ,* 14 (1958), 306-309.

Kelsey, David H. *The Uses of Scripture in Recent Theology.* Philadelphia, 1975.

Kidner, D. "Wisdom Literature of the Old Testament." In *New Perspectives on the Old Testament*. Ed. J. B. Payne. Waco, TX, 1970. Pp. 117-131.

King, Winston L. "Some Ambiguities in Biblical Theology," *Religion in Life*, 27 (1957-1958), 95-104.

Kittel, B. "Brevard Childs' Development of the Canonical Approach," *JSOT*, 9 (1980), 2-11.

Kittel, Rudolph. "Die Zukunft der alttestamentlichen Wissenschaft," *ZAW*, 39 (1921), 84-99.

Klaaren, E. M. "A Critical Appreciation of Hans Frei's *Eclipse of Biblical Narrative*," *Union Seminary Quarterly Review*, 37 (1982), 283-297.

Klaiber, W. "Der eine Gott—die ganze Bibel." In *Mittelpunkt Bibel. Ulrich Fick zum 60. Geburtstag*. Ed. S. Meurer. Die Bibel in der Welt, 20. Stuttgart, 1983. Pp. 167-185.

Klein, G. *Theologie des Wortes Gottes und die Hypothese der Universalgeschichte. Zur Auseinandersetzung mit Wolfhart Pannenberg*. Beiträge zur evangelische Theologie, 37. Munich, 1964.

———. " 'Reich Gottes' als biblischer Zentralbegriff," *EvT*, 30 (1970), 642-670.

———. "Die Fragwürdigkeit der Idee der Heilgeschichte." In *Spricht Gott in der Geschichte?* Fribourg / Basel / Vienna, 1972. Pp. 95-153.

Klein, H. "Leben—neues Leben. Möglichkeiten und Grenzen einer gesamtbiblischen Theologie des Alten und Neuen Testaments," *EvT*, 43 (1983), 91-108.

Knauer, P. "Das Verhältnis des Neuen Testaments zum Alten als historisches Paradigma für das Verhältnis der christlichen Botschaft zu anderen Religionen und Weltanschauungen." In *Offenbarung, geistige Realität des Menschen—Arbeitsdokumentation eines Symposiums zum Offenbarungsbegriff in Indien*. Ed. G. Oberhammer. Vienna, 1974. Pp. 154-170.

Knierim, Rolf. "Cosmos and History in Israel's Theology," *HBT*, 3 (1981), 59-124.

———. "The Task of Old Testament Theology," *HBT*, 6 / 1 (1984), 25-57.

Knight, Douglas A. *Rediscovering the Traditions of Israel*. Missoula, 1973.

———. "Canon and the History of Tradition: A Critique of Brevard S. Childs' *Introduction to the Old Testament as Scripture*," *HBT*, 2 (1980), 127-149.

Knight, D. A., ed. *Tradition and Theology in the Old Testament*. Philadelphia, 1977.

Knight, George A. F. *A Christian Theology of the Old Testament*. London, 1959.

Koch, Klaus. "Der Tod des Religionsstifters," *KuD*, 8 (1962), 100-123.

Köhler, L. "Alttestamentliche Theologie (Literaturbericht)," *TRu*, 7 (1935), 255-276; 8 (1936), 55-69, 247-284.

———. *Theologie des AT*. Tübingen, 1936. Trans. *Old Testament Theology*. London, 1957.

König, Eduard. "Der gegenwärtige Zustand der 'Biblischen Theologie Alten Testaments,' sein eigentlicher Anlass und die Wege zu seiner Verbesserung," *Allgemeine evangelisch- lutherische Kirchenzeitung*, 55 (1922), 242-245.

———. *Theologie des AT kritisch und vergleichend dargestellt*. Stuttgart, 1922.

Koole, J. L. "Het soortelijk gewicht van de historische stoffen van het Oude Testament," *Gereformeerd theologisch tijdschrift*, 65 (1965), 81-104.

————. "Ontwikkelingen op het gebied van de oudtestamentische theologie," *Gereformeerd theologisch tijdschrift*, 67 (1967), 18-26.

Kort, Wesley A. *Story, Text and Scripture: Literary Interests in Biblical Narrative.* University Park / London, 1988.

Kraeling, E. *The Old Testament Since the Reformation.* New York, 1955.

Kraus, H.-J. "Gespräch mit Martin Buber," *EvT*, 12 (1952-1953), 59-77.

————. "Zur Geschichte des Überlieferungsbegriffs in der alttestamentlichen Wissenschaft," *EvT*, 16 (1956), 371-387.

————. *Geschichte der historisch-kritischen Erforschung des AT.* 2nd ed. Neukirchen-Vluyn, 1969.

————. *Die Biblische Theologie: Ihre Geschichte und Problematik.* Neukirchen-Vluyn, 1970.

————. "Theologie als Traditionsbildung?" *EvT*, 36 (1976), 498-507. Repr. in *Biblische Theologie heute.* Ed. K. Haacker. Biblisch-theologische Studien, 1. Neukirchen-Vluyn, 1977. Pp. 61-73.

————. "Probleme und Perspektiven Biblischer Theologie." In *Biblische Theologie heute.* Ed. K. Haacker. Biblisch-theologische Studien, 1. Neukirchen-Vluyn, 1977. Pp. 97-124.

————. *Theologie der Psalmen.* Neukirchen-Vluyn, 1979. Trans. *Theology of the Psalms.* Minneapolis, 1986.

Krecher, J. and H. P. Müller. "Vergangenheitsinteresse in Mesopotamien und Israel," *Saeculum*, 26 (1975), 13-44.

Krentz, Edgar. *The Historical-Critical Method.* Philadelphia, 1975.

Kümmel, W. G. *The New Testament: The History of the Investigation of its Problems.* Nashville, 1972.

————. "Heilsgeschichte im Neuen Testament?" In *Neues Testament und Kirche. Festschrift für R. Schnackenburg.* Freiburg im Breisgau, 1974. Pp. 434-457.

Kuske, M. *Das Alte Testament als Buch von Christus. Dietrich Bonhoeffers Wertung und Auslegung des Alten Testaments.* Göttingen, 1971.

Kutsch, E. *Verheissung und Gesetz.* Beiträge zur *ZAW*, 131. Berlin, 1973.

Lacheman, E. R. "The Renaissance of Biblical Theology," *JBR*, 19 (1951), 71-75.

Ladd, G. E. "The Search for Perspectives," *Interp*, 26 (1971), 41-62.

————. "Biblical Theology, Nature of." In *The International Standard Bible Encyclopedia*, I. Grand Rapids, 1979. Pp. 505-509.

Lakatos, E. "Por una Teologia basada en los hechos," *Rivista Biblica*, 21 (1959), 83-86, 142-144, 197-200; 22 (1960), 140-145.

Lambert, W. G. "Destiny and Divine Intervention in Babylonia and Israel," *Oudtestamentische Studien*, 17 (1972), 65-72.

Lampe, G. W. H. and K. J. Woollcombe. *Essays on Typology.* SBT, 1 / 22. London, 1957.

Landes, G. M. "Biblical Exegesis in Crisis: What is the Exegetical Task in a Theological Context?" *Union Seminary Quarterly Review*, 26 (1971), 273-298.

————. "The Canonical Approach to Introducing the Old Testament: Prodigy and Problems," *JSOT,* 16 (1980), 32-39.

Lang, B. *Die weisheitliche Lehrrede.* Stuttgarter Bibelstudien, 54. Stuttgart, 1972.

Lang, Friedrich. "Christuszeugnis und Biblische Theologie," *EvT,* 29 (1969), 523-534.

Laurin, R. B., ed. *Contemporary Old Testament Theologians.* Valley Forge, PA, 1970.

Leary, A. P. "Biblical Theology and History," *Church Quarterly Review,* 157 (1956), 402-414.

Leeuw, G. van der. "Overzicht van der oudtestamentische theologie," *Ex Oriente Lux,* 14 (1955 / 56), 122-128.

Lehman, Chester R. *Biblical Theology I: Old Testament.* Scottdale, PA, 1971.

Leiman, Sid Z. *The Canonization of Hebrew Scripture: The Talmudic and Midrashic Evidence.* Hamden, CT, 1976.

Lemche, Niels Peter. "Geschichte und Heilsgeschichte. Mehrere Aspekte der biblischen Theologie," *Scandinavian Journal of the Old Testament,* 2 (1989), 114-135.

Lemke, W. E. "Revelation through History in Recent Biblical Theology," *Interp,* 36 (1982), 34-46.

Lentrieccha, F. *After the New Criticism.* London, 1980.

Lerch, D. "Zur Frage nach dem Verstehen der Schrift," *ZTK,* 49 (1952), 350-367.

Lessing, E. "Die Bedeutung der Heilgeschichte in der ökumenischen Diskussion," *EvT,* 44 (1984), 227-240.

Levenson, Jon D. "The Theologies of Commandment in Biblical Israel," *Harvard Theological Review,* 73 (1980), 17-33.

————. *Sinai and Zion: An Entry Into the Jewish Bible.* Minneapolis, 1985.

————. "The Hebrew Bible, the Old Testament, and Historical Criticism." In *The Future of Biblical Studies: The Hebrew Scriptures.* Ed. R. E. Friedman and H. G. M. Williamson. Atlanta, 1987. Pp. 19-60.

————. "Why Jews Are Not Interested in Biblical Theology." In *Jewish Perspectives on Ancient Israel.* Ed. J. Neusner, B. A. Levine, and E. S. Frerichs. Philadelphia, 1987. Pp. 281-307.

————. *Creation and the Persistence of Evil: The Jewish Drama of Divine Omnipotence.* San Francisco, 1988.

————. "The Eighth Principle of Judaism and the Literary Simultaneity of Scripture," *JR,* 68 (1988), 205-225.

Levine, B. A. "Priestly Writers." In *IDB Supplement.* Nashville, 1976. Pp. 683-687.

Licht, J. *Storytelling in the Bible.* Jerusalem, 1978.

Liedke, G. "Die Selbstoffenbarung der Schöpfung," *Evangelische Kommentar,* 8 (1975), 398-400.

Lindbeck, George. "Scripture, Consensus, and Community." In *Biblical Interpretation in Crisis: The Ratzinger Conference on Bible and Church.* Ed. Richard J. Neuhaus. Encounter Series, 9. Grand Rapids, 1989. Pp. 74-101.

Lindblom, J. "Zur Frage der Eigenart der alttestamentlichen Religion." In *Werden und Wesen des Alten Testaments*. Ed. J. Hempel. BZAW, 66. Berlin, 1936. Pp. 128-137.

————. "Vad innebär en 'teologisk' syn pa Gamla Testamentet?" *Svensk Teologisk Kvartalskrift*, 37 (1961), 73-91.

————. *The Bible: A Modern Understanding*. Philadelphia, 1973.

Lohfink, N. *Great Themes from the Old Testament*. Chicago, 1982.

————. "Die Bibel: Bücherei und Buch," *Deutsche Akademie für Sprache und Dichtung. Jahrbuch 1983* (Heidelberg, 1984), 50-64.

Lohse, E. "Die Einheit des Neuen Testaments als theologisches Problem," *EvT*, 35 (1975), 139-154.

Lonergan, Bernard J. F. *Method in Theology*. New York, 1972.

Long, Burke O. and George W. Coats, eds. *Canon and Authority: Essays in Old Testament Religion and Theology*. Philadelphia, 1977.

Longman, Tremper III. *Literary Approaches to Biblical Interpretation*. Foundations of Contemporary Interpretation, vol. 3. Grand Rapids, 1987.

Lönning, Inge. *"Kanon im Kanon."* Zum dogmatischen Grundlagenproblem des neutestamentlichen Kanons. Munich, 1972.

Loretz, O. "Israel und sein Gottesbund. Die Theologie des AT auf neuen Wegen," *Wort und Wahrheit*, 15 (1960), 85-92.

————. *Die Wahrheit der Bibel*. Freiburg im Breisgau, 1964.

Lubsczyk, H. "Die Einheit der Schrift. Zur hermeneutischen Relevanz des Urbekenntnisses im Alten und Neuen Testament." In *Spienter Ordinare. Festgabe für Erich Kleineidam*. Leipzig, 1969. Pp. 73-104.

————. *Die Einheit der Schrift. Gesammelte Aufsätze*. Leipzig, 1989.

Luck, U. *Welterfahrung und Glaube als Grundproblem biblischer Theologie*. Theologische Existenz heute, 191. Munich, 1976.

Luz, U. "Einheit und Vielfalt neutestamentlicher Theologien." In *Die Mitte des Neuen Testaments. Einheit und Vielfalt neutestamentlicher Theologie. Festschrift für E. Schweizer*. Göttingen, 1983. Pp. 142-161.

Lys, D. *The Meaning of the Old Testament*. Nashville, 1967.

Maag, V. "Historische oder ausserhistorische Begründung alttestamentlicher Theologie," *Schweizer Theologische Umschau*, 29 (1959), 6-18.

Mack, B. L. "Wisdom, Myth and Mythology," *Interp*, 24 (1970), 46-60.

Mack, R. "Basic Aspects of Revelation in the Old Testament," *Ghana Bulletin of Theology*, 4 / 8 (1975), 13-23.

MacKenzie, R. A. F. "The Concept of Biblical Theology," *Catholic Theological Society of America: Proceedings*, 10 (1955), 48-73.

————. "The Concept of Biblical Theology," *TToday*, 4 (1956), 131-135.

————. *Faith and History in the Old Testament*. Minneapolis, 1963.

Maier, G. *Das Ende der historisch-kritischen Methode*. Wuppertal, 1974. Trans. *The End of the Historical-Critical Method*. St. Louis, 1977.

————. "Einer biblischen Hermeneutik entgegen? Zum Gespräch mit P. Stuhlmacher und H. Lindner," *Theologische Beiträge*, 8 (1977), 148-160.

Malevez, L. "Les dimensions de l'histoire du salut," *Nouvelle revue théologique*, 86 (1964), 561-578.

Maly, E. H. "The Nature of Biblical History," *The Bible Today,* 1 (1962), 278-285.

Mamie, Pierre. "Peut-on écrire une 'Théologie de l'Ancien Testament'?" *Novum Vera,* 42 (1967), 298-303.

Marböck, J. *Weisheit im Wandel.* Bonner Biblische Beiträge, 37. Bonn, 1971.

Marsh, John. *The Fulness of Time.* London, 1952.

Martens, E. A. "Tackling Old Testament Theology," *JETS,* 20 (1977), 123-132.

————. *God's Design: A Focus on Old Testament Theology.* Grand Rapids, 1981 (copublished in Great Britain as *Plot and Purpose in the Old Testament.* Leicester, 1981).

Martin-Achard, Robert. "Les voies de la théologie de l'Ancien Testament," *Revue de théologie et de philosophie,* 9 (1959), 217-226.

————. *Approche de l'Ancien Testament.* Neuchâtel, 1962.

————. "Remarques sur la signification theeologique de la création selon l'Ancien Testament," *RHPR,* 52 (1972), 3-11.

————. "La théologie de l'Ancien Testament après les travaux de G. von Rad," *Études théologiques et religieuses,* 47 (1972), 219-226.

————. "Old Testament Theologies and Faith Confessions," *Theology Digest,* 33 / 1 (1986), 145-148.

Mattioli, Anselmo. *Dio e l'uomo nella Bibbia d'Israele. Teologia dell'Antico Testamento.* Casale Monferrato, 1981.

Mauser, U. *Gottesbild und Menschwerdung. Eine Untersuchung zur Einheit des Alten und Neuen Testaments.* Tübingen, 1971.

————. "*Eis Theos* und *Monos Theos* in Biblischer Theologie." In *Einheit und Vielfalt Biblischer Theologie.* Ed. I. Baldermann et al. Jahrbuch für Biblische Theologie, 1. Neukirchen-Vluyn, 1986. Pp. 71-87.

Mayo, S. M. *The Relevance of the Old Testament for the Christian Faith: Biblical Theology and Interpretative Methodology.* Washington, D.C., 1982.

Mays, James L. "Exegesis as a Theological Discipline." Inaugural address delivered April 20, 1960. Richmond, VA: Union Theological Seminary, 1960.

————. "Historical and Canonical: Recent Discussion about the Old Testament and Christian Faith." In *Magnalia Dei: The Mighty Acts of God: Essays on the Bible and Archaeology in Memory of G. Ernest Wright.* Ed. Frank Moore Cross et al. Garden City, NY, 1976. Pp. 510-528.

McCarthy, D. J. *Treaty and Covenant.* 2nd ed. AnBib, 21A. Rome, 1978.

McCasland, S. Vernon. "The Unity of the Scriptures," *JBL,* 73 (1954), 1-10.

McComiskey, Thomas E. *The Covenant of Promise: A Theology of Old Testament Covenants.* Grand Rapids, 1985.

McConnell, F., ed. *The Bible and the Narrative Tradition.* New York, 1986.

McConville, J. Gordon. "The Shadow of the Curse: A 'Key' to Old Testament Theology," *Evangel,* 3 / 1 (1985), 2-5.

McEvenue, S. E. "The Old Testament, Scripture or Theology?" *Interp,* 35 (1981), 229-242.

McKane, W. *Prophets and Wise Men.* SBT, 44. London, 1965.

————. "Tradition as a Theological Concept." In *God, Secularization and*

History: Essays in Memory of Ronald Gregor Smith. Ed. E. T. Long. Columbia, SC, 1974. Pp. 44-59.

McKenzie, John L. "God and Nature in the Old Testament," *CBQ,* 14 (1952), 18-39, 124-145.

————. *The Two-Edged Sword: an Interpretation of the Old Testament.* Milwaukee, 1955.

————. "The Task of Biblical Theology," *The Voice of St. Mary's Seminary,* 36 (1959), 7-9, 26-27.

————. *Myths and Realities: Studies in Biblical Theology.* Milwaukee, 1963.

————. *A Theology of the Old Testament.* Garden City, NY, 1974.

McKnight, Edgar V. *Meaning in Texts: The Historical Shaping of Narrative Hermeneutics.* Philadelphia, 1978.

————. *Post-Modern Use of the Bible: The Emergence of Reader-Oriented Criticism.* Nashville, 1988.

Merk, O. *Biblische Theologie des Neuen Testaments in ihrer Anfangszeit.* Marburg, 1970.

Merk, O. "Biblische Theologie II. Neues Testaments." In *Theologische Realenzyklopädie,* VI. Ed. G. Krause and G. Müller. Berlin/New York, 1980. Pp. 455-477.

Metz, J. B. "A Short Apology of Narrative," *Concilium,* 5 / 9 (1973), 84-96.

Mildenberger, F. *Gottes Tat im Wort. Erwägungen zur alttestamentlichen Hermeneutik als Frage nach der Einheit der Geschichte.* Gütersloh, 1964.

————. *Die halbe Wahrheit oder die ganze Schrift.* München, 1967.

————. "Texte—oder die Schrift?" *ZTK,* 66 (1969), 192- 209.

————. "Systematisch-theologische Randbemerkungen zur Diskussion um eine Biblische Theologie." In *Zugang zur Theologie. Fundamentaltheologische Beiträge. Festschrift für W. Joest.* Göttingen, 1979. Pp. 11-32.

Minear, P. S. "Wanted: A Biblical Theology," *TToday,* 1 (1944), 47-58.

Minissale, A. "La 'Teologia' dell'Antico Testamento," *Rivista del clero italiano,* 60 (1979), 179-186.

Miskotte, K. H. "Das Problem der theologischen Exegese." In *Theologische Aufsätze. Festschrift für K. Barth.* Munich, 1936. Pp. 51-77.

————. *Wenn die Götter schweigen.* Munich, 1963. Trans. *When the Gods Are Silent.* London, 1967.

Moeller, Wilhelm and Hans. *Biblische TAT.* Zwickau, 1938.

Momigliano, A. "Time in Ancient Historiography." In *History and Concept of Time.* History and Theory. Supplement, 6. 1966. Pp. 1-23. Repr. in A. Momigliano, *Essays in Ancient and Modern Historiography.* Middletown, CT, 1977. Pp. 161-204.

Morgan, Robert. *The Nature of New Testament Theology.* London, 1973.

Morgan, Robert with John Barton. *Biblical Interpretation.* Oxford / New York, 1988.

Mowinckel, Sigmund. *Prophecy and Tradition: The Prophetic Books in the Light of the Study of the Growth and History of the Tradition.* Avhändlinger utgitt av det Norske Videnskaps-Akademi. Oslo, 1946.

————. *The Old Testament as Word of God.* Nashville, 1959.

Muilenburg, James D. "The Return to Old Testament Theology." In *Christianity and the Contemporary Scene*. Ed. R. C. Miller and H. H. Shires. New York, 1943. Pp. 30-44.

Müller, P.-G. "Altes Testament, Israel und das Judentum in der Theologie Rudolf Bultmanns." In *Kontinuität und Einheit. Festschrift für F. Mussner*. Fribourg / Basel / Vienna, 1981. Pp. 439-472.

Müller-Fahrenholz, G. *Heilsgeschichten zwischen Ideologie und Prophetie*. Fribourg, 1974. Pp. 169ff.

Murphy, R. E. "The Relationship between the Testaments," *CBQ*, 26 (1964), 349-359.

———. "Assumptions and Problems in Old Testament Wisdom Research," *CBQ*, 29 (1967), 407-418.

———. "Eschatology and the Old Testament," *Continuum*, 7 (1969-1970), 583-593.

———. "Christian Understanding of the Old Testament," *Theology Digest*, 18 (1970), 321-332.

———. "The Old Testament as Scripture," *JSOT*, 16 (1980), 40-44.

Murrel, Nathaniel S. "James Barr's Critique of Biblical Theology: A Critical Analysis." Unpublished Ph.D. dissertation, Drew University, 1988.

Muschalek, G. and A. Gamper. "Offenbarung in Geschichte," *Zeitschrift für katholische Theologie*, 86 (1964), 180-196.

Nesbit, W. G. "A Study of Methodology in Contemporary Old Testament Theologies." Unpublished Ph.D. dissertation, Marquette University, 1969.

Nicholson, Ernest W. *Deuteronomy and Tradition*. Philadelphia, 1967.

———. *Exodus and Sinai in History and Tradition*. Richmond, 1973.

———. *God and His People: Covenant and Theology in the Old Testament*. Oxford, 1986.

Nielsen, E. "Det gamle Testamente." In *Teologien og dens fag*. Ed. B. Noack. Copenhagen, 1960. Pp. 13-42.

Nineham, D. E. *The Church's Use of the Bible*. London, 1963.

———. "The Use of the Bible in Modern Theology," *Bulletin of the John Rylands Library*, 52 (1969), 178-199.

North, C. R. "Old Testament Theology and the History of Hebrew Religion," *SJT*, 2 (1949), 113- 126.

Noth, Martin. *Überlieferungsgeschichtlichen Studien: Die sammelnden und bearbeitenden Geschichtswerke im Alten Testament*. 1941. Repr. Tübingen, 1967.

———. "Die Vergegenwärtigung des Alten Testaments in der Verkündigung," *EvT*, 12 (1952-1953), 6-17. Trans. "The 'Re-presentation' of the Old Testament in Proclamation," *Interp*, 15 (1961), 50-60.

———. *The Laws in the Pentateuch and Other Studies*. Philadelphia, 1967.

———. *A History of Pentateuchal Traditions*. Englewood Cliffs, NJ, 1972.

O'Doherty, E. "The Unity of the Bible," *The Bible Today*, 1 (1962), 53-57.

Obayashi, H. "Pannenberg and Troeltsch: History and Religion," *JAAR*, 38 (1970), 401-419.

Oden, Robert A. *The Bible Without Theology: The Theological Tradition and Alternatives to It*. San Francisco, 1987.

Oehler, G. F. *Prolegomena zur Theologie des AT.* Stuttgart, 1845.
———. *Theologie des AT.* 2 vols. Stuttgart, 1873-1874. Trans. *Theology of the Old Testament.* New York, 1883.
Oeming, Manfred. "Bedeutung und Funktionen von 'Fiktionen' in der alttestamentlichen Geschichtsschreibung," *EvT,* 44 (1984), 254-266.
———. "Biblische Theologie — was folgt daraus für die Auslegung des Alten Testaments?" *Evangelische Erziehung,* 37 (1985), 233-243.
———. *Gesamtbiblische Theologien der Gegenwart. Das Verhältnis von AT und NT in der hermeneutischen Diskussion seit Gerhard von Rad.* Stuttgart, 1985.
———. "Unitas Scripturae? Eine Problemskizze." In *Einheit und Vielfalt Biblischer Theologie.* Ed. I. Baldermann et al. Jahrbuch für Biblische Theologie, 1. Neukirchen-Vluyn, 1986. Pp. 48-70.
Ollenburger, Ben C. "Biblical Theology: Situating the Discipline." In *Understanding the Word of God: Essays in Honor of Bernhard W. Anderson.* Ed. James T. Butler, Edgar W. Conrad, and Ben C. Ollenburger. Sheffield, 1985. Pp. 37-62.
———. "What Krister Stendahl 'Meant' — A Normative Critique of 'Descriptive Biblical Theology,'" *HBT,* 8 / 1 (1986), 61-98.
Ollenburger, Ben C., Elmer A. Martens, and Gerhard F. Hasel, eds. *The Flowering of Old Testament Theology: A Reader in Twentieth Century Old Testament Theology,* Winona Lake, IN, 1991.
Orr, James. *The Problem of the Old Testament: Considered with Reference to Recent Criticism.* London / New York, 1906.
Osborne, G. R. "New Testament Theology." In *Evangelical Dictionary of Theology.* Ed. Walter A. Elwell. Grand Rapids, 1984. Pp. 768-773.
Osswald, E. "Theologie des AT — eine bleidende Aufgabe alttestamentlicher Wissenschaft," *TLZ,* 99 (1974), 641-658.
———. "Das Problem der 'Mitte' des Alten Testaments," *Amtsblatt d. E.-Luth. Kirche in Thüringen,* 30 (1977), 192-201.
Östborn, G. *Yahwe's Words and Deeds: A Preliminary Study into the Old Testament Presentation of History.* Uppsala Universitets Årsskrift, 1951, 7. Uppsala / Wiesbaden, 1951.
Ott, H. *Geschichte und Heilsgeschichte in der Theologie Rudolf Bultmanns.* Tübingen, 1955.
Otto, E. "Erwägungen zu den Prolegomena einer Theologie des AT," *Kairos,* 19 (1977), 53-72.
———. "Hat Max Webers Religionssoziologie des antiken Judentums Bedeutung für eine Theologie des AT?" *ZAW,* 94 (1982), 187-203.
Pannenberg, W. "Kerygma und Geschichte." In *Studien zur Theologie des alttestamentlichen Überlieferungen.* Ed. R. Rendtorff and K. Koch. Neukirchen, 1961. Pp. 124-140.
———. *Grundfragen systematischer Theologie.* Göttingen, 1968.
———. *Jesus — God and Man.* Philadelphia, 1968.
———. *Basic Questions in Theology,* 2 vols. Philadelphia, 1970, 1971.
———. "Biblische Theologie." In *Theologie als Wissenschaft.* Stuttgart, 1973. Pp. 384-392.

———. "Glaube und Wirklichkeit im Denken Gerhard von Rads." In H. W. Wolff, R. Rendtorff, and W. Pannenberg, *Gerhard von Rad. Seine Bedeutung für die Theologie. Drei Reden.* Munich, 1973. Pp. 37-54.

Pannenberg, W., ed. *OaG.* 2nd ed. KuD, Beihefte 1. Göttingen, 1963. Trans. *Revelation as History.* London, 1969.

Pannikar, R. "Le temps circulaire: temporisation et temporalité." In E. Castelli et al. *Temporalità e Alienazione.* Archivio di Filosofia. Padua, 1975. Pp. 207-246.

Payne, J. Barton. *The Theology of the Older Testament.* Grand Rapids, 1962.

Pepin, J. *Mythe et allégorie.* Paris, 1958.

Perlitt, Lothar. *Bundestheologie im Alten Testament.* WMANT, 36. Neukirchen-Vluyn, 1969.

Petersen, C. *Mythos im Alten Testament.* BZAW, 157. Berlin, 1982.

Pfeiffer, R. H. "Facts and Faith in Biblical History," *JBL,* 70 (1951), 1-14.

Phythian-Adams, W. J. T. "The Foundations of Biblical Theology," *Church Quarterly Review,* 135 (1942), 1-42.

Piper, Otto A. "Biblical Theology and Systematic Theology," *JBR,* 25 (1957), 106-111.

Pittenger, W. N. "Biblical Religion and Biblical Theology," *JBR,* 13 (1945), 179-183.

Ploeg, J. van der. "Une 'Théologie de l'AT' est-elle possible?" *Ephemer ides theologicae Iovanienses,* 38 (1962), 417-434.

Pokorny, P. "Probleme biblische Theologie," *TLZ,* 106 (1981), 1-8.

Polley, M. E. "H. Wheeler Robinson and the Problem of Organizing an Old Testament Theology." In *The Use of the Old Testament in the New and Other Essays.* Ed. James M. Efird. Durham, 1972. Pp. 149-169.

Porteous, N. W. "Towards a Theology of the Old Testament," *SJT,* 1 (1948), 136-149.

———. "Old Testament Theology." In *The Old Testament and Modern Study.* Ed. H. H. Rowley. London, 1951. Pp. 311-345.

———. "Actualisation and the Prophetic Criticism of the Cult." In *Tradition und Situation. Festschrift für Artur Weiser.* Ed. E. Würthwein and O. Kaiser. Göttingen, 1963. Repr. in *Living the Mystery: Collected Essays.* Oxford, 1967. Pp. 127-141.

———. *Living the Mystery: Collected Essays.* Oxford, 1967.

———. "Old Testament and History," *ASTI,* 8 (1972), 21-77.

Porter, F. C. "Crucial Problems in Biblical Theology," *JR,* 1 (1921), 78-81.

Preus, C. "The Contemporary Relevance of von Hofmann's Hermeneutical Principles," *Interp,* 4 (1950), 311-321.

Preuss, H. D. "Das Alte Testament in der Verkündigung der Kirche," *Deutsches Pfarrerblatt,* 68 (1968), 73-79.

———. *Jahweglaube und Zukunftserwartung.* Beiträge zur Wissenschaft vom Alten und Neuen Testament, 87. Stuttgart, 1968.

———. "Erwägungen zum theologischen Ort alttestamentlicher Weisheitsliteratur," *EvT,* 30 (1970), 393-417.

――――. "Das Alte Testament im Rahmen der Theologie als Kirchlicher Wissenschaft," *Deutsches Pfarrerblatt,* 72 (1972), 356-360.

――――. "Alttestamentliche Weisheit in christlicher Theologie?" *Bibliotheca Ephemeridum Theologicarum Lovaniensium,* 33 (1974), 165-181.

――――. *Das Alte Testament in christlicher Predigt.* Stuttgart / Berlin / Köln / Mainz, 1984.

Priest, John F. "Where is Wisdom to be Placed?" *JBR,* 31 (1963), 275-282.

Procksch, Otto. "Pneumatische Exegese," *Christentum und Wissenschaft,* 1 (1925), 145ff.

――――. *TAT.* Gütersloh, 1949.

Prussner, Frederick C. "The Covenant of David and the Problem of Unity in the Old Testament Theology." In *Transitions in Biblical Scholarship.* Ed. J. C. Rylaarsdam. Chicago, 1968. Pp. 17-41.

Prussner, Frederick C. "A Methodology for Old Testament Theology." Unpublished Ph.D. dissertation, University of Chicago, 1953.

Rad, Gerhard von. "Weiser: *Glaube und Geschichte im Alten Testament,*" *Christentum und Wissenschaft,* 8 (1932), 37.

――――. *Die Priesterschrift im Hexateuch literarisch untersucht und theologisch gewertet.* Stuttgart, 1934.

――――. "Das Christuszeugnis des Alten Testaments: Eine Auseinandersetzung mit Wilhelm Vischers gleichnamigen Buch," *TBl,* 14 (1935), 249-254.

――――. "Gesetz und Evangelium im Alten Testament. Gedanken zu dem Buch von E. Hirsch: *Das Alte Testament und die Predigt des Evangeliums,*" *TBl,* 16 (1937), 41-47.

――――. "Grundprobleme einer biblischen Theologie des AT," *TLZ,* 68 (1943), 225-234.

――――. "Kritische Vorarbeiten zu einer Theologie des AT." In *Theologie und Liturgie.* Ed. L. Hennig. Kassel, 1952. Pp. 11-34.

――――. "Verheissung. Zum gleichnamigen Buch Friedrich Baumgärtels," *EvT,* 13 (1953), 406- 413.

――――. *Theologie des AT,* 2 vols. Munich, 1957, 1960. Trans. *Old Testament Theology,* 2 vols. Edinburgh / New York, 1965.

――――. "Ancient Word and Living Word: The Preaching of Deuteronomy and Our Preaching," *Interp,* 15 (1961), 3-13.

――――. "Typological Interpretation of the Old Testament," *Interp,* 15 (1961), 174-192. Repr. in *EOTH,* pp. 17-39.

――――. "Offene Fragen im Umkreis einer Theologie des AT," *TLZ,* 88 (1963), 401-416.

――――. "Antwort auf Conzelmanns Fragen," *EvT,* 24 (1964), 388-394.

――――. "The Deuteronomic Theology of History in I and II Kings." In *The Problem of the Hexateuch and Other Essays.* New York, 1966. Pp. 205-221.

――――. "The Beginnings of Historical Writing in Ancient Israel." In *The Problem of the Hexateuch and Other Essays.* New York, 1966. Pp. 166-204.

――――. *The Problem of the Hexateuch and Other Essays.* New York, 1966.

Originally published as *Das formgeschichtliche Problem des Hexateuchs.*
Stuttgart, 1938.

———. *Weisheit in Israel.* Neukirchen-Vluyn, 1970. Trans. *Wisdom in Israel.*
London / Nashville, 1972.

———. "About Exegesis and Preaching." In *Biblical Interpretations in Preaching.* Nashville, 1977. Pp. 11-18.

Rahner, K. "Weltgeschichte und Heilsgeschichte." In *Schriften zur Theologie,*
V. 2nd ed. Einsiedeln, 1964.

———. "Bible, Biblical Theology." In *Sacramentum Mundi,* I. Ed. K. Rahner.
London, 1968, Pp. 171-176.

———. "Old Testament Theology." In *Sacramentum Mundi,* IV. London, 1969.
Pp. 186-190.

———. "The Old Testament and Christian Dogmatic Theology." In *Theological
Investigations,* XVI: *Experience of the Spirit: Source of Theology.* London /
New York, 1979. Pp. 177-190.

Raitt, T. M. "Horizontal Revelation," *Religion in Life,* 47 (1978), 423-429.

Ramlot, "Une décade de théologie biblique," *Revue thomiste,* 64 (1964), 65-96;
65 (1965), 95-135.

Ratzinger, Joseph. "Biblical Interpretation in Crisis: On the Question of the
Foundations and Approaches in Exegesis." In *Biblical Interpretation in
Crisis: The Ratzinger Conference on Bible and Church,* ed. Richard J.
Neuhaus. Encounter Series, 9. Grand Rapids, 1989. Pp. 1-13.

Rendtorff, Rolf. " 'Offenbarung' im Alten Testament," *TLZ,* 85 (1960), 833-838.

———. "Hermeneutics des Alten Testaments als Frage nach der Geschichte,"
ZTK, 57 (1960), 27-40.

———. "Die Offenbarungsvorstellungen im Alten Israel." In *OaG.* Ed. W. Pannenberg. 2nd ed. *KuD,* Beiheft 1. Göttingen, 1961. Pp. 21-41. Trans. "The
Concept of Revelation in Ancient Israel." In *Revelation as History.* Ed.
W. Pannenberg. London, 1969. Pp. 23-53.

———. "Geschichte und Wort im Alten Testament," *EvT,* 22 (1962), 621-649.

———. "Alttestamentliche Theologie und israelitisch-jüdische Religionsgeschichte." In *Zwischenstation. Festschrift für Karl Kupisch zum 60. Geburtstag.* Ed. Helmut Gollwitzer and J. Hoppe. Munich, 1963. Pp. 208-222.

———. "Die Entstehung der israelitischen Religion als religionsgeschichtliches und theologisches Problem," *TLZ,* 88 (1963), 735-746.

———. "Der 'Jahwist' als Theologe? Zum Dilemma der Pentateuchkritik." In
Congress Volume: Edinburgh, 1974. Supplements to VT, 28. Leiden, 1975.
Pp. 158-166. Trans. "The 'Yahwist' as Theologian? The Dilemma of Pentateuchal Criticism," *JSOT,* 3 (1977), 2-10.

———. *Das überlieferungsgeschichtliche Problem des Pentateuch.* BZAW, 147.
Berlin / New York, 1977.

———. "I principali problemi di una teologia dell'Antico Testamento," *Protestantesimo,* 35 (1980), 193-206.

———. "Zur Bedeutung des Kanons für eine Theologie des AT." In *"Wenn
nicht jetzt—wann dann?" Aufsätze für Hans-Joachim Kraus zum 65. Geburtstag.* Ed. H.-G. Geyer et al. Neukirchen-Vluyn, 1983. Pp. 3-11.

————. "Must 'Biblical Theology' be Christian Theology?" *Bible Review*, 4 (1988), 40-43.

————. "Covenant' as a Structuring Concept in Genesis and Exodus," *JBL*, 108 (1989), 385-393.

————. "Theologie des AT — Überlegungen zu einem Neuansatz," *Nederduitse Gereformeerde Teologiese Tydskrif*, 30 (1989), 132-142.

Rendtorff, Rolf and Koch, Klaus, eds. *Studien zur Theologie der alttestamentlichen Überlieferungen. Festschrift für Gerhard von Rad zum 60. Geburtstag*. Neukirchen-Vluyn, 1961.

Reventlow, H. Graf. "Grundfragen der alttestamentlichen Theologie im Lichte der neueren deutschen Forschung," *TLZ*, 17 (1961), 81-98.

————. "Die Auffassung vom Alten Testament bei Hermann Samuel Reimarus und Gotthold Ephraim Lessing," *EvT*, 25 (1965), 429-448.

————. *Rechtfertigung im Horizont des Alten Testaments*. Beiträge zur evangelischen Theologie, 58. Munich, 1971. Pp. 41-66.

————. "Die Eigenart des Jahweglaubens als geschichtliches und theologisches Problem," *KuD*, 20 (1974), 199-217.

————. "Basic Problems in Old Testament Theology," *JSOT*, 11 (1979), 2-22.

————. "Der Konflikt zwischen Exegese und Dogmatik. Wilhelm Vischers Ringen um den 'Christus in Alten Testament.'" In *Textgemäss. Aufsätze und Beiträge zur Hermeneutik des Alten Testaments. Festschrift für Ernest Würthwein zum 70. Geburtstag*. Ed. A. H. G. Gunneweg and O. Kaiser. Göttingen, 1979. Pp. 110-122.

————. "Richard Simon und seine Bedeutung für die kritische Erforschung der Bibel." In *Historische Kritik in der Theologie: Beiträge zu ihrer Geschichte*. Ed. Georg Schwaiger. Göttingen, 1980. Pp. 11-36.

————. *Hauptprobleme der alttestamentlichen Theologie im 20. Jahrhundert*. Erträge der Forschung, 173. Darmstadt, 1983. Trans. *Problems of Old Testament Theology in the Twentieth Century*. Philadelphia, 1985.

————. *Hauptprobleme der Biblischen Theologie im 20. Jahrhundert*. Erträge der Forschung, 203. Darmstadt, 1983. Trans. *Problems of Biblical Theology in the Twentieth Century*. Philadelphia, 1986.

————. *The Authority of the Bible and the Rise of the Modern World*. London/Philadelphia, 1984.

————. "Biblische Theologie auf historisch-kritischer Grundlage. Zu einem neuen Buch von Manfred Oeming." In *Einheit und Vielfalt Biblischer Theologie*. Ed. I. Baldermann et al. Neukirchen-Vluyn, 1986. Pp. 201-209.

————. "Zur Theologie des AT," *TRu*, 52 (1987), 237.

Rice, C. "The Preacher as Storyteller," *Union Seminary Quarterly Review*, 31 (1976), 182-197.

Richardson, A. "The Nature of Biblical Theology," *Theology*, 39 (1939), 166-176.

Ridderbos, N. H. "Het Oude Testament en de geschiedenis," *Gereformeerd theologisch tijdschrift*, 57 (1957), 112-120.

Riehm, E. *Alttestamentliche Theologie*. Halle, 1889.

Ritschl, Dietrich. "Johann Salomo Semler: The Rise of the Historical-Critical Method in Eighteenth-Century Theology on the Continent." In *Introduc-*

tion to Modernity: A Symposium on Eighteenth-Century Thought. Ed. Robert Mollenauer. Austin, 1965. Pp. 107-133.

―――. " 'Story' als Rohmaterial der Theologie." In D. Ritschl and H. O. Jones, *"Story" als Rohmaterial der Theologie.* Theologische Existenz heute, 192. Munich, 1976. Pp. 22-24.

Ritschl, D. and H. O. Jones. *"Story" als Rohmaterial der Theologie.* Theologische Existenz heute, 192. Munich, 1976.

Roberts, J. J. M. "Myth versus History: Relaying the Comparative Foundations," *CBQ,* 38 (1976), 1-13.

Robertson, David. *The Old Testament and the Literary Critic.* Philadelphia, 1977.

Robertson, O. Palmer. "The Outlook for Biblical Theology." In *Toward a Theology for the Future.* Ed. D. F. Wells and C. H. Pinnock. Carol Stream, IL, 1971. Pp. 65-91.

Robinson, H. W. *Inspiration and Revelation in the Old Testament.* Oxford, 1946.

Robinson, H. W. "The Theology of the Old Testament." In *Record and Revelation.* Ed. H. W. Robinson. Oxford, 1938. Pp. 303- 348.

Robinson, James M. "Revelation as Word and as History." In *New Frontiers in Theology, III: Theology as History.* New York, 1967. Pp. 1-110.

Rogerson, J. W. *Myth in Old Testament Interpretation.* BZAW, 134. Berlin, 1974.

Rössler, D. *Gesetz und Geschichte. Untersuchungen zur Theologie der jüdischen Apokalyptik und der pharisäischen Orthodoxie.* WMANT, 3. 2nd ed. Neukirchen, 1962.

Rost, L. "Zur Theologie des AT: Eine Übersicht," *Christentum und Wissenschaft,* 10 (1934), 121-124.

Rowley, H. H. *The Unity of the Bible.* London, 1953.

―――. *The Faith of Israel: Aspects of Old Testament Thought.* London, 1956.

Ruler, A. A. van. *The Christian Church and the Old Testament.* Grand Rapids, 1971.

Ruppert, Lothar. "Der Jahwist—Künder der Heilsgeschichte." In *Wort und Botschaft: Eine theologische und kritische Einführung im die Probleme des Alten Testaments.* Ed. Josef Schreiner. Würzburg, 1967. Pp. 88-107.

Rylaarsdam, J. C. "The Problem of Faith and History in Biblical Interpretation," *JBL,* 77 (1958), 26-32.

Saebø, M. "Offenbarung in der Geschichte und als Geschichte. Bemerkungen zu einem aktuellen Thema aus alttestamentlicher Sicht," *Studia Theologica,* 35 (1981), 55-71.

Sanders, J. A. *Torah and Canon.* Philadelphia: Fortress, 1972.

―――. "Adaptable for Life: The Nature and Function of Canon." In *Magnalia Dei: The Mighty Acts of God: Essays on the Bible and Archaeology in Memory of G. Ernest Wright.* Ed. Frank Moore Cross et al. Garden City, NY, 1976. Pp. 531-560.

―――. "Hermeneutics." In *IDB Supplement.* Nashville, 1976. Pp. 402-407.

―――. "Biblical Criticism and the Bible as Canon," *Union Seminary Quarterly Review,* 32 (1977), 157-165.

―――. "Canonical Context and Canonical Criticism," *HBT,* 2 (1980), 173-197.

————. *Canon and Community: A Guide to Canonical Criticism.* Philadelphia, 1984.

————. *From Sacred Story to Sacred Text.* Philadelphia, 1987.

Sandys-Wunsch, John. "G. P. C. Kaiser: La théologie biblique et l'histoire des Religions," *RHPR,* 59 (1979), 391-396.

————. "G. T. Zachariae's Contributions to Biblical Theology," *ZAW,* 92 (1980), 1-23.

————. "Spinoza—The First Biblical Theologian," *ZAW,* 93 (1981), 327-341.

Sandys-Wunsch, John, and Eldredge, Laurence. "J. P. Gabler and the Distinction between Biblical and Dogmatic Theology: Translation, Commentary, and Discussion of His Originality," *SJT,* 33 (1980), 133-158.

Sauter, Gerhard. *Zukunft und Verheissung. Das Problem der Zukunft in der gegenwärtigen theologischen und philosophischen Diskussion.* Zurich / Stuttgart, 1965.

Scharbert, J. "Heilsgeschichte und Heilsordnung des Alten Testaments," *Mysterium Salutis,* 2. Pp. 1076-1144.

Scharbert, J. *Was ist Heilsgeschichte?* Semana Bíblica española, 26. Madrid, 1970.

Schedl, Claus. *Zur Theologie des AT: Der göttliche Sprachvorgang in Schöpfung und Geschichte.* Vienna, 1986.

Schlier, Heinrich. "The Meaning and Function of a Theology of the New Testament." In *Dogmatic vs. Biblical Theology.* Ed. H. Vorgrimler. Baltimore, 1964. Pp. 88-90.

————. "Biblical and Dogmatic Theology." In *The Relevance of the New Testament.* London / New York, 1968. Pp. 26-38.

Schmid, H. H. *Wesen und Geschichte der Weisheit.* Berlin, 1966.

————. *Gerechtigkeit als Weltordnung.* Beiträge zur historichen Theologie, 40. Tübingen, 1968.

————. "Schöpfung, Gerechtigkeit und Heil. 'Schöpfungstheologie' als Gesamthorizant biblischer Theologie," *ZTK,* 70 (1973), 1-19.

————. *Altorientalische Welt in der alttestamentlichen Theologie. Sechs Aufsätze.* Zürich, 1974.

————. "Das alttestamentliche Verständnis von Geschichte in seinem Verhältnis zum gemeinorientalischen Denken," *WuD,* 13 (1975), 9-21.

————. *Der sogenannte Jahwist. Beobachtungen und Fragen zur Pentateuchforschung.* Zürich, 1976.

————. "Unterwegs zu einer neuen Biblischen Theologie? Anfragen an die von H. Gese und P. Stuhlmacher vorgetragenen Entwürfe Biblischer Theologie." In *Biblische Theologie heute.* Ed. K. Haacker. Biblisch-theologische Studien, 1. Neukirchen-Vluyn, 1977. Pp. 75-95.

————. "Ich will euer Gott sein, ihr sollt mein Volk sein. Die sogenannte Bundesformel und die Frage nach der Mitte des Alten Testaments." In *Kirche. Festschrift für G. Bornkamm.* Tübingen, 1980. Pp. 1-25.

————. "Vielfalt und Einheit alttestamentlichen Glaubens." In *"Wenn nicht jetzt, wann dann?" Aufsätze für Hans-Joachim Kraus zum 65. Geburtstag.* Ed. H.-G. Geyer et al. Neukirchen-Vluyn, 1983. Pp. 13-22.

————. "Was heisst 'Biblische Theologie.'" In *Wirkungen hermeneutischer Theologie. Festschrift für G. Ebeling.* Zurich, 1983. Pp. 35-50.

————. "Creation, Righteousness, and Salvation: 'Creation Theology' as the Broad Horizon of Biblical Theology." In *Creation in the Old Testament.* Ed. Bernhard W. Anderson. IRT, 6. Philadelphia / London, 1984. Pp. 102-117.

Schmidt, J. M. "Vergegenwärtigung und Überlieferung," *EvT,* 30 (1970), 169-200.

Schmidt, L. "Die Einheit zwischen Altem und Neuen Testament im Streit zwischen Friedrich Baumgärtel und Gerhard von Rad," *EvT,* 35 (1975), 119-139.

————. "Hermeutische und biblisch-theologische Fragen." In H. J. Boecker et al., *Altes Testament.* Neukirchener Arbeitsbücher. Neukirchen-Vluyn, 1983. Pp. 288-307.

Schmidt, Sebastian. *Collegium Biblicum in quo dicta Veteris et Nova Testamenti iuxta sierem locorum communium theologicorum explicantur.* Argentorati, 1671; 2nd ed. 1676.

Schmidt, W. H. "'Theologie des AT' vor und nach Gerhard von Rad." In *Verkündigung und Forschung.* Beiheift zur EvT, 17. Munich, 1972. Pp. 1-25.

————. *Das erste Gebot. Seine Bedeutung für das Alte Testament.* Theologische Existenz heute, 165. Munich, 1979.

————. *The Faith of the Old Testament: A History.* Oxford / Philadelphia, 1983.

————. "Vielfalt und Einheit alttestmentlichen Glaubens. Konstruktionsversuch an einem Pfeiler der Brücke 'Biblische Theologie.'" In *"Wenn nicht jetzt, wann dann?" Aufsätze für Hans-Joachim Kraus zum 65. Geburtstag.* Ed. H.-G. Geyer et al. Neukirchen-Vluyn, 1983. Pp. 13-22.

————. "Die Frage nach der 'Mitte' des Alten Testaments im Spannungsfeld von Religionsgeschichte und Theologie." In *Gott loben das ist unser Amt. Festschrift für D. J. Schmidt.* Ed. K. Jürgensen et al. Kiel, 1984. Pp. 55-65.

————. "The Problem of the 'Centre' of the Old Testament in the Perspective of the Relationship Between History of Religion and Theology," *Old Testament Essays,* 4 (1986), 46-64.

Schmithals, W. "Schriftauslegung auf dem Weg zur Biblischen Theologie. Kritische Bemerkungen zu einem Buch von Peter Stulmacher," *Reformierte Kirchenzeitung,* 117 (1976), 282- 285.

Schmitt, R. *Abschied von der Heilsgeschichte? Untersuchungen zum Verständnis der Geschichte im Alten Testament.* Europäische Hochschulschriften, 25 / 195. Frankfurt / Bern, 1982.

Schofield, J. N. *Introducing Old Testament Theology.* Philadelphia, 1964.

————. "Otto Procksch." In *Contemporary Old Testament Theologians.* Ed. R. B. Laurin. Valley Forge, 1970. Pp. 91-120.

Schrage, W. "Die Frage nach der Mitte und dem Kanon im Kanon des Neuen Testaments in der neueren Diskussion." In *Rechtfertigung. Festschrift für E. Käsemann zum 70. Geburtstag.* Ed. J. Friedrich et al. Tübingen, 1976. Pp. 415-442.

Schulz, S. *Die Mitte der Schrift.* Stuttgart, 1976.

Schwarzwäller, K. "Das Verhältnis Altes Testament—Neues Testament im Lichte der gegenwärtigen Bestimmungen," *EvT,* 29 (1969), 281-307.

Scullion, J. J. "Recent Old Testament Theologies: Three Contributions," *Australian Biblical Review*, 24 (1976), 6-17.

Seebass, H. "Der Beitrag des AT zum Entwurf einer biblischen Theologie," *WuD*, 8 (1965), 20-49.

―――. *Biblische Hermeneutik.* Uni-Taschenbücher, 199. Stuttgart, 1974.

―――. "Zur Ermöglichung biblischer Theologie," *EvT*, 37 (1977), 591-600.

―――. "Biblische Theologie," *Verkündigung und Forschung*, 27 (1982), 28-45.

―――. *Der Gott der ganzen Bibel. Biblische Theologie zur Orientierung im Glauben.* Freiburg / Basel / Vienna, 1982.

―――. "Geschichtliche Vorläufigkeit und eschatologische Endgültigkeit des biblischen Monotheismus," *Zukunftshoffnung und Heilserwartung in den monotheistischen Religionen.* Ed. A. Falaturi et al. Freiburg im Breisgau, 1983. Pp. 49-80.

―――. "Ist biblische Theologie möglich?" *Judaica*, 41 (1985), 194-206.

―――. "Gerechtigkeit Gottes. Zum Dialog mit Peter Stuhlmacher." In *Einheit und Vielfalt Biblischer Theologie.* Ed. I. Baldermann et al. Jahrbuch für Biblische Theologie, 1. Neukirchen-Vluyn, 1986. Pp. 115-134.

Seeligmann, I. L. "Erkenntnis Gottes und historisches Bewusstsein im alten Israel." In *Beiträge zur alttestamentlichen Theologie. Festschrift für W. Zimmerli.* Göttingen, 1977. Pp. 414-445.

Sekine, M. "Vom Verstehen der Heilsgeschichte. Das Grundproblem der alttestamentlichen Theologie," *ZAW*, 75 (1963), 145-154.

Sellin, E. *Das Alte Testament und die evangelische Kirche der Gegenwart.* Leipzig, 1921.

―――. *Alttestamentliche Theologie auf religionsgeschichtlicher Grundlage.* 2 vols. Leipzig, 1933.

―――. *Theologie des AT.* Leipzig, 1933.

Semler, Johann Salomo. *Abhandlung von freier Untersuchung des Canon.* 4 vols. Halle, 1771-1775.

Sheppard, Gerald T. *Wisdom as a Hermeneutical Construct. A Study in the Sapientializing of the Old Testament.* BZAW, 151. Berlin, 1980.

Siedl, S. "Das Alte und das Neue Testament. Ihre Verschiedenheit und Einheit," *Theologisch-praktische Quartalschrift*, 119 (1971), 314-324.

Siegwalt, G. *La Loi, chemin du Salut. Étude sur la signification de la loi de l'Ancien Testament.* Neuchâtel, 1971.

―――. "Biblische Theologie als Begriffe und Vollzug," *KuD*, 11 (1979), 254-272.

Simon, U. *History and Faith in the Biblical Narrative.* London, 1975.

Simpson, C. A. "Professor Procksch's Theology of the Old Testament," *Anglican Theological Review*, 34 (1952), 116-122.

Sitarz, Eugen. *Höre Israel! Jahwe ist einzig: Bausteine für eine Theologie des AT.* Stuttgart, 1987.

Smart, James D. "The Death and Rebirth of Old Testament Theology," *JR*, 23 (1943), 1-11, 124-136.

―――. *The Interpretation of Scripture.* London, 1961.

————. *The Strange Silence of the Bible in the Church: A Study in Hermeneutics*. Philadelphia, 1970.

————. *The Past, Present, and Future of Biblical Theology*. Philadelphia, 1979.

Smend, Rudolf. "J. Ph. Gablers Begründung der biblischen Theologie," *EvT*, 22 (1962), 345-367.

————. "Universalismus und Partikularismus in der Alttestamentliche Theologie des 19. Jahrhunderts," *EvT*, 22 (1962), 169-179.

————. *Elemente alttestamentlichen Geschichtsdenkens*. Theologische Studien, 95. Zurich, 1968.

————. *Die Mitte des AT*. Theologische Studien, 101. Zurich, 1970.

————. "Heinrich Ewalds Biblische Theologie." In *Festschrift für Wolfgang Trillhaas*. Ed. H. W. Schütte and F. Wintzer. Göttingen, 1974. Pp. 176-191.

————. "Tradition and History: A Complex Relation." In *Tradition and Theology in the Old Testament*. Ed. D. A. Knight. Philadelphia, 1977. Pp. 49-68 (= "Überlieferung und Geschichte. Aspekte ihres Verhältnisses." In *Zu Tradition und Theologie im Alten Testament*. Ed. O. H. Steck. Biblisch-Theologische Studien, 2. Neukirchen, 1978. Pp. 9-26).

————. "Theologie des Alten Testament." In *Verifikationen. Festschrift für G. Ebeling*. Tübingen, 1982. Pp. 11-26.

Smith, M. "The Common Theology of the Ancient Near East," *JBL*, 71 (1952), 135-147.

————. "The Present State of Old Testament Studies," *JBL*, 88 (1969), 19-35.

Snaith, N. H. *The Distinctives Ideas of the Old Testament*. London, 1944.

Soggin, J. A. "Alttestamentliche Glaubenszeugnisse und geschichtliche Wirklichkeit," *TZ*, 17 (1961), 385-398.

————. "Geschichte, Historie und Heilsgeschichte," *TLZ*, 89 (1964), 721ff.

————. "God and History in Biblical Thought." In J. A. Soggin, *Old Testament and Oriental Studies*. Biblica et Orientalia, 29. Rome, 1975. Pp. 59-66.

————. "Den gammaltestamentliga theologin efter G. von Rad," *Svensk exegetisk Årsbok*, 47 (1982), 7-20.

————. "Teologia dell'Antico Testamento oggi. Dopo Gerhard von Rad," *Protestantesimo*, 39 / 1 (1984), 1-17.

Spicq, C. "L'avènement de la Théologie Biblique," *Revue biblique*, 35 (1951), 561-574.

————. "Nouvelles réflexions sur la théologie biblique," *RSPT*, 43 (1958), 209-219.

Spina, F. A. "Canonical Criticism: Childs versus Sanders." In *Interpreting God's Word for Today: An Inquiry into Hermeneutics from a Biblical Theological Perspective*. Ed. J. E. Hartley and R. L. Shelton. Anderson, IN, 1982. Pp. 165-194.

Spriggs, D. C. *Two Old Testament Theologies: A Comparative Evaluation of the Contributions of Eichrodt and von Rad to our Understanding of the Nature of Old Testament Theology*. SBT, 2 / 30. Naperville, IL, 1974.

Stade, Bernhard. "Über die Aufgaben der biblischen Theologie des AT," *ZTK*, 3 (1893), 31-51.

————. *Biblische Theologie des AT*, 2 vols. Tübingen, 1905, 1911.

Staerk, Willy, "Religionsgeschichte und Religionsphilosophie in ihrer Bedeutung für die biblische Theologie des AT," *ZTK*, 4 (1923), 289-300.

Steck, K. G. *Die Idee der Heilsgeschichte.* Theologische Studien, 56. Zurich, 1959.

Steck, Odil Hannes. "Theological Streams of Tradition." In *Tradition and Theology in the Old Testament.* Ed. D. A. Knight. Philadelphia, 1977. Pp. 183-214 (= "Strömungen theologischer Tradition im Alten Israel." In *Zu Tradition und Theologie im Alten Testament.* Ed. O. H. Steck. Biblisch-theologische Studien, 2. Neukirchen-Vluyn, 1978. Pp. 27-56).

Steck, Odil Hannes, and Barth, Hermann. *Exegese des Alten Testaments.* Neukirchen-Vluyn, 1971.

Steimle, E. "Preaching and the Biblical Story of Good and Evil," *Union Seminary Quarterly Review,* 31 (1976), 198-211.

Stek, John H. "Biblical Typology Yesterday and Today," *Calvin Theological Journal,* 5 (1970), 133-162.

Stendahl, Krister. "Biblical Theology, Contemporary." In *IDB,* I. Pp. 418-432.

———. "Method in the Study of Biblical Theology." In *The Bible in Modern Scholarship.* Ed. J. P. Hyatt. Nashville, 1965. Pp. 266-273.

———. "The Bible as a Classic and the Bible as Holy Scripture," *JBL,* 103 (1984), 3-10.

———. "Biblical Theology: A Program." In *Meanings: The Bible as Document and as Guide.* Philadelphia, 1984. Pp. 11-44.

———. *Meanings: The Bible as Document and as Guide.* Philadelphia, 1984.

Sternberg, Meir. *The Poetics of Biblical Narrative.* Bloomington, 1987.

Steuernagel, Carl. "Alttestamentliche Theologie und alttestamentliche Religionsgeschichte." In *Vom Alten Testament. Festschrift für K. Marti.* Ed. K. Budde. BZAW, 41. Giessen, 1925. Pp. 266-273.

Stoebe, H.-J. "Das Verhältnis von Offenbarung und religiöser Aussage im Alten Testament," *Acta Tropica,* 21 (1964), 400-414.

———. "Überlegungen zur Theologie des AT." In *Gottes Wort und Gottes Land. H.-W. Hertzberg zum 70. Geburtstag.* Ed. H. Graf Reventlow. Göttingen, 1965. Pp. 200-220.

Stolz, F. "Monotheism in Israel." In *Monotheismus im Alten Testament und seiner Umwelt.* Ed. O. Keel. Biblische Beiträge, 14. Fribourg, 1980. Pp. 143-184.

Strange, John. "Heilsgeschichte und Geschichte. Ein Aspekt der biblischen Theologie," *Scandinavian Journal of the Old Testament,* 2 (1989), 100-113.

———. "Replik an Niels Peter Lemche," *Scandinavian Journal of the Old Testament,* 2 (1989), 136-139.

Strauss, H. "Theologie des AT als Bestandteil einer biblischen Theologie," *EvT,* 45 (1985), 20-29.

Strecker, G. " 'Biblische Theologie.' Kritische Bemerkungen zu den Entwürfen von Hartmut Gese und Peter Stuhlmacher." In *Kirche. Festschrift für G. Bornkamm.* Tübingen, 1980. Pp. 425-445.

Stroup, G. W. *The Promise of Narrative Theology.* Atlanta, 1981.

Stuhlmacher, P. *Gerechtigkeit Gottes bei Paulus.* 2nd ed. FRLANT, 95. Göttingen, 1966.

————. *Schriftauslegung auf dem Wege zur biblischen Theologie.* Göttingen, 1975. Trans. *Historical Criticism and Theological Interpretation of Scripture.* Philadelphia, 1977.

————. "Biblische Theologie und Kritische Exegese," *Theologische Beiträge,* 8 (1977), 88-90.

————. "Zum Thema: Biblische Theologie des Neuen Testaments." In *Biblische Theologie heute.* Ed. K. Haacker. Biblisch-theologische Studien, 1. Neukirchen-Vluyn, 1977. Pp. 25-60.

————. "Das Gesetz als Thema biblischer Theologie," *ZTK,* 75 (1978), 251-280.

————. *Vom Verstehen des Neuen Testaments: Eine Hermeneutik.* Göttingen: Vandenhoeck & Ruprecht, 1979.

————. " '. . . in verrosteten Angeln," *ZTK,* 77 (1980), 222-238.

————. "Biblische Theologie als Weg der Erkenntnis Gottes. Zum Buch von Horst Seebass: Der Gott der ganzen Bibel." In *Einheit und Vielfalt Biblischer Theologie.* Ed. I. Baldermann et al. Jahrbuch für Biblische Theologie, 1. Neukirchen-Vluyn, 1986. Pp. 91-114.

Stuhlmueller, C. "The Influence of Oral Tradition upon Exegesis and the Senses of Scripture," *CBQ,* 20 (1958), 299-326.

Syreeni, Kari. "Teologia, hermeneutiikka ja 'toisenlainen hermeneutiikka'," *Teologinen aikakauskirja,* 91 / 3 (1986), 293-296.

Talmon, S. "The Old Testament Text." In *Qumran and the History of the Biblical Text.* Ed. F. M. Cross and S. Talmon. Cambridge, MA, 1975. Pp. 1-41.

Teeple, H. M. "Notes on a Theologian's Approach to the Bible," *JBL,* 79 (1960), 164-166.

Tengström, S. "Kristen tolkning av Gamla Testamentet," *Svenk exegetisk Årsbok,* 48 (1983), 77-101.

Terrien, S. *The Elusive Presence: Toward a New Biblical Theology.* San Francisco, 1978.

————. "The Play of Wisdom: Turning Point in Biblical Theology," *HBT,* 3 (1981), 125-153.

————. "Biblical Theology: The Old Testament (1970-1984). A Decade and a Half of Spectacular Growth," *BTB,* 15 / 4 (1985), 127-135.

TeSelle, S. *Speaking in Parables: A Study in Metaphor and Theology.* London/ Philadelphia, 1975.

Thils, G. "La théologie de l'histoire. Note bibliographique," *Ephemerides Theologicae Lovanienses,* 26 (1950), 87-95.

Thiselton, Anthony. *The Two Horizons: New Testament Hermeneutics and Philosophical Description.* Grand Rapids, 1980.

Toombs, L. E. "Old Testament Theology and the Wisdom Literature," *JBR,* 23 (1955), 193-196.

Towner, W. S. "The Renewed Authority of Old Testament Wisdom for Contemporary Faith." In *Canon and Authority: Essays in Old Testament Religion and Theology.* Ed. G. W. Coats and B. O. Long. Philadelphia, 1977. Pp. 132-147.

————. "Is Old Testament Theology Equal to Its Task? A Response to a Paper by Rolf Knierim," *HBT,* 6 / 1 (1984), 73-80.

Tracy, David. *The Analogical Imagination: Christian Theology and the Culture of Pluralism.* New York, 1981.

Tracy, David, and Lash, Nicholas, eds. *Cosmology and Theology.* New York / Edinburgh, 1988.

Tsevat, M. "Theology of the Old Testament—A Jewish View," *HBT,* 8 / 2 (1986), 33-50.

Tucker, Gene M., Petersen, David L., and Wilson, Robert R., eds. *Canon, Theology, and Old Testament Interpretation: Essays in Honor of Brevard S. Childs.* Philadelphia, 1988.

Uffenheimer, B. "Biblical Theology and Monotheistic Myth," *Immanuel,* 14 (1982), 7-24.

Van Seters, J. *In Search of History: Historiography in the Ancient World and the Origins of Biblical History.* New Haven / London, 1983.

Vanhoozer, Kevin J. "A Lamp in the Labyrinth: The Hermeneutics of 'Asthetic' Theology," *Trinity Journal,* NS 8 (1987), 25-56.

Vatke, Wilhelm. *Die biblische Theologie wissenschaftlich dargestellt,* I: *Die Religion des Alten Testaments.* Berlin, 1835.

Vaux, R. de. "A propos de la Théologie Biblique," *ZAW,* 68 (1956), 225-227.

———. "Method in the Study of Early Hebrew History." In *The Bible in Modern Scholarship.* Ed. J. P. Hyatt. Nashville, 1965. Pp. 15-17.

———. "Peut-on écrire une 'théologie de l'AT'?" In *Bible et Orient.* Paris, 1967. Pp. 59-71. Trans. "Is it Possible to Write a 'Theology of the OT'?" In R. de Vaux, *The Bible and the Ancient Near East.* Garden City, NY, 1971. Pp. 49-62.

———. "Presence and Absence in History: The Old Testament View," *Concilium,* 5 (1969), 5-12.

Vawter, B. "History and Kerygma in the Old Testament." In *A Light Unto My Path: Old Testament Studies in Honor of Jacob M. Myers.* Ed. H. Bream et al. Philadelphia, 1974. Pp. 475-492.

Veijola, T. "Finns det en gammaltestamentlig teologi?" *Svensk exegetisk Årsbok,* 48 (1983), 10-30.

———. "Ilmoitus kohtaamisena. Vanhan testamentin teologinen perusstruktuuri," *Teologinen aikakauskirja,* 90 / 5 (1985), 381-390.

———. "Vanhan testamentin teologia ja 'historiallinen hermeneutiikka'," *Teologinen aikakauskirja,* 91 / 2 (1986), 118-121.

———. "Vanhan testamentin tutkimus ja teologia eilen ja tänään," *Teologinen aikakauskirja,* 91 / 3 (1986), 180-189.

Verhoef, Pieter A. "Some Thoughts on the Present-day Situation in Biblical Theology," *Westminster Theological Journal,* 33 (1970), 1-19.

Vetter, D. *Jahwes Mit-Sein ein Ausdruck des Segens.* Arbeiten zur Theologie, 45. Stuttgart, 1971.

Vicary, D. R. "Liberalism, Biblical Criticism, and Biblical Theology," *Anglican Theological Review,* 34 (1950), 114-121.

Vischer, W. *Das Christuszeugnis des AT.* Zurich, 1934. Trans. *The Witness of the Old Testament to Christ.* London, 1949.

Vogels, Walter. "Biblical Theology for the 'Haves' and the 'Have-nots'," *Science et Esprit,* 39 (1987), 193-210.

Vorgrimler, Herbert, ed. *Dogmatic vs. Biblical Theology.* Montreal, 1964.

Vos, G. *Biblical Theology.* Grand Rapids, 1948.

Vriezen, Th. C. *Hoofdlijnen der Theologie van het Oude Testament.* Wageningen, 1954. Trans. *An Outline of Old Testament Theology.* 2nd ed. Newton, MA, 1970.

————. "Geloof, openbaring en geschiedenis in de nieuwste Oude-Testamentische Theologie," *Kerk en Theologie,* 16 (1956), 97-113, 210-218.

Wacker, B. *Narrative Theologie?* Munich, 1977.

Wagner, S. "Zur Frage nach einem Gegenstand einer Theologie des AT." In *Fides et Communicatio. Festschrift M. Doerne.* Ed. D. Rössler et al. Göttingen, 1970, 391-411.

————. "'Biblische Theologien' und 'Biblische Theologie,'" *TLZ,* 103 (1978), 791-793.

Walkenhorst, K.-H. "Theologie der Psalmen. Eine kritische Stellungnahme zur biblischen Theologie von Hans-Joachim Kraus," *Zeitschrift für katholische Theologie,* 104 (1982), 25-47.

Wallace, D. "Biblical Theology: Past and Future," *TZ,* 19 (1963), 88-105.

Walther, James Arthur. "The Significance of Methodology for Biblical Theology," *Perspective,* 10 (1969), 217-233.

Ware, J. H. "Rethinking the Possibility of a Biblical Theology," *Perspectives in Religious Studies,* 10 (1983), 5-13.

Watson, Philip S. "The Nature and Function of Biblical Theology," *ExpTim,* 73 (1962), 195-200.

Watts, John D. W. *Basic Patterns in Old Testament Religion.* New York, 1971.

Weinrich, H. "Narrative Theology," *Concilium,* 5 / 9 (1973), 46-56.

Weinrich, M. "Grenzen der Erinnerung. Historische Kritik und Dogmatik im Horizont Biblischer Theologie. Systematische Vorüberlegungen." In *"Wenn nicht jetzt, wann dann?" Aufsätze für Hans-Joachim Kraus zum 65. Geburtstag.* Ed. H.-G. Geyer. Neukirchen-Vluyn, 1983. Pp. 327-338.

Weinsheimer, Joel C. *Gadamer's Hermeneutics: A Reading of Truth and Method.* New Haven / London, 1985.

Weiser, Arthur. *Glaube und Geschichte.* Stuttgart, 1931.

Weiss, Meir. *The Bible From Within: The Method of Total Interpretation.* Jerusalem, 1984.

Wellek, R. and A. Warren. *Theory of Literature,* 3rd ed. New York, 1977.

Wells, Paul Ronald. *James Barr and the Bible: Critique of a New Liberalism.* Phillipsburg, NJ, 1980.

Wernberg-Möller, P. "Is There an Old Testament Theology?" *Hibbert Journal,* 59 (1960), 21-29.

West, C. "On Frei's *Eclipse of Biblical Narrative,*" *Union Seminary Quarterly Review,* 37 (1982), 299-302.

Westermann, C., ed. *Probleme alttestamentlicher Hermeneutik. Aufsätze zum Verstehen des Alten Testaments.* TBü, 11. Munich, 1960. Trans. repr. *EOTH.* Atlanta, 1979 (= *Essays on Old Testament Interpretation.* London, 1963).

———. "Sinn und Grenze religionsgeschichtlicher Parallelen," *TLZ*, 90 (1965), 489-496.

———. "The Way of the Promise through the Old Testament." In *OTCF: A Theological Discussion*. Ed. Bernhard W. Anderson. New York, 1969. Pp. 200-224.

———. *The Old Testament and Jesus Christ*. Minneapolis, 1970.

———. "Das hermeneutische Problem in der Theologie." In C. Westermann, *Forschung am Alten Testaments: Gesammelte Studien*, II. Munich, 1974. Pp. 68-84.

———. "Zu Zwei Theologien des AT," *EvT*, 34 (1974), 96-112.

———. *Theologie des AT in Grundzügen*. Göttingen, 1978. Trans. *Elements of Old Testament Theology*. Atlanta, 1982.

———. *What Does the Old Testament Say About God?* Atlanta, 1978.

———. "The Interpretation of the Old Testament." In *EOTH*. Ed. C. Westermann. Repr. Atlanta, 1979. Pp. 40-49.

———. "Remarks on the Theses of Bultmann and Baumgärtel." In *EOTH*. Ed. C. Westermann. Repr. Atlanta, 1979. Pp. 123-133.

———. "Aufgaben einer zukünftigen Biblischen Theologie." In C. Westermann, *Erträge der Forschung am Alten Testament: Gesammelte Studien*, III. TBü, 73. Munich, 1984. Pp. 201-221.

Wharton, J. A. "The Occasion of the Word of God: An Unguarded Essay on the Character of the Old Testament as the Memory of God's Story with Israel," *Austin Presbyterian Seminary Bulletin (Faculty ed.)*, 84 (1968), 5-54.

Whybray, R. "Old Testament Theology—A Non-existent Beast?" In *Scripture: Meaning and Method. Essays Presented to Anthony Tyrell Hanson for His Seventieth Birthday*. Ed. B. P. Thompson. Pickering, North Yorkshire, 1987. Pp. 168-180.

Wilch, J. R. *Time and Event*. Leiden, 1969.

Wilckens, U. "Über die Bedeutung historischer Kritik in der Bibelexegese." In *Was heisst Auslegung der Heiligen Schrift?* Ed. W. Joest et al. Regensburg, 1966. Pp. 85ff.

Wildberger, Hans. "Auf dem Wege zu einer biblischen Theologie," *EvT*, 19 (1959), 70-90.

Wink, Walter. *The Bible in Human Transformation: Toward a New Paradigm for Biblical Study*. Philadelphia, 1980.

———. *Transforming Bible Study*. Nashville, 1988.

Wolfe, R. E. "The Terminology of Biblical Theology," *JBR*, 15 (1947), 143-147.

Wolff, H. W. "Hauptprobleme alttestamentlicher Prophetie," *EvT*, 15 (1955), 116-168.

———. "Zur Hermeneutik des Alten Testaments," *EvT*, 16 (1956), 140-180. Trans. "The Hermeneutics of the Old Testament," *Interp*, 15 (1961), 439-472. Repr. in *EOTH*. Ed. C. Westermann. Atlanta, 1979. Pp. 160-199.

———. "The Old Testament in Controversy: Interpretive Principles and Illustration," *Interp*, 12 (1958), 281-291.

———. "Das Alten Testament und das Probleme der existentialen Interpretation," *EvT*, 23 (1963), 1-17.

————. *Anthropology of the Old Testament*. London / Philadelphia, 1974.
————. "The Understanding of History in the Old Testament Prophets." In *EOTH*. Ed. C. Westermann. Repr. Atlanta, 1979. Pp. 336-355.
————. "The Elohistic Fragments in the Pentateuch." In W. Brueggemann and H. W. Wolff, *The Vitality of Old Testament Traditions*. 2nd ed. Atlanta, 1982. Pp. 67-82. First translated in *Interp*, 26 (1972), 158-173. Originally published as "Zur Thematik der elohistischen Fragmente im Pentateuch," *EvT*, 29 (1969), 59-72.
————. "The Kerygma of the Deuteronomic Historical Work." In W. Brueggemann and H. W. Wolff, *The Vitality of Old Testament Traditions*. 2nd ed. Atlanta, 1982. Pp. 83-100. Originally published as "Das Kerygma des deuteronomischen Geschichtswerks," *ZAW*, 73 (1961), 171-186.
————. "The Kerygma of the Yahwist." In W. Brueggemann and H. W. Wolff, *The Vitality of Old Testament Traditions*. 2nd ed. Atlanta, 1982. First translated in *Interp*, 20 (1966), 131-158. Originally published as "Das Kerygma des Jahwisten," *EvT*, 24 (1964), 73-98.
Wolff, H. W., ed. *Probleme biblischer Theologie. Gerhard von Rad zum 70. Geburtstag*. Munich, 1971.
Wolff, H. W., Rendtorff, R., and Pannenberg, W. *Gerhard von Rad: Seine Bedeutung für die Theologie*. Munich, 1973.
Wrede, William. "The Task and Method of 'New Testament Theology.'" In R. Morgan, ed., *The Nature of New Testament Theology*. SBT, 2 / 25. Naperville, IL, 1973. Pp. 68-116.
Wright, G. Ernest. *The Old Testament Against Its Environment*. SBT, 1 /.2. London / Chicago, 1950.
————. *God Who Acts: Biblical Theology as Recital*. SBT, 1 / 8. London / Chicago, 1952.
————. "Reflections Concerning Old Testament Theology." In *Studia Biblica et Semitica. Festschrift Th. C. Vriezen*. Wageningen, 1966. Pp. 376-388.
————. *The Old Testament and Theology*. New York, 1969.
————. "Historical Knowledge and Revelation." In *Translating and Understanding the Old Testament: Essays in Honor of Herbert Gordon May*. Ed. H. T. Frank and W. L. Reed. Nashville, 1970. Pp. 279-303.
————. "The Theological Study of the Bible." In *The Interpreter's One-Volume Commentary on the Bible*. Nashville, 1971. P. 983.
Würthwein, E. "Bemerkungen zu Wilhelm Vischer, *Das Christuszeugnis des Alten Testaments*," *Deutsche Theologie*, 3 (1936), 259-273.
————. "Amos-Studien," *ZAW*, 62 (1950), 10-52.
————. "Zur Theologie des AT," *TRu*, 36 (1971), 185-208.
Young, Edward J. *The Study of Old Testament Theology Today*. London, 1958.
————. "What is Old Testament Biblical Theology?" *EvQ*, 31 (1959), 136-142.
Zahrnt, H. "Religiöse Aspekte gegenwärtiger Welt- und Lebenserfahrung. Reflexionen über die Notwendigkeit einer neuen Erfahrungstheologie," *ZTK*, 71 (1974), 94-122.
Zenger, E. "Die Mitte der alttestamentlichen Glaubensgeschichte," *Katechetische Blätter*, 101 (1976), 3-16.

————. "Beobachtungen zur Komposition und Theologie der jahwistischen Urgeschichte." In *Dynamik im Wort; Lehre von der Bibel; Leben aus der Bibel. Festschrift des Katholischen Bibelwerks in Deutschland.* Stuttgart, 1983. Pp. 35-54.

Zimmerli, W. "Verheissung und Erfüllung," *EvT,* 12 (1952-1953), 34-59. Trans. "Promise and Fulfillment," *Interp,* 15 (1961), 310-338. Repr. in *EOTH.* Ed. C. Westermann. Atlanta, 1979. Pp. 89-122.

————. " 'Offenbarung' im Alten Testament. Ein Gespräch mit R. Rendtorff," *EvT,* 22 (1962), 15-31.

————. "G. von Rad, Theologie des AT," *VT,* 13 (1963), 100-111.

————. "Die historisch-kritische Bibelwissenschaft und die Verkündigungsaufgabe der Kirche," *EvT,* 23 (1963), 17-31.

————. "Alttestamentliche Traditionsgeschichte und Theologie." In *Probleme Biblischer Theologie. Gerhard von Rad zum 70. Geburtstag.* Ed. Hans Walter Wolff. Munich, 1971. Pp. 632-647.

————. *Grundriss der alttestamentlichen Theologie.* Theologische Wissenschaft, 3. Stuttgart, 1972. Trans. *Old Testament Theology in Outline.* Atlanta, 1978.

————. "Erwägungen zur Gestalt einer alttestamentlichen Theologie," *TLZ,* 98 (1973), 81-98.

————. *Studien zur alttestamentlichen Theologie und Prophetie.* TBü, 51. Munich, 1974.

————. "Zum Problem der 'Mitte des Alten Testaments'," *EvT,* 35 (1975), 97-118.

————. "Biblische Theologie I. Altes Testament." In *Theologische Realenzyklopädie,* VI. Ed. G. Krause and G. Müller. Berlin / New York, 1980. Pp. 426-455.

————. "Biblical Theology," *HBT,* 4 (1982), 95-130.

————. "Biblische Theologie," *Berliner Theologische Zeitschrift,* 1 (1984), 5-26.

Zirker, Hans. *Die kultische Vergegenwärtigung der Vergangenheit in den Psalmen.* Bonn, 1964.

Zobel, H.-J. "Altes Testament—Literatursammlung und Heilige Schrift," *TLZ,* 105 (1980), 81-92.

Zwanger, C. " 'Kritischer müssten mir die Historisch- Kritischen sein!' Hinter Barth zurück," *EvT,* 43 (1983), 370-379.

Zyl, A. H. van. "The Relation Between the Old Testament and the New Testament," *Hermeneutica* (1970), 9-22.

Index of Subjects

actualization, 8, 75-77
allegory, 96, 192
anachronism, 116
analogy, principle of, 99, 128, 150,
153, 154, 180, 198
annunciation, 88
anthropocentrism, 128
anthropology, 17, 39-42, 63, 110,
113, 158
antitype, 179, 180. *See also* type;
typology
apocalyptic, 62, 93, 150
approach
book-by-book, 62, 70
canonical, 5, 89, 96, 98, 107-110,
114, 135, 136
constructive, 58
critical 13-17, 20, 21, 30, 46, 47,
62, 72, 73, 75, 76, 77, 82, 91,
93, 94, 96, 98-104, 110, 115-
120, 123, 125, 127-132, 138,
188, 189, 196-199
descriptive, 16, 31-33, 89. *See
also* descriptive task
diachronic, 71-79
formation-of-tradition, 77, 79-85,
86, 104. *See also* tradition
historical, 20, 33, 51, 60, 92, 94,
96, 162, 200. *See also* criticism: historical; method: historical-critical
history-of-religions, 9, 18, 19, 23,
24, 50, 96, 104, 112, 190. *See
also Religionsgeschichte*
literary, 7-9, 13, 62, 89, 95, 96,
99, 100, 104, 112, 132-138,
176, 201-203
longitudinal, 205. *See also*
theme: logitudinal
methodological, 204-206
multiplex, 111-114, 183, 184,
191, 205, 207
multi-valent, 163
sociological, 90

topical-thematic, 68
traditio-historical, 51, 60, 71-79,
92, 94, 96
unilinear, 114, 205
archeology, 202
authority, 13, 16, 20, 45, 56, 57,
95, 106, 107, 121, 137

Biblical theology
critical, 13-17, 20, 21, 30, 46, 47,
62, 72, 73, 75-77, 82, 91, 93,
94, 96, 98-104, 110, 115, 116-
120, 123, 125, 127-132, 138,
188, 189, 196, 197-199
definition of, 11, 16
historical discipline, 14, 16, 17,
18
history of, 76, 92, 115, 116, 126,
202
nature of, 17
new, 103-111
Roman Catholic, 2, 3
"synthetic modern," 96, 97
Biblical Theology Movement, 2,
27, 104
biblicism, 185
bipolarity/bipolar, 89, 91
blessings, 69
bruta facta, 115, 131

canon, 14, 32, 43, 45, 46, 55, 60,
66, 67, 81, 85, 95, 100, 104, 106-
109, 113, 129, 130, 133, 135-137,
144, 165, 184, 185, 204
"canon within the canon," 66, 67,
107
canonical criticism, 67, 109
canonization, 85, 105, 205
cause-effect, 197, 198
center, 3, 4, 9, 40, 42, 44, 47, 51-
54, 58, 60, 63, 64, 66, 70, 74, 80,
81, 83, 86, 92, 97, 107, 110, 112,
113, 115, 129, 139, 140, 142-146,
148-164, 166-171, 194, 203, 204

Christ. *See* Jesus Christ
Christ-event, 149, 150, 174, 181
Christ-message, 174
Christianism, 19
Christomonism, 173, 178
close reading, 135
communion concept, 2, 87, 143
comparative religion, 104, 183.
    See also approach: history-of-
    religions
confession, 68, 71, 121, 149
conservatism, 18, 20, 22
context, 5, 21, 30, 32, 33, 38, 101,
    104, 107, 108, 110, 126, 130,
    176, 178, 181, 184-186, 188, 190,
    192, 202, 207
continuity, 68, 80, 85, 87, 145,
    171, 172, 174, 184
covenant formula, 40
creation theology, 54, 171
Creator, 55, 93, 154
credo, 147
crisis, 1, 2, 69, 70, 125, 164, 194,
    198, 208
criticism
    canonical, 67, 109
    content, 66, 167
    historical, 17, 46, 82, 83, 95, 98,
        100, 108, 131. *See also* ap-
        proach: historical; method: his-
        torical-critical
    literary, 7-9, 13, 62, 89, 95, 96,
        99, 100, 104, 112, 132-138,
        176, 201-203
    new, 135, 136
    philosophical, 17
cult, 4, 54, 56, 61, 62, 64, 65, 67,
    69, 70, 76, 148, 156, 157, 205

Decalogue, 68, 69
descriptive task, 4, 16, 18, 28-34,
    36, 37, 45, 46, 49, 56, 58, 59, 63,
    68, 82, 89, 96, 101, 103, 107-
    109, 143
Deuteronomist, 78, 147
developmentalism, 19, 20
dialectic, 86-89, 91-94, 177
dialectical theology, 18
discontinuity, 145, 172-174, 184,
    187
dissimilarity, 184, 207
disunity, 172, 187

dogmatic theology. *See* systematic
    theology
doom, 54
dual concept, 4, 63, 66, 142, 156
dualism, 11, 120

election, 45, 64, 65, 67, 70, 88, 89,
    92, 141, 149, 157, 159, 169, 192,
    204
Enlightenment, 10, 13, 18, 101, 197
error, 118, 122
eschatology, 41, 150, 156, 177, 179
event(s), 73, 120, 121, 123-126,
    129-131, 147, 149, 150, 158, 169,
    174, 177, 179, 181, 182, 185,
    192, 193, 198, 201, 204
evolution, 23, 25
exegesis, 15, 21, 77, 96, 101, 102,
    133, 176, 179, 185, 196, 199, 202
existence, 39, 52, 64-67, 70, 78, 79,
    104, 118, 128, 164, 169, 189
exodus, 192, 204, 205
experience, historical, 72, 197,
    199, 201

fact(s), 17, 37, 72, 81, 99, 111, 118,
    120, 121, 124-126, 128, 131, 132,
    147, 150, 168, 173, 174, 176,
    180, 184, 188, 190
facticity, 99, 118, 124, 125
failure, 132, 142, 173-175
faith, 6, 18, 25, 26, 30, 36, 54, 57,
    59, 64, 66, 72, 73, 77, 86, 88, 90,
    97, 99-101, 106, 109, 111, 115-
    118, 121, 122, 126, 129, 131,
    139, 143, 147, 148, 158-160, 163,
    167, 170, 173, 176, 188, 189,
    200, 201, 205
feeling, 18
fiction, 99, 116, 138
fulfillment, 142, 149, 150, 174,
    176, 181-183, 189, 192
fundamentalism, 95
Fundamentalist-Modernist con-
    troversy, 27
future, 3, 4, 17, 34, 37, 40, 55, 56,
    62, 70, 85, 94, 95, 97, 105, 127,
    141, 148, 149, 163, 170, 182,
    193, 205

God
    acts, activity of, 6, 8, 22, 71, 73,

93, 122, 131, 168-170, 176,
195, 198, 203
center, 148-164, 166-171, 194,
203, 204
doctrine of, 11, 12, 17, 22, 40,
41, 113, 153, 166
eternal, 45, 141
existence, 169
holiness of, 141, 159
kingdom of, 41, 113, 142, 159,
177, 205
kingship of, 49, 141
Lord of history, 22
lordship, 141
presence of, 5, 44, 69, 86-88, 94,
170
reality of, 199
rulership of, 64, 141, 159, 192
self-disclosure of, 169, 170, 201,
203
word of, 14, 45, 57, 91, 119, 138,
195
God-hypothesis, 116, 125
God-talk, 61
gospel, 81, 87, 101, 141, 173, 175,
189
grace, 64

Hagiographa, 43
happening, 92, 120, 125, 197
Hebraism, 19, 87
Hegelianism, 19
Heilsgeschichte, 73, 110, 125, 127,
147, 183. See also salvation history
Hexateuch, 69, 77, 149
historical-critical method. See approach: historical; criticism: historical; method: historical-critical
historical experience, 72, 197, 199,
201
historical Jesus, 118, 119
historical theology, 33, 79, 100, 101
historicism, 24, 25, 48, 49
historicity, 73, 99, 118, 119, 175
historic progression, 42-44, 61,
109, 119
Historie, 73, 110
historiography, 73, 119, 123, 131,
132
history
critical picture of, 13-17, 20, 21,

30, 46, 47, 62, 72, 73, 75-77,
82, 91, 93, 94, 96, 98-104, 110,
115-120, 123, 125, 127-132,
138, 188, 189, 196-199
faith picture of, 115, 118
history of Israel, 4, 23, 26, 111,
117, 118, 121, 128, 131, 147,
173, 174, 175, 202
history of religions. See approach:
history-of-religions
history of tradition, 73, 85, 115,
116, 128-131, 153, 182. See also
tradition
history of transmission, 115-117,
128-131, 153, 182, 202
"howness," 123

imagination, 99
incarnation, 175
inspiration, 13, 15, 16, 20, 22, 95,
206
interpretation, 10, 25, 30-32, 46,
56, 57, 63, 64, 67, 73, 77, 93, 95,
108, 115, 122, 124-126, 129, 130,
136, 146, 148, 150, 153, 174,
177, 178, 184-186, 188, 189, 196,
199, 200, 201, 203
introspection, 73

Jamnia, 55, 85
Jesus Christ, 22, 26, 43, 57, 77, 81,
85, 92, 93, 93, 101, 118, 119,
146, 149, 150, 161, 174-182, 192,
193
Jewish scholarship, 6, 7, 34-38
Judaism, 19, 37, 87, 157
judgment, 31, 48, 54, 55, 70, 84,
93, 141, 147, 148, 170, 183, 184,
192, 195, 196, 201

Kantianism, 126, 131
kerygma, 71, 73, 118, 119, 124, 149
kingdom of God, 41, 113, 142, 159,
177, 205
knowledge, 13, 26, 40, 55, 95, 163,
170

law, 5, 20, 43, 45, 46, 64, 65, 67,
70, 93, 102, 157, 173, 175, 189
legend, 96, 116
liberalism, 13, 25, 75, 97
life, 18, 24, 30, 41, 49, 53, 56, 61,

65, 69, 85, 92, 110, 134, 157,
180, 186, 189, 190, 192, 205
literary
approach/criticism, 7-9, 13, 62,
89, 95, 96, 99, 100, 104, 112,
132-138, 176, 201-203
paradigm, 8, 100, 132, 136, 138
study, 7-9, 13, 62, 89, 95, 96, 99,
100, 104, 112, 132, 133-138,
176, 201-203
literature, 7, 34, 38, 45, 46, 89, 90,
92, 98, 100-102, 106, 133, 134-
138, 147, 162, 166, 167, 169, 188

magic, 23, 64, 65, 67, 70
man, 3-5, 16, 20, 22, 26, 39, 41,
42, 48-50, 55, 56, 63-66, 74, 75,
91, 92, 94, 111, 124, 126, 128,
134, 142, 143, 147, 156, 158,
160, 169, 170, 174, 175, 181,
193, 195, 196, 200, 205
Marcionism, 186
meaning, 22, 30, 35, 45, 49, 63, 65,
77, 90, 93, 121, 122, 125, 126,
127, 128, 130-132, 135, 175-178,
184, 188, 195-197, 199-202
mercy, 93
Messiah, 178
method
biblical-exegetical, 15
confessional, 51, 73, 74, 100,
108, 120, 133, 143, 148, 153
cross-section, 26, 47-60, 107,
113, 143
descriptive, 16, 30-33, 89. See
also descriptive task
diachronic, 71-79
dogmatic-didactic, 39-42
evolutionary, 23
formation-of-tradition, 77, 79-85,
86, 104
genetic-progressive, 42-47
grammatical-historical, 20-25
historical-critical, 13, 16, 17, 20,
30, 72, 75, 76, 82, 115, 116,
117, 119, 120, 125, 127-129,
131, 132, 188, 189, 197-199
historical-theological, 194-196
multiplex, 111-114. See also approach: multiplex
"New Biblical Theology," 103-111
thematic-dialectical, 86-94

theological, 38
topical, 60-71
traditio-historical, 51, 60, 71-79,
92, 94, 96
Moses, 42, 43, 63, 64, 68, 110, 180
multiplex canonical OT theology,
111-114, 194-208
myth, 96, 121, 138, 150, 174

narrative, 74, 100, 102, 132, 136-
138
natural theology, 98
neo-Kantianism, 131
neologist, 15
"new criticism," 135, 136
nonnormative, 33, 34, 37, 108
normative, 26, 28, 30-34, 40, 56,
73, 96, 99, 101, 104-108, 134,
135, 136-138

objective/objectivity, 6, 8, 25, 26,
31, 32, 34, 48, 108, 125, 126,
198, 200

paradigm, 5, 99, 132, 134-136, 138
particularism, 19
past, 6, 9, 35, 40, 75, 76, 102, 104,
111, 122, 126, 127, 132, 141,
148, 149, 170, 201
Pentateuch, 43, 45, 69, 70, 77, 79,
157
philology, 34, 95
philosophical theology, 15
philosophy, 18, 19, 25, 33, 48, 195
Pietism, 12, 14
positivism, 119, 126, 131
premise, 8·?, 151, 155, 179
prescriptive, 34, 96, 101
present, 3, 6, 8, 9, 13, 22, 26, 28,
30, 35, 40, 42, 45, 56, 63, 68, 75-
77, 85, 97, 102, 104, 105, 111-
113, 117, 118, 125, 126-128, 131,
141, 157, 159, 163, 166, 170-172,
174, 182, 186, 192, 195, 204, 205
presupposition, 33, 126, 128, 154,
155, 173, 206
Priestly Writers, 3, 78, 79, 93, 150
principle
dogmatic, 12, 15-17, 21, 39, 42,
55, 56, 60, 63, 98, 100, 113,
158, 198
historical, 49

historico-genetic, 18, 21
of analogy, 128
of coherence, 87
of congeniality, 49
of consent, 99
of criticism, 99
of selectivity, 49, 53, 62
systematic, 49
progressive revelation, 4, 43, 52
promise, 5, 44, 52-54, 110, 113,
142, 149, 150, 159, 173-176, 181,
182, 183, 189, 192
proof, 11, 12, 15, 22, 131, 175-177
proof-texts, 11, 12, 15, 22
prophecy, 69, 93, 102, 148, 149,
175, 176
prophets, 3, 20, 43, 46, 54, 55, 62,
63, 67, 69-71, 87, 110, 130, 141,
147-149, 174, 196, 205
Protestant Orthodoxy, 11, 12
proto-history, 120
providence, 88, 89

rationalism, 13, 14, 17, 18
reality, 32-34, 61, 73, 86, 87, 91,
92, 118, 121, 123-128, 131, 132,
139, 141, 189, 195, 197, 199,
201, 205
reason, 13, 17, 45, 62, 83, 131,
174, 197
reconstruction, 17, 23, 30, 31, 63,
73
reductionism, 91, 177
relativity, 200
relevance, 58, 117, 122, 129, 147,
175, 184
religion, 4, 17-21, 23, 25, 26, 33,
40, 48, 49, 55, 63, 90, 97, 104,
108, 111, 112, 122, 131, 132,
136, 141, 154, 173, 175, 183,
184, 202
Religionsgeschichte, 18, 23-25. See
also approach: history-of-religions
remnant, 196
resurrection, 88, 92, 161
re-telling, 74, 75, 92. See also
actualization
revelation, 4, 13, 20, 23, 25, 41-45,
52, 55, 61, 62, 64, 71, 72, 77, 91,
106, 109, 110, 116, 126, 127,
129, 131, 134, 137, 146, 150,

158, 169-171, 173, 193, 196, 198,
203, 204
righteousness, 164, 166

Sabbath, 87, 154
salvation, 5, 20-23, 26, 39, 41-43,
48, 49, 54, 55, 70, 71, 92, 110,
115, 118, 123, 125, 127, 128,
130, 131, 141, 148, 149, 150,
158, 163, 169, 170, 175, 176,
179, 192, 193, 195, 201
salvation history, 22, 110, 115,
118, 125, 127, 128, 130, 131,
148, 149, 150, 163, 179, 193. See
also Heilsgeschichte
self-interpretation, 10
self-revelation, 55, 146, 169, 171
Sitz im Leben, 186
sociology, 91
"sola scriptura," 10, 11
soteriology, 39-42, 63, 69, 113, 158
story, 96, 97, 99, 115, 133-138
stratum, strata, 3, 78, 79, 93, 150
structure, 4, 15, 17, 20, 40-43, 49,
52, 53, 55, 61, 63, 64, 69, 70, 90,
92, 94, 102, 107, 113, 114, 128,
142, 152, 154, 156, 157, 158,
161, 174, 184, 202, 207
structuralism, 95, 98
subjective, 26, 48, 53, 157, 164, 181
supernatural, 99, 197
supernaturalism, 13, 18
symbol, 139
synchronic, 102
systematic theology, 12, 15-17, 21,
33, 37, 39, 42, 47, 55, 56, 59, 96,
101, 102, 111, 125, 164, 190, 196
systematization, 50, 141, 158, 164-
166, 168, 204

"Tanakh Theology," 36
tension, 19, 43, 51, 88-90, 124,
144, 148-150, 186, 207
testimonies, biblical
depth 1-5, 7-21, 23, 25, 27, 29-
34, 36, 37, 42, 47, 49, 51, 54,
58-61, 66, 67, 75, 77, 80-91, 93-
108, 111, 114, 121, 123-125,
129, 130, 132-139, 142, 143,
155, 156, 158-160, 163, 164,
169, 171, 172, 177, 185, 186,

188, 190, 193-201, 203, 205,
207, 208
diversity, 1-5, 7-21, 23, 25, 27,
29-34, 36, 37, 42, 47, 49, 51,
54, 58-61, 66, 67, 75, 77, 80-
91, 93-108, 111, 114, 121, 123-
125, 129, 130, 132-139, 142,
143, 155, 156, 158-160, 163,
164, 169, 171, 172, 177, 185,
186, 188, 190, 193-201, 203,
205, 207, 208
kerygmatic, 194-196
multiform, 144, 145, 182, 184,
207
multiplex, 145, 189, 207
text(s)
what it (they) mean(s), 29-32,
59, 63, 64, 83, 90, 102, 103,
109, 185, 194
what it (they) meant, 6, 29, 30-
32, 36, 63, 83, 89, 90, 102,
103, 109, 60, 63, 98, 100, 113,
158, 198
"thatness," 123
theme(s)
blessing-promise, 52, 54. See
also promise
longitudinal, 53, 54, 114, 171,
205, 206
presence, 5, 44, 69, 86-88, 94,
170
theocracy, 177
theology of the Hebrew Bible, 1-31,
33-77, 79-83, 85-87, 89, 90, 91-
115, 117, 118, 120, 125, 127-131,
133, 136, 137, 138-145, 148-166,
168, 170-172, 185, 186, 188, 189,
190, 194, 196, 198-208
tôrāh, 45
tradition(s)
biblical, 81, 84, 104
foundation of, 79, 80, 81, 83
historical, 71-73, 81, 157. See
also approach: formation-of-
tradition; history of tradition

Traditionsgeschichte. See history of
tradition
transcendence, 99, 197, 199
transfiguration, 88
Trinity, 178
truth, 6, 25, 37, 48, 99, 123, 130,
137, 138, 187, 198, 199
type, 37, 143, 147, 165, 173, 179,
180, 185, 188, 189
typology, 178-180, 183, 192

unity, 4, 21, 24, 44, 46, 49-54, 61,
64, 70, 76, 78, 80, 84, 85, 87, 91,
102, 112, 114, 124-128, 131, 132,
139, 141, 143, 145, 151, 152,
155, 157, 158, 160, 162, 165,
167, 171, 172, 176, 177, 179,
180, 187, 191-193, 197, 205-207
universalism, 19, 150

victory, 69

war, 10, 18, 25, 28, 69
Wellhausenism, 116
wisdom literature, 45, 46, 92, 147
wisdom theology, 65, 69, 87, 92,
156, 171, 205
word, 14, 22, 45, 57, 72, 88, 91,
100, 116, 119, 124, 125, 129,
131, 138, 141, 148-150, 158, 169,
176, 182, 186, 191, 195, 198. See
also God: word of
world, 3, 22, 30, 35, 41, 50, 54, 92,
93, 142, 144, 147, 153, 164, 168-
171, 194, 200
worldview, 30
worship, 43, 93, 157, 158, 169,
205

Yahweh, 40, 55, 56, 61-63, 68-70,
87, 116, 123, 126, 129, 140, 143,
144, 146, 147, 149, 151, 153,
154, 157, 160, 162, 164, 168,
170, 174, 182, 183. See also God
Yahwist, 78, 79, 93

Index of Authors

Achtemeier, E., 59
Ackroyd, P., 76, 107, 168
Adar, Z., 202
Albright, W. F., 120, 152
Alt, A., 120, 157
Alter, R., 99, 137, 138
Ammon, A. A. von, 15
Amsler, S., 172, 187
Anderson, B. W., 35, 76
Anderson, G. W., 77
Andrew, M. E., 152
Astruc, J., 13
Auvray, P., 187

Baab, O. J., 26, 27, 158, 159
Baier, J. W., 12
Baker, D. L., 6, 161, 167
Barnett, T. A., 38
Barr, J., 34, 37, 57, 94-98, 111, 112,
   124, 133, 134, 158, 173, 178,
   179, 191, 192, 198, 203
Barth, C., 72, 74, 131, 155
Barth, K., 195
Barth, M., 2
Barton, J., 98, 111, 132, 135, 136
Bauer, B., 19
Bauer, G. L., 15, 17, 18, 39, 48, 172
Baumgärtel, F., 61, 72, 74, 121,
   122, 130, 152, 168, 170, 174-176,
   179, 187
Baumgarten, W., 13
Baur, F. C., 20
Beauchamp, P., 159
Beck, J. T., 22
Benoit, P., 38, 173
Benson, J. E., 13
Berlin, A., 137
Bertholet, A., 23
Betti, E., 35
Betz, O., 12, 38, 40
Beyerlin, W., 123
Birch, B. C., 163
Blackman, C., 124
Blenkinsopp, J. A., 27, 46, 67, 112

Braaten, C. F., 124, 198
Braun, F. M., 38, 183, 191
Bright, J., 94, 120, 187, 192
Bruce, F. F., 163, 166, 187, 192
Brueggemann, W., 39, 76, 78, 86,
   88-90, 94, 103
Buber, M., 4
Budde, K., 25
Bultmann, R., 61, 122, 173-176,
   187, 195
Burden, J. J., 38
Burrows, M., 27, 190
Büsching, A. E., 14

Calovius, A., 12
Cazelles, H., 187
Childs, B. S., 2, 5, 6, 27, 29, 31,
   32, 36, 45, 47, 60, 67, 85, 89-91,
   95-98, 103-112, 135-137, 183,
   186, 188-191, 196, 202
Chubb, T., 13
Clements, R. E., 5, 8, 36, 38, 39, 44-
   46, 59, 77, 79, 83, 103, 140
Coats, G. W., 78, 79, 107
Cobb, J. B., Jr., 198
Collins, J. J., 39, 94, 98-101, 111,
   126, 137, 138
Cölln, D. G. C. von, 15, 19
Conzelmann, H., 116
Cordero, M. G., 39, 41
Craig, C. T., 25
Crenshaw, J. L., 65
Cullmann, O., 73, 183, 186, 193
Cunliffe-Jones, H., 29

Davidson, A. B., 24
Davies, G. H., 71, 140
Day, G. E., 21
Deissler, A., 3, 27, 39, 168
Dentan, R. C., 2, 10, 12, 14, 15, 18-
   21, 23, 25, 38-42, 47, 48, 157,
   159
Deutschmann, J., 12
Diem, H., 184, 185

Diest, H. A., 11
Dietrich, W., 98, 128, 134, 165, 166
Dillmann, A., 23
Dodd, C. H., 192
Duhm, B., 40, 144
Dulles, A., 32, 75, 103, 195
Durham, J. I., 140
Dyrness, W., 5, 39

Ebeling, G., 10, 11, 13, 14, 130,
    172, 197
Eichhorn, J. G., 17
Eichrodt, W., 1, 24, 26, 29, 43, 47-
    51, 54, 58-60, 72, 86, 91, 110,
    111, 120, 121, 123, 139, 140,
    141, 143, 150, 155, 159, 163,
    178, 180, 185, 189, 190, 192
Eissfeldt, O., 26, 33, 48, 51, 59, 108
Eliot, T. S., 135
Ellis, P. F., 78
Enders, H., 202
Ernesti, J. A., 15
Ernst, W., 39, 47, 162
Ewald, H., 22, 23

Fackre, G., 137
Fannon, P., 158, 160
Feiereis, K., 47
Feiner, J., 191
Fensham, F. C., 159
Festorazzi, F., 38
Filson, F. V., 187, 190, 191, 199
Fischer, A., 11
Fohrer, G., 3, 4, 27, 39, 63-67, 69,
    70, 111, 124, 140, 142-144, 152,
    156, 160, 169, 181, 186, 188, 189
France, R. T., 191, 192
Frank, H. T., 1
Freedman, D. N., 29, 78, 85
Frei, H. W., 75, 132, 137, 138
Fretheim, T. E., 78
Fridrichsen, A., 29
Fries, J. F., 18
Fritsch, C. T., 10, 38
Frizzell, L. E., 86
Frör, K., 184
Fuller, D. P., 126
Funk, R. W., 197

Gabler, J. P., 15-18, 21, 26, 28, 34,
    36, 46, 49, 83, 102, 109, 190
Gadamer, H.-G., 35, 84

Gamper, A., 128
Gese, H., 80, 81-85, 96, 103-105,
    109, 187
Geyer, H.-G., 58, 125
Gilkey, L. B., 75
Glait, O., 11
Goldberg, M., 137
Goldingay, J., 36, 38, 56-60, 103
Goppelt, L., 192
Goshen-Gottstein, M. H., 7, 35, 36
Gottwald, N. K., 47, 51, 89-91, 132
Graf, K. H., 6, 7, 23, 38, 56, 72, 74,
    83, 84, 102, 168
Grässer, F., 82
Grelot, P., 172, 187, 193
Groves, J. W., 59, 75-77, 84
Gundry, R. H., 191
Gundry, S. N., 111
Gunneweg, A. H. J., 38, 39, 82, 85,
    105, 162, 163, 173, 175
Guthrie, D., 95

Haacker, K., 80
Haag, H., 191
Haevernick, H. A. C., 20
Hahn, H. F., 20
Halbe, J., 74
Hamilton, W., 127
Hanson, P., 5, 6, 7, 36, 57, 59, 86,
    88, 89, 161
Harnack, A., 186
Harrelson, W., 105, 152, 163
Harrington, W. J., 2, 3, 187, 189,
    190, 191
Harvey, V. A., 33, 38, 72
Hasel, G. F., 2, 11, 39, 40, 44, 59,
    64, 66, 72, 74, 103, 108, 112,
    115, 116, 150, 158, 170
Hauerwas, S., 137
Hayes, J. H., 8, 65
Haymann, C., 12
Heinisch, P., 26, 27
Hempel, J., 117, 122-124
Henry, C. F. H., 75, 137
Herbert, A. S., 1
Herrmann, S., 152, 156, 157, 160
Heschel, A. J., 168
Hesse, F., 71, 117-120, 123, 125,
    131, 173, 175, 176, 185, 187
Hicks, R. L., 38
Higgins, A. J. B., 187
Hinson, D. F., 39, 41

Hirsch, E., 186
Hirsch, E. D., 35
Hitzig, F., 23
Hofius, O., 166
Hofmann, J. C. K. von, 22
Høgenhaven, J., 101, 102, 160
Honecker, M., 72, 118, 147, 148, 155
Hoppe, J., 128
Hornig, G., 14
Hufnagel, W. F., 15
Hyatt, J. P., 11, 29, 103

Imschoot, P. van, 27, 158

Jacob, E., 1, 2, 11, 12, 29, 38, 87, 158, 168, 169
Janowski, H. N., 81
Jasper, F. N., 187
Jepsen, A., 168
Jones, H. O., 134

Kähler, M., 25, 198
Kaiser, G. P. C., 18
Kaiser, O., 82, 162
Kaiser, W. C., 5, 39, 44, 52-54, 69, 159
Kantzer, K. S., 111
Käsemann, E., 197
Kautzsch, E., 48
Kayser, A., 24, 140, 202
Kelsey, D. H., 30, 31, 75, 103
King, W. L., 53
Kittel, R., 23
Klein, G., 125, 141, 159
Kneucher, J. J., 23
Knierim, R., 106, 152, 163-166, 169
Knight, D. A., 71, 78, 80, 83, 84, 85, 106
Knight, G. A. F., 158
Köberle, J., 117
Koch, K., 125, 170
Köhler, A., 116
Köhler, L., 26, 49, 141, 155, 158, 159
König, E., 24, 25, 49
Kort, W. A., 136
Kraeling, E., 25, 38
Kraus, H.-J., 2, 3, 10, 12-19, 21, 22, 23, 39, 46, 48, 58, 73, 82, 83, 85, 112, 129, 130, 131, 188-190, 196, 199, 202, 203

Krentz, E., 99
Kuenen, A., 23
Kümmel, W. G., 13-17
Kutsch, E., 47, 55

Ladd, G. E., 22, 197, 198
Lampe, G. W. H., 192
Landes, G. M., 203
Lang, B., 187
Laurin, R. B., 106
Lehman, C. K., 4, 27, 39, 42-44, 103
Leiman, S. Z., 55, 85
Lentrieccha, F., 135
Lessing, E., 15
Levenson, J. D., 7, 36, 37
Levine, B. A., 7, 36, 78
Licht, J., 134
Lindblom, J., 168
Lipenius, M., 11
Locke, J., 13
Loersch, S., 78
Lohfink, N., 78, 173, 187
Lohr, M., 191
Long, B. O., 78, 107
Longman III, T., 135
Lönning, I., 66
Lubsczyk, H., 47
Lucas, R., 179
Luther, M., 11

Maag, V., 72
McCarthy, D. J., 47, 55, 140, 202
McComiskey, T. E., 55
McConnell, F., 137
McEvenue, S. E., 58, 78, 105, 106
McKenzie, J. L., 4, 27, 39, 46, 60-62, 64, 69-71, 188, 191
MacKenzie, R. A. F., 32
McKnight, E. V., 132, 133, 137
Maier, G., 82
Maius, J. H., 12
Martens, E. A., 5, 38, 39, 59
Martin-Achard, R., 38
Mattioli, A., 55, 56
Mauser, U., 58, 187
Mayo, S. M., 6
Mendenhall, G. E., 47, 120, 140
Menken, G., 22
Merendino, R. P., 78
Merk, O., 10-12, 14, 16-19, 39, 63
Michaelis, J. D., 13

Mildenberger, F., 74, 119, 120, 185, 200
Miskotte, K. H., 145, 168, 187
Moeller, W. and H., 26
Moltmann, J., 150
Mowinckel, S., 78, 98
Müller, P.-G., 162
Murphy, R. E., 163, 164, 165, 173, 178, 181, 187, 189
Nicholson, E. W., 55, 78
Nineham, D. E., 187
Noack, L., 19
North, C. R., 25, 57, 133, 161, 168
Noth, M., 40, 79, 120, 144, 203

Obayashi, H., 126-128
Oberman, H., 10
O'Collins, G. G., 126
Oden, R. A., 133, 138
O'Doherty, E., 187
Oehler, G. F., 20, 21, 42, 43, 140
Oeming, M., 58, 84
Ollenburger, B. C., 36, 59, 103
Osborn, R. T., 126
Osswald, E., 38, 119, 122-125, 199

Pannenberg, W., 76, 110, 124-128, 131, 150, 174-176, 180
Payne, J. B., 27, 159, 191
Perlitt, L., 19, 47, 55, 140
Petersen, D., 97
Pfeiffer, R. H., 124
Piepenbring, C., 24
Pinnock, C. H., 191
Porteous, N. W., 25, 38, 48, 59, 76
Porter, F. C., 140
Preuss, H. D., 6, 65, 170, 173, 187
Priest, J. F., 105
Procksch, O., 22, 26, 27, 50
Prussner, F. C., 8, 47, 159

Rad, G. von, 1, 3, 22, 27, 29, 38, 45, 47, 48, 51, 52, 59, 60, 61, 67-76, 80, 81, 84, 86, 87, 91, 92, 93, 94, 96-98, 104, 109, 110, 115-117, 119-123, 125, 127, 129, 130, 132, 145-151, 153, 155, 156, 157, 160, 163, 175, 178, 179, 180-184, 186, 189, 190-192, 196, 198, 199, 200, 206
Ramlot, L., 38
Ratzinger, L., 75, 168

Reed, W. L., 1
Reisner, E., 197
Rendtorff, R., 58, 79, 123, 125, 128, 129
Reuss, E., 24
Reventlow, H. G., 6, 7, 8, 38, 56, 72, 74, 83, 84, 102, 168
Ringgren, H., 202, 203
Ritschl, D., 98, 134
Robertson, D., 113, 138
Robertson, O. P., 191
Robinson, H. W., 26
Robinson, J. A. T., 2
Robinson, J. M., 119, 120, 129, 182, 198
Rogerson, J. W., 212
Rössler, D., 128, 151
Rowley, H. H., 25, 38, 187, 189, 190, 192, 193
Ruler, A. A. van, 172, 177, 187
Rylaarsdam, J. C., 47, 124, 159
Sanders, J. A., 46, 67, 76, 96, 106, 109
Sauter, G., 125
Schäfer, P., 55
Schlier, H., 202
Schmid, H. H., 54, 79, 82, 83, 160, 169
Schmidt, L., 61
Schmidt, S., 12
Schmidt, W. H., 38, 151-154, 162, 191
Schmithals, W., 82
Schnackenburg, R., 160
Schofield, J. N., 27
Scholder, K., 13
Schulz, H., 152
Schulz, S., 40
Scott, R. B. Y., 65
Scullion, J. J., 38
Seebass, H., 84, 141, 144, 159, 163, 166, 187
Seitz, G., 78
Sekine, M., 123
Sellin, E., 26, 49, 141, 158, 159
Semler, J. S., 13, 14, 15
Seters, J. van, 79
Siedl, S., 187
Siegwalt, G., 82, 187
Smart, J. D., 104, 105, 172, 187, 189
Smend, R., 16, 24, 28, 40, 139, 143, 144, 151, 157, 160, 166

Smith, M., 21, 90
Soggin, J. A., 119, 120
Spener, P. J., 12
Spicq, C., 32, 33, 191
Spina, F. A., 96, 109
Spriggs, D. C., 47, 48, 58
Stade, B., 24, 40, 144
Staerk, W., 25
Staiger, E., 202
Stamm, J. J., 152
Stammler, E., 81
Steck, O. H., 78
Stek, J. H., 192
Stendahl, K., 11, 28, 29, 32, 34, 36,
  46, 59, 63, 83, 89, 102, 103, 109,
  134-137, 200
Sternberg, M., 99, 137, 138
Steudel, J. C. F., 20
Steuernagel, C., 25, 190
Stoebe, H.-J., 74, 168
Strange, J., 20, 129, 187, 189
Stuhlmacher, P., 58, 80-85, 85, 99,
  166
Sturm, R., 82

Talmon, S., 56, 202
Tappert, T. G., 12
Taylor, S., 21
Terrien, S., 5, 39, 69, 86-88, 91, 94,
  103, 105
Thiselton, A., 35
Thompson, R. J., 23, 57, 161
Tindal, M., 13
Toland, J., 13
Towner, W. S., 163, 164
Tracy, D., 137
Troeltsch, E., 126, 128, 199
Tsevat, M., 7, 34, 35
Tucker, G. M., 97

Vanhoozer, K. J., 137
Vatke, W., 19, 20
Vaux, R. de, 32, 33, 40, 120, 191
Verhoef, P. A., 191, 193
Vielhauer, P., 151
Vischer, W., 26, 176-178, 187
Vorgrimler, H., 202
Vos, G., 27, 43, 190
Vriezen, T. C., 1, 2, 4, 27, 39, 50,
  51, 54, 87, 91, 103, 111, 131,
  142, 143, 146, 152, 159, 177,
  179, 193

Wagner, S., 40, 58, 79, 82, 83,
  168
Walther, J. A., 5, 59, 120, 150, 153,
  174
Warren, A., 135
Watson, P. S., 29
Weidner, J. C., 12
Weinfeld, M., 78
Weinsheimer, J. C., 35
Weippert, M., 120
Weiser, A., 123, 124, 155
Weismann, C. E., 12
Weiss, M., 135, 202
Wellek, R., 135
Wellhausen, J., 19, 23, 24, 40, 143,
  151
Wells, P. R., 97, 191
Wernberg-Möller, P., 29
West, C., 132
Westermann, C., 3, 5, 39, 45, 66,
  75, 78, 86, 88, 91-94, 103, 116,
  122, 153, 156, 161, 169, 173,
  174, 181, 187, 175, 181, 182,
  189, 192
Wette, W. M. L. de, 18-20
Wharton, J. A., 133
Whybray, R., 57, 79, 160, 161
Wilckens, U., 13, 128, 151, 197
Wildberger, H., 141, 159
Wilken, R. L., 126
Wilson, R. R., 97, 151
Witter, J. B., 13
Wolff, H. W., 41, 150, 153, 170,
  179, 184, 190, 192
Woollcombe, K. J., 192
Wrede, W., 11, 28, 34, 36, 46, 83,
  102, 109
Wright, G. E., 1, 26, 27, 29, 38, 39,
  47, 50, 51, 66, 98, 117, 120, 155,
  158, 159, 173, 178, 194
Würthwein, E., 10, 38, 39, 162

Young, E. J., 27, 38

Zachariä, G. T., 14, 15
Zedler, J. H., 12
Zenger, E., 169
Zimmerli, W., 3-5, 27, 38-40, 45,
  67-70, 83, 85, 92, 112, 129, 152-
  155, 157, 158, 162, 169, 174,
  181, 187, 192, 193
Zyl, A. H. van, 187